Contents

Foreword by William H. Willimon | *ix*
Acknowledgments | *xi*

Prelude: Why Literary Ministers? | 1

Interlude: "The Collar" by George Herbert | 13

1   Heroism and Suffering | 23

      Romero, The Mission, Becket, Murder in the Cathedral,
      The Power and the Glory, Gilead

Interlude: *Diary of a Country Priest* by Georges Bernanos | 39

2   The Counselor/Confessor | 43

      George Eliot, E. M. Forster, A. S. Byatt

Interlude: *Scenes of Clerical Life* by George Eliot | 61

3   Fools for Christ | 69

      Tristram Shandy, The Vicar of Wakefield, Bleak House,
      The Warden, Monsignor Quixote, Heavens Above!,
      Rowan Atkinson's vicars

Interlude: Barbara Pym and Jan Karon | 91

4   The Collared Detective | 97

      Brother Cadfael mysteries, Father Brown stories,
      The Name of the Rose

Interlude: *Cry, the Beloved Country* by Alan Paton | 115

5   Passion, for Better and for Worse | 121

      The Scarlet Letter, The Crucible, Racing Demon, Priest

Contents

Interlude: *The Book Against God*, a Novel by James Wood | 135

6   Failure, for Worse and for Better | 139

     Jane Eyre, Middlemarch, Margaret Oliphant, Jane Austen, John Updike, Clint Eastwood

Interlude: *Doubt, a Parable* by John Patrick Shanley | 157

7   Disaster | 161

     A Portrait of the Artist as a Young Man, Brand, The Spire, Light in August, Rain

Interlude: *Pale Rider*, directed by Clint Eastwood | 177

8   Frustration: The Collar on Screen | 181

     The Thorn Birds, Footloose, 7th Heaven, Keeping the Faith, The Vicar of Dibley, Rev.

Interlude: The Bing Crosby and Richard Burton Movie Priests | 205

9   Clergy Wives and Daughters: The Concealed Collar | 217

     A Clergyman's Daughter, Bed Among the Lentils, The Rector's Wife, Candida

Interlude: *The Bell* by Iris Murdoch | 237

10   The Canadian Collar | 241

     The Stone Angel, Such is My Beloved, As For Me and My House, Good to a Fault, Robertson Davies, Ralph Connor, Stephen Leacock, Warren Cariou

Interlude: *Lights and Shadows of Clerical Life* by William Cheetham | 271

Postlude: *Corpus permixtum* | 277

     Bibliography | 283
     Index | 293
     Scripture Index | 305

The Collar

Reading Christian Ministry in Fiction, Television, and Film

Sue Sorensen

The Lutterworth Press

For all ministers, ordained or not, rashly following a Lord who
"saved us and called us with a holy calling" (2 Tim 1:9).
And especially, with love, for Michael.

The Lutterworth Press
P.O. Box 60
Cambridge
CB1 2NT
United Kingdom

www.lutterworth.com
publishing@lutterworth.com

ISBN: 978 0 7188 9364 4

British Library Cataloguing in Publication Data
A record is available from the British Library

First published by The Lutterworth Press, 2014

Copyright © Sue Sorensen, 2014

Published by arrangement
with Cascade Books

Foreword

The more I wander in the rather abstract and ethereal realm of theology and philosophy, reading required of me by my professions,
clerical and academic, the greater my appreciation for the truth that can
be told only through fiction. In an age of thin descriptions and reduction-
istic assessments, fiction portrays human life as complex and mysterious
as God means it to be. Our conventional, socially acceptable, governmen-
tally sanctioned modes of explanation—sociology, psychology, econom-
ics—seem simple compared to the depth and subtlety, the insight and
candor of good fiction. In seeking discernment about who we are and
why we live as we do, I have found Flaubert always to be a more trustworthy guide than Freud, Mann better than Kant.

As a Christian clergyman it is understandable why I have such high
regard for the narrative arts. The faith of Jews and Christians is generated
by and accountable to story. Scripture is first a story of how we came to be,
a rendition of God as author of life, a long saga of a God who gratuitously,
in love, became entangled with the triumphs and tragedies of Israel. And
something there was in the nature of Jesus Christ that demanded to be
handled by story. We think that sometime in the late first century Mark
invented a literary device that was previously unknown—the gospel—in
order to tell the truth about Jesus. The gospel itself is a story about God
before it is propositions or principles about God.

My generalizations about the fecund, perceptive, evocative power
of fiction are particularly true when one sets out to understand us clergy.
Clergy are interesting to the world as those who dare to stand at that fate-
ful intersection between God and humanity. Called to the task of point-
ing humanity upward toward the sacred, we notably have our feet stuck
in the muck and mire of earth. The clerical collar around our necks both
reveals and conceals who we really are or wish to God we were. Those of
us who are yoked in service to God and to our congregations in this very
political, public role can be adept at hiding the truth about ourselves.
Therefore some of our very best novelists and dramatists have attempted
to pry into the recesses of our clergy souls, investigating what lies beneath

our collars and, in the process have produced some of our most engaging—and truthful—narrative art.

Professor Sue Sorensen offers lively, compelling evidence that fiction about clergy is one of the best ways to discover who clergy are and what clergy are for. Even if you are uninterested in the realm of the spirit, you are sure to be engaged by her astute depiction of human, all-too-human clergy. In her fast-paced, wide-ranging sweep of novels, plays, movies, and television shows about those of us who wear the collar, fresh insights abound on nearly every page. She is judicious in her judgments, gentle in her criticism, and so very insightful. Sorensen is not only a wonderful reader of fiction but she also reveals herself to be someone who knows us clergy quite well, down deep, collar on or off.

By interweaving her engaging, perceptive reading of these works of art with surprisingly appropriate biblical citations she reminds us that scripture itself is art in service of divine truth. Something about the truth of the God of Israel and the church could not be told without the use of poetry, saga, myth, and parable. Sorensen shows how fictional depictions of us clergy have dismissed us, ridiculed us, idealized us, idolized us, and also told truth about us that could be revealed in no other way.

Throughout the years of my own vocation I have been an avid consumer of novels, short stories, and movies about clergy. I have even ventured into the writing of fiction myself. Clergy have been an enduring theme in British fiction and film. Douglas Alan Walrath (in *Displacing the Divine*) shows how novels about clergy can be said to be an obsession of American writers from the very first. (Sorensen's reading of Hawthorne is wonderful.) And now Sorensen adds to the clergy fiction canon the Canadians—as well as contemporary movies and television—greatly increasing our appreciation for the fictional representation of women and men of God.

I've read close to a hundred clergy novels and yet Sue Sorensen introduced me to some new ones I had missed. Her discussion of Canadian clergy fiction is delightful and, I expect, unprecedented.

Anyone who wears the collar or who must put up with those who do, or anyone who loves novels, television, or film is sure to enjoy this quite wonderful book.

William H. Willimon
Bishop, the United Methodist Church, retired; Pastor, Duke Memorial
United Methodist Church, Durham, North Carolina; Professor of
the Practice of Christian Ministry, Duke University; and author of
Incorporation, a novel about a church and its clergy

Acknowledgments

An early presentation of research findings on fictional and cinematic portrayals of women in ministry was given to the Christianity and Literature Study Group at the Congress of the Humanities and Social Sciences in Toronto in May, 2006. A version of chapter 10 on the representation of Canadian clerics in fiction is forthcoming in *Studies in Religion/ Sciences religieuses*. I am appreciative for the responses received from several Winnipeg congregations between 2007 and 2009 when I presented the adult Christian education seminar "Ministry: Coming Soon to a Screen Near You." And as a recipient of the Canon Denys Ruddy Memorial Scholarship for study in Theology, Liturgy, Spirituality, or Christianity and the Arts I was able to experience a time of research and writing at Gladstone's Library in Wales in 2012.

I am very grateful to my two loving and encouraging Christian communities in Winnipeg—Canadian Mennonite University, where I teach, and First Lutheran Church, with whom I worship. The students, faculty, and staff at CMU are inspiring; here I am privileged to witness real peacebuilding and reconciliation every single day. The people of First Lutheran make me happy to be alive, and I am particularly thankful for my pastor, Michael Kurtz, whose generous and vital spirit inhabits so much of what I discuss in *The Collar*.

Finally, to that same Michael Kurtz, my husband, my most enormous thanks, for your love, companionship, and calm assurance, and to my sons, Peter and Theo, my gratitude and love.

Why Literary Ministers?

In the presence of God and of Christ Jesus, who is to judge the living and the dead, and in view of his appearing and his kingdom, I solemnly urge you: proclaim the message; be persistent whether the time is favorable or unfavorable; convince, rebuke, and encourage, with the utmost patience in teaching. For the time is coming when people will not put up with sound doctrine, but having itching ears, they will accumulate for themselves teachers to suit their own desires, and will turn away from listening to the truth and wander away to myths. As for you, always be sober, endure suffering, do the work of an evangelist, carry out your ministry fully. (2 Tim 4:1–5)[1]

He sits on the edge of a chair in the background. He has colourless eyes, fixed earnestly, and a face almost as pale as the clerical bands beneath his somewhat receding chin. His forehead is high and narrow, his hair mouse-coloured. His hands are clasped tight before him, the knuckles standing out sharply. This constriction does not mean that he is steeling himself to speak. He has no positive intention of speaking. (Max Beerbohm, "A Clergyman")[2]

In Graham Greene's powerful and strange 1940 novel *The Power and the Glory* we follow a character called only the priest or the whisky priest. An alcoholic who has fathered a child, he has little respect for himself and is accorded none by the officials of his country, Mexico, which has

---

1. All biblical quotations are taken from the New Revised Standard Version unless otherwise noted.

2. Beerbohm, *And Even Now*, 238.

purged the nation of all clergy. The whisky priest is on the run. He is the last priest, and he carries on a clumsy and clandestine ministry until at last he is captured and executed. Like all of Greene's religious characters, the priest is a complicated amalgam of bad and good: he is weak and full of uncertainties, but he is also stubbornly faithful and self-sacrificing. He would agree with anyone who said he could not possibly be the stuff of a martyr, and yet that is what he becomes. He has no name because his importance as a man is nothing. For Greene, it is his identity as a Roman Catholic priest that matters. He is a priest to the end.

In one of Eugene Peterson's many wonderful books about the Christian ministry, *The Contemplative Pastor*, he tells an anecdote about his congregation getting ready to go on retreat. Peterson, as their pastor, is late to arrive at the gathering place. Once, he tells us, they would have waited obediently for him. But he has recently been on sabbatical, and the congregation has become less reliant on their pastor. They are more vitalized and independent. After waiting for a while, they leave without him. When Peterson does arrive, he is delighted to find that he has lost his place of prominence.

Here are two distinct tales located at very different places along a continuum of stories about Christian ministry. These stories both, in their own ways, tell important truths about what ministry is for and what it looks like. Ministry is at the same time a high calling and a frustrating, changeable job that is encased in complex notions of servanthood. There are thousands of other stories that are quite different from Greene's and Peterson's. The Christian ministry provides such a rich heritage of stories because it is, in fact, one of the "oldest professions." For example, since Christians can claim an inheritance from the history of the Hebrew people, the Old Testament contains hundreds of injunctions for and glimpses of the lives of priests. We also encounter priests and ministers in Chaucer, Shakespeare, Jane Austen, George Eliot, Marilynne Robinson. Because religion has always been one of the most pressing themes that occupy writers, we constantly meet pastors and ministers in novels, plays, films, and poems because they are the readily grasped representatives of religion. Dostoyevksy in *The Brothers Karamazov* gives us Father Zossima not just as a character but as a symbol of certain ideas about holiness, humility, foolishness, miracles, irony, death. In chapter 6 of Gustave Flaubert's *Madame Bovary* the village priest fails utterly to help Emma Bovary when she turns to him for moral guidance. Flaubert's description of him is devastating:

The full light of the setting sun upon his face made the cloth of his cassock, shiny at the elbows and frayed at the hem, seem paler. Grease and tobacco stains ran along his broad chest, following the line of the buttons, growing sparser in the vicinity of his neckcloth, in which rested the massive folds of his red chin; it was dotted with yellow spots that disappeared beneath the coarse hair of his greyish beard. He had just eaten his dinner, and was breathing noisily.[3]

Flaubert, the scathing social critic, in those three descriptive sentences tells us volumes about his opinions of the Roman Catholic Church in France in the nineteenth century. Whether such portrayals have been fair or not, any candidate for the ministry knows that she or he is entering one of those occupations (the law is another) that are rife with provocative stereotypes and about which everyone has an opinion.

That I can call this book *The Collar* and safely assume that most readers will successfully arrive at my topic indicates the ministry's strong cultural associations. (For the few who hoped for a book about the training of dogs, my apologies.) And that many (if not most) pastors do not even wear clerical collars in the twenty-first century is even more of an indication how powerful the old associations and symbols are. In 1994 and 2011 two films simply titled *Priest* could tap into a complex range of expectations—about duty, mystery, reverence, sexual frustration, confession, confidentiality—that allowed filmmakers to leap instantly into their particular stories. One has to think hard to come up with a roster of movies or plays starring plumbers, postal workers, or accountants—although all of these professions outweigh the ministry in numerical terms. Ask an average person to name a handful of movies or television shows about ministers, and there should be few hesitations: *The Bells of St. Mary's, The Keys of the Kingdom, A Man Called Peter* for an older generation; *The Preacher's Wife, The Vicar of Dibley, Rev.* for a younger generation. Gregory Peck, Bing Crosby, Robin Williams, Richard Burton, and Max von Sydow have played priests or pastors more than once and developed recognizable clerical screen personas. Indeed, possibly there are young people who have internalized Rowan Atkinson's line "In the name of the Father, the Son, and the holy goat" from *Four Weddings and a Funeral* and accept it as sound liturgical form. In a tiny and splendid Wallace and Gromit animated short film, "The Autochef," one of Wallace's inventions that goes hopelessly awry is a cooking and serving robot. One of the signs

3. Flaubert, *Madame Bovary*, 80.

3

that the robot is about to go berserk is its sudden and maniacal utterance, "More tea, vicar?" For some reason the only line that is funnier than this is the robot's last word before it blows up: "Knickers."[4]

Why should ministry attract so much cultural attention? For Christians, one substantial reason, although largely unacknowledged, is that we are all ministers. Most of us do not think of ourselves in this manner from day to day, but unconsciously we must be studying pastoral actions and attitudes for models of what we should be doing or not be doing. John Patrick Shanley's excellent *Doubt*, with a cast of two nuns and a priest, attracted attention both as a Broadway play and as a Hollywood film, and the questions Shanley raises about honesty, manipulation, and compassion are hardly restricted to the clergy. E. M. Forster's Mr. Beebe, in the 1908 novel *A Room with a View*, is one of my favorite literary vicars because of his crucial but unassuming role as a social mediator. On the other hand, Reverend Arthur Dimmesdale in Hawthorne's *The Scarlet Letter* and Reverend Samuel Parris in Arthur Miller's *The Crucible* are disturbing reminders of just how fallen and flawed all Christian mortals are.

Ministry is also fascinating as a cultural artifact because it has been and continues to be the most personal of the professions. As we advance into the twenty-first century our respect for certain key members of society—lawyers, physicians, professors, soldiers, pastors—may become less and less obvious, but there is no doubt that our civilization will never completely lose its conviction that specific careers involve such dedication that a strong sense of vocation or calling is required, in addition to specialized training. Historically, the ministry was one of three professions accepted automatically as having high social status (the other two being the law and medicine). We can see this in Jane Austen's novels. Mr. Elton in *Emma*, with no special personal recommendations, nevertheless has an immediate invitation to events for the social elilte. Whether we consider Austen's century or our own, the fact is that the only professional with whom ordinary people are likely to have contact—everyday, if they wish—is the parson, pastor, preacher, priest, or minister. (I will use a variety of these terms throughout my study.) Parson, after all, derives from a word that denotes "person," and pastors are, etymologically speaking, shepherds. They are an intriguing mixture of the exalted and the humble. In centuries past, they were among the few men accorded the

---

4. "The Autochef," *Wallace and Gromit's Cracking Contraptions.*

status of gentleman, but they were also, in England at any rate, considered the representative, accessible gentlemen of a parish. Often the only literate person for miles around, the cleric would be the go-to person for a large variety of needs: not only to officiate at solemn occasions and preside over the sacraments, but to teach, keep a community's records, and distribute charitable aid. This combination of privileged status with familiarity and availability makes the character of the pastor endlessly interesting to us. And the ministry has probably changed less than almost any other profession.

Justin Lewis-Anthony notes that while medicine, law, and other professions have become conglomerated or more corporate, the parson today remains "in solitary splendor."[5] And within that solitary splendor the most basic needs have been met for centuries: among the pastor's most crucial tasks is to listen, to sit with people and acknowledge their humanness.

Ministry has been studied profusely over the generations and so there is a mass of material regarding the pastoral life. Larry Witham claims that at least 485 surveys of the ministry were made between 1930 and 1970.[6] And because study for the ministry is, alone among the professions, lodged in or near the humanities wing of universities, it is closely tied to history, classics, philosophy, and English; these are fields traditionally given to contemplation. The thousands of handbooks, meditations, and polemics involving the ministry range across many disciplines—psychology, sociology, communications, ethics. The medical profession has comparatively few such works written in the vernacular and accessible to the layperson. The following books are all titles published since 1990 that I encountered randomly in the small library of my Christian university: *Walking Through the Valley: Understanding and Emerging from Clergy Depression; Fit to Be a Pastor: A Call to Physical, Mental, and Spiritual Fitness; The Pastor as Minor Poet: Texts and Subtexts in the Ministerial Life; The Country Preacher's Notebook; Clergy Killers: Guidance for Pastors and Congregations Under Attack.* Older titles can be winsome; titles I have seen over the years include *How to be a Minister and a Human Being; They Cry, Too! What You Always Wanted to Know about Your Minister but Didn't Know Whom to Ask;* and (a personal favorite) *Your Pastor's Problems.*

---

5. Lewis-Anthony, *If You Meet George Herbert on the Road, Kill Him*, 34.

6. Witham, *Who Shall Lead Them?*, vii.

But this lively publishing activity does not mean that there is anything close to a solid or definite agreement about what Christian ministry is, how it works itself out in daily life. The profession is an astonishingly diverse one. Nearly every ministry handbook offers a list of key attributes that a pastor should have, and I am always intrigued by how various these lists are. Dietrich Bonhoeffer's *Life Together* offers these: holding one's tongue, meekness, listening, helpfulness, bearing, proclaiming, authority. John Stott in *The Preacher's Portrait* claims five key roles: steward, herald, witness, father, servant. Eugene Peterson's *Five Smooth Stones for Pastoral Work* lists these focal points: directing prayer, telling stories, sharing pain, saying no to sin and the dominant culture, building community. And to cast the clerical eye over the more ancient texts can be a prelude to dejection. Who feels confident after reading George Herbert's admonishment about being "exceeding exact in his Life, being holy, just, prudent, temperate, bold, grave in all his ways"?[7] And then there are the mighty injunctions in 1 and 2 Timothy and Titus, the pastoral epistles: "Proclaim the message; be persistent whether the time is favorable or unfavorable; convince, rebuke, and encourage, with the utmost patience in teaching." This sounds reasonable, even if the word "utmost" gives one pause, but this manageable job description is followed by some unnerving imperatives and ultimates: "always be sober, endure suffering, do the work of an evangelist, carry out your ministry fully" (2 Tim 2:5).

All of this is to say that while there may be thousands of studies of the ministry, the ministry is fascinating and important enough to bear one more. And the ministry deserves close attention because of the tremendous strains involved. Like physicians and lawyers, pastors lead unpredictable and stressful lives, much of it under an intense public gaze; unlike physicians and lawyers, pastors are only modestly recompensed for their hard work. It is not for me to say with any certainty that the ministry is more stressful than it ever was—I suspect that the challenges were always arduous, with a brief respite perhaps in the religious golden era of nineteen fifties America—but it is certainly now no less stressful than it ever was. Here, for example, is the complaint of the prominent American preacher and teacher Barbara Brown Taylor, in her 2006 memoir:

> I gave myself to the work the best way I knew how, which sometimes exhausted my parishioners as much as it exhausted me. I thought that being faithful meant always trying harder to live

7. Herbert, *The Country Parson*, 56.

a holier life and calling them to do the same. I thought that it meant knowing everything I could about scripture and theology, showing up every time the church doors were open, and never saying no to anyone in need.[8]

The notion that people feel called to be so arduously holy and then do such exhausting work is worth our thoughtful attention. Eugene Peterson informs us "in the fifty years that I have lived the vocation of pastor . . . defections and dismissals have reached epidemic proportions in every branch and form of the church."[9] Marva Dawn asks, "Why is it so hard to serve God these days? Everywhere I go, pastors and lay people tell me how discouraged they are."[10] To be a pastor, says G. Lee Ramsey Jr. "is a recipe for heartache followed by failure."[11]

Married as I am to a hard-working pastor, and with many friends in church leadership, I take this crisis language seriously. But I also remember Martin Luther's words "O worthless religion of this age of ours, the most godless and thankless of all ages!" in 1520.[12] Consider Søren Kierkegaard's bitter invectives in the eighteen fifties about the failings of the church. "We play at believing, play at being Christians," he sneers; "we go and twaddle with one another, or let the priest twaddle to us."[13] It was ever thus, and perhaps ever thus shall be. The nature of ministry prompts passionate views, and we should be grateful that such passion still abounds, even when that passion is transformed into anger and grief.

Before this subject becomes too distressing, recall this delightful passage from Mark Twain's *Huckleberry Finn*:

> It was pretty ornery preaching—all about brotherly love, and such-like tiresomeness; but everybody said it was a good sermon. . . . It did seem to me to be one of the roughest Sundays I had run across yet.[14]

In 1885, Twain's famous book points to those of us who might be accused of absent-minded piety, and advises us to hold on just a minute. Similarly, in Shaw's *Candida* (1898) a straight-talking Londoner says, "A

8. Taylor, *Leaving Church*, 226.

9. Peterson, *The Pastor*, 5.

10. Dawn, *The Sense of the Call*, 1.

11. Ramsey, *Preachers and Misfits, Prophets and Thieves*, 43.

12. Luther, *On the Babylonian Captivity of the Church*, 43.

13. Kierkegaard, *Attack upon "Christendom,"* 191.

14. Twain, *Huckleberry Finn*, 176.

clorgyman is privileged to be a bit of a fool, you know: it's ony becoming in 'is profession that he should."[15] Yes, the ministry is a profession of vital importance, but it is also delightfully strange, even absurd. We need to look at it from a variety of angles and look at it honestly, making do with the least possible amount of mystification and false reverence.

My desire to contemplate ministry's many facets makes literary analysis a sound choice. One can study the ministry by way of denominational comparisons, or by way of biblical injunctions, or through the history of women in the church. But, with James Wood I hold that fiction "gives the best account of the complexity of our moral fabric."[16] Fiction is flexible and warm-blooded, suggestive rather than prescriptive. (I include film, for the purposes of this book, in my rather open definition of fiction.) Literature about the ministry allows us to explore ministry as lived by individuals, not as stipulated in denominational handbooks. Statistical reports need to be embodied, and perhaps that embodiment involves getting to know Geraldine Granger, the fictional vicar of Dibley, played by Dawn French on BBC television. The seminary study of ministry tends to be abstract; the precise details of an imagined pastor's life in John Updike's novel *A Month of Sundays* or Marilynne Robinson's *Gilead* open the way to authentic, sympathetic comprehension. Clergy literature also allows the communication of pressures and pains that might not be able to find an appropriate place in official channels. The awfulness and stupidity of the clerical characters in the nineties British television series *Father Ted* can be cringe-inducing, but the laughter is beneficial, puncturing as it does so many pointlessly sanctimonious anxieties about the church. The flawed but far from wicked character of Arthur Dimmesdale in *The Scarlet Letter* has been for 150 years a necessary reminder that clerics like everyone else have desires that can be powerful or hurtful.

What I hope is clear from the outset is my interest not in those books and movies that are comforting, anodyne, and "inspirational," but rather my trust in the sometimes difficult and prickly world of literary fiction and film. Although kindly, gentle novels and movies about the ministry have their place, and I do mention them from time to time, their usefulness is limited. The well-meaning but insipid clerics found in the television show *7th Heaven* or the old movies *The Bells of St. Mary's* and *Going My Way* are not rooted in anything resembling real church

---

15. Shaw, *Candida*, 140 (with Shaw's idiosyncratic spelling).

16. Wood, *How Fiction Works*, 178–79.

life, which is more messy and complicated. The upright and relatively untroubled pastor can never be as valuable to the reader or viewer as Shaw's struggling Major Barbara or Greene's whisky priest. An evening with a cup of cocoa and a slim Barbara Pym or Jan Karon novel may provide some relief to a cleric smarting from the day's parish cruelties, but for real understanding I propose a large measure of Tennessee Williams and Sinclair Ross—*The Night of the Iguana* and *As For Me and My House* demand to be considered and reconsidered; they stay in one's active memory longer than Karon's Father Tim novels. And because worthwhile literature demands full attention and considerable interpretative energy, I try not to summarize or categorize too quickly. Many of the works in this study resisted being sorted, although for the sake of the reader I have provided an organizational framework. For the integrity of the stories and the characters, however, I have let some of them stand alone in "Interlude" sections of close reading, where the literary works and the pastors they contain belong to themselves and not to a taxonomy.

There is something extreme about the ministry that makes this profession a truly fascinating subject, one that cannot be fully fixed or delineated. Justin Lewis-Anthony, in his provocative book *If You Meet George Herbert on the Road, Kill Him*, provides an anguished and nearly endless list of the demands we make of our ministers.

> We want a priest who is always available, who is always on the end of the telephone, who is always out visiting, who is good with old people, good with young people, brings new families into church, looks after the old families of the church community, makes the church grow, keeps the church the same, preaches well, is the first to arrive and the last to leave, keeps a happy family, attends every meeting, and so on, until the last syllable of recorded time.[17]

So many heightened expectations assail us when we immerse ourselves in the many tangled aspects of the ministry that an artistic outlet is useful, even just to name and expel irritation. But literary art can do more. The tributes and affection that poured out for Marilynne Robinson's picture of the ministry in her 2004 novel *Gilead* demonstrate the considerable power of literary art. *Gilead* has been, I believe, genuinely inspirational, perhaps even life-saving for many people in the church. No writing of "A New Creed" (as in the United Church of Canada), no reworking of

---

17. Lewis-Anthony, *If You Meet George Herbert*, 163.

the Thirty-Nine Articles can even begin to suffice as full explanations of church leadership and membership. But a poem like George Herbert's impassioned "The Collar" or an explosive work like *Elmer Gantry* (which exists now as an opera, as well as a novel and film) helps to provide a more all-embracing view of the possibilities and, yes, perversions of the ministry. As Horton Davies said in 1959, in one of the first books to take seriously the literary treatment of pastors: "Since complacency is the chief enemy of the Christian church, the critical novelist, whether this is his intention or not, can play the Socratic role of a gadfly, stinging the comatose Church into awareness of its dangerous condition."[18] At the very least, the representation of the church in art can prompt stimulating questions. Who, I wondered as I embarked on this book, invented the color "clerical gray" and what does it mean for the profession to be encumbered with this middling, unexciting hue? And why is it inevitably funny (and it is) that a pack of rascals in P. G. Wodehouse's short story "The Great Sermon Handicap" expend much energy establishing odds and placing bets on the length of sermons in English country churches? Would it be as amusing to put the length of lawyers' summations at the center of a comic story?

My personal incentives for working through some of the masses of clerical references in literature and film were several. As I noted earlier, my husband is a member of the clergy, so I have an intimate investment in observing cultural representations of his profession. While closely surveying his work and the work of his clerical friends and colleagues over the years, I have been amazed by the manifold demands of this strange but wondrous career. He has strength of character and bears up exceedingly well. But recently he told me of a colleague who was floundering and said to me, shaking his head, "I would have thought he had more grit." Whether or not Michael always knew that being a pastor would require grit, he certainly knows it now. Ministry is a tough profession, and it is increasingly hard to attract good candidates. The seminaries of most denominations are overly quiet places in our century. There is now less prestige attached to this profession. The hours are long, the financial compensation underwhelming. Two of my motives for this study are to unpack some of the cultural factors that might make the ministry such a hard sell, and to determine whether literary and cinematic works have been misrepresentative, misleading, or even harmful. I do want this book

18. Davies, *A Mirror of the Ministry in Modern Novels*, 8.

to be of practical use to the church and helpful for my often beleaguered friends in the ministry.

This is not a definitive survey of literary and cinematic clerics through the ages. I have chosen themes that resonate with the needs of the church today, in the twenty-first century, and have paid close attention to clerical types that insist on recurring over the generations. Many of the portrayals I examine arise from contemporary fiction and film, but this is not entirely the case. The nineteenth century provides a rich and timeless store of ministers. Just recently I retrieved from our university library the little-known 1879 Canadian novel *Lights and Shadows of Clerical Life*, by William Cheetham, and was instantly captivated by how discerning and modern Cheetham's descriptions of church life seem to me. As for geographic range, this study is unusual, I think, in not being exclusively fixed on British or American models. My examples are taken in the main from three cultural landscapes: the United States, the United Kingdom, and Canada, and I partake happily of examples from Protestant and Roman Catholic traditions.

A great deal has been written and said about the divide—a longstanding one—between the established or mainstream aspect of the church and the evangelical stream. This is one of those issues that, it seems, will never go away. (This ecclesiastical division is at the heart of Margaret Oliphant's novel *Phoebe Junior*, as one example. It was published in 1876. Take away the candles and crinolines, and the story could almost be set at the current time, with its high church/low church tensions.) From time to time I will have to address this divide in my book, but I signal to the reader straight away my partial impatience with such categories. There has been so much energy squandered, in my opinion, defining one's own category of Christian over and against other categories of Christian that the church is in grave danger of losing its true purpose and identity. One matter that exercises me is the continued use of the term *evangelical* to connote a certain range of characteristics that have little to do with evangelism, a word (*euangelion* in Greek, Latinized as *evangelium*) that means, after all, "gospel" or "good news." My own denomination, the Evangelical Lutheran Church in Canada (ELCIC) is not what most people think of as evangelical. Although a re-envisioning process for this terminology is not a main objective of this book, I thought it best to put my impatience with such factionalism frankly before the reader.

Another somewhat controversial matter concerns my decision about how to handle portrayals of women in ministry. In early outlines of this book I gave female ministers a "room of their own." There was a chapter just for them. However, I have decided that surely 2013 (the date of my current writing) is as good a time as any to work more positively within Paul's declaration that "there is no longer male or female" (Gal 3:28). While not all denominations have fully welcomed women into the leadership of the church, Christianity overall has at last achieved a respectable standing on this issue. My own work, feminist as it is, on the cultural representation of clergy feels most comfortable if I impose the least number of divisions on the clerics under scrutiny.

Finally, I hope that *The Collar* mediates between an accessible style and a scholarly one. I am an academic but also an enthusiastic church member, and I care about the audience of this book, just as I care about the real flesh-and-blood pastors I have known all my life. To all of them I dedicate this book, and I have a word of comfort for them. The enmity that our society, and its cultural artifacts, sometimes shows to the ministry indicates that the church, in this age, is still a contender. If the church were no longer significant there would be no need for moviemakers, as an example, to pursue pastors with such mocking or condescending vigor. Of course, mockery is not the only scenario to be encountered. Nevertheless, there would be no purpose in creating a clergy buffoon or charlatan if the church no longer mattered. We are still here, and still breathing.

"The Collar" by George Herbert

I struck the board, and cried, "No more!
　　　　I will abroad.
What! shall I ever sigh and pine?
My lines and life are free; free as the road,
　　Loose as the wind, as large as store.
　　　　Shall I be still in suit?
Have I no harvest but a thorn
To let me blood, and not restore
What I have lost with cordial fruit?
　　　　　　Sure there was wine
　　Before my sighs did dry it; there was corn
　　　　Before my tears did drown it.
Is the year only lost to me?
　　　　Have I no bays to crown it?
No flowers, no garlands gay? all blasted?
　　　　　　All wasted?
　　Not so, my heart; but there is fruit,
　　　　　　And thou hast hands.
　　　　Recover all thy sigh-blown age
On double pleasures; leave thy cold dispute
Of what is fit and not; forsake thy cage,
　　　　　　Thy rope of sands,
Which petty thoughts have made, and made to thee
　　Good cable, to enforce and draw,
　　　　　　And be thy law,
　　　While thou didst wink and wouldst not see.
　　　　　　Away! take heed;
　　　　　　I will abroad.

Call in thy death's-head there; tie up thy fears;
　　　　He that forbears
　　　To suit and serve his need
　　　　Deserves his load."
But as I raved, and grew more fierce and wild
　　　　At every word,
　Methoughts I heard one calling, "Child";
　　　And I replied, "My Lord."[1]

Of the two greatest metaphysical poets, John Donne and George Herbert, Herbert in the past was understood as calm, dutiful, and single-minded, especially placed next to the passionate and complicated Donne. It is true we possess Donne's poems of sensuality as well as his religious verses, while Herbert left us only religious poems; we can judge Donne's skill as a preacher by his printed sermons, while Herbert, also a seventeenth-century parson, left us none. Until recently, critics assumed that Herbert was (compared to Donne, at any rate) acquiescent, quiet, secure, modest, as Stanley Fish pointed out with some exasperation in 1978, and he then went to some lengths to demonstrate that Herbert was as "restless and secure, precarious and stable"—just as full of metaphysical paradox—as his friend Donne.[2] One of the first to redress the imbalance in the ways Herbert and Donne are seen was T. S. Eliot, who did much to rehabilitate the reputation of all the metaphysical poets. In his short study of Herbert in 1962 Eliot said this: "To think of Herbert as the poet of a placid and comfortable easy piety is to misunderstand utterly the man and his poems."[3]

When I came across these remarks, which assumed that a case needed to be made for George Herbert's complexity, I was puzzled. The first poem by Herbert I ever read, and one that is still my favorite, is "The Collar," a poem fizzing and spitting with impatience, daring, and apparent irreverence.

Like Donne, Herbert was a devoted man of the church, but both were slow in taking holy orders. Initially each was ambitious, brilliant, and worldly, expert in an astonishing array of matters; to some minds their submission to the church must seem a tremendous waste of their

1. Herbert, "The Collar," *The Country Parson, The Temple.* All quotations of Herbert's poetry in this chapter are from this source.

2. Fish, *The Living Temple*, 46.

3. Eliot, *George Herbert*, 14.

gifts. In their poems both dare to argue vociferously with God, to plead with him as if he is a lover or a close comrade. While Donne's religious poems are less about his life as a priest but rather his life as a Christian, some of Herbert's most notable poems are explicitly about the trials of the priestly life. Yes, many of the poems in Herbert's only collection, *The Temple*, can be read as expressions of the problems and joys of the Christian life more generally, but several of them apprehensively and anxiously probe a priestly way of life that will never quite fit Herbert's personality, even though he is completely convinced of the rightness of the cause. "The Priesthood," "Aaron," "The Windows," and of course, "The Collar" are all profound ruminations on the difficulties of the minister's vocation.

"The Collar," unlike many seventeenth-century poems, is delivered conversationally, if a conversation can be imagined to rush and roar in near-monologue as this one does. The voice is a modern one to our ears, with its short, clipped demands and complaints, its repetitions ("I will abroad"), and its crankiness. The poem seems to belie its age by disdaining order and good form, with the poem's narrative arc beginning in that very contemporary place, the end. (We too often forget that the twentieth and twenty-first centuries did not invent fragmentation or unconventional structure.) The reader enters into the space of the poem just as the speaker launches into his furious finale, shouting his defiance at God for ruining his life and denying him pleasure and opportunity. "I struck the board, and cried, No more" is the first line; we neither know the precise cause of the speaker's anger nor does it matter. What we need to do is catch both the legitimacy of his complaint and his petulance. He is rightly frustrated by the leanness and harshness of his life: "No flowers, no garlands gay? all blasted? / All wasted?" But he is also enmeshed in petty, selfish concerns, indicated by the frequency of the pronoun "I" and the way the poem's short lines rush along heedlessly in one long stanza, refusing to stop and consider whether there might not be another, more sensible way. The poem also, cleverly, does not at first sight make much use of rhyme, and the ragged lines look disordered. For thirty-two lines, the speaker raves unchecked, and only in the last four lines is a turnaround indicated; he steps back from his fit of temper in line 33 and in lines 35 and 36 acquiesces with great suddenness: "Methoughts I heard one calling, *Child*: / And I replied, *My Lord*."

That's it. *Child. My Lord.* The reader wants to turn the page to follow up the story. And then what? Does the Lord tell the speaker what to do with all this anguish? Does God suggest what rules to follow that might work better, what work to undertake that could be less maddening? No. The storm inherent in the human personality is immediately obedient, recognizing in all humility its master's voice. The humility, I think, is shown to be most real in Herbert's decision to end the poem so immediately. To go on, to explain would be to exercise human ingenuity too much; the lesson is that the speaker must obey. When reading this poem aloud to my students, I often wish that there were helpful punctuation marks for the final exchange between God and the man. Is *Child* querulous? Is the naming an exclamation? Stage directions would be agreeable. Is the reply *My Lord* an appropriately gracious one? Is this tiny exchange of words loving or regretful? (While I am asking my fussy or naïve questions, my colleague Paul Dyck at Canadian Mennonite University bids me look at the meter of the last two lines. The rhythms have been uncertain, but when God speaks, common meter—the most common rhythm for old hymns—enters and establishes peace.)

"The Collar" is full of movement and fierce vitality, a little one-act play familiar to anyone who has ever shaken a fist at the heavens and muttered irreverent oaths through gritted teeth. The disappointments the speaker has suffered need not be confined to the work of the church; the festering irritations are widely applicable. But it is, after all, called "The Collar," and while we are invited to hear *choler* and *caller* in the word— and I think both the speaker and God call on each other, although only the fallible speaker gives into choler—Herbert has chosen the spelling of this homophone because his calling as a man of the cloth is most clearly at stake. While today we might think of a clerical collar as the obvious symbol that is choking Herbert's speaker (and, let us be frank, Herbert himself), it would be more appropriate to think of liturgical vestments as confining him, particularly the stole, which symbolizes the yoke of Christ that the priest has accepted. And while "the board" that is struck in the poem's first breath can be a homely and ordinary table, suitable for the domestic argument that is underway—"What? Shall I ever sigh and pine?" sounds like the griping and bellyaching that occurs in one's own kitchen—when combined with the collar of the title, the board becomes much more. This is the table of Holy Communion, and Herbert wants to hear our gasp of shock when we realize that the speaker is pounding on the communion table in a fit of rage. Even a postmodern, liberal Protestant such as myself pales at sacred furnishings handled in such a manner.

The lovely thing about "The Collar" is that it is precisely and only the minister who presides at that table and is thoroughly at home with it who would use it in such a manner. It is, in a way, the table he is sharing with the Lord, an intimate part of the equipment of his pastoral work. Why should he not pound on it? Is it not his, at least a little? On further reflection, the reader should recognize that the table, as representative of Christ's sacrificial love for the Church, can stand up to this battering and a whole lot more. The Lord can bear any amount of abuse from his priest. This does not mean that God is not hurt by the speaker's rant, but certainly God is wholly in control of the situation, as the simplicity of God's one word answer, "*Child,*" demonstrates.

The notion that a minister, and a godly one, as the last line proves, could be so angry at God and have the courage to publish that anger, was liberating when I first read this poem so many years ago. I had known ministers all my life, and although in my tradition they dressed casually, turned up in the post office, and watched many of the same television shows the rest of us did, like nearly everyone I suspected they were ridiculously patient people, touched with some special gift of goodness. Later, I would read other Herbert poems, such as "The Windows," where the poet almost moans or snarls the first lines: "Lord, how can man preach thy eternal word? / He is a brittle crazy glass" (with "crazy" here having simply the meaning of flawed, unsound). "The Windows" deals with one particular aspect of ministry, the poet asking how good preaching can be achieved. But, unlike "The Collar," Herbert's "The Windows," which compares the sermon to a stained glass window, is orderly, with a tidy conceit and something like a pat ending. "The Priesthood" also deals methodically with the motif of God as potter, making a useful vessel even out of the "foul and brittle" clay that the speaker feels himself to be. "The Collar" is more akin to Herbert's poems of despair and longing like "Affliction" (of which there are five, more than any other of his repeated titles, with even "Prayer" and "Praise" being used three times only). "Kill me not ev'ry day" is the first line of "Affliction (II)" and the final phrase is "all my future moan." In these poems there are no startling revelations or straight answers; God does not provide ease in a flash and sometimes does not provide ease at all.

These are the poems of a real man and a real priest: painful, exuberant, intense. It is helpful to place the priesthood poems of *The Temple* alongside Herbert's other major work, the prose treatise *The Country*

Parson, sometimes called *The Priest to the Temple.* According to some clergy within the Church of England, Herbert's *The Country Parson* sets up impossibly lofty standards for clerical behavior. In the recent book *If You Meet George Herbert on the Road, Kill Him*, Justin Lewis-Anthony rails against the tradition of "Herbertism":

> Herbert has been, and continues to be, used as an exemplar, *the* exemplar for the English parson. Whether you are High Church, Low Church, Evangelical, Charismatic, whatever, Herbert is portrayed as the prototype of the pastor, teacher, preacher, almoner, negotiator, gentleman, scholar. He is *Ur-*Vicar, the *Echt-*Rector.[4]

These super-vicars that Herbert supposedly promotes are, says Lewis-Anthony, "not just representatives of the Church of England, they *are* 'the Church of England' in any given place" and are "omni-present, omni-competent and omni-affirming." If all you read of *The Country Parson* is this devastating passage from the first chapter, "Of a Pastor," one can see the rightness of Lewis-Anthony's complaint:

> A Pastor is the Deputy of Christ for the reducing of Man to the Obedience of God. This definition is evident, and contains the direct steps of Pastoral Duty and Authority. For first, Man fell from God by disobedience. Secondly, Christ is the glorious instrument of God for the revoking of Man. Thirdly, Christ being not to continue on earth, but after he had fulfilled the work of Reconciliation, to be received up into heaven, he constituted Deputies in his place, and these are Priests. And therefore St. *Paul* in the beginning of his Epistles, professeth this: and in the first to the *Colossians* plainly avoucheth, that he *fills up that which is behind of the afflictions of Christ in his flesh, for his Body's sake, which is the Church.* Wherein is contained the complete definition of a Minister. Out of this Charter of the Priesthood may be plainly gathered both the Dignity thereof, and the Duty: The Dignity, in that a Priest may do that which Christ did, and by his authority, and as his Vicegerent. The Duty, in that a Priest is to do that which Christ did, and after his manner, both for Doctrine and Life.[5]

I am not a parson, country or otherwise, but I can imagine the sting a cleric might feel under the snap of some of Herbert's phrases.

4. Lewis-Anthony, *If You Meet George Herbert on the Road, Kill Him*, 6, 46–47.
5. Herbert, *The Country Parson*, 55 (emphasis in original).

The emphasis on obedience and duty is sobering enough but it is terrifying to think of oneself either as Christ's "deputy" or (worse) Christ's "viceregent." I would not know whether to laugh or cry at the unbearable simplicity of "the complete definition of a Minister"—the parson must merely and simply take Christ's place.

There are severe-sounding words in this passage that seem to guarantee a pastor's unpopularity: the pastor is to *reduce* us to obedience, and we are reminded that Christ came to *revoke* us. However, we misapprehend if we read too much negativity here. If the pastor must reduce his parishioners, in early seventeenth century usage that means he is to bring them back from error. If Christ revokes believers, he restores them to a good life. Some of the vocabulary that George Herbert uses in *The Country Parson* has descended in tone over the centuries. Words that now sound fierce were in some cases more positive in their original connotation; this is the case, for example, with the way Herbert uses *mortify, condescend,* and *censure* in his book.

If read carefully and patiently, the famous "complete definition of a Minister" emphasizes not only obedience and duty, but joy. Christ, after all, is the "glorious instrument of God," and Herbert wants ministers to take their strength from Christ. Concentrate on Christ, on dignity and duty, he says, and the rest will follow. Even more helpful is to turn back to the previous page, "The Author to the Reader," and note not only that this preface emphasizes Herbert's desire to "please" God (the word is used twice) but that he wants to describe the character of a pastor's "love." The vocabulary is gentler. The key sentence of the opening of *The Country Parson,* however, is this one, and we should often recall it to mind: "I have resolved to set down the Form and Character of a true Pastor, that I may have a Mark to aim at: which also I will set as high as I can." Herbert is writing a guidebook to inspire his own ministry, setting up a series of objectives for himself. Being the man he was, Herbert made his standards sufficiently demanding to be worthy of a calling he knew was a high calling indeed.

The Country Parson and the poems in *The Temple* are companion pieces, the former setting forth the ideals, while the latter reveals how the "various strategies of didacticism are actually acted out," as John N. Wall Jr. has put it.[6] To see the daunting injunctions of *The Country Parson* as a series of commands is to see only a tiny portion of what Herbert

6. Wall, "Introduction," *The Country Parson, The Temple,* 28.

intended. The dialectical movement between the ideal and the actual in the two books should, hopefully, create a third way: a dynamic, embodied, workable portrayal of what ministry might be like. (Similarly, says Christine Wohlberg in her study of *The Country Parson* called *All Possible Art*, Herbert was the advocate of a middle way between high church elitism and Puritanical plainness. He was advocating balance in an era when conflict between Anglo-Catholics and Dissenters was real and sometimes agonizing.) There is also a sense that Herbert realizes that the profession of ministry is already in social jeopardy (in *The Country Parson* see chapter 28, "The Parson in Contempt"). Thus lofty goals must be established. The author knows his guidebook is idealistic, but ideals are needed to try to turn the situation around.

There are other elements which make the tone of *The Country Parson* hard for today's reader to grasp. One point to remember is that Herbert's era was one of the last great ages of rhetoric. He was well trained in the rigid conventions of classical rhetoric at Cambridge, where he was a leading scholar and even held the position of Public Orator, demonstrating that he was among the best rhetoricians in a time of masterly rhetoric. *The Country Parson* would have been recognizable to its first readers as, among other things, a type of courtesy or conduct book, a guide to correct behavior. The genre was well-known and readers would expect the author to delineate sharply the rules of comportment for a gentleman who happens (in this case) to be a minister. What we may not see today is how unusual Herbert's relatively personal manner would be in such a conduct book. See for example, his advice about being a companionable storyteller while traveling; Herbert suggests the parson provide "sometimes some short, and honest refreshments, which may make his other discourses more welcome, and less tedious" ("The Parson in Journey").[7]

What makes *The Country Parson* truly remarkable is that, unusual for its time, this is a book about relationships, about community. Herbert is not interested in the parson in isolation, because then he would be no minister at all. His aim is an enlightening portrayal of how the parson and the people interact. The parson should bless them frequently (chapter 26), give thanks and bear their sins to God (chapter 6), praise them (chapter 7), and most importantly teach them. Chapter 21, on catechizing, ought to be the dullest of chapters, but Herbert's instruction catches

---

7. Herbert, *The Country Parson, The Temple,* 78.

fire in this chapter. He emphasizes the delight that will result for all parties during the process of truly good and meaningful catechism.

Those readers who still worry that George Herbert sets impossible standards for the clergy of any age, or who worry alternatively that *The Country Parson* places too much emphasis on appearance ("his apparel plain, but reverend, and clean, without spots, or dust, or smell; the purity of his mind breaking out, and dilating itself even to his body, clothes, and habitation"),[8] should take notice of the brief, beautiful expressions that appear to have crept into *The Country Parson* from its more ecstatic sister volume, *The Temple*:

> The pulpit is his joy and his throne. (62)

> His Parish being all his joy and thought. (78)

> Do well, and right, and let the world sink. (97)

> Now Love is his business, and aim. (109)

Yes, Herbert does say that "The Country Parson desires to be all to his Parish, and not only a Pastor, but a Lawyer also, and a Physician" (87) and that it is necessary that his wife should be, of course, a skilled healer (69). But alongside these exacting injunctions are plenty of homely remarks, like the one in which a pastor is required "to be on God's side, and be true to his party" (80). I think the statement that demonstrates most clearly the intimate relation between *The Temple* and *The Country Parson* is this one, in the chapter on preaching: "He often tells them, that Sermons are dangerous things, that none goes out of Church as he came in, but either better, or worse" (62–63). The sharp edges of ministry, the fears and disappointments, are as evident in this simple but explosive sentence as in "The Collar" when the speaker shouts at himself to "leave thy cold dispute / Of what is fit and not; forsake thy cage, / Thy rope of sands."

No one should go out of church as he or she came in. No one should enter *The Country Parson* or *The Temple* as she or he came in. Herbert desires with all his considerable being that ministry, and the experience of being a Christian generally, should change us every day. It involves risk and anguish, passion and love. Herbert's two books, four hundred years old, reveal the ministry in a fully-embodied, terrifying manner that will, if read rightly, even now change lives.

---

8. Ibid., 57. References to subsequent passages are given parenthetically.

1

Heroism and Suffering

Do not be ashamed, then, of the testimony about our Lord or of me his
prisoner, but join with me in suffering for the gospel. (2 Tim 1:8)

Therefore, when we feel pain, when we suffer, when we die, let us turn to this,
firmly believing and certain that it is not we alone, but Christ and the church
who are in pain and are suffering and dying with us. . . . We set out upon the
road of suffering and death accompanied by the entire church.
(Martin Luther, *Fourteen Consolations*)[1]

A remarkable turn has occurred during the last half century in the
Christian attitude toward religious heroes. For centuries veneration
of martyrs was a fundamental part of the worship experience; while one
might assume this is a predominantly Roman Catholic reality, the story
of Thomas Becket has been important for both Anglicans and Catholics,
and in the radical Reformation tradition of the Mennonites, the book
The Martyrs Mirror is acknowledged traditionally as having a place second in importance only to the Bible. Foxe's *Book of Martyrs* is similarly
a product of the Reformation. Yet in my lifetime the place of martyrdom
in the worship experience has become questionable, if not objectionable.
In Robertson Davies's 1970 novel *Fifth Business*, Dunstable Ramsay begins a career as historian and mythographer in part because of his early
exposure to Foxe's *Book of Martyrs*. The action is set in the early twentieth century; this late twentieth-century reader found the protagonist's

1. Luther, *Fourteen Consolations*, 163.

tolerance, and even fondness, for martyrs' tales bizarre, although Davies's magnificent storytelling skills carried the day.

The subject of martyrdom makes me uncomfortable, I freely admit, and I suspect, based on a lifetime of observing other Christians at worship (admittedly mostly Protestants), my feelings are widely shared. Two men who could be considered the most important Christian martyrs of the past century, Dietrich Bonhoeffer and Martin Luther King Jr., are more usually termed political martyrs, killed for their determined stances against Nazism and racism, respectively. Only a few generations ago they would have more definitely been designated Christian heroes—people who suffered pain, disgrace, torture, and death, following the example of Christ. While there were certainly other ways of being entered in either Alban Butler's Catholic *Lives of the Fathers, Martyrs and Other Principal Saints* (1756–1759) or Sabine Baring-Gould's Anglican *Lives of the Saints* (1872–1877), for the majority of Christian history the customary way of distinguishing oneself as a hero in the church has been to die for love of God and God's church. As James Doyle says in the Preface to the 1895 edition of Butler's authoritative collection of tales, "here the doctrines of the Catholic Church are presented to us passing through the *ordeal* of time."[2]

I will say little here about the way in which the current avoidance of stories of suffering and death marks the cowardice and comfortableness of our era. There is truth in that. But in our century the transformation of notions of Christian heroism has been, in many ways, a necessary and valuable one. For one thing, the unrelenting violence of most martyrologies has done little enough to "guide our feet into the way of peace" (Luke 1:79). Additionally, as Gerard Manley Hopkins tells us in his poem "Pied Beauty," God is also in the "dappled things," in "skies of couple-colour as a brinded cow," and for many (if not most) Christians such lovely but homely particulars suggest the numinous more commendably than any tale of flaying or beheading. This chapter, then, details some of the fictional representations of martyrology in recent times, but takes note of a lessening emphasis on violent suffering, until we arrive at Marilynne Robinson's astonishing work *Gilead*, a novel which proposes a gentle new ideal of Christian hero, one who dies slowly, lovingly, peacefully.

---

2. Doyle, preface to *Lives of the Martyrs*, 8 (my emphasis).

The Willing Sacrifice

> I would like to make an appeal in a special way to the men of
> the army. . . . Brothers, you are part of our own people. You kill
> your own campesino brothers and sisters. And before an order
> to kill that a man may give, the law of God must prevail that
> says: Thou shalt not kill. No soldier is obliged to obey an order
> against the law of God. . . . In the name of God, and in the name
> of this suffering people whose laments rise to heaven each day
> more tumultuous, I beg you, I ask you, I order you in the name
> of God: Stop the repression![3]

Oscar Romero, Roman Catholic Archbishop of San Salvador, delivered
these words during a long Lenten homily one day before he was assas-
sinated on March 24, 1980. Romero's words are used nearly verbatim in
John Duigan's film *Romero*, released in 1989 and starring Raul Julia. The
highlight of Romero's March 23 sermon is when he moves from request
to order, attempting to use his authority to compel the soldiers to his
point of view. Neither request nor order succeeds for the historical Archbishop, but in the years since 1980, in artistic and inspirational terms, his
words and example have been notable.

Part of the appeal of Romero's dramatic life and death is the distance he traveled in the three years he was Archbishop. As a priest, Oscar
Romero had been a conservative, with little patience for the liberation
theology so prevalent in the Latin American church. However, during
his term as Archbishop, six priests were murdered and Romero became
increasingly outspoken about government corruption and his nation's
neglect of the poor and vulnerable. Increasingly he allied himself with the
poor; the collection of his writings called *The Violence of Love* is replete
with statements like this one: "A church that does not join the poor, in
order to speak out from the side of the poor against the injustices committed against them, is not the true church of Jesus Christ."[4]

In some respects John Duigan's film does not stray far from docu-
mentary, but it has little need to. Such a recent martyr in the church is
well documented. What distinguishes this film is Raul Julia's fine and
subtle performance as Romero, a man not known for his passionate nature and one who had little personal charisma. Julia, without histrionics,

3. Quoted in Brockman, *The Word Remains*, 217.
4. Romero, *The Violence of Love*, 202.

demonstrates how remarkable was Romero's transformation from dull and careful conservative to someone who preached radical openness, as evidenced in these words from 1978:

> Everyone who struggles for justice, everyone who makes just claims in unjust surroundings is working for God's reign, even though not a Christian. The church does not comprise all of God's reign; God's reign goes beyond the church's boundaries. The church values everything that is in tune with its struggle to set up God's reign. A church that tries only to keep itself pure and uncontaminated would not be a church of God's service to people.[5]

It must have been tempting in the film *Romero* to make this personality shift overly melodramatic, but Duigan and Julia resist the temptation. It is precisely the passionate martyrdoms of the past that they counter with their film. Their Romero is dogged, grim, almost plodding. He does little that is more remarkable than refusing stubbornly to be untrue to his principles, demonstrating to the audience the potential that anyone has to be heroic. It is Romero's environment that is unusual, rather than the man; given another era or another place Oscar Romero might have been ordinary. But his response to circumstances that were vicious and inhumane moves him out of the category of the ordinary. Still, the message is there: he did not have a particularly startling or eloquent message, nor did he have supernatural powers or strength. He was, however, obstinately committed to the ideal that the church must represent the downtrodden.

Romero's martyrdom in this film does resemble prevailing notions of religious martyrdom: he is calm in the face of death; he appears prophetically to see his end coming; he dies in the act of serving others. Like other martyrs over the centuries he is marked by loneliness and isolation. But the novelty in Romero's martyrdom is his insistence that God's reign is not only about or for Christians. Before his death Romero came to a wide and all-embracing view of God's love that appears to dissolve boundaries between the secular world and the church. Although responsibility for Romero's death has been variously attributed to military forces protected by the government of El Salvador, to U.S.-trained opposition death squads, and to the rebel forces who did not welcome his pacifist

5. Ibid., 115.

approach, Romero's statement that the "church does not comprise all of God's reign" must have also unsettled Romero's superiors in the church.

Romero at first seems different in its politics than the other great nineteen eighties film about religious leaders making the ultimate sacrifice, Roland Joffe's *The Mission*. While *Romero* ultimately promotes a radically open view of the church's responsibility and membership, *The Mission* looks very old-school in its allegiance. Father Gabriel, played by Jeremy Irons, is a devoted servant of the church, sent to convert the forest-dwelling Guarani nation in South America. Father Gabriel's remote mission is presented in idealized terms as a place of education and tranquility. (Although Robert Bolt's screenplay purports to be based on actual events in the eighteenth century, this is a European vision of the events, and somewhat patronizing to the aboriginal peoples in the story.)

The twist in *The Mission* occurs when Spanish missionaries, of which Father Gabriel is one, are ordered to abandon the missions they have painstakingly created because these colonized territories in Paraguay are being reassigned to Portugal. In refusing to leave the mission, Father Gabriel is, on the one hand, standing up for the institution of the church as he understands it. But on the other hand, Father Gabriel's stance can be interpreted as his transfer of allegiance to the Guarani people, who are presented in Joffe's film as the true people of God, sincere in their worship and unwavering in their principles (unlike the Europeans, who are seen to have no firm principles). It is arguable that Father Gabriel dies, with his parishioners, for a very ancient church. But it could also be said that Father Gabriel dies in the act of becoming a new kind of priest, or even the priest of a new vision of Christianity.

In key scenes in this film we watch Jeremy Irons in the act of translation, both literal and figurative. So much of ministry is about translation, taking biblical stories and unpacking them for a congregation, explaining the history and theology, making scripture appropriate for the times. What we see Father Gabriel ultimately performing, however, is translation that goes the other way. Looking out to the secular world, he reads the actions of the Europeans and recognizes that the orders he has received are not part of God's plan for a healthy creation—far from it. So he becomes a spokesman for the Guarani against the church, carrying in the final battle scene a cross that has become the cross of the Guarani, not the cross of the Holy Mother Church that Father Gabriel once served.

Transformation of Character

In analyzing *Romero* and *The Mission* I have been emphasizing elements of Christian martyrdom that seem under revision, but one can begin to see this shift in early- and mid- twentieth century's fictional representations of the twelfth-century martyr, Thomas Becket. Of the many depictions of Becket I have chosen two famous ones: T. S. Eliot's 1935 verse drama *Murder in the Cathedral* and Jean Anouilh's 1959 play *Becket* (*Becket, ou L'Honneur de Dieu*), which was the basis for the 1964 film with Richard Burton as the Archbishop and Peter O'Toole as Henry II. Archbishop Becket's story is not unlike Archbishop Romero's in that it involves a tremendous change in sensibility. Becket's shift, however, was ethical, moving as he did from thoroughgoing man of the world to ascetic, in opposition to Romero's political conversion. But in some aspects, Becket's death is the template for the sacrificial deaths of Father Gabriel and Archbishop Romero. Once the friend of a king who gave him supreme power in the church and expected the appointee to obey the royal will, Becket suddenly becomes loyal only to God, and is murdered at the king's command. Becket stands against political and secular authorities who challenge his view of what the church should be—and all of these martyrs also stand against collaborationist factions within the church itself.

Both Anouilh and Eliot emphasize aspects of Becket's ordinariness; it is perhaps that quality in Becket that has prompted over the centuries such loyalty among the lower classes (most noticeable in Chaucer's *Canterbury Tales*). In Anouilh's play Becket's last words, for example, are not majestic and stirring but plaintive, even peevish. In Edward Anhalt's English screenplay Becket's penultimate lines are weary: "It is here now, the supreme folly. This is its hour. O Lord, how heavy thy honour is to bear"; his last words express understated pity for his persecutor ("Poor Henry").[6] *Murder in the Cathedral* has Becket say at one point, rather wonderfully, one of my favorite Eliot lines (used again in the poem *Burnt Norton*): "Human kind cannot bear very much reality."[7] But the difference between the two plays is in the degree of faith: Anouilh is not overly interested in the religious aspect of the story and Eliot most certainly is.

6. Anouilh, *Becket*, directed by Peter Glenville, English adaptation by Edward Anhalt (this and all subsequent quotation is my own transcription from the film).

7. Eliot, *Murder in the Cathedral*, 69.

> A Christian martyrdom is never an accident, for Saints are not
> made by accident. Still less is a Christian martyrdom the effect
> of man's will to become a Saint, as a man by willing and con-
> triving may become a ruler of men. A martyrdom is always the
> design of God, for His love of men, to warn them and to lead
> them, to bring them back to His ways. It is never the design of
> man; for the true martyr is he who has become the instrument
> of God, who has lost his will in the will of God, and who no lon-
> ger desires anything for himself, not even the glory of becoming
> a martyr.[8]

This is Eliot's Becket: predicting his own end and the upheaval that that
end will cause. The priest as the instrument of God who has made his
will over to God—this is the pattern we expect. Anouilh's Becket, on
the other hand, stands more simply as refusal to compromise with the
worldly authority that he once represented. "One can always manage the
church. We must come to a sensible little arrangement with God" is a
typical line for the early Becket. An hour later in the viewing experience
he has cleanly switched sides: "The kingdom of God must be defended
like any other kingdom. Gentlemen, it is a supreme irony that the worldly
Becket, the profligate and libertine, should find himself standing here at
this moment. But here he is, in spite of himself."[9]

Both Eliot's and Anouilh's Beckets are seen as strong-willed men
learning to submit to God's stronger will, but the principles involved in
Anouilh's play are more straightforward. Anouilh's Becket is an individual, and the playwright is interested in the ways in which individualism
threatens the powers that be. Becket has been wholly the king's man, but
when he removes that loyalty the king will do almost anything to halt this
assertion of independence. In Eliot's version of the story, the king does
not even appear. For Eliot, the drama involves Becket and God, and (to
a lesser extent) the People, represented not only by the Chorus but also
by the Tempters, Priests, and Knights. But without the king in view, the
situation is no less dangerous; indeed it is more dangerous. The demands
put upon Becket by the People to live, to die, to protect and shield are
frightening and extreme. In the Gospel of John and several other places
in the Gospels, Christ insists on the hatred that is the prerequisite of his
service and sacrifice: "If the world hates you, be aware that it hated me
before it hated you. If you belonged to the world, the world would love

8. Ibid., 49.
9. Anouilh, *Becket*.

you as its own. Because you do not belong to the world, but I have chosen you out of the world—therefore the world hates you" (John 15:18–19). In *Murder in the Cathedral* this unreasoning animosity is palpable. Currents of hatred swirl around Becket for no good reason, and even the love of the People can be destructive. At the end of the play the Chorus, having the last word, admits they "fear the blessing of God, the loneliness of the night of God, the surrender required, the deprivation inflicted"[10] and yet they know they too have played their awful part in compelling Becket toward his violent end, forcing him to undergo the sacrifice that they cannot bear.

For the most part, the deaths of Archbishop Romero and Father Gabriel in *Romero* and *The Mission* are unaccompanied by hagiographical élan. In the films, the directors are clear that no miracles are attributable to these men before or after their deaths; the stories are resolutely grounded in realism; the action ends in each case with their deaths. The stories about Thomas Becket in the past were different, in that Becket's death was immediately seen, by way of miracles, to make a difference. But these twentieth-century versions of Becket's story, by Eliot and Anouilh, stop short of potential miracles. We are grounded in death, selflessness, in strength of will.

What purpose do tales of martyrdom have for readers and viewers of our time? Our world continues to be a violent one, and there is no doubt that clerics and ordinary believers right now are dying for their faith under one oppressive regime or another. Those suffering under such circumstances must find strength and inspiration from stories of previous martyrs. But for the average comfortable Christian in the West today, different lessons arise from works like *The Mission, Romero, Becket,* and *Murder in the Cathedral*. One lesson is best summarized in the repeated phrase of the Chorus in Eliot's play about "living and partly living." The average Christian is like this, "living and partly living," simultaneously conscious and unconscious of God's presence and the Christian's duty to do God's will.

> We do not wish anything to happen.
> Seven years we have lived quietly,
> Succeeded in avoiding notice,
> Living and partly living.[11]

10. Eliot, *Murder in the Cathedral*, 87.
11. Ibid., 18.

Heroic Christian leaders like Oscar Romero and Thomas Becket demonstrate the possibility of going beyond this halfway stage, becoming fully alive in relationship with God. It feels odd to think of someone who dies for love of Christ as fully alive but, when we think about this, it should not be odd at all. Another lesson arising from these tales of martyrdrom is the value of single-mindedness. Words like *submission*, *instrument*, and *surrender* in Eliot's drama do not play well for us in our time, but think instead of a determined sense of purpose, or complete and utter attention. This aspect of the martyrs' stories is needed in our era, when nearly all people, pastors included, experience so many distracting voices, clamoring bits of information, and cries for help spinning around and enveloping us at all times. Martyrdom, in other words, is not about death, although dying may well happen. For a Christian, death can hardly be the point. The heroic Christian act is rather identifying oneself as being a Christian to the detriment of all other claims. Nothing could be simpler, or more challenging.

Stripped to Essentials

In 1938 English novelist Graham Greene, a convert to Roman Catholicism since 1926, visited Mexico, which had endured at that point several years of anti-clerical purges by ostensibly leftist governments hostile to the church. Greene, both a leftist and a Catholic, was fascinated by this situation and wrote a fiction and a non-fiction book about the Mexican situation. The novel is one of Greene's most famous books, *The Power and the Glory*, published in 1940. At the center of the novel is an unnamed priest on the run, a weak, alcoholic, and despairing man whose sins are many and who (in his own eyes and in the eyes of others) is almost impossible to imagine as a hero. He summarizes his own life in this way: "a caricature of service: a few communions, a few confessions, and an endless bad example."[12] Yet by the end of the book, when he is captured and executed, it does appear that Greene asks us to entertain the notion that the whisky priest, as he is named, is a martyr for the Christian church.

Greene's Catholic novels are difficult for Protestants to negotiate, or at least difficult for this Protestant to negotiate. Suffering and sin are foremost in novels like *The Power and the Glory*, *The Heart of the Matter*, and

---

12. Greene, *The Power and the Glory*, 208. References to subsequent passages are given parenthetically.

The End of the Affair, and the insistence that human beings are powerless to save themselves by their own efforts is relentless. There is an intense sense of Catholic separateness in Greene's stories; the characters are isolated not just from humanists, but from other Christians, and although there is pride involved in this separation, there is also misery. In *The Power and the Glory* the priest desperately needs to confess his sins, but for this he needs another priest; he desperately guards the elements of the Eucharist because, as one of the last priests in Mexico, he is the gateway to communion with God. Saying a Mass in a remote village, the priest believes that "God was here in the body for the first time in six years" (71). Greene's focus on sin and the mysterious movements of God's grace are certainly applicable and interesting for any Christian reader, although some references to Catholic dogma may be puzzling for Protestants.

In *The Power and the Glory* we should put aside doctrinal matters and concentrate on the priest. Although the reader may disagree with the priest's belief that the Christian's first duty is to save his own soul (65), the emphasis in the novel on the importance of duty is salutary. Horton Davies sees Greene's novel as "a modern version of the book of Jonah, as man's attempt to evade God and God's pursuit of him"[13] but I do not see the whisky priest as evading God. Whatever else is wrong with the priest—and there is much that is wrong—his sense of duty, however often he betrays it, is strong. Greene cannot be easily described as a modernist—his style is too straightforward and accessible—but in his portrayal of self-haunted, alienated humanity he can be aligned with other literary modernists like Faulkner and Joyce. One of the many valuable elements of personality that twentieth-century souls have lost, according to Greene, is that sense of duty that can propel an individual through arduous situations. In *The Power and the Glory* we observe the priest failing in his responsibilities time and again, but as his life is pared down to its most primitive qualities, his sense of duty resurrects itself and allows him to retain some dignity at the end. He truly believes that "when he was gone it would be as if God in all this space between the sea and the mountains ceased to exist" (65); this is a real sorrow for him as he prepares for execution.

Duty is a difficult word for us these days, and has been for many decades. But it is a concept still worth our attention. Perhaps it needs another name, as so many abused concepts do, but duty can make all the

---

13. Davies, *A Mirror of the Ministry*, 103.

difference in a challenging situation. To use a commonplace example, it is necessary to offer condolence and support when a neighbor faces the death of a loved one. We may not want to; it may not be convenient; we may not even like the person to whom we are offering sympathy nor have respect for the person who has died. But duty, especially Christian duty, demands in a time of mourning or crisis that we act. In this novel, the price of duty for the priest is costly; several times he is on the verge of escaping this oppressive region and saving himself but he is called back to hear a dying man's confession. Each time he turns back automatically, wearily and unhappily, but dutifully.

In *The Power and the Glory* the strangeness of the religious concepts can have the happy effect of forcing us to think about the qualities of Christian leadership or the strictures of doctrine that we claim adherence to and those we actually enact. It is thought-provoking, to say the least, when the whisky priest tells a woman in the confessional that loving God means "wanting to protect Him from yourself" (173). This, to me, is such a strange idea that I am forced anew to consider what relationship to God I actually ascribe to. (Just how honest and open can the relations between follower and deity be?) And when the priest experiences bouts of inappropriate giggling, the reader cannot help but be reminded, in a useful way, of the comic ironies involved in God's condescension to become part of humankind. There are not a lot of moments of humor or grace in Graham Greene's rather grim Catholic novels, but when these moments arrive they are significant, and the delight (or potential delight) in laughter marks the giftedness of creation, creating communion and community, almost despite the actions of the individuals involved.

> Now they were both tired out and the mule simply sat down. The priest scrambled off and began to laugh. He was feeling happy. It is one of the strange discoveries a man can make that life, however you lead it, contains moments of exhilaration; there are always comparisons which can be made with worse times: even in danger and misery the pendulum swings. (59)

The Power and the Glory is a novel that prompts questions about whether we should be reading allegorically. Does the priest represent Christ and the *mestizo* who betrays him Judas? Do the priest's journeys point toward the stations of the cross? Is the priest's relatively happy and safe time with the upright Lutherans, the Lehrs, some sort of "take this cup from me" time of temptation? I think useful analysis can be done along these lines, but ultimately the priest as priest is more interesting. In relatively prosperous times he has been a fallen priest; in terrible times, he is challenged to become a redeemed and redeeming priest. He is stripped of much that we consider the trappings of humanity, but when we see what is left that is intrinsic to his vocation, we are moved and enlightened, even if we do not share Greene's doctrinal beliefs. (Although we may admire the priest for protecting the elements of the Eucharist so assiduously, and pouring himself into his duty as a confessor and baptizer, it may be less easy for us to accept the deaths attributable to him in his journey toward martyrdom: the lieutenant pursuing him shoots, unwillingly, three hostages in an attempt to force the people of the region to give up the priest.) Despite his many sins and weaknesses, the priest stripped down to essentials becomes a profound blessing; there should be argument about whether the essentials that Greene demonstrates are in fact the essentials at all, but the exercise is a good one.

The Serene Hero

An emphasis on heroism in Christian leadership has led me into lengthy consideration of martyrdom, and the direction was not absolutely necessary. One could find portrayals of clergy being heroic in less violent films and novels: I do find Reverend Farebrother in George Eliot's *Middlemarch* an exemplary cleric in many respects, and the recent BBC television comedy *Rev.* shows us a good priest who does not undergo torture or death but nevertheless suffers daily a million tiny humiliations as he patiently tries to serve God. But it is undeniable that we expect a truly impressive priest in literature to die for the faith rather than live for the faith.

As an example of an important work of fiction that explores the possibility of holy service that is serene and gentle, Marilynne Robinson's much-loved 2004 novel *Gilead* is unsurpassed in its beauty and depth. While not everyone would agree that John Ames, the pastor at the center of *Gilead*, fulfills the definition of a hero, nearly everyone could agree about his goodness. When *Gilead* was published, there was a sense in North American literary circles of relief and joy. I can recall thinking how wondrous it was to meet a protagonist so trustworthy, moving, and humble, and yet absolutely human, fallible, and recognizable. Here was hope for contemporary literature, for ethics, and for religion. *Gilead* is that rare thing: a lovely and profoundly wise book about faith, about the tremendous gift that is existence, about human love and sorrow and loneliness.

The plot is both simple and urgent: an aging pastor with a heart condition wants to leave a record of his life to his son; in a parallel plot the pastor awkwardly attempts to minister to his troubled godson, the wayward son of his best friend, also a pastor. There is much to treasure in *Gilead*. It is a version of (and a complication of) the prodigal son parable that does not end easily. Is the novel also a portrait of America, its frayed edges, its small hopes? Yes, and most certainly *Gilead* is a celebration of the tiny mysteries that allow everyday living to be so miraculous; for example, the friendship and rivalry of the two ministers, Ames and Boughton, is both a source of frustration and sustenance to them. Daily, Ames is simultaneously enthralled by the world around him and saddened that so few people see the glory he does: "Wherever you turn your eyes the world can shine like transfiguration. You don't have to bring a thing to it except a little willingness to see. Only, who could have the courage to see it?"[14] And then there is the enigma of the understated but passionate love of this sixty-seven-year-old cleric for a woman in her thirties and for their young son, a character who remains shadowy but unforgettable on the edge of the story.

As a minister, Ames in some respects would appear to be colorless, diminished. He is aging and sick, able to do less and less. He suffers in imagination the weight of his hundreds of sermons in the attic of his home. He serves a small congregation in the middle of nowhere. At one point he says to his diary, in quiet exasperation, "This afternoon I came back from a fairly discouraging meeting at the church—just a few people came, and absolutely nothing was accomplished. That is the kind of thing that wears me out."[15] But his shy enactments of forgiveness and service, his tiny offerings of good counsel are lovely. In his humility he has opened himself up completely to the experience of God's creation. Significantly, Robinson removes nearly all direct references to Ames's denomination so that this can be a pure portrait of the ministry, of faith as opposed to institution; an American reader attuned to denominational distinctions can construe that Ames is Congregationalist, but the type of church Ames serves is less important than comprehending Christian service in its essence.

14. Robinson, *Gilead*, 245.
15. Ibid., 195.

Gilead is constructed along similar lines to the novel *Diary of a Country Priest* by Georges Bernanos, and John Ames explicitly has that book, which he admires, in mind as he narrates his own story. In each book there is the same diary format, the same last days, the same almost ludicrous clarity of vision (at times), the same fierce commitment to vocation, the same overpowering and often unexpected love for people, the same sleeplessness. But the experience of reading these two novels about country priests could not be more different. Bernanos emphasizes the frustration and isolation of his unnamed priest. Robinson provides her priest not only with a solid name, but a definite community, one that is flawed but marked by real tenderness. No matter how resolute is the priest's love of God in Bernanos, my question persists: is he doing more harm than good? Robinson's minister lives through similar situations, but there is no need to ask this question. John Ames is doing good. To watch the daily unfolding of small acts of goodness is a pleasure.

Particularly important is the novel's investigation of forgiveness: how hard it is not only to forgive but to be forgiven. If Graham Greene asks us to reconsider the neglected concept of duty, Marilynne Robinson urges us to contemplate forgiveness: a concept not so abased, but nevertheless bandied about with too much ease. Above I noted that *Gilead* (and its sequel *Home*) is an investigation of the story of the prodigal son. Over the space of these two novels, Robinson's slow and careful unraveling of the story of black sheep Jack Boughton, the godson of John Ames, is masterful. One element that is sometimes lost in our reading of this ancient parable is the complex nature, the multiple signification of prodigality. Who is prodigal in the biblical story, and in Robinson's novel? Is the emphasis properly on the prodigious amount of sin that needs to be forgiven, or is it on the prodigality of the father's (or godfather's, or God's) gifts? Do we need to think more about squandered inheritance or about extravagant grace? Is it the bitterness of the dutiful brother that is prodigal? And is it any less difficult to be on the side of "good" prodigality, to be the one doing the forgiving and blessing, than to be the one on the "sinning" side? John Ames agonizes over the life of young Jack Boughton, and his evidently loftier moral position does not give him the comfort one might expect. Reviewing this novel, James Wood described it as "fiercely calm" and also "demanding, grave and lucid."[16] This assessment is accurate, but it misses some of the ache and loneliness of John Ames's meditation.

16. Wood, "Acts of Devotion," *New York Times*.

The inducement is understandable that artists in search of high drama should want to portray the ideal church leader as someone in dire circumstances, as one who endures death for God's glory. For many people during the past century (and longer) the church has come to seem less and less relevant, and so the extreme portrait of heroic cleric as martyr might seem once again necessary, as a jolt to the sensibilities of a bored and alienated audience. Just before T. S. Eliot wrote *Murder in the Cathedral* he wrote his Choruses for *The Rock* (1934), which are not terribly well known. *The Rock* mingles the dour atmosphere of *The Waste Land* (produced before Eliot's conversion) with his newer Christian emphasis on the church as a light for a world immersed in darkness and fear. But even that church, whose light Eliot repeatedly describes as *little*, is tainted, the view of it sour or tired; most people consider it useful only for weddings.

In the face of this modern (and postmodern) estrangement from Christian life, it might look as if the only way to awaken interest in Christian leadership is to court extremity, to play variations on the theme of martyrdom and sacrifice. But this is to comply too easily with the dubious expectations of secular culture. Martyrdom's stress on violence fits in all too well with the violence inherent in the rest of contemporary life. Marilynne Robinson's *Gilead* shows beautifully how another way is possible, a way of peace and small revelations. Nearly every page of John Ames's book contains a small but breathtaking word of advice: "There are a thousand thousand reasons to live this life, every one of them sufficient" or "I feel sometimes as if I were a child who opens its eyes on the world once and sees amazing things it will never know any names for and then has to close its eyes again."[17] To have such delicate and beautiful principles is heroic enough.

17. Robinson, *Gilead*, 243, 57.

The Diary of a Country Priest

by Georges Bernanos

Written in 1936 and translated into English the same year, *The Diary of a Country Priest* (*Journal d'un curé de campagne*) was immediately awarded a distinguished prize by the French Academy and is a much-loved novel in France. In English-speaking countries, the book has been less influential but is nevertheless held in high regard, particularly by Roman Catholics, and one can without difficulty find both the novel and the 1951 film adaptation by Robert Bresson described as masterpieces. Recently an online commentator praised its "frightening and poetic penetration into the very life of things" and its "universal character,"[1] while in *Religion and Literature* Ann M. Begley in 2001 affirmed confidently that the miserable unnamed curé is presented by Bernanos as the exclusive owner of a "deep inner life" while all around him are the *mediocrés*, "tepid souls who emphasize exterior signs of respectability." For the unhappy and unhealthy protagonist, God is "a loving companion, a joyous experience, a living friendship," says Begley,[2] while Rachel Murphy claims this:

> Strangely, mysteriously, by the end of the novel there is such a clear sense of wholeness, of an unbroken worldview, that one senses in the thrust of the priest's obscure life a divine purpose; an unfolding of a flower; a life beautiful in its very hiddenness, its seeming poverty.[3]

1. Murphy, review of *Diary of a Country Priest*.
2. Begley, "Georges Bernanos' Love Affair with God," 38, 42.
3. Murphy, review of *Diary of a Country Priest*.

It is possibly already evident by my tone that in reading these commentators I hardly recognize the novel I have read. I am grateful to Horton Davies for his exemplary *A Mirror of the Ministry in Modern Novels* (1959), but I balk at his judgment that Bernanos has written "the supreme fictional account of the fool for Christ's sake."[4] As a work of fiction, *The Diary of a Country Priest* is a disaster. Purporting to be a journal, it consists of long complicated conversations on convoluted theological issues faithfully recorded by Monsieur le Curé at the end of each exhausting day. For the non-Catholic the theological points so fiercely debated can be baffling, while for any reader the voices of the various characters surely resemble each other too much to be distinguishable. (This may be the fault of the translation by Pamela Morris, which seems decidedly problematic.) But it is the novel's status as a work of religious significance that troubles me more. The entire novel is one long cry of pain. I have no doubt that the priest loves God, but his belief in his vocation, his ability, and his fellow human beings is so tangled and thwarted that nearly every page delivers some encounter with doubt or conflict or humiliation. Reading *The Diary of a Country Priest* is, in my opinion, a debilitating experience. Here is a typical passage:

> Last night after writing this, I knelt at the foot of my bed and prayed that Our Lord might bless my resolutions. Suddenly I was overwhelmed by a sense of destruction, a feeling that all the dreams, hopes and ambitions of my youth had been broken down. I got into bed shivering with fever, and never slept till dawn.[5]

The unnamed priest is dying; we eventually find out he has stomach cancer, although his manic mood swings and crazily erroneous image of his own well-being make one suspect tuberculosis for some time. He refuses to be a good steward of his health and declines steadily, until at the end of the novel he is dead, offering these last words: "Grace is everywhere" (253). The novel has been praised for the priest's radical honesty with himself, yet he tears pages out of his journal, refusing to share them with the reader. While reading this novel and considering its date, I wondered if it were a modernist experiment of the sort being attempted at the time by Hemingway or Joyce. Should the priest be deemed unreliable,

---

4. Davies, *Mirror of the Ministry*, 84.

5. Bernanos, *Diary of a Country Priest*, 33. References to subsequent passages are given parenthetically.

like the narrator in Fitzgerald's *Great Gatsby* or Ford Madox Ford's *The Good Soldier*? Is irony being utilized as a compositional strategy? There is a hallucinatory quality in some of the prose that might suggest a modernist experiment.

At this point the reader is asking whether I ought to be communicating my bafflement so transparently. But this experience of being so completely out of step with critical opinion is rare enough for me that I think it worth investigating. One feature to contemplate in this novel by Bernanos is that this is palpably a tale of martyrdom, yet I am uncertain what the martyrdom is for. "Monks suffer for souls, *our* pain is on behalf of souls. This thought came to me yesterday evening and remained all night long beside my bed, a guardian angel" (27) is another typical passage from the curé, and a few pages later he returns to the theme: "'Suffer on behalf of others.' I whispered this comforting thought to myself all night, but my angel did not return" (30). In mid-century French intellectual life, the existential emphasis on freedom was prevalent; freedom, no matter how hellish, was often the subject of Sartre and Camus. The long-standing French feud between an anti-clerical intelligentsia and faithful Catholics is also a factor in the novel; Bernanos is reacting against a society he saw dominated by a soulless secularism. "I began to write," he said, "to try to escape from this disgusting era."[6]

One of the few commentators to make sense of Bernanos is Graham Greene, who in an essay described his fictions as "open wounds that refuse, like stigmata, to heal."[7] Mark Bosco, discussing the influence on Greene of French Catholic writers like Bernanos and Mauriac, says that Greene appreciated Bernanos for denouncing the "distortion of Christianity into respectable and genteel mediocrity."[8] Greene, with his ambiguous, tortured, sometimes disgusted believers, does something of the same thing in his novels. However Greene writes with lucidity and discrimination, while Bernanos writes in an excessive, anguished style that the sympathetic reader calls "ardent"[9] but the present reader finds distasteful.

I offer one more scene of this priest's troubling courtship of martyrdom from Bernanos's novel. The curé throughout the novel struggles to pray; there are many scenes like the following, and they are all agonizing.

6. Quoted in Hoen, "Georges Bernanos."
7. Quoted in Bosco, *Graham Greene's Catholic Imagination*, 43.
8. Ibid., 42.
9. Begley, "Georges Bernanos' Love Affair with God," 43.

> I have watched all night: day is beginning. My window has been open, and I am shivering. I can hardly hold this pen, but I seem to be breathing more freely, to be calmer. Though I got no sleep, this cold which goes right through me does just as well. An hour or two ago when I was praying, squatting on my heels with my cheek against the wooden table, I suddenly felt such a hollow emptiness, I thought I was going to die. It made me happy. (162)

To be charitable, what *The Diary of a Country Priest* can prompt in the reader is a profound contemplation of servanthood. What does it mean to serve God wholly and completely? What lengths would most Christians go in their fidelity to Christ? As someone who believes that God desires us to experience fulfillment and joy, I take issue with a writer like Bernanos, who insists on the difficulty of serving God. But it is a worthwhile exercise, this contemplation of sacrifice, this examination of just how absolute we are willing to be in our religious efforts. Yet it is not merely servanthood that the curé desires and inhabits so intensely. He longs to identify entirely with Christ, to enter into Christ's pain and death. He does so, but the reason for this self-immolation refuses to become clear for me. Grace may well be everywhere, as the dying curé says, but one has to search too violently and interpret too ingeniously to find the grace in this story.

2

The Counselor/Confessor

And the Lord's servant must not be quarrelsome but kindly to everyone, an apt
teacher, patient, correcting opponents with gentleness. (2 Tim 2:23–25)

A concept of God is always conceived in relation to a
concept of person and a concept of a community of persons.
(Dietrich Bonhoeffer, *Sanctorum Communio*)[1]

The language of Christian leadership and discipleship can be daunting. *Righteous* is one word that has always made me skittish, as has
godly. I shy away from using *pious* if I can help it. But all are still good
words, worthy and meaningful, and have only become spoiled by misuse
and exploitation. There are also humbler words for followers of Christ
which, for some reason, bear up better: *gentle, kind, patient*. Long before
I knew the line was Milton's, I would, as an impatient youth, mutter to
myself, teeth clenched, "They also serve who only stand and wait." This
aspect of ministry—listening, accepting, waiting, and then listening
some more—seems in some respects so straightforward that we take it
for granted. But if it really is easy, then this should be one of the tasks of
ministry that the ordinary layperson can leap right into. I doubt that it is
as easy as we think, but nevertheless, we should leap, because people are
desperate to be heard and desperate for neighbors to be present to them,
to walk and stand and sit with them.

1. Bonhoeffer, *Sanctorum Communio*, 34.

The Listener

In 1978, British novelist A. S. Byatt published the first in a series of four novels that have been called the "Powerhouse Quartet" or the "Frederica Quartet." I have always called them the Potter novels, as they begin with the three Potter children: Stephanie, Frederica, and Marcus, growing up in Yorkshire in the fifties, although the story of the Potters is considerably complicated by Byatt's myriad intellectual concerns and the dozens of minor characters, often allegorical, that she insists upon. The Potters are precociously talented and intellectual, and in the Potter quartet (especially the latter two books), Byatt's style eventually becomes erudite and self-conscious. But the first two books, *The Virgin in the Garden* and *Still Life*, promised an enjoyable and epic grappling with English culture in the fifties and sixties, similar to Anthony Powell's series *A Dance to the Music of Time;* by the time she reached *Babel Tower* and, especially, *A Whistling Woman*, her prose would be encased with what the *Guardian* called "a blizzard of symbols."[2]

Since there is so much going on in Byatt's work, no critical notice has been taken of one attractive but unassuming creation, the clergyman Daniel Orton. Daniel is a marvelous character, functioning as he does like a solid counterweight to the highly cerebral Potters in the Potter Quartet. He is an overweight working class Yorkshireman bemused by the Potters' linguistic and aesthetic interests, and against all expectation he marries the clever Stephanie and—again against all expectation—makes her supremely happy. ("He was so strong, so ingenious, so much there," Stephanie thinks in *The Virgin in the Garden*.)[3] The Orton marriage, heartbreakingly short (Stephanie dies at the end of the second Potter novel), is one of the great and mysterious marriages in fiction, and Daniel Orton is one of the most moving and least known clerical characters in twentieth-century fiction.

Daniel is a definite kind of cleric, "psychologically acute, doctrinally simple," someone who responds to the needs of those around him with every fiber of his being. He becomes involved with people in dire situations, especially the antisocial, the severely depressed, and women with damaged or dead children. Although not full of "book learning" like the Potters, he is smart, imaginative, and—that rare thing—an amazingly

2. Macfarlane, review of *A Whistling Woman*.
3. Byatt, *The Virgin in the Garden*, 296.

helpful listener. In *The Virgin in the Garden* one of the characters is startled when Daniel mentions *King Lear* in a sermon: could he possibly have read it? But it is soon impressed upon us that Daniel just "knows Lear."[4] Daniel's knowledge and goodness are deep-rooted, profound, and almost beyond language. Byatt makes him fat because, I think, Daniel's physicality is a large part of his success as a parson; he loves with his whole being, and his being is enormous.

I have included Daniel Orton in this chapter about ministers who function primarily as counselors or social workers, but such a designation might sound more condescending than is meant. Daniel toward the end of the Potter books more or less defrocks himself and becomes a "Listener" on a telephone help line, and while he will be an unhappy and somewhat broken man his entire life (he never recovers from his wife's death), his dedicated work as a Listener is crucial. He accompanies people during the most painful events of their lives, taking their pain into himself and settling it alongside his own never-healed grief. One of Daniel's critical attributes is that he refuses to see his calling as complicated, although he is far from stupid: he is dedicated to simple and sometimes grim work that helps the people who need help most. This is one of the reasons why his marriage to the erudite Stephanie works; he sees that her bookishness is not the only part of her personality, but that they share "a pastoral compulsion. She filled the cottage with the lost and unhappy."[5] Their intense erotic life allows Stephanie occasionally to attain the wholeness Daniel more naturally possesses; making love to him she see this "as the only time in her life when her attention had all been gathered in one place—body, mind, and whatever dreams or makes images." Making love to her, Daniel thinks only, "I am *here*."[6]

As a young person, Daniel is converted during a speech by an evangelist at his school. The visitor "bleakly" tells the boys that "what was required was that people should use their lives. . . . Christ came that they might have life more abundantly. Not happiness, life." Daniel is immediately and permanently gripped, physically and spiritually, by the sense of his vocation to help others.

> What was needed, he came to see, was someone practical, someone completely committed to *practical* solutions. He used this

4. Ibid., 173, 39.
5. Byatt, *Still Life*, 20.
6. Byatt, *Virgin*, 281–82.

word to himself in a sense perhaps uniquely his own. . . . To be practical was to deal directly with pain, poverty, horror, quite directly.[7]

There is a sense of "biological urgency" in his faith that recurs in his courtship of Stephanie. His large and warm physical presence allows her to step outside of language; the chapter in *The Virgin in the Garden* about their courtship on a cold Yorkshire beach is a wonderful thing, with the lovers reduced to the basics of "I want, I want, I want" and understanding each other perfectly.[8] In the two books that follow the death of Stephanie, the plot sidelines Daniel, because the Orton marital experiment of living and loving somehow outside language is smashed, and other characters become central to Byatt's increasingly hyper-intellectual interests. Alone in widowhood, Daniel distrusts language more than ever, but the distinct fulfillment that once arose from his devotion to a life of Christian action is forever gone.

If I have made Daniel Orton sound too primitive or simple, I have done the character a disservice. For one thing, much of Daniel's energy arises from a strong sense of rage that he keeps under control. In *Still Life*, Stephanie and Daniel's marriage becomes tightly constrained when Daniel's annoying mother and Stephanie's neurotic brother come to live with them and Stephanie undergoes two unexpected pregnancies early in the marriage. Additionally, Daniel's vicar is embroiled in sexual wrongdoing, and Daniel and Stephanie are painfully aware of all of these problems. Where Daniel's natural instincts might be to create a rewarding explosion, instead he tries to be the civilized young rector that everyone expects him to be, and as a result his entire life implodes.

Everything goes wrong for Daniel, but after a time of mourning he manages to go back to work, and continues to save lives. In *Babel Tower* he saves, among others, the antisocial Jude, whose pornographic dystopian book *Babbletower* occupies a major part of the action. Jude is introduced to us as a caller to Daniel's helpline, and Daniel's interactions with the irritating Jude are instructive:

> "Remember there is no God."
> "So you have said before."
> "And because there is no God, do as thou wilt shall be the whole of the law."

7. Ibid., 53–55 (emphasis in original).
8. Ibid., 183.

"So you have also said before."

"If you knew what that meant. If you really knew. You would not sound so complacent."

"I hope that is not how I sound."

"You sound stolid, you sound blinkered, you sound one-dimensional."

"You never let me say much, to sound anything."

"You are not supposed to mind that. You are supposed to listen to what I have to say to you."

"I do listen."

"I abuse you. You don't respond. I can hear you turning the other cheek. You are a Christian parson or person. I waste your time. You waste your own time, since there is no God."[9]

Daniel does this sort of work, more or less patiently, for years, and he does it marvelously well. He is not a doormat; although he tries to be a peacemaker he can be stubborn and argumentative as needed. He dislikes Jude intensely but cares for him purposefully. When he hears of the suicide of a troubled woman he has been accompanying on a difficult journey, he does not pray for her: "He was not that kind of priest. He had metaphorically shaken a large fist, impotently, at some looming energy-field, and got on with his work, his work."[10]

Long after forgetting other characters in Byatt's Potter Quartet, I remember Daniel Orton perfectly. When his wife becomes pregnant, he recognizes the fact instantly and approaches her with the word "Annunciation," because, he says, she looks "just as stunned as if you'd seen an angel."[11] He is a strikingly tangible character and his care for those who are not cared for by others raises provocative and necessary questions about the difficulties of pastoral duty: How does a cleric, after all, usefully minister to the mad, the annoying, the antisocial? Most do not bother. Daniel does. Daniel is also a refutation of the notion that many church leaders are cool, if not cold, in their temperaments and dealings with others. His warmth is remarkable.

---

9. Byatt, *Babel Tower*, 9–10.

10. Ibid., 10.

11. Byatt, *Virgin*, 297.

The Intermediary

One of A. S. Byatt's intellectual ancestors is George Eliot. *Middlemarch*, the preeminent novel of the nineteenth century, is replete with clergy-men, including the memorably insensitive and haughty Casaubon, but there is one who strikes me as a precursor to Daniel Orton, and he is the kind, unassuming, though not unruffled Camden Farebrother. *Middle-march* is a network or web of complicated interrelationships and one of the nexus points of stability and certainty in the novel is Farebrother. Like Daniel Orton, Farebrother is rarely seen in the pulpit but is instead out and about in community, talking to people, helping them, making con-nections. Farebrother is an intermediary in the best sense and when the novel's heroine, Dorothea Brooke, also takes on the role of intermediary (especially in the domestic dispute between Tertius Lydgate and his wife Rosamond), it is tempting to believe that Dorothea has, at least in part, learned this skill from Farebrother.

Farebrother's name, in a sense, tells it all, although it is telling in a different way than Casaubon's name is. (Eliot's evocation of respected seventeenth-century scholar Isaac Casaubon in the naming of fictional Edward Casaubon is ironic.) Farebrother actually does function as a brother and a representative of equanimity and equilibrium in the com-munity of Middlemarch. If one sees *Middlemarch* as having three major marital plot strands—the marriages of Dorothea and Casaubon (and later Will Ladislaw), of Lydgate and Rosamond, and of Mary Garth and Fred Vincy—Farebrother plays an important role as conciliator in two of the strands. Farebrother watches his friend Lydgate's faltering marriage and medical career with concern and offers help; more successfully, Fare-brother is used as envoy from Fred Vincy to Mary Garth. (In Dorothea's section of the plot, it is actually she and Lydgate who act as conciliators for Farebrother, securing him a living so that he may better support the unmarried and widowed women of his household.)

Before I get too wound up in my praise of Farebrother, however, it must be admitted that the sort of conciliatory work he represents is not always successful. In the case of his friend Tertius Lydgate, the ad-vice of Farebrother is rejected, and Lydgate carries on in his essentially self-destructive course until he dies, prematurely, at the age of fifty. Even more painfully, Farebrother's work as intermediary between Fred and Mary ruins his own chances for marital happiness, since Farebrother also admires Mary and would, in some respects, be a more appropriate husband for her. Yet this interconnectedness is a fundamental characteristic of *Middlemarch* and the benefits outweigh the dangers.

As a pastor, Camden Farebrother is observed as having "a desire to do with as little pretense as possible."[12] We are told that "his preaching was ingenious and pithy, like the preaching of the English Church in its robust age, and his sermons were delivered without book," and also that he is "sweet-tempered, ready-witted, frank, without grins of suppressed bitterness or other conversational flavours which make half of us an affliction to our friends" (178). Although we see less of Farebrother in the latter chapters of the novel, when the plot concentrates on the various dilemmas of Dorothea and Lydgate, in chapter 80 Farebrother is present to notice Dorothea's reaction to some news about Will Ladislaw. Readers have always been perplexed by how slow Dorothea is to realize that she is in love with Will; Farebrother, in contrast, is "quick in perception," realizing she loves Will before she does. Farebrother can be gently self-mocking; in renouncing the possibility of marrying Mary Garth he wryly says to himself that he has made "a very good imitation of heroism" (676).

Farebrother is, unintentionally, placed at the center of one of the most contentious issues in the town of Middlemarch when he and another preacher, the harshly righteous Evangelical Mr. Tyke, are debated as candidates for the chaplaincy of a new hospital. Lydgate, an inexperienced newcomer, is caught in a vicious battle of wills when the hospital directors meet to make the decision. Like the reader, Lydgate assumes this is a relatively minor issue and that Farebrother, as a man with splendid pastoral skills, is the obvious choice. Nearly all of chapter 18 is given over to exhaustive coverage of the directors' meeting and by the end of that chapter everyone knows just how intricate and unscrupulous Middlemarch politics can be. Farebrother loses the chaplaincy and Lydgate loses for the reader a good deal of his moral traction.

It is not until chapter 50 that this wrong is put right, when Lydgate suggests to Dorothea, now a widow, that Farebrother is the right man for the church at Lowick. The living is hers to offer, as Casaubon's heir, and she agrees. The conversation they have about Farebrother and the "apostolic" Tyke (whose temperaments are evident in their respective names) is enlightening. Lydgate begins:

---

12. Eliot, *Middlemarch*, 173. References to subsequent passages are given parenthetically.

> [Farebrother] is only a parson among parishioners whose lives he has to try and make better. Practically I find that what is called being apostolic now, is an impatience of everything in which the parson doesn't cut the principal figure. I see something of that in Mr. Tyke at the Hospital: a good deal of his doctrine is a sort of pinching hard to make people uncomfortably aware of him.

Dorothea responds:

> I have been looking into a volume of sermons by Mr. Tyke: such sermons would be of no use at Lowick—I mean, about imputed righteousness and the prophecies in the Apocalypse. I have always been thinking of the different ways in which Christianity is taught, and whenever I find one way that makes it a wider blessing than any other, I cling to that as the truest—I mean that which takes in the most good of all kinds, and brings in the most people as sharers in it. It is surely better to pardon too much, than to condemn too much. (495)

This is Dorothea's creed, but it is also Farebrother's. Earlier I noted that *Middlemarch* can be seen as a web or network, and indeed many commentators have remarked upon the thorough use of this metaphor by George Eliot. It is worth reminding ourselves, however, that the community's interconnectedness is not always a happy thing. For example, the narrowness of the town's ideas threaten to crush Lydgate's ambitions; early on the narrator wryly notes that the town "counted on swallowing Lydgate and assimilating him very comfortably" (154). If we think of webs, we must think also of spiders consuming their prey. If the reader occasionally senses that Reverend Farebrother would be happier somewhere else doing something else, this is, I think, a correct impression. He is doing a good job in Middlemarch, but he is far from perfectly happy. Even the egotistical Lydgate eventually recognizes the power of the strong ties that bind people for good and ill; he says to Dorothea that Farebrother has not "done more" with himself because "it's uncommonly difficult to make the right thing work: there are so many strings pulling at once" (494).

There are two aspects of Farebrother that demonstrate he is not completely comfortable in his clerical role. One is that he plays cards for money, and his reputation in Middlemarch suffers because of it. Lydgate recognizes that the gambling is not integral to the man, but that Farebrother needs money to support his family. Once he and Dorothea intervene to get Farebrother a better living, the rector abandons the whist table. The other issue is that he is a talented amateur natural scientist. Some critics have taken this inclination toward science to mean that Farebrother has made a "dubious vocational choice," as Kerry McSweeney puts it.[13] But I see Farebrother's scientific studies as evidence of how well-rounded and accomplished he is and, more importantly, we ought to compare Farebrother's well-conducted research with the unhealthy and obsessive research that both Lydgate and Casaubon undertake. Farebrother has the humility to say, with great quietness, "I fancy I have made an exhaustive study of the entomology of the district" (172). He knows where to stop his taxonomy before it becomes a mania. One of George Eliot's most important authorial intentions in *Middlemarch*—and she has many—is to warn against the sort of devastating intellectual ambition that believes it can encompass and categorize an entire field of knowledge.

By the end of the novel we see that in addition to Farebrother there is another good minister in Middlemarch, and indeed she may be more effective at ministry than he is. This is Dorothea, unordained of course, but doing the kind of reconciliatory work that Farebrother has done, but with more passion (a word constantly associated with her is "ardor"). In the early chapters, Dorothea's passion is often foolish, but she is only nineteen, and by the conclusion she has suffered and become wiser. But she still has the necessary "ardor" to take spirited action during the novel's final crisis, while Farebrother hesitates. Lydgate's reputation as a physician and man of honor is in question, and Farebrother does not step forward to help. Dorothea refuses to wait and see, uttering an impetuous cry to Farebrother that has become one of the novel's touchstone sayings: "What do we live for, if it is not to make life less difficult to each other?" (733–34). McSweeney notes that in the final analysis Dorothea is the "moral exemplar" of *Middlemarch*, and not Farebrother or any of the admirable Garth family, because Dorothea contains enough egotism in her personality to make her a force for change.[14] Casaubon, Lydgate, and Rosamond have too much egotism; Farebrother has not enough. "I am not a model clergyman—only a decent makeshift" is his own judgment (176). Whether egotism (in the right proportion) is the right term to describe the quality that makes Dorothea different, there is no doubt that she ultimately has more courage than the vicar.

13. McSweeney, *Middlemarch*, 54.
14. Ibid., 27.

Still, Farebrother is an admirable clergyman, particularly when lined up against his clerical rivals in the novel: Casaubon, Tyke, and the ineffectual Cadwallader. Farebrother is assigned one of the novel's other memorable aphorisms: "character," he says, "is not cut in marble—it is not something solid and unalterable. It is something living and changing, and may become diseased as our bodies do" (734–35). This is one of the principles close to George Eliot's heart; as a meliorist she ascribed to the view that human moral progress is achievable, but as an artist (and a realist) she knew the contrary possibility: that change is not necessarily positive.

Waiting and Watching

The love story of Mary Garth and Fred Vincy in *Middlemarch* is often eclipsed in critical comment; it is certainly a less complex matter than the other major marriage plots. But Mary Garth is of special interest to those studying the representation of clergy because of her firm and unusual insistence that the man she loves must not be a clergyman. This is not because Mary is not a devout Christian (she is) and it is not because she does not respect her vicar Mr. Farebrother (she does). However, it has been proposed by the Vincy family that Fred should also be a clergyman, and Mary stands against it. This is an odd state of affairs in a Victorian story, because many Victorian gentlemen (both inside and outside of fiction) happily acceded that a career in the church was advantageous, providing social respect and a decent possibility of advancement. One of the reasons that *Middlemarch* is such a remarkable book is that George Eliot sharply probes this slovenly attitude toward vocation. Nearly all her major characters are either searching hard for their vocation or are chastened when they get it wrong. Mary Garth is uncommon in her insistence that being a clergyman means something very precise, and Fred Vincy is not the right man for the job, no matter how ferociously she loves him. As she puts it:

> His being a clergyman would be only for gentility's sake, and I think there is nothing more contemptible than such imbecile gentility. I used to think that of Mr. Crowse, with his empty face and neat umbrella, and mincing little speeches. What right have such men to represent Christianity—as if it were an institution for getting up idiots genteelly—. (516)

Mary Garth's pronouncement is an advantageous spot to move our attention to the fine and earnest 1859 novel by George Eliot, *Adam Bede*. I have occasion elsewhere in this study to discuss the situation of unordained women who function as ministers. This happens, for example, in novels about clergy couples, where the wife can be a more effective pastor than her husband. One remarkable portrait of an unordained but admirable (and relatively honored) female minister is Eliot's character Dinah Morris in *Adam Bede*, but Dinah suits this present chapter about ministers who serve as counselors and confessors. Dinah does not have to worry about entering an "institution for getting up idiots genteelly," as Mary Garth puts it, because Dinah will never be offered a "living" or given the opportunity to climb the ecclesiastical ladder to achieve a deanery. Dinah, however, is remarkably content with her situation because she is a Methodist, and she exists within a (not untroubled) tradition of Methodist lay preaching that was (for a time) open to women. Any Methodist of the time (the action of *Adam Bede* begins in 1799), or even George Eliot's time, was by definition outside of established and conventional religion. So Dinah's position as an itinerant lay preacher is not remarkably different from male preachers in her own tradition. Eliot places the action of *Adam Bede* in 1799 in order that Dinah may be part of the historical moment when Methodists allowed women preachers. For several decades at the end of the eighteenth-century female preaching was accepted; by the early nineteenth century this was no longer the case, and Methodist women would have to wait until the twentieth century to regain their position as church leaders.

Adam Bede probably should be called *Dinah Morris*. The orthodox view of the plot emphasizes Adam's love for the gorgeously inappropriate Hetty Sorrel, who comes to a bad end because of her own love for the gorgeously inappropriate Arthur Donnithorne. But the animating spirit that propels the characters out of their moral disarray, raising the tone of the novel above a conventional tale of thwarted passion, originates in Dinah. Although George Eliot painstakingly details Dinah's sermons and prayers, it is Dinah's commitment to pastoral care that is most remarkable. Dinah works in a mill in order to be close to the working poor who need her most; when called to the bedside of a sick person she immediately puts on her bonnet and goes. We see her ministering to Adam Bede's querulous mother, Lisbeth, when her husband dies and later, again, when Lisbeth is ill. Through Dinah's "still sympathy and absence from exhortation" she brings a "greater quietness of spirit" to people like Lisbeth.[15] These scenes are rehearsals for the intense drama near the conclusion of the novel, where Hetty, condemned to death for child murder, is visited by Dinah in prison and only Dinah can prompt from Hetty her confession. (She has not murdered her illegitimate child, but abandoned it.)

The chapters depicting Dinah's death watch with Hetty are remarkable. The ostensible hero of the book, Adam, is waiting miserably nearby, passively hoping that Hetty's sentence will be stayed (and, at the last moment, it is). He should be more actively at work on Hetty's behalf, because he was once her betrothed, but his own bitterness and sexual jealousy keeps him from action. Not only does Dinah approach the prison in the evening hours, alone in a time when women in polite society rarely walked unaccompanied, she elects to stay with Hetty in her unlit cell and later rides with her to the place of execution. After Dinah procures Hetty's confession, Hetty refuses to leave off her grip on Dinah, finding her only comfort in close physical proximity to Dinah. When Adam finally enters Hetty's cell he sees that Hetty "was clinging close to Dinah; her cheek was against Dinah's. It seemed as if her last faint strength and hope lay in that contact, and the pitying love that shone out from Dinah's face looked like a visible pledge of the Invisible Mercy" (505). The onlookers who watch Hetty and Dinah in their cart ride to the gibbet ("a sight that some people remembered better even than their own sorrows") gaze at Dinah "with a sort of awe" (506).

It is difficult to describe the effect of *Adam Bede* in the same chapter as *Middlemarch*. *Adam Bede* is sweeter and more conventional, but more than that, Eliot is writing a work of nostalgia for a previous era of English history. The more sophisticated later Eliot will not provide us with speeches like this one—

> Jesus, thou present Saviour! Thou hast known the depths of all
> sorrow: thou hast entered that black darkness where God is not,
> and hast uttered the cry of the forsaken. Come Lord, and gather
> of the fruits of thy travail and thy pleading. (496)

—which marks the beginning of Dinah's long prison cell exhortation that finally breaks down Hetty's reserve. Even in Dinah's silence there is an antiquated extravagance:

---

15. Eliot, *Adam Bede*, 158. References to subsequent passages are given parenthetically.

> Dinah began to doubt whether Hetty was conscious who it was
> that sat beside her. She thought suffering and fear might have
> driven the poor sinner out of her mind. But it was borne in upon
> her, as she afterwards said, that she must not hurry God's work:
> we are overhasty to speak—as if God did not manifest himself
> by our silent feeling, and make his love felt through ours. She
> did not know how long they sat in that way, but it got darker and
> darker, till there was only a pale patch of light on the opposite
> wall: all the rest was darkness. But she felt the Divine presence
> more and more—nay, as if she herself were a part of it, and it was
> the Divine pity that was beating in her heart and was willing the
> rescue of this helpless one. (494)

Much of Dinah's ministry, strangely enough, involves her eyes, described
as "shedding love [rather] than making observations" and "so simple, so
candid, so gravely loving, that no accusing scowl, no light sneer could help
melting away before their glance" (67). Knowing that the reader must be
suspicious of the supposed eloquence of this untutored evangelist, Eliot
provides, in our first exposure to Dinah, a well-educated outsider who
happens upon the scene of her outdoor sermon. The stranger thinks to
himself that she is "a sweet woman . . . but surely nature never meant
her for a preacher" (67); later he will notice that because of her plaintive,
calm, fluent honesty "she had thoroughly arrested her hearers" (71).

It will be clear that Dinah Morris's acceptance of Hetty Sorrel's confession is unlike the usual rite of confession that we see in novels and
movies featuring Roman Catholic priests. Dinah, as a Methodist, does
not consider confession a sacrament, nor does she assign penance to
Hetty. Roman Catholic confession is frequently invoked as a plot element
in fiction, even a gimmick, because of the secret nature of the confession.
This secrecy plays well into the structural needs of murder mysteries and
melodramas, but more interesting than secrecy is the relationship that
should grow between one who submits and one who receives a confession.

Despite the melodramatic plot and language, the portrayal of
Dinah Morris is affecting and thoughtful, and can hardly help but be
inspirational. Toward the end of the novel, Dinah is humanized when
she realizes her love for Adam Bede; previously she has seemed a little
too perfect. Some critics have explicitly, and with good cause, compared
Dinah to Christ.[16] But her feelings for Adam force her into a time of exacting contemplation. She believes in her vocation as a preacher, she has

16. Hodgson, *Theology in the Fiction of George Eliot*, 47.

been well accepted, and she has no plans to be a wife. Eliot does not rush Dinah through this time of self-scrutiny, although no reader will be foolish enough to think that the happy ending is not just over the horizon. But one of the modern touches in *Adam Bede* is the "division in my heart" that Dinah feels in regard to the marriage question. She tells Adam that her ministry has been "like a land I have trodden in blessedness since my childhood" (554) and since she now feels conflicted she worries that there will be no peace for her and Adam. The last time we hear of Dinah preaching, she picks up a testy child in her congregation and holds him on her lap while she finishes her sermon (548); this scene presages the Epilogue, where Dinah has entered domesticity and functions as wife and mother and only occasionally talks "to the people a bit in their houses," as Adam puts it (583). Because the Epilogue is so short, we do not know the precise details of how Dinah and Adam have responded to the 1803 injunction barring Methodist women from preaching; it may be that there has been marital tension around this moment. But the proscription likely makes small difference in Dinah's life. Whether she can officially be called preacher or not, her primary pastoral gifts were always comfort, service, and eloquent presence in illness and anxiety.

The Instigator

My last clerical counselor may seem a minor one compared to these quite astonishing and inspirational figures in Byatt and Eliot. But *A Room with a View* is a comedy, and it is a remarkable accomplishment that E. M. Forster is able to invest Mr. Beebe, the vicar of Summer Street, with a certain amount of devilish flair and allow him to be one of the instigators of the liberation and joy at the heart of Forster's novel. In comedies (or even in tragedies—consider poor Friar Laurence in *Romeo and Juliet*) clergymen often function as obstacles. They are the humorless, oblivious, or repressive forces that young lovers—or others seeking delight—must either subvert or succumb to. Mr. Beebe's very name sets him up to be the conventional comic vicar, bumbling and irrelevant, more than a bit of a fool. And to an extent Mr. Beebe does function like a fool in the plot, but in Forster's world a fool may have different meanings than expected.

Like the other pastors in this chapter, Mr. Beebe functions as an intermediary; his seemingly innocuous task at the novel's beginning is to negotiate between Mr. Emerson, who has "rooms he does not value," and Miss Bartlett and Miss Honeychurch, promised that their Florence hotel rooms would have a view of the Arno. This small action kicks the entire plot into motion. Mr. Emerson is a radical, whom Mr. Beebe describes drolly as having the "merit—if it is one—of saying exactly what he means."[17] Miss Bartlett is a figure of propriety, functioning as young Lucy Honeychurch's chaperone on her European tour; in Miss Bartlett's opinion, to exchange hotel rooms with a man and his handsome son can only lead to scandal. Miss Bartlett is correct—after a series of comic misunderstandings and misadventures, Lucy Honeychurch and George Emerson do run away together. Strangely enough, everyone (including Mr. Beebe) is appalled at Lucy and George at the novel's end—everyone, that is, except Miss Bartlett, who just possibly has had her heart turned toward joy by the strange chain of events set in motion by Mr. Emerson's tactless truth-telling and Mr. Beebe's social mediation. It is easy enough to say that *A Room with a View* is a love story about two young people who are held apart for a time by convention, but even more romantic and singular is the subtle inner transformation of the spinster Charlotte Bartlett into someone who (like the Emersons) learns to say "Yes," however quietly, to life.

Acting as a kind of Chorus to this instigating action of *A Room with a View* are the elderly and seemingly proper Miss Alans, Teresa and Catharine, who assure Lucy and Miss Bartlett that "there are people who do things which are the most indelicate, and yet at the same time—beautiful" (15). And throughout Forster's novel the Dionysian cry to enjoy living, even if it means at times flirting with the indecent, arises from other unlikely sources. My intention is to point out a few of the scenes where it is Mr. Beebe's Dionysian interventions that move the plot toward joyous fulfillment, even though he may not be fully conscious or wholly approving of his own interventions.

One must halt here, however, and say a word about how an early twentieth-century Church of England parson could possibly be in harmony with Dionysian ideas. To grasp E. M. Forster one must be open to such possibilities. For Forster, Dionysian joy need not be inaccessible just because one is the sort of Englishwoman who goes for visits to Tunbridge Wells or sits on little mackintosh squares in the Italian countryside. Forster's early works are heavily invested in neo-pagan ideas; his short 1911 tale "The Story of a Panic" outlines (in darker tones than he allows in the

17. Forster, *A Room with a View*, 13. References to subsequent passages are given parenthetically.

sunny *A Room with a View*) what happens when the power of the god Pan is not acknowledged. Richard Ellmann reminds us that "almost to a man, Edwardian writers rejected Christianity" and Forster was part of this abdication; these writers then felt free to look to other religious traditions to express their need to be "religious about life itself."[18] For Forster the Dionysian ideal was a way of expressing his notions about a life force, about ecstasy and spontaneity.

There is no doubt that Mr. Beebe does not actually or even potentially worship Dionysus, but some of his actions put him in delightfully Dionysian terrain. His decision to swim naked with George Emerson and Lucy's brother Freddy in an idyllic woodland pool is unexpectedly one more occasion that drives Lucy into George's arms. Lucy's fiancé Cecil is confused and embarrassed when the naked swimmers are discovered, but Lucy is poised enough to return the bow that a naked George makes to her. As this wondrous scene of innocent transgression concludes, Forster's narrator says that the pool "had been a call to the blood and to the relaxed will, a passing benediction whose influence did not pass, a holiness, a spell, a momentary chalice for youth" (141).

The mixed Christian and pagan language of that tumultuous and anarchic chapter, mock-innocently called "Twelfth Chapter," when other chapters in *A Room with a View* are given titles like "How Miss Bartlett's Boiler was so Tiresome" and "Lying to Cecil," indicates the exuberant possibilities that may pass from spirited people like the Emersons to more ordinary folk like the Honeychurches and Mr. Beebe. We see this ecstatic potential in a smaller way in Mr. Beebe's appreciation for the way Lucy plays Beethoven piano sonatas. While Charlotte Bartlett may hope that Mr. Beebe's polite intervention in the affair of the Emerson bedroom exchange "is a guarantee of a sort that they will not presume on this" (18), the alert reader will notice that Mr. Beebe's fuller attention is on Lucy's passionate musicality:

> Does it seem reasonable that she should play so wonderfully, and live so quietly? I suspect that one day she will be wonderful in both. The water-tight compartments in her will break down, and music and life will mingle. Then we shall have her heroically good, heroically bad—too heroic, perhaps, to be bad or good. (99)

---

18. Ellmann, *Edwardians and Late Victorians*, 192, 196.

It is always a little difficult to explain why Mr. Beebe, after a speech such as this, should be listed among Lucy's antagonists on the last page of the novel, when she and George most evidently have broken through all water-tight compartments. But it does not do to reason too closely when reading Forster; the currents of passion and rectitude sometimes get disconcertingly crossed. Let it be enough to say that Mr. Beebe, who loves Beethoven, swims nude, and jovially demands good food as soon as he enters a parishioner's house, is on the side of the angels in Forster's book. Forsterian angels do look something like satyrs, but they do more good than harm if one gives in to them.

This selection of texts has been very English and very interrelated—Eliot, Forster, and Byatt have a distinct set of links to each other—but while the clerics examined in this chapter may be far from representative, I do trust they make up for that in their stimulating qualities. To be a counselor, an intermediary, or a confessor is no small thing. It may not be necessary that these functions are carried out by a Christian minister, but it is a credit to Christianity when they are. These are vital roles in community; we could not survive a day as a human race without such mediators. When I speak of the mediating and counseling role of a pastor I hope that a sense of sanctity is not lost: the words seem mundane, but the task is holy. Theologian Douglas John Hall is exercised about the way Protestants have downplayed the holiness of such tasks:

> In their distaste for a Catholicism that elevated the clergy
> . . . many Protestant denominations rushed to the opposite side
> of the arena and propounded a concept of ministry in purely
> pragmatic terms. Ministry then is seen as a function, a task, a
> job—no doubt necessary to order and good government in the
> church, and no doubt a work for which some are better quali-
> fied than others, yet possessing no special quality, no aura of
> sanctity, no mystique, perhaps not even a sense of "call."[19]

The belief that Christ is the first and most crucial mediator ("For there is one God; there is also one mediator between God and humankind, Christ Jesus, himself human, who gave himself a ransom for all"—

19. Hall, *Bound and Free*, 3–4.

1 Tim 2:5–6) should illumine for us the resultant importance of the pastor as mediator. One thoughtful analyst of this aspect of ministry is Dietrich Bonhoeffer, who in *Life Together* writes that "Jesus made authority in the fellowship dependent upon brotherly service. Genuine spiritual authority is to be found only where the ministry of hearing, helping, bearing, and proclaiming is carried out."[20] Bonhoeffer's list of seven vital traits of ministry highlights qualities that should be marked in the personality of a mediator. Holding one's tongue, meekness, listening, helpfulness, bearing, and proclaiming are the first six traits, with authority named last, since Bonhoeffer insists that authority be based on all the previous traits. A similar insistence on the Christian's leader's position in the midst (not at the pinnacle) of community comes from Rowan Williams, who uses both "mediate" and "in the middle" several times in his 2004 address "The Christian Priest Today": the priest's "fundamental task is that of announcing in word and action in the middle of the community what the community is and where it is." He also uses the language of immersion, involvement, intersection, interpretation—and also, noticing: "We can't uncover the face of Christ in people unless we have the habit of real attention to human faces in all their diversity."[21]

One of the most moving and profound examples of this mediating and confessional relationship is in Tim Robbins's movie *Dead Man Walking*. A nun and a death row inmate spend the last week of his life in companionship; she urges him to admit his crime and be sorrowful, but for the most part she is simply with him, sometimes in silence. She listens; sometimes she pushes back; always she shares his loneliness and fear. Her presence, patience, and acceptance provide the impetus for his final confession more than any promise of absolution or salvation. Confession can stereotypically look like a simple binary relation, or even seem rather passive. You receive my words; I receive your words. In Robbins's film, confession is active, demanding, messy. Observing fictional and cinematic pastors who have strong listening and counseling skills and who prompt revelatory and liberating confession can help us recognize and promote this significant aspect of true Christian ministry. The counselor priest is often underrated and undervalued; quiet listening and unconditional support are less conspicuous than eloquent preaching. But the counselor pastor probably saves more lives.

20. Bonhoeffer, *Life Together*, 108.
21. Williams, "The Christian Priest Today."

Scenes of Clerical Life

by George Eliot

First serialized in *Blackwood's Edinburgh Magazine* in 1857, the three stories in *Scenes of Clerical Life* were the first works of fiction by an author who went by the name George Eliot. The public did not know the true identity of this gentleman then, although once *The Mill on the Floss* was published in 1860 it became known that the author was Marian (or Mary Ann) Evans. By the time of her death in 1880, George Eliot was one of the Victorian era's eminent writers and certainly the most serious of the century's popular novelists. That George Eliot *was* a popular novelist is rather astonishing today; although her plots could be conventional and even clichéd, her style often veered toward "philosophical Latinity," as commentator Grace Rhys said in 1910.[1] Yet George Eliot, for all her considerable erudition, was a fashionable and beloved author, and we know that Queen Victoria was an admirer, writing in her journal of the "deep impression" that *Adam Bede*, George Eliot's 1859 novel, made upon her.[2] This success came about even though the writer lived from 1854 with a married man who could not obtain a divorce, George Henry Lewes; it is generally recognized that the high standards of morality personally embodied by George Eliot and George Henry Lewes overcame those Victorian social norms that were supposedly so rigid.

Another point that might have counted harshly against George Eliot, and certainly lost her the approval of members of her family, is that she was one of the nineteenth century's foremost agnostics. Unlike

1. Rhys, "Introduction," *Scenes of Clerical Life.*
2. Quoted in Haight, *George Eliot,* 335.

Dickens, who made Christian gestures when he felt it was useful to do so, George Eliot instigated in her family what she called a "Holy War" when she refused to attend church services from the time she was in her early twenties.[3] Up until that point she had been an extremely devout young woman, but after reading deeply in the continental "higher criticism" of the time (later becoming the first English translator of key works by David Friedrich Strauss and Ludwig Feuerbach), she lost faith in the divinity of Christ and the sacredness of the Bible.

Why then should her first book consist of such well-rounded and sympathetic portrayals of clergymen? Indeed, when *Scenes of Clerical Life* appeared, many readers assumed its author must be a clergyman, someone devoted to the church and undeniably studious. The book brims over with profound knowledge of the ecclesiastical controversies of the time, especially concerning the rapidly widening breach between those of Evangelical or "low church" tendencies and those belonging to a "high church" party. George Eliot's fascination with the church and with religion never abated through her life. This is in part because, while she could not agree with the creeds of Christianity, she nevertheless saw it as "the highest expression of the religious sentiment that has yet found its place in the history of mankind."[4] It is generally accepted that George Eliot's philosophical beliefs are closely related to Christian doctrine, yet she would not accede to belief in a god or savior. She was, in a sense, a highly Christianized humanist, one who in 1842 wrote to a friend that she had to value moral decisions that have no eye on salvation but instead make "that choice of the good for its own sake."[5] She had that superlative faith in the capability of the human being that has become progressively harder to accept in the century and a half since then.

It is surprising, casting an eye over the other major novelists of the nineteenth century, that it is George Eliot whose interest in and knowledge of the church predominates. Jane Austen and Charlotte Brontë were both the daughters of clergymen and made no break with the church; Brontë married a clergyman in the last year of her life. Charles Dickens's *A Christmas Carol* has practically become a secular scripture welded onto the Christmas season, and he wrote an earnest book for his children called *The Life of Our Lord*. None of these prominent novelists

3. Ibid., 44.

4. Ibid., 331.

5. Ibid., 44.

rebelled against the church as George Eliot did. Neither did any of them write with anything close to the absorption and knowledge which she demonstrated when she turned her attention to the church. Oliver Lovesey claims that the *Scenes* can be termed a "clerical anatomy" in which "critical self-reflection about fiction, and particularly about characterization" is tested by contrasting "clerical stereotypes" with "particularized individual characters."[6] But George Eliot's first book of fiction is more warmly engaged with the church than that.

George Eliot's intense involvement with clerical matters is a fascinating puzzle, but one that can be explained in part by the key doctrine of George Eliot's humanist religion. That is the doctrine of sympathy. The notion is central to understanding her intentions in *Adam Bede* and *Middlemarch*, but in *Scenes of Clerical Life* it is outlined most plainly. And who does the author ask us to contemplate with sympathy? In large part, it is those who are usually expected to be the conductors of sympathy to others: the clergy. Nothing wrenches at George Eliot's considerable faculties of compassion like the situation of a clergyman, especially a mediocre clergyman.

> The Rev. Amos Barton, whose sad fortunes I have undertaken to relate, was, you perceive, in no respect an ideal or exceptional character; and perhaps I am doing a bold thing to bespeak your sympathy on behalf of a man who was so very far from remarkable,—a man whose virtues were not heroic, and who had no undetected crime within his breast; who had not the slightest mystery hanging about him, but was palpably and unmistakably commonplace; who was not even in love, but had had that complaint favourably many years ago. 'An utterly uninteresting character!' I think I hear a lady reader exclaim— Mrs. Farthingale, for example, who prefers the ideal in fiction; to whom tragedy means ermine tippets, adultery, and murder; and comedy, the adventures of some personage who is quite a 'character.'
>
> But, my dear madam, it is so very large a majority of your fellow-countrymen that are of this insignificant stamp. At least eighty out of a hundred of your adult male fellow-Britons returned in the last census are neither extraordinarily silly, nor extraordinarily wicked, nor extraordinarily wise; their eyes are neither deep and liquid with sentiment, nor sparkling with suppressed witticisms; they have probably had no hairbreadth

6. Lovesey, *The Clerical Character in George Eliot's Fiction*, 22.

escapes or thrilling adventures; their brains are certainly not pregnant with genius, and their passions have not manifested themselves at all after the fashion of a volcano. They are simply men of complexions more or less muddy, whose conversation is more or less bald and disjointed. Yet these commonplace people—many of them—bear a conscience, and have felt the sublime prompting to do the painful right; they have their unspoken sorrows, and their sacred joys; their hearts have perhaps gone out towards their first-born, and they have mourned over the irreclaimable dead. Nay, is there not a pathos in their very insignificance—in our comparison of their dim and narrow existence with the glorious possibilities of that human nature which they share?[7]

I quote at such length from "The Sad Fortunes of the Reverend Amos Barton," the first of the three stories in *Scenes*, because it is precisely this sort of passage that George Eliot produces time and again in her fiction. This one is beautifully typical. She pleads for readers to turn with love and patience to the least likely person in their vicinity. She asks us to contemplate with sorrow the characters that other authors would turn into mere villains (the most famous of these the unlikeable Casaubon in *Middlemarch*). And the wonderful surprise is that often the least likely, least likeable person in one's neighborhood, in a George Eliot story, turns out to be the parson, and so she prompts us to practice our sympathy on him. Amos Barton dutifully goes to preach salvation to the workhouse poor, using images of "chosen vessels, of the Paschal lamb, of blood as a medium of reconciliation" (27) and is utterly incomprehensible to his listeners. To his own congregation he preaches a roaring sermon on the Incarnation, "an extremely argumentative one." But, the narrator wryly notes, "as it was preached to a congregation not one of whom had any doubt of that doctrine, and to whom the Socinians therein confuted were as unknown as the Arimaspians" (36), Mr Barton merely bewilders them. This happens not because he is a scholar: the narrator gently lets us know that Barton's grasp of biblical languages is weak, as is his grasp of dogma. He is inclined to mix up the Evangelical and Tractarian doctrines that his uneducated parishioners understand better than he does. As a farmer's wife, Mrs. Hackit, notes, "I *like* Mr Barton. I think he's a good sort o' man, for all he's not overburthen'd i' th' upper story" (14).

7. Eliot, *Scenes of Clerical Life*, 43–44. References to subsequent passages are given parenthetically.

Like the titles of the other stories within *Scenes of Clerical Life*, the title "The Sad Fortunes of the Reverend Amos Barton" has idiosyncratic ironic tones. Because he is "not overburthen'd i' th' upper story," Amos Barton brings most of his hardships on himself. He has too many children, lives beyond his means, and is not terribly perceptive. But George Eliot's irony is a serious kind, with only minor playful or derogatory elements. Amos Barton is an inadequate minister and unwise husband, but he is not a bad man, and the author asks us to withhold our judgment until we see him suffer. And suffer he does, on the death of his wife, so much so that

> his recent troubles had called out their better sympathies, and
> that is always a source of love. Amos failed to touch the spring
> of goodness by his sermons, but he touched it effectually by his
> sorrows; and there was now a real bond between him and his
> flock. (74)

It turns out that Amos Barton's best attribute as a human being is his suffering; his "sad fortunes" make him a better parson partly because they bring out the ministering ability in others. Likewise in "Mr. Gilfil's Love Story," which I will not analyze since it has the least ecclesiastical content of the three, there is very little "love story," and in "Janet's Repentance," the final and best story, the reader may be baffled for some time why Janet, who is the nearly-broken victim of an abusive husband, needs to be acquainted with repentance at all. These subtle ironies do work themselves out. Janet has lost faith in herself and in goodness; although George Eliot does not use the term, the contemporary reader will likely understand Janet to be an alcoholic. She does need to repent—of her lost love of self and humanity.

There are fewer divisions between cleric and layperson in George Eliot's novels than in, for example, the novels of Anthony Trollope, whose clergy are rarely occupied with arduous parish tasks and sometimes seem to have little contact with their parishioners at all. George Eliot counters with Mr. Cleves. Mr. Cleves secures one paragraph in "Amos Barton," but in this brief appearance we know much about how the best sort of minister gets along in community.

> To a superficial glance, Mr. Cleves is the plainest and least cleri-
> cal-looking of the party; yet, strange to say, *there* is the true par-
> ish priest, the pastor beloved, consulted, relied on by his flock;
> a clergyman who is not associated with the undertaker, but

> thought of as the surest helper under a difficulty, as a monitor who is encouraging rather than severe. Mr. Cleves has the wonderful art of preaching sermons which the wheelwright and the blacksmith can understand; not because he talks condescending twaddle, but because he can call a spade a spade, and knows how to disencumber ideas of their wordy frippery. (55, emphasis in original)

In George Eliot's hands clerical life does of course involve the life of the cleric, but it expands to include absolutely everyone in the parish. The entire community becomes entangled in theological matters. In "Janet's Repentance," men gather in the public house to debate matters pertaining to the high church/low church divide (cottage preaching, Sunday night lectures, and the extempore sermon); the women gather in parlors and have debates that are at least as knowledgeable, and probably more so (they discuss liturgical issues, the doctrine of justification by faith, and read the latest religious books). One of the remarkable things about "Janet's Repentance" is the way in which this female side of clerical life is revealed.

It must be conceded that even George Eliot understands how many church-going women are interested in preachers for very personal and romantic reasons. There is less of this sort of thing than one encounters in Jane Austen's *Emma*, for example, where the clergyman Mr. Elton's entire narrative purpose seems to entail marriage to someone or other, but George Eliot's narrator does remark the "susceptibility towards the clerical sex" (223) notable in many middle-class women with not enough to occupy them. (How intriguing that clerics have an entire gender assigned to them.) But for the most part communities like the one drawn in "Janet's Repentance" really do have a meaningful "clerical life." This concern with the church is not a mere pastime but includes much that is vital and necessary, and the whole community is in on it. George Eliot invests an extraordinary amount of time and energy to illustrate how many varieties of faith there are, even in a little English village, and how they can coexist helpfully, although this is not always the case. In "Janet's Repentance" religious doctrine alters lives for good or ill; Janet's husband becomes obsessed with persecuting the evangelical parson, Mr. Tryan, and dies a raving madman, while Janet herself has her heart turned back toward life by Mr. Tryan's intense sympathy for and with her.

"Janet's Repentance" is, among other things, a vivid and realistic psychological portrait of the currents within an abusive marriage—daring for its time. The only factor that is capable of tearing Janet away from her blank subjection to her cruel husband is Mr. Tryan's willingness to show Janet his own vulnerability. That Janet is innately moral is demonstrated by the narrator's description of her as an arum lily (232)—lilies being associated with purity and Christ's passion—and also by the "sacramental" (290) kisses bestowed on a neighbor who gives Janet shelter. But only Mr. Tryan's feeling that "her anguish was not strange to him; that he entered into the only half-expressed secrets of her spiritual weakness" (300) can bring her back to wholeness. Mr. Tryan's redemptive relationship with Janet is described in terms of grave looks and moments of intense intuition, of mute standing in the presence of suffering, but he also is able to articulate to her that "in speaking to me you are speaking to a fellow-sinner who has needed just the comfort and help you are needing" (298).

That Mr. Tryan's doctrine is at times a bit "narrow," that he desires Janet more than he ought even though he is antagonistic to the world and the flesh (266)—these faults are made clear by George Eliot's narrator. Of the many parsons in *Scenes of Clerical Life* he is overall the most admirable, but the author never wants us to wander too far from the notion that he might be the best of a bad lot. And it is this unexpected badness—usually ineptitude and egotism, not evil—that makes George Eliot's clergymen such beautiful specimens to practice our sympathy on. The more we love them, the better chance that they will love in turn, and do the good works they were called to do.

> The blessed work of helping the world forward, happily does not wait to be done by perfect men; and I should imagine that neither Luther nor John Bunyan, for example, would have satisfied the modern demand for an ideal hero, who believes nothing but what is true, feels nothing but what is exalted, and does nothing but what is graceful. The real heroes, of God's making, are quite different: they have their natural heritage of love and conscience which they drew in with their mother's milk; they know one or two of those deep spiritual truths which are only to be won by long wrestling with their own sins and their own sorrows; they have earned faith and strength so far as they have done genuine work; but the rest is dry barren theory, blank prejudice, vague hearsay. Their insight is blended with mere opinion; their sympathy is perhaps confined in narrow conduits of doctrine,

> instead of flowing forth with the freedom of a stream that blesses every weed in its course; obstinacy or self-assertion will often interfuse itself with their grandest impulses; and their very deeds of self-sacrifice are sometimes only the rebound of a passionate egoism. So it was with Mr. Tryan. (265–66)

The patience, compassion, and forgiveness one might expect to find in clerical fiction moves, under George Eliot's guidance, in the opposite direction than we imagined. Only someone highly attuned to the religious history of George Eliot's era will even notice how much of the morality in *Scenes of Clerical Life* springs from human interaction, as opposed to supernatural belief. For reasons of her own, she retained many conventional references to God, as in the above references to "heroes, of God's making," and thus the reader informed of George Eliot's agnosticism may be baffled for a time. Yet her depiction of Christian community, in all its variety and fallibility, is among the most valuable and truthful of the many Victorian depictions of clerical life. And that is because she moves past the doctrinal struggles that obsessed and paralyzed many Victorians and rushes straight back to the primal matter of suffering, sympathy, and love. Not only do her ministers take part in this primal movement, but so do the best of George Eliot's laity, making clerical life a truly community effort.

3

Fools for Christ

But God chose what is foolish in the world to shame the wise; God chose what is weak in the world to shame the strong; God chose what is low and despised in the world, things that are not, to reduce to nothing things that are, so that no one might boast in the presence of God. (1 Cor 1:27–29)

If I, even for a moment, accept my culture's definition of me, I am rendered harmless. I can denounce evil and stupidity all I wish and will be tolerated in my denunciations as a court jester is tolerated. I can organize their splendid goodwill and they will let me do it, since it is only for weekends.
(Eugene Peterson, *The Contemplative Pastor: Returning to the Art of Spiritual Direction*)[1]

The above quotation by Eugene Peterson is one of my favorite descriptions of the relationship between culture and priesthood. There are many wonderful aspects to Peterson's paragraph. One is the phrase "splendid goodwill." Secular culture appreciates the beauty and history of the church—or, more precisely, secular culture values church buildings and church ceremonies—and wants priests in attendance to provide blessings and go through appropriate celebratory motions whenever there is a commencement or inauguration. One can almost hear Peterson's sigh when he says that this splendid goodwill must be "organized." It is not inspired or joyously spontaneous. What looks like a triumphal

1. Peterson, *The Contemplative Pastor*, 16.

procession to the outside world can be yet another humdrum job from the viewpoint of the narthex.

Contrasting this is the priest's real job: denouncing evil and stupidity. Peterson's sharp, simple declaration sits steadfastly and angrily in this paragraph full of frustration. Although the priest may be tolerated and looked down upon like a court jester, Peterson is fully aware of the important role a jester should have in the public sphere. The jester must be a truth-teller, and a courageous one. However, the essential word in Peterson's passage is "if." *If* the priest accepts culture's definition of him as a court jester, then he is rendered harmless. Peterson has no intention of accepting this posture. Paul in 1 Corinthians admonishes his readers to embrace an identity of court jester servanthood that includes becoming "the rubbish of the world, the dregs of all things" (4:13). For Paul, to be slandered, reviled, hungry, and weak is to experience a new kind of power. Only "fools for the sake of Christ" (4:10) can be found "turning the world upside down" (Acts 17:6) in the eccentric and radically unconventional way that the early church required—and still does require. This is the court jester as earth-shaker, image-smasher. At the very least, it could be Pastor David Inqvist of Garrison Keillor's Lake Wobegon, turning up to meet visiting clerics with ice cream cone in hand and wearing a t-shirt with the motto "Lutherans: It could be worse": unassuming, cheerful, willing to provoke laughter.[2]

Literature and film and especially television are full of clerical court jesters. Many of these portrayals are humiliating for the church, or at their least harmful they merely make clergy look weak and ineffectual. One thinks of *Father Ted*, the nineties BBC television series in which several priests have been banished to an island where their stupidity, lechery, and drunkenness can cause the least possible harm. Mr. Collins, from Jane Austen's *Pride and Prejudice*, is the favorite comic clergyman of many. Mr. Collins is pompous, worldly, and wholly unaware how unattractive and unintelligent he is. Nearly his entire conversation in *Pride and Prejudice* is about his noble patroness, Lady Catherine de Bourgh, about whose "affability" and "condescension" he can never cease speaking, and before whom he will "earnestly endeavour to demean" himself at every opportunity.[3] The Bennett sisters in Austen's novel are told that Mr. Collins, inheritor of their father's estate, comes "prepared to admire

2. Keillor, *Pontoon*, 216.

3. Austen, *Pride and Prejudice*, 47, 50.

them" but none leap at the compliment, even when it is accompanied by the report that Lady Catherine has condescended to advise Mr. Collins about the installation of shelves in the parsonage closets. Father Mulcahy in the television show *M*A*S*H* (and its more severe cinematic predecessor) is a nice enough fellow, but largely he exists as a surface for jokes to bounce off, as when Hawkeye declares that "It's amazing he doesn't go deaf from the sound of the commandments breaking around us."[4] There is rarely an episode where Father Mulcahy does anything effective about the moral mayhem going on about him; the chaos of war continues and Father Mulcahy stands there, smiling wanly, stammering shyly. In season 3, Colonel Blake gets a big laugh by bumping into the priest, uttering an angry oath, and then saying, "Oh, I'm sorry, Father. I thought you were a regular person."[5]

Unworldly and Roisterous

The comic clergyman is one of the oldest and most firmly established literary types. The caricature is in wide use today, but it was just as vigorous in 1759 when Laurence Sterne began his infamous multi-volume fiction project *The Life and Opinions of Tristram Shandy, Gentleman* and a few years later when Oliver Goldsmith published *The Vicar of Wakefield* in 1766. Only a handful of eighteenth-century novels have a large readership today, and these two are among the most durable productions of that era. The eighteenth century was, in many respects, the nursery of what we today recognize as the novel. The conventions of prose fictions were still unsettled, and experiments in realism were definitely experiments. Melodrama, sentiment, and well-worn plot devices were welcomed. Reading Defoe's *Moll Flanders* or Fielding's *Tom Jones* is an unusual experience for the twenty-first-century reader; the mixture of satire, picaresque romp, and sententiousness is definitely an acquired taste. But what is intriguing is the already-settled expectation that the clergyman is a sure-fire supplier of comedy.

The Vicar of Wakefield is the more typical of the eighteenth-century novels under consideration here. Reverend Primrose is offered to us as

4. "Dear Dad," *M*A*S*H*, season 1, directed by Gene Reynolds, written by Larry Gelbart.

5. "Rainbow Bridge," *M*A*S*H*, season 3, directed by Hy Averback, written by Larry Gelbart and Laurence Marks.

a genial and unworldly man who has a larger family than he can manage. His wife and daughters are silly and vain, and his children get into predicament after predicament that Primrose is not fully equipped to handle. Like many comic clergymen, Primrose has one obsession: trivial to the outside world but of foremost importance to him. He has written a treatise on his belief that a Church of England priest should not remarry if he is widowed, and this is the only rigorous intellectual work he has ever undertaken. The novel's plot is a lengthy and circuitous trial of Primrose's character, as he is stripped of his fortune and prestige and is eventually imprisoned for debt. He is, of course, patient, charitable, and unwavering in his faith and eventually all is restored.

The tone of *The Vicar of Wakefield* is, in my view, troubling, although most critics seem content to assess Goldsmith's novel as presenting "the moral struggles of the ordinary man."[6] The simplicity and unassuming goodness of the vicar are captured in pronouncements such as this one: "The greatest stranger in this world, was he that came to save it. He never had an house, as if willing to see what hospitality was left remaining amongst us."[7] But Primrose can also be pompous and sententious:

> If we commit a smaller evil, to procure a greater good, certain guilt would be thus incurred, in expectation of contingent advantage. And though the advantage should certainly follow, yet the interval between commission and advantage, which is allowed to be guilty, may be that in which we are called away to answer for the things we have done, and the volume of human actions is closed for ever. (139)

Promoting his campaign against clergy remarriage, the vicar tells readers that he has written an "epitaph for my wife, though still living, in which I extolled her prudence, economy, and obedience till death" (41), and describing his children he says they had "but one character, that of being all equally generous, credulous, simple, and inoffensive" (40). One of the issues that must be taken into account when assessing the manner of Goldsmith's book is that the vicar is the first-person narrator. Occasionally the statements seem parodic, but is this the vicar's intention, or Goldsmith's? Does the vicar grasp the flaws in himself and his family, or present them accidentally? Or is it possible that the twenty-first-century

6. Coote, "Introduction," *The Vicar of Wakefield*, 11.

7. Goldsmith, *The Vicar of Wakefield*, 57. References to subsequent passages are given parenthetically.

reader is failing to fully comprehend the sentimentality and sensibility so valued at the time?

Putting aside the problems of tone, *The Vicar of Wakefield* delivers a portrait of a certain type of clerical life that has been durable. The vicar is an indulgent parent, weak and pleasure-loving: "To say the truth, I was tired of being always wise, and could not help gratifying their request, because I loved to see them happy" (73). He does not seem terribly religious, nor does he seem worn out by his parish duties. Describing an early idyllic period before his children come to grief in various forms, he writes, "We were generally awaked in the morning by music, and on fine days rode a hunting" (41). The severe reader, or even the merely realistic reader, will recognize that the vicar needs at the least to have his priorities rearranged. But if we expect that the challenges that beset Primrose will alter him, we are mistaken. At the novel's end, the family is more or less as they always were (even after seduction, fire, prison, and the apparent death of one daughter). They have endured, that is all. There is no doubt that the Primroses have suffered, but what have they learned?

Those who view *The Vicar of Wakefield* as an exemplary portrayal of a minister may cite the vicar's prison life as his accomplishment. He does, apparently, have a salutary effect on his fellow inmates, although on his first arrival this is achieved not by prayer or moral exhortation but by the expedient of standing everyone a drink (153). Later, admittedly, he finds work for them to do, acts as a moral arbiter in disputes, and "in less than six days some were penitent, and all attentive" (161). The most prominent action performed by the vicar in prison is the preaching of a sermon, which takes up an entire chapter. This sermon seems offered to us as proof of Primrose's worth, and it is not without elegance and solace. But the entire import of his message is that after death earthly miseries will be dissolved in the pleasures of heaven. "Bliss" is the key word of his sermon; for the "fortunate" this bliss will be "unutterable," "unending," and "our truest comfort" (174–76). The sermon neither mentions God nor Christ, although "providence" is invoked four times and "religion" seven times. (Indeed Jesus Christ is not named in the entire novel, and the word "Christian" occurs only twice.)

I would like to focus on two terms in my assessment of *The Vicar of Wakefield*. One is "exemplary" and the other is "providence." Goldsmith's novel does not use "exemplary," but the critic Stephen Coote does, and the term is helpful in understanding the impact of Reverend Primrose's story. For Coote, Primrose is a "good, an unremarkable man" and "an exemplary Christian" whose only major fault is intellectual pride.[8] To describe a literary character as exemplary suggests at first the character is a positive example, although it is possible that the word means merely "illustrative" or "typical." But "exemplary" can also have a definition that opposes a positive or beneficial application: "He took an exemplary vengeance" is the Oxford English Dictionary citation that sits closest in time (1735) to Goldsmith's novel.

In other words, if Primrose is an exemplary parson, it could mean either that he is fit for imitation or offered as a deterrent. I suspect Primrose has generally been taken as a beneficial example; although Goldsmith might have intended a gently ironic portrayal of the ministry, Primrose has usually been seen as a good sort. How Primrose should be read today is another matter; if I had my way, readers would agree that Primrose is a poor example of what a Christian minister should be. This is in large part because Christianity—and Christ himself—is so little mentioned in the novel. Religion is what Reverend Primrose vaguely serves, not Christ, and the lazy and passive appeals in his sermon to providence rather than to an incarnate, vital living God indicate a thin and anemic belief.

> Why man should thus feel pain, why our wretchedness should be requisite in the formation of universal felicity, why, when all other systems are made perfect by the perfection of their subordinate parts, the great system should require for its perfection, parts that are not only subordinate to others, but imperfect in themselves? These are questions that never can be explained, and might be useless if known. On this subject providence has thought fit to elude our curiosity, satisfied with granting us motives to consolation. (173)

The phrase "satisfied with granting us motives to consolation" indicates Primrose's complacent faith. It is a relief to turn to the eighteenth century's other famous literary cleric, Parson Yorick in Sterne's *Tristram Shandy*. Yorick is not a main player in Sterne's strangely postmodern novel (written several centuries before anyone thought of postmodernism or even modernism), but he is a key figure both at the beginning and conclusion of this wild, massive, bawdy, anarchic tale. Yorick is given the last word in the novel—if it is the last word or if it is a novel. We do not know that Sterne intended the novel to end where it did, in volume 9, or if he

8. Coote, "Introduction," *The Vicar of Wakefield*, 11.

intended the work to be other than literary mayhem and shenanigans. As the narrator himself says, in volume 1, "In a word, my work is digressive, and it is progressive too,—and at the same time."[9] Whatever the book in fact is, Yorick has its celebrated last line when he declares that a particular anecdote (but really the entire novel) is a cock and bull story "and one of the best of its kind, that I ever heard" (588).

By that line alone one can begin to assess Parson Yorick's character. He has a keen sense of judgment and a keen capacity for enjoyment. He is a participant in the ridiculous debates that go on *ad nauseum* among the men who live in and visit the Shandy household (while the women go about with the real business of life—having babies and doing all else that needs doing), but he is more sensible than the insufferable pedant Walter Shandy or the innocent Uncle Toby. Yorick's good sense is evident in his support of midwifery. The debate about whether a female midwife or a "man-midwife" (the idiotic Dr. Slop) should be allowed to deliver baby Tristram is an important dispute in the novel (and indeed this dispute is one of many eclipsing the actual birth of Tristram—at the novel's end his birth is famously in abeyance and indeed has receded from the novel's action, now four years behind where it was at the beginning). In any case, it is Yorick and his wife who have promoted midwifery in the community and Yorick himself who has "cheerfully" paid the midwife's licencing fee of eighteen shillings and four pence (13). Dr. Slop, on the other hand, when Walter Shandy insists that he be the one to deliver the baby, makes a mistake with the forceps and breaks Tristram's nose. Score one for Yorick.

Yorick's place at the book's beginning is more complicated. For fifteen pages in volume 1 we are given a sustained sketch (or what counts for the digressive Sterne as a sustained sketch) of the life and then, surprisingly, the touching death of Yorick. On pages 31 and 32 of the Penguin Classic are the black pages of mourning for Yorick, among the first of the novel's typographical eccentricities. In the book's chaotic time scheme Yorick's death will be postdated and he remains alive on the last page, yet Sterne is unusually reverent in the manner he presents Yorick's death in the early pages. This is possibly because in Yorick the author has (sentimentally) represented his own oncoming death and has made the cheerful Yorick an alter ego for himself. Yorick is merry and "mercurial"

---

9. Sterne, *Tristram Shandy*, 64. References to subsequent passages are given parenthetically.

and known for his indiscretion; it is said that "he had but too many temptations in life, of scattering his wit and his humour,—his gibes and his jests about him" (24–25). Because gravity is inimical to his personality, Yorick finds himself in the occasional tight spot, but refuses to "stoop" to refute any "illiberal report" that is "injurious to him" but instead trusts "to time and truth to do it for him" (291). One of *Tristram Shandy*'s most notorious comic episodes involves a hot chestnut down the trousers of a fellow cleric, codenamed Phutatorius (politely, "copulator"). Phutatorius resents Yorick and is inclined to believe that Yorick is responsible for the hot chestnut. It is hard to say anything for certain about *Tristram Shandy*; likely Yorick is innocent but he is, after all, mercurial.

Yorick represents what Laurence Sterne calls the Cervantick character (302), and sometimes Shandeism.

> True Shandeism, think what you will against it, opens the heart and lungs, and like all those affections which partake of its nature, it forces the blood and other vital fluids of the body to run freely through its channels, makes the wheel of life run long and cheerfully round. (303)

Obvious references to Cervantes's madcap hero Don Quixote and to *Hamlet*'s jester Yorick indicate the value that Sterne places on the truth-telling aspects of clowning, seen in the best possible sense. The jester or fool in ancient times was a person with wit who entertained and questioned, and who was given license to criticize (with slyness and cleverness) those in power. The jester never takes himself seriously, but he does take position and responsibility seriously. Similarly, the madness of Don Quixote could be strangely clear-eyed and courageous compared to the narrowness and cowardice evident in the "real" world around him. Sterne's Parson Yorick, even more than the Shandy family members, represents the best of Shandeism. (One assumes that young Tristram, if he can manage to emerge from his shadowy semi-existence, might be another fine example of Shandeism.)

While one is polishing up Yorick as a shining example of a classic fool one can almost forget that he is a Christian minister. Even more surprising is the fact that his author, Laurence Sterne, was also a minister of the Church of England. Bearing in mind the mainstream eighteenth-century taste for roisterous, racy literature makes its production by a prominent clergyman a little more understandable, but only just. Sterne's novel was both popular and notorious in its time, and one of the things that he did with his notoriety was to publish his own sermons—under Yorick's name. The sermons are usually judged as measured and ortho- dox; the unaware reader might never connect the sermons with the au- thor of *Tristram Shandy*.

All of this is to say that Laurence Sterne appears to have been a sincere Christian pastor. One can make a variety of judgments about Sterne's novel—I like Christopher Ricks's assessment of "delightfully unkempt"[10]—but about the character of Yorick we can speak with some certainty. He stands against the stale and conventional and for joy. To encounter the free-spirited and large-hearted, unpretentious Yorick so early in English literary history is bracing and encouraging. If he were not in danger of being overwhelmed by *Tristram Shandy*'s multifarious jokes and digressions, its parodies and frisky exuberance, I would say that Yorick is a highly laudable fool for Christ, one who clears away preten- sion and makes way for simple happiness. However, it is to be feared that Yorick's literary example soon becomes submerged, for the next clerical fools are not so salutary.

The Bigmouth

Although Charles Dickens, the most popular novelist of the next cen- tury, had no special interest in clerical characters (especially compared to nearly all other Victorian novelists), in 1853 he offered in *Bleak House* one of my favorite ecclesiastical fools: the wonderfully oily clergyman Mr. Chadband. My literary delight in Chadband is matched, however, by my distinct unease with the license Dickens employs in skewering this ecclesiastical type. Dickens means the character to be funny, and he is, but the portrayal is also quite terrifying. Mr. Chadband is a heartless and arrogant creature, but so is Dickens heartless in his pitiless criticism of evangelical vacuity. Here are Chadband's opening lines, as he and his wife appear at the home of the Snagsbys for tea and platitudes:

> "My friends," says Mr. Chadband, "peace be on this house! On the master thereof, on the mistress thereof, on the young maidens, and on the young men! My friends, why do I wish for peace? What is peace? Is it war? No. Is it strife? No. Is it lovely, and gentle, and beautiful, and pleasant, and serene, and joyful?

10. Ricks, "Introductory Essay," *Tristram Shandy*, xxiv.

Oh, yes! Therefore, my friends, I wish for peace, upon you and upon yours."[11]

This is the "Chadband style of oratory" (307) which is "widely received and much admired," or so says the novel's "public" narrator, who happens to be given to irony (there are two narrators). Chadband will hold forth in this prolix manner on refreshment, animals, humility, or any topic that arbitrarily presents itself, and is known to orate for four hours or more. Of no regular denomination, Chadband is a freelance minister, although he prefers to call himself a vessel, while his detractors call him a "gorging vessel" (304).

First described as a "large yellow man with a fat smile and a general appearance of having a good deal of train oil in his system," Chadband is then compared to "a bear who has been taught to walk upright . . . very much embarrassed about the arms, as if they were inconvenient to him and he wanted to grovel" (305). Dickens never fails to remind the reader of Chadband's animal appetites, so incompatible with his ostensibly spiritual discourse, and Dickens takes special pleasure in emphasis, at least a half dozen times, of Chadband's oiliness. The oleaginous character of Chadband is literal—he is a greedy, sweating, fat man—but it is also emblematic of his unctuousness and his dodgy personality.

Chadband is all rhetorical flourish and exaggeration, with no content. He attracts followers merely because he has a perverse sort of charisma (Mr. Snagsby reports drily that Mrs. Snagsby "likes to have her religion rather sharp" [303]). Dickens makes it transparent that this ministry is entertainment, if it is anything, and Chadband's entertainment value is dependent on personal taste. He specializes in blessings; on arriving and leaving, his verbosity shows notable bravado: "May this house live upon the fatness of the land; may corn and wine be plentiful therein; may it grow, may it thrive, may it prosper, may it advance, may it proceed, may it press forward!" (313).

All of this might seem no more than an occasion for a small laugh at the clergy's expense. Is Chadband so different from Mr. Collins in Austen's *Pride and Prejudice*, a vain and stupid man whose inability to see his own moral and intellectual unattractiveness allows the reader the guilty pleasure of feeling superior? The situation is worse, I believe, because Chadband attempts to make a humiliating example of a character at the

---

11. Dickens, *Bleak House*, 305. References to subsequent passages are given parenthetically.

moral center of *Bleak House*, and in doing so Chadband makes an enemy of the sensitive reader. Chadband goes after Jo, the illiterate and homeless crossing-sweeper at the heart of many of the novel's complex character networks. Jo is a victim and a nobody ("I don't know nothink" is his constant refrain as he tries to stay out of harm's way) but he is trustworthy and honest—one of Dickens's examples of untutored, natural morality.

Knowing nothing of Jo, Chadband assumes Jo *is* nothing, a "young hardened Heathen" (414), and uses him as an exhibit of deficiency. Jo is "devoid" (a word Chadband repeats incessantly) of everything, but especially he is devoid of truth, or as Chadband puts it, the "light of Terewth" (411). After a rambling disquisition that slips into inapt references to eels, elephants, and gazelles, Chadband's homily on Jo's inadequacy is ended only when Mrs. Snagsby has hysterics (and poor Jo has fallen asleep). Despite Jo's lowly status, Dickens allows him to have the last word, of sorts, when the narrator reports that, despite Jo's supposed lack of knowledge, "he knows the Reverend Chadband and would rather run away from him for an hour than hear him talk for five minutes" (415). Although the novel's Chadband scenes are largely comic in purpose, one of them is concluded with especial poignancy when Jo (always sent away with scraps of meat from the sympathetic Mr. Snagsby) is juxtaposed with the mighty symbol of the Christendom that Chadband supposedly represents, but represents so appallingly.

> And there [Jo] sits, munching and gnawing, and looking up at the great cross on the summit of St. Paul's Cathedral, glittering above a red-and-violet-tinted cloud of smoke. From the boy's face one might suppose that sacred emblem to be, in his eyes, the crowning confusion of the great, confused city—so golden, so high up, so far out of his reach. (315)

The Pawn

Anthony Trollope, unlike his acquaintance and rival Dickens, did make much of the clerical theme in his novels, particularly in the six novels usually known as the Barchester Chronicles. The first of these novels, *The Warden* (1855), will suffice to indicate Trollope's characteristically loose deployment of the comic cleric. Although Trollope's Barchester novels are thoroughly sown with clergymen (and, importantly, clergy wives, often more capable and ambitious than the husbands), one reads Trollope with a sense that nearly any institution would do for his mildly satirical fiction. Archdeacon Grantly, Dr. Stanhope, Bishop Proudie, and the rest could be involved in maneuvering and plotting in Parliament or the law—professions that Trollope likewise wrote about. They are defined in terms of power and loyalty, money and ambition; a few are sincerely faithful, but most are interested in the church as a source of prestige and prosperity. Archdeacon Grantly, one of the more worldly clerics, is described starkly as wanting "success on his own side and discomfiture on that of his enemies," and more slyly in this way: "He did not believe in the Gospel with more assurance than he did in the sacred justice of all ecclesiastical revenues."[12] Grantly's Christian name is Theophilus, "friend of God" in Greek, and Trollope expects us to smirk at this incongruity.

To contrast the power-hungry clergy of Barchester, Trollope gives us Mr. Harding in *The Warden*, a good and simple man who falls afoul of the machinations and vendettas of others. He is the sort of gentle pastor who does no harm and a little good; he is elderly, kind, unassuming, and loving. His only passion is music, which puts him above Primrose in *The Vicar of Wakefield*, whose passion is a trifling thesis about remarriage, but music also, rather regrettably, is the main reason he went into the church. *The Warden* revolves around the scandal stirred up against Mr. Harding when the terms of his wardenship of Hiram's Hospital are aired in the newspapers. This medieval charity was set up to care for indigent old men, but in the centuries since the charity was created, the estate has done well, and now the warden of the charity has an income of eight hundred pounds while the old men get a few pence. (In comparison, Mr. Harding's other job as precentor of the cathedral nets him only eighty pounds.) A crusading reformer makes an example of Mr. Harding's position to demonstrate the inappropriate affluence of the church; after painful deliberation, old Mr. Harding resigns the wardenship. Trollope's point is sharply made: the wealth of the church charity is inappropriate, but no one benefits from exposing Mr. Harding. The old men in the Hospital are neglected in future, and Mr. Harding is unnecessarily humiliated. He has been caught in the crossfire between rival factions: those who wish to attack church privilege and those who will defend the institution in any circumstance.

The reader will discover that little actual ministry is evident in a Trollope novel. Many parlors are visited and many delegations to bishops

12. Trollope, *The Warden*, 65, 32.

and lawyers take place, but worship is rarely in sight and parish duties are far in the background. Even Mr. Harding, one of the best of Trollope's clergymen, does not exactly overtax himself in the service of his parishioners. Thus the humor of a Trollope novel can be subtle. If Mr. Harding is a clerical clown it plays out this way: he is a small man trying to do a bit of good in a huge religious corporation badly damaged by corruption and greed. The comedy of *The Warden* is reminiscent of Chaplin's comic turns as the Little Tramp: both Harding and the Tramp are slightly ridiculous, well-meaning, downtrodden, and ultimately pitiable. *The Warden* contains a nice scene where Harding travels to London to confer with society lawyer Sir Abraham Haphazard and while waiting for him goes ineptly in search of a cup of coffee. He enters a cigar divan, a posh gentleman's smoking club, and is childishly pleased but bewildered by its opulence; he falls asleep there.

Happily Absurd

Graham Greene's novels can be sorted (by his own categorization) into two columns: his novels and his entertainments. *Monsignor Quixote* (1982), one of his later fictions, has aspects of both. Greene's novels are generally seen to be his serious works, often with an emphasis on imperialism, political corruption, and Roman Catholic doctrine; his entertainments are more light-hearted works or thrillers like *Our Man in Havana* or *The Third Man*. This taxonomy was abandoned by Greene in his later years, but it is intriguing to look at *Monsignor Quixote* in both ways. The tone is sprightly and good-tempered, the main characters (in imitation of *Don Quixote*) bumbling through the Spanish countryside, drinking too much wine and getting into ridiculous conflicts. Father Quixote and his friend the Mayor go on a vague quest, visiting shrines and tombs but also brothels and pornographic films because of Quixote's radical innocence. Despite its surface daftness, Greene manages to engage with serious religious questions in the novel, usually in the realm of Christian character and the nature of faith. Although the conclusion of the novel is not particularly tragic, as in Greene's more serious Catholic novels *The End of the Affair, The Power and the Glory,* and *The Heart of the Matter,* Father Quixote's death after presiding at a final invisible sacrament of communion while sleepwalking is both outlandish and moving.

As with the best kind of comic clerics in this chapter, Father Quixote represents Christian love at its most basic. He has no ambition and little learning but is dutiful and sincere. Elevated to the position of Monsignor when he offers aid to a bishop in a manner that can only be called quixotic, Father Quixote is then exposed to the pitiless attention of church authorities who cannot bear that so simple a man should be allowed distinction. As a consequence of the absurd adventures with his "Sancho," Quixote is stripped of his priestly identity and barred from hearing confessions or presiding at mass. This is when things turn serious. As in *The Power and the Glory*, this destruction of priestly authority is devastating. In *Monsignor Quixote,* the priest calls it a "sentence of death,"[13] while in *The Power and the Glory* the last priest in Mexico, on the run, is in despair because he can hear confessions but "was the only one left who hadn't repented, confessed, been absolved."[14] The Mexican priest is caught and executed in *The Power and the Glory* because he feels compelled to hear the confession of a criminal, even though he knows it will lead to his own death.

This attention to the Roman Catholic sacraments is a preoccupation of Graham Greene's. An adult convert to Catholicism, Greene (like Evelyn Waugh) always gives emphasis to confession and the Eucharist in his fiction. On their own, the priests of *Monsignor Quixote* and *The Power and the Glory* are not impressive: Quixote is innocent to the point of absurdity, and the Mexican whisky priest is, as his nickname suggests, a drunk and has also broken his vows of chastity. But in their roles as priests, they acquire nobility and dignity. In *Monsignor Quixote* this dignity is most evident at the last moment; injured and dying, Father Quixote cannot be prevented from taking and offering communion in a trance-like Eucharist. Whether that dignity is undermined by the fact that the words of the mass are garbled—his last uttered phrase is "By this hopping"[15] as an invisible Host is offered—is a matter of opinion and taste, as it is with many of the comic clerics we have been considering.

I count Father Quixote among the comic priests in this chapter who are offered as positive examples rather than derisory ones. Throughout *Monsignor Quixote* the priest prays for everyone; at the tomb of Franco

13. Greene, *Monsignor Quixote*, 208.

14. Greene, *The Power and the Glory*, 172.

15. Greene, *Monsignor Quixote*, 250. References to subsequent passages are given parenthetically.

he tells Sancho that he would pray even for Stalin or Judas. "There are degrees of evil, Sancho—and of good. We can try to discriminate between the living, but with the dead we can't discriminate. They all have the same need of our prayer" (113). His humility is absolute. Visiting a cathedral he feels "as though he were an infinitely small creature set on the slide of a microscope" (151), and he quietly refuses to accede to another priest's estimation that the church must be ruled with a firm hand.

> "A child has to be educated through discipline. And we are all children, monsignor."
> "I don't think a loving parent would educate by fear."
> "I hope this is not what you teach your parishioners."
> "Oh, I don't teach them. They teach me." (74)

This elderly priest is a priest errant, one who does battle, for example, on behalf of the sanctity of the Virgin Mary when her image is used in a crass money-raising scheme. Don Quixote in Cervantes's seventeenth-century tale was a knight errant, and in each case the term errant is usually seen to describe their wandering or rambling aspect. It is not incorrect, however, to hear suggestions of "error" or "erring" in the word; the etymology is interrelated. Quixote is both a wandering hero (or priest) and one who makes mistakes. Both Quixotes are flawed, but gain a nobility from their imperfections because they contemplate them and attempt to learn from them. This is more obvious in Greene's simpler tale. As Father Quixote explores the world, he discovers the limitations of his knowledge and feels chagrin. Unlike the typical Graham Greene character, Father Quixote throughout his existence has experienced no conflict between the desires of the flesh and the demands of Christian morality. He has never known lust, and it is characteristic of him that he feels inadequate and guilty because of his goodness.

> How can I pray to resist evil when I am not even tempted? There is no virtue in such a prayer. He felt completely alone in his silence. . . . He prayed in his silence: O God, make me human, let me feel temptation. Save me from my indifference. (141)

The most unusual aspect of Father Quixote's personality is his insistence on the importance of doubt in the Christian life. He dreads certainty, and has a dream about Christ being saved from the cross by angels, so there was "no final agony" (76)—for Quixote this dream is a nightmare. He "felt on waking the chill of despair felt by a man who realizes suddenly that he has taken up a profession which is of no use to no one" (77). Faith, not certainty, is of paramount importance; he believes that human beings cannot survive without faith.

The silliness of Father Quixote's final mass (can the priest be in his right mind if the liturgy includes the words "by this hopping"?) might seem to undermine the serious theological points Graham Greene is making in the novel, but I like to think that Quixote's devotion to ministry and his utter faithfulness overrule the addled quality of his final priestly action. And his final priestly action is generously to offer invisible communion to his unbelieving friend Sancho; Quixote's dying confidence that the gift of the Host will be well received may mark a turning point in Sancho's life.

The Pure Buffoon

In 1963, Peter Sellers starred in a small satirical film, *Heavens Above!*, one of those low-budget British films not seen much abroad, and certainly one of Sellers's lesser known films. The plot concerns a mild and gentle Anglican parson named John Smallwood who is confused with another cleric named John Smallwood. The wrong Smallwood—Sellers—is given a plum church job for which his own unassuming behavior would never have qualified him. One of the lovely things about this amiable satire is that everyone assumes that Reverend Smallwood is stupid because he is gentle. But he is the only one to get the joke that he has been given the wonderfully named parish of Orbiston Parva because of a "clerical error."

The descriptions of this movie can make Smallwood seem a holy idiot who falls afoul of his worldly parish. But Smallwood is aware of what he is doing and how the community may react to him. He is innocent, but not ignorant, acting on principle throughout, and this baffles nearly everyone. His preaching is sharp, although it is delivered in a deceptively childlike manner.

> As this is my first sermon, I think I ought to tell you that I'm not a good Christian. But I want to be. So I'm trying. . . . This town is full of people who call themselves Christians. But from what I've seen I wouldn't mind taking a bet that there aren't enough real Christians around to feed one decent lion. . . . Well, I tell you

what I'm going to do. I'm going to try to reopen negotiations
with the Kingdom of God.[16]

One of the moral targets that Smallwood has in his sights is the local
commercial enterprise Tranquillax, a combination laxative, sedative, and
stimulant. No one expects the mild little priest to be the one to declare
this staple commodity in the local economy "worthless," but he does, and
in a sermon, and the trouble begins.

This low-key comedy is unusual in part because narrative conventions lead us to expect that Smallwood will be an utter failure in his gentle
and principled ministry. And he is, for a while. At the beginning he fails
to get Christ's message across to his plainly uninterested parishioners.
In the middle of the movie, however, Smallwood unexpectedly converts
the richest woman in the parish and together they start up an enormous
free food depot. Previously she had been devoted to her fat lapdogs, but
now she gives shelter to the homeless in her mansion. There are amusing
scenes in which she tries to give free food to people who cannot comprehend what Lady Despard could possibly be doing. The vicar puts up signs
around the community:

> Good Neighbour Fellowship (Non-Denominational): As from
> 23rd next, the Church Hall will be open as a centre for a scheme
> to distribute goods FREE to those who feel in need. The purpose
> is Christian Unity and rediscovery of the Christian joy of giv-
> ing. Signed J. Smallwood, Vicar, Holy Trinity Vicarage, Orbiston
> Parva.

Suddenly people accept and appreciate what Smallwood is doing. At the
center of the film is a brief and shining glimpse of the heavenly kingdom.

But then things go terribly wrong. Local business cannot stand for
the free produce being distributed in the community, and eventually riots
break out. Lady Despard loses heart. Smallwood offers himself up as a
sacrifice to the mob, in order for peace to be maintained. He makes this
speech: "I came down here to Orbiston Parva because I wanted to serve.
Well, it looks as though I've failed. What you want, I can't give, and what
you need, you don't want." This has no salutary effect, and it begins to
look again as if "Nobody takes parsons seriously these days anyway," as
Sir Geoffrey Despard says. He is the son of the wealthy benefactress, Lady

16. *Heavens Above!*, directed by John Boulting and Roy Boulting, written by John
Boulting and Frank Harvey (this and all subsequent quotation is my own transcription
from the film).

Despard, and has earlier accused her of "sucking up to the Almighty" with her good works.

At some point in this film parallels between John Smallwood and Jesus Christ make themselves manifest, and the viewer may wonder how this little man was maneuvered into position as apotheosis. Smallwood is without exception patient and forgiving, never angry, generous with absolutely all he has. He gives over his home and food to the reprobate lazy and itinerant Smith family, with its eleven children, for no other reason than this is what he does. The only thing that seems to dishearten him is a small thing. After the newly-baptized Smiths run off with all his money (and the lead tiles from the church roof), they leave him a "Dere Vicar" note that makes his face fall.

The solution of the church is to make him the new Bishop to outer space. It might look as though the authorities want to blast him into orbit, but they only hope he will sit quietly at the isolated northern see of his bishopric and stay out of trouble. Once there, Smallwood voluntarily takes the place of a frightened astronaut, partly because that is the sort of thing he does, and partly because he knows the world has no place for him. The film ends with John Smallwood being sent into space.

The smart comedy of this little-known film offers us a familiar type of clergy buffoon with the beautiful twist that this vicar actually is living out Christ's injunction to love, feed, forgive, bless, and give life. The wonder of it is that there is no agonizing struggle; this is not a drama or a tragedy. Peter Sellers as a vicar beautifully plays out the notion that an intelligent but committed person can just do this, almost involuntarily. No one expects Christ-like living to be so comically easy. And ultimately it is not at all easy; Smallwood's ministry does not exist in the end, because he was too good for this world.

The Idiot

One of the most memorable and devastating portrayals of a cleric in recent movie history is Rowan Atkinson's turn as Father Gerald in the popular *Four Weddings and a Funeral*, directed in 1994 by Mike Newell and written by Richard Curtis, who created *The Vicar of Dibley* in the same year. Wedding number two is performed by Father Gerald. He appears wearing a biretta but does not seem to know what to do with it, and uncomfortably takes it off before the ceremony. He starts off nervously but correctly, until he says "Holy Goat" instead of "Holy Ghost" and then proceeds to blunder after blunder.[17] He hopelessly tangles the names of the couple, uses the phrase "awful wedded wife," and finishes up with a reference to the "Holy Spigot" instead of "Holy Spirit." There are constant reaction shots in this scene to the congregation; barely contained hysterical laughter is engulfing the younger set while the older people are horrified. When Father Gerald manages to finish up the ceremony more or less successfully, Atkinson's face is a picture of childlike smugness. His smirk underscores his pathetic lack of responsibility; Bernard and Lydia have practically done the wedding themselves, since they had to correct the priest throughout the entire service. Father Gerald is a fool through and through.

It is a justifiably famous comic scene, and wonderfully performed. Is it harmless or dangerous? Atkinson himself claimed in a 2011 interview with the London *Times* that originally he believed his satirical characterizations of clerics were "exaggerated," or even "unreasonable satires." Some of his sketches originated on the television sketch show *Not the Nine O'Clock News*, where Atkinson made a specialty of awkward, off-color, or inappropriately rude vicars. But, he went on to say his attitude was now different, because

> so many of the clerics that I've met, particularly the Church of England clerics, are people of such extraordinary smugness and arrogance and conceitedness who are extraordinarily presumptuous about the significance of their position in society. Increasingly, I believe that all the mud that Richard Curtis and I threw at them through endless sketches that we've done is more than deserved.[18]

Keeping Mum, a more recent Rowan Atkinson film, revisits the foolish clerical character he has perfected, but softens him. This vicar, the emphatically named Reverend Goodfellow, is well-meaning but inept. Asked to play football in a charity game, he is useless in goal, to the distinct embarrassment of his children. He fusses about trivia while his daughter and wife are off having sexual adventures that he misses entirely; he forgets to pick up his young son from school. Typical of his prayer is one he attempts to offer when a mysterious new housekeeper,

---

17. *Four Weddings and a Funeral*, directed by Mike Newell, written by Richard Curtis (this and all subsequent quotation is my own transcription from the film).

18. Quoted in Taylor, "Rowan Atkinson."

Grace, comes to the vicarage; his family impatiently waits for the mean-dering and dull prayer to fizzle out, which it does. The plot of this black comedy pivots on the identity of Grace as a criminally insane murderer (and the long-missing mother of the vicar's wife); she materializes as a kind of mutant Mary Poppins to bring harmony to the vicarage, and this actually works for a while. Grace, for example, teaches Goodfellow how to tell jokes to make him a more effective public speaker; this is success-ful, although one gets the sense that Goodfellow does not understand the jokes himself. Grace also, unfortunately, murders anyone who annoys the Goodfellow family, in an attempt to protect and help them, and eventu-ally the body count is too high not to attract notice.

This farce is premised on the notion that encompassing an unworld-ly and dim vicar with a foul-mouthed, adulterous wife and a murderous mother-in-law will inevitably be hilarious. If you push certain buttons on your plot-o-matic, comedy will ensue; set aside the detail that the com-edy is broad and clichéd. The parish of Little Wallop has a population of sixty-seven, a sign tells us, and the enduring topic of controversy in the parish involves the flower arranging committee. Reverend Goodfellow lacks confidence and must practice sermons in his empty church, and he never gets the hang of correct microphone usage. Giving an address at a convention on "God's Mysterious Ways" he manages, of course, to call it "Cod's Mysterious Ways."[19] Goodfellow recovers some of his dignity by the end of the film, but the film itself does not, relying as it does on the formula of idiot vicar with an unintelligent parish that cannot raise its level of concern above the flower rota.

The same clerical clown inhabits a little tale called *The Vicar of Nibbleswicke* by Roald Dahl, published in 1991 after Dahl's death in 1990. A publication that benefited a dyslexia charity, Dahl's gleefully tasteless little book may or may not be for children, but it probably is, since Dahl's children's books never circumvented the vulgar, even (or especially) in works like *The Witches* and *Matilda*. The vicar in Dahl's book has a rare kind of (fictional) dyslexia, whereby he reverses the spelling of spoken words when he is under stress. Thus, his name (Lee) becomes "eel" and he is a "rotsap" rather than a "pastor." The comic crux of the story comes when he counsels new communicants not to gulp communion wine, but to sip it, and later when he suggests a new way for the congrega-tion to park their cars. The words "sip" and "park" are reversed, and his

19. *Keeping Mum*, directed by Niall Johnson, written by Richard Russo.

reputation is nearly ruined. However, he is finally fitted up with a mirror so he can walk backward while preaching, which solves his problem and, it is reported, "it added a nice crazy touch to what was normally a dreary proceeding." The final line of Dahl's story can almost be guessed: "and for the rest of his life he became a lovable eccentric and a pillar of the parish."[20]

In the movie *Heavens Above!* a heartless archdeacon has a line that has stayed with me. During an argument about the mission of the church and the controversies that surround Reverend Smallwood, the archdeacon suddenly says, "I don't see any reason to keep bringing God into it." It is a telling line of dialogue. If you remove God from the equation, much of what the church does seems bizarre, even comic. Occasionally even a work that does "bring God into it"—like Greene's *Monsignor Quixote*—remains bizarre and comic. It is an accepted procedure in comic writing to find a dignified situation or personality and attempt to puncture it. There is humor that is life-giving and valuable (as in *Tristram Shandy*, *Heavens Above!*, and *Monsignor Quixote*) and then there is cruel humor, where the very nature of clerical life is automatically risible, and thus the office is rendered ineffectual. Such clerics are compromised creatures who have given over the dignity of their office, and seem complacently implicated in the laughter aimed at them.

20. Dahl, *The Vicar of Nibbleswicke*, 40.

Barbara Pym and Jan Karon

If you tell people you are at work on a book about clerical figures in literature, Barbara Pym and Jan Karon are two names hopefully offered as a gift to appease the harried researcher. Each is representative of a particular stream of literature in her own nation. Pym captured the parish affairs of mid-century English towns of a certain sort, and perfected the portrayal of the anxious, foolish, yet tamely erotic vicar. Here are two examples from *Jane and Prudence* (1953). The focalizing intelligence is Jane, a vicar's wife:

> He used to be so attractive, she thought, but being a clergyman and a husband had done their worst for him, rubbed off the bloom, if that was the right word.[1]

> "Edward Lyall is charming, don't you think?" she went on. "I thought he looked rather tired tonight. It must be exhausting to be admired like that, and one feels that politicians aren't quite so used to it as the clergy are."[2]

Jan Karon's works are also gentle comedies, although less funny than Pym's. Her clergyman is Father Tim Kavanagh, an Episcopal priest in a southern American town. Set in the present time, the Mitford stories feature basically good people and their occasionally discontented but good minister. There is less of a sense in Karon's books, as compared to Pym's, that she is intent on gentle mockery of church leaders. When Father Tim becomes smitten with his neighbor Cynthia in the second Mitford book, *A Light at the Window*, Karon's prose almost slips into Harlequin or Mills

1. Pym, *Omnibus*, 551.
2. Ibid., 568.

and Boon style: "Her eyes were like sapphires, smoky and deep with that nearly violet hue that always caught him off-guard."[3] One cannot imagine Pym offering that sentence, unless to do something sarcastic with it.

Pym's books are moderately well-known today, although her career suffered in the sixties and seventies and she could no longer find a publisher. In 1977, in one of those moments that gladden an author's heart, her reputation was rescued when various prominent writers were asked to provide to the *Times Literary Supplement* their nominees for most underrated author of the twentieth century. Lord David Cecil described her books as "the finest examples of high comedy to have appeared in England during the past seventy-five years"; Philip Larkin praised her "small poignancies."[4] Her books began to circulate once more, including ones she had written and put in a drawer. When a commentator today wants to explain how Jane Austen's plots can be adapted to the present time, Pym is often evoked. I am not sure I can agree with Merritt Moseley, who remarked in 1990 about Pym's "present state of renown,"[5] but a look at the website of the Barbara Pym Society does turn up a list of twenty-six book-length studies published about her since 1985.

Pym created a certain smart spinster heroine: resolutely colorless, sometimes mousy and passive, apparently resistant to passion, keenly observant. These women often report that they say things "stupidly," undercutting and demeaning themselves. Yet these protagonists, in an odd but agreeable wish-fulfillment move, can be pursued in a mild way by men. The women may not desire or even realize this. Often Pym's women are involved in hopeless admiration of vicars, married or unmarried; they do not really want to marry the vicars but enjoy worshiping them from afar. (Jane in *Jane and Prudence*, who marries a vicar, is an exception.) Some of Pym's comedy is not completely accessible to a non-British audience; there is a high-church-versus-low-church ruckus going on throughout the books that Pym's characters find absorbing but North Americans may find puzzling. The vicars are human and fallible, often vague or self-centered. Jane's husband, Nicholas (the despair of his archdeacon), delightedly buys himself little soaps in the shape of animals and learns to dry his own tobacco to save money. It is up to the women in the novels to preserve sanity.

3. Karon, *A Light at the Window*, 7.

4. "Reputations Revisited," 67.

5. Moseley, "A Few Words about Barbara Pym," 75.

"I thought Mr. Latimer's sermon last week was very fine," [Miss Doggett] said, still on the same subject. "He is a really gifted preacher, such a command of language. And those quotations were really quite obscure. Anyone can see that he is a very well-read man."[6]

The genius of Pym's novels lies in their affectionate piercing of the Anglican vicar before he gets too full of himself. Without making the vicar an outright fool, Pym's observant, affectionate, but independent women make certain that arrogance cannot get a foothold. This is my favorite passage of Pym, from *Crampton Hodnet*, a novel written in the forties not published until after Pym's 1980 death. In this scene, the young curate Mr. Latimer talks with Miss Morrow at a church affair, a "Sale of Work":

"How much longer will it last?" he asked in a low voice. "It's five o'clock now."

"It will last as long as *you* stay here," said Miss Morrow. "Surely you can see that?"

Mr. Latimer heaved a scarcely perceptible sigh. "Do you think that if a thunderbolt suddenly fell out of the sky onto this hideous embroidered tea cosy it would end then?" he asked.

"The tea cosy would be spoilt and nobody would be able to buy it, but why would the Sale of Work end?" said Miss Morrow.

"Are there no sick people I ought to visit?" asked Mr. Latimer hopefully.

"There are no sick people in North Oxford. They are either dead or alive. It's sometimes difficult to tell the difference, that's all," explained Miss Morrow.[7]

Here is another fine passage, from *Some Tame Gazelle:*

The new curate seemed quite a nice young man, but what a pity it was that his combinations showed, tucked carelessly into his socks, when he sat down. Belinda had noticed it when they had met him for the first time at the vicarage last week and had felt quite embarrassed. Perhaps Harriet could say something to him about it. Her blunt jolly manner could carry off these little awkwardnesses much better than Belinda's timidity. Of course he might think it none of their business, as indeed it was not, but Belinda rather doubted whether he thought at all, if one were to judge by the quality of his first sermon.[8]

6. Pym, *Crampton Hodnet*, 78.

7. Ibid., 31–32.

8. Pym, *Omnibus*, 3.

Without Miss Morrow, Belinda, and Harriet, these vicars and curates might run amuck or become hopelessly mired in their insufficiencies. Pym's apparently downtrodden ("timid," "embarrassed") but secretly excellent women provide a necessary corrective, a brisk reconfiguration of the unexpectedly complicated moral balance that is an English parish. They explain. They doubt. They notice. This corrective was especially needed when the Church of England was an all-male affair, but is always needed. When a character in Pym says "But, of course, we mustn't forget that a man's a man however he wears his collar, must we?" we may smile, but the remark is profound.[9] This fine-tuning of ecclesiastical attitude is the sort of thing missing from Jan Karon's novels, where the atmosphere can become too wholesome and sacrosanct.

There is a distant nobility about the depiction of Father Tim Kavanagh that appears to me unwarranted; there is also a kind of conspiracy to keep him unmarried that seems unhealthy in present-day America. (It is clear from the beginning that Tim and Cynthia will wed, but the actual wedding is not presented until the sixth Mitford novel, *A Common Life*.) Although Father Tim does finally marry, an unreal aura of inexperience remains about his character. In the first novel his friend the bishop discusses the state of clerical marriage in a highly unnatural manner.

> I cannot exhort you to go out and marry, Timothy, but I will say that these ten years with Martha have brought an ease to the stress which was plundering my own soul. . . . As I recall from our days in seminary . . . you were fairly smitten with Peggy Cramer, but when your feelings for her began to interfere with your calling, you broke the engagement.[10]

These are, I remind you, Protestant ministers of the late twentieth century. How could a wife be called merely an "ease to stress" and how exactly do wives "interfere" with one's calling? Why does the bishop's language include "exhort" and "smitten"? If an actual present-day bishop wrote a letter to a restless and tired pastor like this one in the first chapter of *At Home in Mitford*, that bishop should be disciplined.

> You ask if I have ever faced such a thing as you are currently facing. My friend, exhaustion and fatigue are a committed priest's steady companions, and there is no way around it.[11]

9. Pym, *Crampton Hodnet*, 126.

10. Karon, *At Home in Mitford*, 5.

11. Ibid., 4.

The atmosphere of the Mitford series is resigned, gentle, comforting, and ultimately a little smug. Sorrow is occasionally invoked, but rarely felt. Father Tim gets tired, but is unacquainted with despair. He dreams of a wife with a face of "girlish sweetness."[12] Karon's writing is deliberately nostalgic and pastoral; people go for walks and work in gardens, as they do in Pym (and in Austen), but in Mitford such scenes are deliberately enlisted to provide security to the reader. In the first Mitford novel, Father Tim converts a criminal accidentally when the man overhears Father Tim speaking in the church. The "man in the attic," jewel thief George Gaynor, has been hiding in the church building, and descends when Father Tim's goodness finally overwhelms him. It is true that religious moments can be serendipitous, but there is something disturbing about Father Tim's lack of consciousness in his ministry to Gaynor. Should a Christian minister be so unaware?

I feel the need to tread carefully here, because Jan Karon's books have brought pleasure to millions of readers. She is one of those authors that can safely be recommended to the sensitive older person; Christian bookstores feel assured that they can display Karon's books prominently. One of Karon's supporters is Lauren Winner, who has said that the first two Mitford novels were critical in her conversion to Christianity. She has written in *Books and Culture* that

> one of the things Jan Karon does terrifically well is create, and plunge readers into, a kind of close-knit community that few of us today experience in real life. Tacitly, her novels suggest that this community is possible not because the novels are set in a small town but because they depict the body of Christ—the kind of community possible in, if not always realized by, the church.[13]

Winner is a professor at Duke Divinity School. But Karon's depiction of community, for me, is too soothing and simplistic to serve in the successful negotiation of contemporary life. For one thing, change makes the people of Mitford deeply uncomfortable. In *Out to Canaan* the town's mayor, Esther Cunningham, has been in power for "eight great terms" and Father Tim is one of those who support the "stickin' with Esther" campaign.[14] Surely a series which has prompted cookbooks and bedside companions should make us think twice about its depth or shrewdness.

12. Ibid., 10.
13. Winner, "Sherry with Father Tim."
14. Karon, *Out to Canaan*, 234.

And just why does Father Tim's church have a "fine Norman tower" in North Carolina?

Ultimately neither Pym nor Karon makes strenuous demands of the reader, but at least Pym can be enigmatic. Pym's vicars and rectors could stand some improvement and therefore should be at least mildly thought-provoking, although the books do function principally as entertainment. Her novels require some ingenuity on the part of the reader, since her characters are not always as straightforward as they seem. Nor, as Karl Miller once said in the *New York Review of Books*, it is always possible to tell how genuine is her interest in religion:

> Her interest in religion is anthropological, skeptical, sardonic;
> it may also be romantic; whether and in what way it is pious, I
> can't be sure. For all I can tell, she may be an "Anglican atheist":
> a term of Orwell's, which has been applied to Larkin.[15]

Jan Karon's background, on the other hand, is in advertising, and this is evident. It does not do to be too ambiguous in such a world, so she has painted the church community in Mitford with broad strokes. I do not want to say that I cannot conceive of how the Mitford books could lead to conversion nor how they help to sustain belief once there. But I have to say it: the Christian life has always been and always will be tough and ridiculous—even painful and dangerous—and this is not detectable in Karon's novels.

15. Miller, "Ladies in Distress."

4

The Collared Detective

Although I am the very least of all the saints, this grace was given to me to
bring to the Gentiles the news of the boundless riches of Christ, and to make
everyone see what is the plan of the mystery hidden for ages
in God who created all things. (Eph 3:8–9)

Country parsons suggest some sociological experiment: give a reasonably
educated middle-class Englishman a modest income, a house in the country,
and job security for life, and see what he will do. (Thomas Hinde, *A Field
Guide to the English Country Parson*)[1]

G. K. Chesterton in 1901 wrote that "not only is the detective story a
perfectly legitimate form of art, but it has certain definite and real
advantages as an agent of the public weal."[2] In 1929 Dorothy L. Sayers
made a similar claim in her imposing *Omnibus of Crime*, stating that by
the nineteenth century "the detective steps into his right place as the pro-
tector of the weak—the latest of the popular heroes, the true successor
of Roland and Lancelot."[3] Joining Sayers and Chesterton, W. H. Auden
in a 1948 essay wrote that the "job of detective is to restore the state of
grace in which the aesthetic and the ethical are as one."[4] Auden also said
that the wish "which the detective story addict indulges is the fantasy of

1. Hinde, *Field Guide*, 4.
2. Chesterton, "A Defence of Detective Stories," 158.
3. Sayers, "Introduction," *Omnibus of Crime*, 12.
4. Auden, "The Guilty Vicarage," 21.

being restored to the Garden of Eden, to a state of innocence."[5] Claiming that the detective story has a moral function, especially a highly moral function, has always been a challenging task, and even today few critics or practitioners are convincing when making lofty claims for detective fiction. Sayers was inclined to admit that "pure perversity" or the need to exercise our "animal faculties of fear and inquisitiveness" could be perfectly sound explanations for the popularity of mystery stories and crime fiction.[6]

But these three writers were strong adherents of the notion that there is a restless and hungry aspect in human personality that desperately needs the ingenuity and questing spirit found within Romantic forms like detective stories. And what Sayers, Chesterton, and Auden held in common aside from their love of mysteries was their Christian faith. While Auden was a poet rather than a mystery writer, and Sayers generally avoided including her strong theological ideas within her Lord Peter Wimsey mysteries, Chesterton enthusiastically placed himself right at the center of the conversation about whether the church and the detective story truly have anything to say to each other. He is best remembered for his Father Brown mystery stories, by far the greatest achievement in the field of clerical mystery. Chesterton explored the religious ramifications of detective fiction not only in his enigmatic and sometimes whimsical Father Brown stories, but in essays and newspaper articles as well. In a 1912 article Chesterton declares Christ as a kind of good detective because he "insists on really knowing all the souls that he loves."[7] Going further, he claims the entire Church to be "the only thing that ever attempted by system to pursue and discover crimes, not in order to avenge, but in order to forgive them. . . . Its specialty—or, if you like, its oddity—was this merciless mercy; the unrelenting sleuthhound who seeks to save and not slay."[8] The elevated and even mystical ideals Chesterton sets out for his sort of detective story mean that the Father Brown stories cannot strike the average reader as plausible or realistic. One does not turn to Chesterton for ordinary characters or everyday plots, although Father Brown is a keen observer of simple details. But one does turn to

5. Ibid., 24.
6. Sayers, "Introduction," *Omnibus of Crime*, 9.
7. Chesterton, "The Divine Detective," 239.
8. Ibid., 236.

Chesterton for detective fiction that resonates with moral robustness and significance.

Joseph Bottum in a 2011 *Books and Culture* essay makes large claims for a preponderance of clerical detective fiction on the market, saying that 10 percent of the perhaps three thousand English-language mysteries released annually "touch on religion in some clearly recognizable way."[9] Bottum cites a researcher who has counted at least "219 different clerical detectives in mainstream mystery fiction" and is himself animated about the apparent flood, in the past few decades, not only of mysteries involving medieval monks, but also those with Anglican women clergy as detectives.[10] Yet for all this ostensible activity, there is no clerical detective who approaches what Chesterton accomplished with Father Brown. The names that Bottum presents for our inspection—Prioress Eleanor, Reverend Callie Anson, Deaconess Theodora Braithwaite, Brother Barnabas—are generally unfamiliar, while the more familiar characters (I think of Ralph McInerny's Father Dowling and Andrew Greeley's Father Ryan) exist within books that are, under stern evaluation, unremarkable, with little religious interest to differentiate their plots from formulaic drugstore mystery.

Bottum is right when he points to grace as the hallmark of a certain kind of detective story, although I am inclined to call attention to how rarely such grace appears.

> The explicit presence (or worry about the absence) of grace is what, at last, distinguishes the best religious mysteries and what marks off the genre from other kinds of mystery fiction. A detective story is religious if it superadds an awareness of redemption to the fallen world assumed by all mysteries. If it sees the chance of God's grace down in a universe of sin.[11]

Auden was one of the boldest, most self-revealing commentators of this genre. He suspected, he said, that the "typical reader of detective stories is, like myself, a person who suffers from a sense of sin."[12] (Intriguingly, he also said that artists, physicians, scientists, and the clergy are unusually devoted fans of detective fiction.) However, to use the form of a religious whodunit to resolve notions of sin and forgiveness, evil and redemption

9. Bottum, "God and the Detectives," 2.

10. Ibid., 8, 2.

11. Ibid., 10.

12. Auden, "The Guilty Vicarage," 23.

is all too likely to throw things thoroughly off balance—unless that story is in the hands of a master. This is because there is a mathematic or geometric element in many detective stories (think of the Agatha Christie books featuring diagrams); to contemplate grace and salvation in such a story can be ridiculous or painful. Only a few mystery writers manage at all well the addition of the spiritual to the more material and worldly whodunit. Auden thought that Chesterton's Father Brown was one of only three successful detectives in the entire history of the detective genre.

The Roman Connection

One does not have to ponder clerical detective fiction long before observing that the Roman Catholic Church dominates the field. I submit that the best known clerical detectives are Father Brown, Brother Cadfael, and William of Baskerville, with the last trailing a good deal behind since he occurs in just one book, Umberto Eco's *The Name of the Rose*, while Father Brown and Brother Cadfael star in successive adventures. All have been successfully adapted to the screen, big and small, with Ellis Peters's Cadfael mysteries making the most impressive transition due to the considerable gifts of Sir Derek Jacobi in the television role. Cadfael, William of Baskerville, and Father Brown excel at detection largely for the reasons that other great detectives, such as Sherlock Holmes, do. They are simultaneously rational and intuitive (although in differing measures), have prodigious memories, and exhibit extraordinary skills of observation. But they have additional gifts and advantages.

One reason for the appeal of the Roman cleric in mystery stories is the binding nature of the confessional. Alfred Hitchcock knew well the ironic power of the confessional, where a crime can be revealed and simultaneously buried. In his 1953 film *I Confess* Father Michael Logan (Montgomery Clift) is forced to conceal the identity of a murderer who has deliberately set out to frame Father Logan for the murder. Father Logan, principled and sincere, is trapped in a deadly position where he knows he must willingly remain. Adding a Roman Catholic backdrop to a mystery provides scenic exoticism of a sort (especially if set in medieval times, like the Cadfael stories and *The Name of the Rose*); the Roman church also supplies a distinct hierarchy for the detective to chafe and occasionally rebel against. More importantly, the celibacy of a Roman priest or monk defines for such detectives a solitary existence; they are capable of those long periods of contemplative thought necessary for crime-solving, even if they live in monastic community. The detective, being a stock figure of Romantic art, is necessarily an isolated figure. (Revisionist authors have tried several times to provide an updated Sherlock Holmes with a romantic partner, but he functions best alone.)

I suspect the most important reason Roman Catholic priests and monks dominate the genre of clerical detective fiction is that the Roman church has been able to hold on to ancient conceptions of religious mystery better than most Protestant churches. Add this to the rigorous intellectual tradition of the Roman Catholic church, for example within the Dominican, Augustinian, and Jesuit religious orders, and you have a rich dual heritage in accord with the passion and discipline found in the Gospels and (particularly) in Paul's epistles. When Paul writes to the Ephesians, declaring the gospel of Christ, he wants "to make everyone see what is the plan of the mystery hidden for ages in God who created all things" (Eph 3:9). This wonderful conjunction of "plan" and "mystery" is what a Roman cleric should almost effortlessly be able to bring to the detective genre.

Brother Cadfael, for example, is learned (he is an expert in herbology) yet staunchly worshipful of the relics of the martyred Saint Winifred. Father Brown is both a proponent of logic and of miracles, although what he claims as miracle may be unexpected. As a comparative example of what happens when you put a Protestant cleric in a detective mystery, see *The Mysteries of Reverend Dean* (2008) by Hal White. White's elderly detective lacks dignity (he is fat, he waddles) and White never plausibly explains why Thaddeus Dean should be so capable and ingenious at crime solving. The ecclesiastical landscape is bland. One assumes that an author chooses to deploy clerical detectives because such characters are superbly placed: they can go everywhere, they know human nature, they are patient. Their cleverness is underrated. But the downside of choosing clerical detectives is that if they become mere sleuthhounds, they appear cold and callous; they lose the benevolence and reverence so necessary to the portrayal of a believable minister. Removing the cleric from the protective and very interesting confines of the Roman church is dangerous for a detective story; the exposed Protestant cleric is liable to look foolish. A Methodist clerical detective would seem too transparent, but who knows what wonders a talented writer of mysteries may produce in the future?

Chesterton and the Joy of Paradox

The Father Brown stories began in 1911 with *The Innocence of Father Brown*, a collection that contains the most memorable stories, and continued until the nineteen thirties. Chesterton never gave into the temptation, as did Arthur Conan Doyle, to write a full-length novel for his detective, and that was all to the good. There are fifty-two Father Brown stories, and as with Sherlock Holmes stories, they work best with single incidents, tightly constrained action, and quickly sketched characters. Chesterton's love of analogy and paradox means that his plots tend to center on one device or puzzle that must be set parallel to another idea or, alternately, set on its head for the solution to become clear. The beauty of the paradox-driven detective story is that much that is vital to Christian belief is paradoxical.

The first and the most significant Father Brown Story, "The Blue Cross," is set during a Eucharistic Congress taking place in London. The narrative keeps Father Brown at a distance until nearly the end. The apparently more primary and charismatic figures are Flambeau, called the "colossus of crime," and the policeman trailing him, the supposedly brilliant Valentin.[13] The real detective is Father Brown, with "a face as round and dull as a Norfolk dumpling" and "eyes as empty as the North Sea" (18). He is presented as short, simple, and pitiful; both Valentin and Flambeau misapprehend him entirely. (The first-time reader will fare no better. Chesterton makes sure we are in the dark about Father Brown's capabilities, and refuses to even provide his name until the story is more than half over.) What Father Brown does in "The Blue Cross" is prophesy a crime that never happens. The crime disintegrates because he is able to prevent it and (more importantly) save the soul of the wrongdoer. Father Brown dangles the bait of a valuable jeweled cross, a relic he is taking to the Eucharistic Congress. Flambeau takes the bait, pretending to be a fellow priest and fastening himself to Father Brown's side, and Father Brown proceeds to lead him on a bizarre odyssey all over London.

They visit a restaurant and Father Brown throws soup at a wall; they pass a greengrocer's shop and he disarranges the price tags. He smashes a window; he forces Flambeau to overpay a luncheon bill. Valentin follows this trail of oddities and eventually draws close enough to overhear Flambeau and Father Brown discussing theology on Hampstead Heath.

---

13. Chesterton, *The Annotated Innocence of Father Brown*, 16. References to subsequent passages are given parenthetically.

When Flambeau turns violent and demands the cross, he discovers that Father Brown has already sent it into safekeeping, after a complicated parcel exchange. Flambeau, unable to steal the cross, must instead listen to Father Brown's gentle lectures on reason, truth, and justice. At the end of the story both Flambeau and Valentin bow to Father Brown as their master.

The story is known for its use of topsy-turvy reasoning. Father Brown, in his journey across London with Flambeau, subjects him to a peculiar series of tests. Father Brown is a champion of logic, but he uses disorder to lead to the orderly judgment that Flambeau is not a priest but a criminal. Since Flambeau raises no objection to paying a bill that is too high nor to any of the other oddities, Father Brown proves to himself that Flambeau is up to no good; as a bonus, the priest lays a trail of strangeness for the police to follow. Father Brown appears the picture of innocence, and in a sense he is the exemplar of purity, but he demonstrates to Flambeau that he can anticipate and understand every move of a devious criminal mind. "How in blazes do you know all these horrors?" is Flambeau's exasperated cry. Father Brown's response: "Has it never struck you that a man who does next to nothing but hear man's real sins is not likely to be wholly unaware of human evil?" (39).

Father Brown's commitment to reason (he says he also knows Flambeau is not a priest because Flambeau's "priestly" conversation attacks the rational) added to his knowledge of human beings and their fallenness are his equipment for detection. Valentin, the official detective, can only tag along behind the imaginative and courageous amateur detective. In his decision to keep a look out for "any sort of queer thing" (27), Valentin is partly successful but his methods are too passive. Father Brown, in crafting the queer things, is at the heart of the action that Valentin merely follows. The police officer is also unable to grasp Father Brown's illogical logic. Valentin falls too strongly under the spell of the bizarre, which Father Brown would never do, even though it sometimes appears he does. Of Valentin, Chesterton writes, "[W]hen he could not follow the train of the reasonable, he coldly and carefully followed the train of the unreasonable. Instead of going to the right places . . . he systematically went to the wrong places" (21). This only works to a degree. The trick of a Chesterton story usually involves discerning the rational core of the apparently absurd action.

Father Brown's methods will be the methods of many clerical detectives to come. He knows human sin so well that few criminals can outsmart him. He is unassuming, a "bumpkin" (38), and can accomplish much without being noticed. He is intelligent but humble, well-educated but unambitious for himself. He believes in truth and is unlikely to give into the ennui and pessimism that grip secular detectives. But the distinguishing mark of Father Brown's crime solving is that he wants to turn the wrongdoer not toward right, but toward God. "The Blue Cross" takes place during a Eucharistic Congress, and this is not a mere device which allows Father Brown to takes his precious silver relic to London. Eucharistic congress—the fellowship of the Lord's table, the communion of true believers—is precisely what Father Brown desires for and with Flambeau. He does not want to capture or punish but to save him, so they can join together in thanksgiving, which is, after all, what "Eucharist" means. Nor is the cross only a valuable object to steal. Father Brown holds the cross aloft before Flambeau; both Flambeau and Valentin see the cross as bait, but for Father Brown it is a promise, a consolation. Indeed it is a way of life. Father Brown, at the beginning of the story, is seen clumsily dropping the parcel with the cross in it, thus putting it in danger by naïvely talking about it to complete strangers. Valentin and Flambeau write him off as a booby. But, in another of Chesterton's contrarieties, Father Brown reverences the true cross more than anyone. The cross that Father Brown loves cannot be dropped or stolen.

In another fine story, "The Queer Feet," Father Brown once again saves Flambeau from himself and from damnation. (That Flambeau and Father Brown lock horns again is strange, rather like Wile E. Coyote and the Road Runner going up against each other over and over.) This is also a story with lovely religious reverberations, as Evelyn Waugh knew when he placed a reading of it within a key scene in his novel *Brideshead Revisited*. Once again there is a setting that is symbolically significant: the action takes place at a dinner for a club called the Twelve True Fisherman, and the theft (which once again Father Brown foils before it actually happens) is of valuable silver. But this is no ordinary silver. The plunder that Father Brown recovers and restores to the club is a set of silver fish knives and fish forks. Father Brown solves this crime before it becomes a crime by listening to the sound of footsteps, the "queer feet" of the title. He repeatedly hears rapid steps going up a passage, but when they go back down the steps are slow. He places this observation alongside his realization of the "one indispensable mark" central to a crime at a club of this sort: that lower class waiters and upper class gentlemen wear the same costume, a black coat. One man could pretend to be both. Father Brown catches the thief alone and turns his heart (again); then he releases him.

Here the cleverness of the story (and its lovely simplicity) is combined with a theological commentary well laced with irony. Unlike the Eucharistic Congress, the club of the Twelve True Fisherman is offered up as a parody of Christian fellowship. The club is "select" (64), not open to all. They insist upon "luxurious privacy" (66) and meet in a hotel which is a "topsy-turvy product . . . a thing which paid not by attracting people, but actually turning people away" (65). That Father Brown bothers to save the silver fish knives and fish forks is a tribute not to this corrupt association but to the master whom he serves, whose symbol was a fish. Christ, Father Brown knows, would have been repulsed by the ostentatious wealth of these particular fishermen. It is doubtful whether the club members grasp the lesson which Father Brown offers them in his telling of the tale:

> Father Brown got to his feet, putting his hand behind him. "Odd, isn't it," he said, "that a thief and a vagabond should repent, when so many who are rich and secure remain hard and frivolous, and without fruit for God or man?" (78)

Then follows his renowned description of how he is the only true fisher of men in the vicinity. He has hooked Flambeau for the church and let him go, to exercise his free will, but Flambeau can be brought back "with a twitch upon the thread" (79).

Father Brown is on the spot for this foiled crime because he has been involved in the ultimate drama: he was called to the hotel to be with a dying man. Father Brown is, literally, doing life-and-death work. He has taken a man's confession and happens to overhear Flambeau's queer feet while writing a letter to amend some wrong on behalf of the dead man. Unlike other detectives, Father Brown comes to the aid of those who need him—both criminal and victim—not when he is ensconced in armchair or office, but while he is performing sacred offices, offices so holy that other characters barely comprehend their magnitude. Additionally, Father Brown comes to the solution by an amalgam of reason and mysticism—once again I am reminded of the "plan of the mystery" mentioned by Paul in Ephesians. He listens to and notices everything, but then goes into a kind of dreamy, visionary state, and comes to his conclusions suddenly and instinctively. The way Chesterton puts it is this:

> Father Brown's figure remained quite dark and still; but in that instant he had lost his head. His head was always most valuable when he had lost it. In such moments he put two and two together and made four million. (71)

Father Brown's success as a detective comes about as a result of his love of truth and his respect for all people. (Often in the Father Brown stories we hear of the respect one should have for crime as a work of art.) He allows himself visionary moments but never forgets his reverence for reason and science. His detecting skills are, I think, neither here nor there for him; he is more importantly a spiritual diagnostician and healer. As Auden said, "His prime motive is compassion, of which the guilty are in greater need than the innocent."[14] Father Brown's ministry has taught him the worth of silence and discretion. In "The Hammer of God" he uncovers the crime of a fellow cleric but sets the man free to make his own decision; the other clergyman immediately turns himself in. Like his creator, Father Brown is intrigued by all of life; he is curious and open to delight and awe. In "The Blue Cross" Chesterton says, "The most incredible thing about miracles is that they happen" (19), but what he and Father Brown identify as miracles would surprise us (an example: clouds come together to form the shape of an eye). Father Brown notices things because he is in love with God's creation. Above, I cited a book called *The Mysteries of Reverend Dean*; while reading that book I made a note to myself that said: "How does this amateur detective know so much about angle of knife penetration?" Even in some laudable Sherlock Holmes stories, one wonders how Holmes knows about those poisons impossible to detect. But Father Brown's observations are indelibly part of his being. As with Chesterton himself, Father Brown is filled with a sense of curiosity (and a resulting collection of esoteric facts) about, quite literally, everything. This omnivorous interest is part of his vocation. Chesterton wrote in 1913, "It is very difficult to find an unimportant subject, or even an uninteresting subject. I have gone through most of my life looking for an uninteresting subject—or even an uninteresting person. It is the romance of my life that I have failed to find either of them yet."[15]

14. Auden, "The Guilty Vicarage," 22.
15. Chesterton, "Bacon and Shakespeare, Again," 419.

Medieval Mystery

It is, perhaps, a mistake to gaze so closely at Father Brown and then turn one's attention to other collared (or cowled) detectives. But it cannot be denied that other clerical detectives in truth do look thin in comparison. There is a sense that, along with Conan Doyle's Sherlock Holmes, Chesterton's Father Brown sets the standard for a great deal of the detective fiction that follows. Although Arthur Conan Doyle began writing mysteries before Chesterton, in 1887 as opposed to 1911, they published alongside each other for the better part of two decades, and Chesterton, at any rate, was appreciative of the other's work. In a 1927 piece in praise of Sherlock Holmes, Chesterton says that "everybody who has written a detective story has felt his long, angular shadow upon the page,"[16] and many readers and writers now also feel the shadow of the very short priest resembling a Norfolk dumpling. But Chesterton occasionally finds fault with the great detective. In one story, Holmes tells Watson to "cut out the poetry" because Watson has been describing a moss-covered brick wall in a case study. Chesterton springs to Watson's defense. "Why the devil should not the poor brute be allowed to notice moss?" argues Chesterton. "The moss may turn out to be as important as the bricks."[17]

Here Chesterton's criticism of Conan Doyle arises because of Holmes's uneven use of logic. Chesterton is hardly the first to notice Conan's Doyle's fallibility in this area, but it is surprising how many readers still carelessly describe Holmes as a cold creature of pure reason. Not so fast, says Chesterton. "As a matter of mere logic," he points out drily, "if all details may be of importance" (and they are), then bricks and moss have equal claim on our attention.[18] Attentive followers of Holmes know that he often does, like Father Brown, use his neighboring faculties of reason and intuition mutually. However, in the clerical detective fiction that trails behind Chesterton and Conan Doyle in the years to come, the influence of reason dominates.

Edith Pargeter's novels about Brother Cadfael, for instance, emphasize her medieval detective as a man of action *and* a man of knowledge. Although Cadfael can show emotion and does have strong loyalties and antipathies, generally he solves crimes by putting one foot in front of

16. Chesterton, "The World of Sherlock Holmes," 237–38.

17. Ibid., 239.

18. Ibid.

another, methodically working through motives, means, and opportunities. Pargeter, writing as Ellis Peters, began the Cadfael series in 1977 with *A Morbid Taste for Bones*, finishing in 1994 with the twenty-first Cadfael title, *Brother Cadfael's Penance*. The books are more historical than mysterious, with Pargeter providing finely-detailed descriptions of all aspects of twelfth-century manufacturing, travel, warfare, diplomacy, and religion. The pace is appropriately slow, with precise attention to the complex bonds of kinship which hold together a very tribal Britain. Although each novel usually does feature a murder or two for Cadfael to solve, several matters predominate over detection in the Cadfael books. These are the machinations and ambitions of the monks and priests among whom Cadfael works; the parallels Pargeter suggests between the twelfth century and our own time; and Cadfael's own remarkable personality. It is probably this last that has won so many followers. Cadfael combines military knowledge, political acumen, and brilliant skills as a healer with his determination to be the humblest possible man of the cloth. It is an unusual and winning blend.

Possibly no fiction writer outside Anthony Trollope has depicted so vividly the complex interactions of people who work within the church, the tactics, loyalties, and bargains that mark the lives of men (nearly all these church people are men) thought to be withdrawn from society but in truth as socially involved as anyone else. One of the ironies of Pargeter's books is that Cadfael has had two lives, and his cloistered life is just as full of dangers, plots, and treachery as his first life as a soldier. Cadfael has been a man of the world, a Crusader, but he is now devoted to the arts of peace and healing. He may have turned from war and acquisition to mercy and worship, but around him are characters for whom the church is an important business, a profession like any other, rather like the men he knew in the army.

In *Brother Cadfael's Penance*, we accompany Cadfael to some very uncertain peace talks between King Stephen and Empress Maud, rivals for the English throne. Pargeter is a good medievalist, and I would not be the one to challenge her grasp of history, but the manner in which many of the characters talk about war and peace has a distinctly twentieth-century ring. I assume this is a deliberate anachronism on her part; there is a pessimistic modernity, for example, in this description of a worship service at the close of the failed peace talks:

> Compline, the last office of the day, which should have signified
> the completion of a cycle of worship, and the acknowledge-
> ment of a day's effort, however flawed, and a day's achievement,
> however humble, signified on this night only a final flaunting of
> pride and display, rival against rival.[19]

The presiding Bishop chides the rulers with being unwilling to take on
the responsibility of curing the nation of its ills. Indeed several of the
church's representatives speak with a weary pacifism more likely in the
twentieth century. The novel ends with one of the chief warriors turning
his back on the bloodshed and taking the cross.

This is what Cadfael has done, in turning from Crusader to Bene-
dictine monk and healer. Cadfael seems our representative: a modern
man in medieval garb who wants to cure rather than hurt and has no
great confidence in might or politics. He is both in and out of the world,
and thus ideally placed to appeal to modern readers and to function as a
detective. His detecting methods are solid and familiar: in *Brother Cadfael's Penance*, for example, he examines the body, determines the murder weapon, inspects the crime scene, searches the victim's possessions,
and retraces the man's recent actions. His best attributes as a detective,
aside from his expertise in the field of herbology and his extraordinary
acquaintance with both the material and spiritual realms, are honesty,
discipline, patience, and compassion.

Here is where I would like to turn aside from Cadfael as a detective
and examine more precisely what sort of man of the cloth Edith Pargeter
has given us in Cadfael. The question of how to be in the world but not
of the world—a pressing dilemma for many Christians and certainly for
many pastors—is the central question in the Cadfael books. Although I
do not recall that Cadfael ever struggles explicitly with a text like John
17, where Jesus gives direction to his disciples with repeated use of the
phrases *in the world* and *of the world* (or *from the world*), the thorny and
intricate implications of that Gospel passage could be said to form the
foundations of Cadfael's existence.

> But now I am coming to you, and I speak these things in the world
> so that they may have my joy made complete in themselves. I
> have given them your word, and the world has hated them be-
> cause they do not belong to the world, just as I do not belong to
> the world. I am not asking you to take them out of the world, but

19. Peters, *Brother Cadfael's Penance*, 68.

> I ask you to protect them from the evil one. They do not belong
> to the world, just as I do not belong to the world. Sanctify them
> in the truth; your word is truth. As you have sent me into the
> world, so I have sent them into the world. And for their sakes
> I sanctify myself, so that they also may be sanctified in truth.
> . . . I made your name known to them, and I will make it known,
> so that the love with which you have loved me may be in them,
> and I in them. (John 17:13–19, 26)

There is a strong and sometimes confusing current of movement in John 17, an insistent iteration of words like *coming* and *sending, belonging* and *protecting, sanctity* and *hatred.* But ultimately the commandment is clear: the key word in the final verse of John 17 is *love.* Although Cadfael is supremely interested in the entire world, and is often provoked to anger by the actions of Brother Jerome and Prior Robert, the unkind members of his brotherhood, nevertheless he is committed to work on behalf of Christ. The tensions and contending loyalties he feels within himself are expressed in phrases like "an impossible paradox, a void that weighed heavier than stone" and a "challenging contention . . . with himself. He had indeed taken vows, and he felt the bonds they wound about him tightening."[20] More often than not, however, Cadfael conveys tranquility.

The central problem in the final Cadfael book is not really a crime to solve—although there is one, almost forgotten for chapters at a time—but Cadfael's apparent apostasy. He must leave the abbey to find and rescue the son he fathered years ago in the Crusades. He feels remorse at quitting his community, but sets for a time love for his son over his love of the monastic life. Once his mission is over, however, he is genuinely penitent and returns to the abbey not knowing whether the abbot and brothers will accept him again. Cadfael is described during this time as both "erect and apart, again solitary" and full of "willing submission to the claims of community."[21] At beginning and end of the book, he prostrates himself on the floor of the abbey church, in front of the high altar. His worldly mission into the world of war, politics, and illegitimate children necessitates sincere penitence, even though his actions out in that other world are actions of compassion and reconciliation. But nothing makes Cadfael more profoundly happy than his return to the abbey, nearly always described by Pargeter in terms of "community." It is not a perfect community, but it is the best model of its kind in that time.

20. Ibid., 100, 22.
21. Ibid., 18.

Brother Cadfael, for all his cleverness and skill, is willing and grateful to strip his existence back to practically nothing: a cloak, a donkey to ride, a few herbs. This movement—not retreat, I think—into simplicity must be done not once, but repeatedly. The offices of the day's worship cycle in the abbey are insistent and imperative; Cadfael will halt almost anything to be in attendance at Matins, Lauds, Prime, and so on. And then the cycle—so primal and basic—begins again. Edith Pargeter presents medieval Christianity, with all its flaws, as a deeply relevant and resonant configuration; at the same time she slyly gives us in Cadfael a very modern man. Although he willingly lives within the sometimes suffocating rules of his order, if in real trouble he will go "directly to the source of all strength, all power, all faithfulness,"[22] concentrating on God alone. In this direct communion with God he can be understood by us rather like a present-day cleric, or how a present-day cleric ought to be.

The key line in the Father Brown stories is possibly this one, from "The Hammer of God": "I am a man . . . and therefore have all devils in my heart."[23] This idea that the ultimate detective, and perhaps the ultimate cleric, needs to be the normal, characteristic human being *par excellence* (if such a paradoxical concept is viable) also permeates Umberto Eco's 1980 novel *The Name of the Rose*. Eco's detective, the fourteenth-century Franciscan monk William of Baskerville, is erudite, observant, and worldly wise, but he also has a keen appreciation for human frailty. Eco has chosen medieval Christendom as his background so that he can people *The Name of the Rose* with extremist churchmen who believe that religion cannot survive without fear, and that reason and faith must be inimical to each other. This is a starker version of our own times. William's well-rounded and sensible character stands out in relief against the fanatics and hysterics of the abbey where he has been asked to investigate a series of murders. When the villain, at the book's close, succeeds in destroying by fire the entire abbey, including the magnificent library, William says grimly, "It was the greatest library in Christendom. . . . Now

22. Ibid., 14.
23. Chesterton, *Innocence of Father Brown*, 195.

the Antichrist is truly at hand, because no learning will hinder him any more."[24]

William is the lone voice of sanity and wisdom in *The Name of the Rose*. Even his novice Adso, the book's narrator, does not really comprehend what William stands for, and the last we hear of William is this melancholy statement by Adso: "I learned much later that he had died during the great plague."[25] Although no one in the fourteenth century can comprehend William's true worth, the reader is expected to see him as the great ancestor of Sherlock Holmes and, even better, an ancestor of our own era's most brilliant thinkers. Eco's clerical detective is a hero because he champions the life of the ordinary, fallible human being against the impossible ideals and tortuous ethical standards of medieval church leaders. Most importantly, William stands up for the power of ordinary human laughter.

It is a strange plot. It turns out that the villain, the librarian Jorge, has been trying to prevent the second volume of Aristotle's *Poetics*—a treatise on comedy thought to be lost—from seeing the light of day. To prevent laughter, to prevent the discussion of laughter, and certainly to prevent anyone from acceding to Aristotle's belief that laughter is beneficial, Jorge poisons the book, so that all who read it are killed. Eventually, in a bizarre parody of Ezekiel, Jorge will himself eat the book he has poisoned. He destroys himself and the knowledge of laughter's goodness in one devastating act. Just before Jorge does this, he engages in the sort of ethical dispute, with the detective, which often occurs prior to the denouement of a mystery. After listening to Jorge's demented condemnation of laughter, William responds with this précis of the Aristotle they have found:

> Comedy does not tell of famous and powerful men, but of base and ridiculous creatures, though not wicked; and it does not end with the death of the protagonists. It achieves the effect of the ridiculous by showing the defects and vices of ordinary men. Here Aristotle sees the tendency to laughter as a force for good, which can also have an instructive value: through witty riddles and unexpected metaphors, though it tells us things differently from the way they are, as if it were lying, it actually obliges us to examine them more closely.[26]

24. Eco, *The Name of the Rose*, 491.
25. Ibid., 499.
26. Ibid., 472.

Throughout the book, in a preview of the methods that Sherlock Holmes will use centuries later, William insists on the importance of curiosity and of examining everything—no matter how small—with exquisite care. The universe is "talkative," he says early on, and "it speaks not only of the ultimate things (which it does always in an obscure fashion) but also of closer things, and then it speaks quite clearly."[27] It is the job of the detective, and the man of God, to listen, to notice, to read the signs.

William of Baskerville does not succeed in convincing many people in his own era—there is a sense of disintegration and loss at the end of the book (and the movie: the film starring Sean Connery is comparable to the book but easier to navigate). Eco is confident that William's assertions will be understood by twentieth- and twenty-first-century readers. When William says, at the climax of the action, "God created the monsters, too. And you. And He wants everything to be spoken of," we feel the wind of modernity, at its most liberating and therapeutic, sweeping through the church.[28]

For Eco, *everything* is to be listened to, spoken of. For Pargeter/Peters, being in the world and being of the world create a constant and necessary tension. For Chesterton, compassion and wonder are key. These are the elements of successful detective work as undertaken by William of Baskerville, Brother Cadfael, and Father Brown. But these are also the elements of successful ministry as embodied in these three clerics. While detective stories for most of us are entertaining distractions, a few clerical detective stories resound with genuine lessons for how meaningful and redemptive ministry might be achieved. Eco, Chesterton, and Pargeter/Peters realize their goals by providing a glimpse of the "plan of the mystery" so important to Saint Paul. Logical *and* passionate, their clerical detectives discover wrongdoers on God's behalf, not on behalf of human law.

27. Ibid., 24.
28. Ibid., 478.

Cry, the Beloved Country

by Alan Paton

There are certain works of art that insist the world is a huge web of connections, that wherever you turn you will encounter someone who is somehow in relation with you, that small actions are bound by unseen gossamer threads to a million other small actions. George Eliot's magisterial novel *Middlemarch* is one of these stories of connection as is, in a less optimistic way, Charles Dickens's *Bleak House*. There has been a vogue for films of this style in recent years, sometimes called hyperlink films: *Traffic, Contagion, Crash, Syriana*. Read or viewed in a harshly realistic or critical frame of mind, these works can seem too heavily involved in coincidence. It turns out that nearly everyone in *Middlemarch* is somehow related to everyone else; surely there are too many cousins. But with an open attitude, the observer can see the truths about human community that need to be constantly examined and re-examined, and how these works of art (which are usually complicated in form, with many characters) help us to understand the intensive nature of community.

Alan Paton's novel about South Africa, *Cry, the Beloved Country*, is one such work. The cast of characters is not large as in Dickens or George Eliot, but nearly everyone in the novel is bound to everyone else. Considering the racial situation of South Africa, this was a bold move on Paton's part in 1948, and feels bold even today, after apartheid. (Intriguingly, this book was written before apartheid and—while this is too complex a matter to go into—to read this book now and attempt to tally all the varied stages of South African life in the past sixty years or so is mind boggling.)

At the center of the web of connections are two fathers—one black, one white—whose sons are both dead by the end of the novel. The black son, Absalom, has killed the white son, Arthur, in a bungled burglary. It is likely that Absalom did not mean to kill Arthur, but did so out of panic, and the deep and painful irony of this killing is that Arthur Jarvis was a friend to the black community, working as an activist on their behalf. Absalom had no knowledge of this. In the first half of the novel some of the connections and coincidences seem bitter and unhelpful. The black father, Stephen Kumalo, travels from his rural village to Johannesburg to help his troubled sister Gertrude. Once she is located—and the help offered to her is first accepted and then discarded, as she also discards her children—Kumalo sets off to find the next troubled member of his family, his son Absalom. The quest to find Absalom is meandering, exhausting for Kumalo but fascinating for the reader. Each time he meets someone who has seen Absalom, we have another glimpse of a South Africa that is unexpected, lovely, and dreadful. Kumalo's own brother John is appalling and self-interested, but strangers come on board to help in the quest, which leads slowly in all sorts of directions. We begin to accumulate a picture of this wonderful but distressed nation, with all its tribal and linguistic variety and political and economic tensions. Running parallel to the story of Kumalo's search for Absalom is the news of the murder of a prominent white man, and it is some time before the two plotlines intersect. The most distinguished passage of Paton's novel, containing the title phrase, occurs at the point when the murder is reported but it is not known that Absalom Kumalo is the murderer.

> Sadness and fear and hate, how they well up in the heart and mind, whenever one opens the pages of these messengers of doom. Cry for the broken tribe, for the law and the custom that is gone. Aye, and cry aloud for the man who is dead, for the woman and children bereaved. Cry, the beloved country, these things are not yet at an end. The sun pours down on the earth, on the lovely land that man cannot enjoy. He knows only the fear of his heart.[1]

Alan Paton skillfully keeps in hand these two views at all times—the land is lovely and beloved, the land is fearful and broken. Both the black and white communities are involved at all levels; there are imperfections

---

1. Paton, *Cry, the Beloved Country*, 104–5. References to subsequent passages are given parenthetically.

on both sides. Kumalo Senior, a humble and gentle man for the most part, is not flawless; this is not a naïve book about white demons and black victims, although Kumalo does think (and Paton seems to concur) that "the white man has broken the tribe" and "it cannot be mended again" (56). But more importantly, the nation of South Africa must simply move forward, as if it were a family. The main religious message of the novel is, I believe, that God's love cannot be explained or fathomed but it can be lived. Christian living is humble and generous and sorrowful. But the secular reader can, if she wishes, strip the Christian aspect out (with loss, of course) and still gain a great deal from this book. The major point is that there is only so much understanding that can be gained about something as painful as racism or violence: at crucial stages people must forgive and move on.

The second half of the novel, after the violence, relates the slow and unexpected alliance of the two fathers. They do not become friends, exactly, since they speak and meet only rarely. But from their first meeting there is mutual respect and sorrow. They acknowledge the suffering of the other, quietly, and there is no hatred. From that basis, and because of the intervention of a small white grandson who is described as having "brightness" within him and functions as a catalyst of goodness, the two men gradually and almost wordlessly work together to improve Kumalo's village. The white man, Jarvis, is wealthy and lives on a hill overlooking the village. Encouraged by the small boy and moved by Kumalo's integrity, Jarvis sends an elemental series of gifts to the village. An agricultural expert, a dam, milk rations, a new church—these come close to the essentials of earth, water, fire, and air (if one accepts milk as a kind of fuel or fire of life and the church as representative of spirit, or air). At the end of the novel the unhopeful and volatile situation of murder has unexpectedly resolved into peace and hopefulness. Kumalo's final prayer, as he performs a vigil on the day his son is to be executed, involves turning aside from "fruitless remembering" and instead giving constant and reiterated thanks, particularly for the mysterious fact that it has been "given to one man to have his pain transmuted into gladness" (309–10).

It is not one man who is thankful, but explicitly at least two—and the actions of these two forgiving and forgiven fathers will have exponential reactions of forgiveness and growth throughout their interlinked communities.

I have said nothing so far of the fact that Stephen Kumalo is a pastor or, using the marvelous Zulu word, *umfundisi*. The novel works well enough without the clerical element, but the ecclesiastical identity of Kumalo adds distinct richness to *Cry, the Beloved Country*. I have avoided mention of Kumalo as pastor because I believe Paton's intention is to demonstrate how any two people can achieve the fruitful and gracious friendship that occurs between Jarvis and Kumalo: in its laconic simplicity their joint project cries out to be duplicated. There are two aspects of Kumalo's ministerial identity that are, however, significant. One is that Kumalo's journeys throughout Johannesburg would have been impossible without the loving help of two other clergymen, Reverend Msimangu and Father Vincent. One black, one white, they anticipate the helpful alliance of the two grieving fathers. Although Kumalo has not known them before, in the city they house him, reassure him, help him find a lawyer, aid him financially, function as his brothers, pray and worship with him, and do everything and anything to aid him. Most importantly, they accompany him without question or complaint. This tireless walk alongside the one who suffers is offered quietly and modestly as a solution that indeed has been taken up as standard peacemaking practice in Africa (and elsewhere) in the past few decades. Again, it is not necessary to the plot of the book that Msimangu and Vincent be pastors, but the bonus part of the relationship involves the supreme value of prayer, and this would be unlikely to occur in a secular novel. Here is one of my favorite parts of *Cry, the Beloved Country*, a loving injunction from Father Vincent, who tells the faltering Kumalo that "Sorrow is better than fear. Fear is a journey, a terrible journey, but sorrow is at least an arriving" (140):

> And do not pray for yourself, and do not pray to understand the ways of God. For they are secret. Who knows what life is, for life is a secret. . . . We do what is in us, and why it is in us, that is also a secret. It is Christ in us, crying that men may be succoured and forgiven, even when He Himself is forsaken. . . . I shall pray for you, he said, night and day. That I shall do and anything more that you ask. (142)

The other valuable aspect of Kumalo's clerical identity is the way his presence binds together his village. Paton's writing style is both basic and lyrical, with elements of folktale. The cadences are slow, dignified, and unlike anything in the mainstream of the European or North American literary tradition. This style works well in a scene where Kumalo returns to his village after his long and painful trip to Johannesburg.

> Kumalo shakes hands with his friend, and they all set out on the narrow path that leads into the setting sun, into the valley of Ndotsheni. But here a man calls, umfundisi, you are back, it is a good thing that you have returned. And here a woman says to another, look, it is the umfundisi that has returned. One woman dressed in European fashion throws her apron over her head, and runs to the hut, calling and crying more like a child than a woman. It is the umfundisi that has returned. She brings her children to the door and they peep out behind her dresses to see the umfundisi that has returned. (255)

The significance of the umfundisi's return is not made explicit, but it does not have to be. The reticence of the description makes the esteem for Kumalo in the village all the more apparent. His mere presence is a matter of joy and hope.

5

Passion, for Better and for Worse

And others are those sown among the thorns: these are the ones who hear
the word, but the cares of the world, and the lure of wealth, and the desire for
other things come in and choke the word, and it yields nothing.
(Mark 4:18–19)

In these communities of sinners, one of the sinners is called pastor and given
a designated responsibility in the community. (Eugene Peterson, *Working the
Angles: The Shape of Pastoral Integrity*)[1]

Words in the English language are always on the move: rising and
falling in connotation and denotation. One of the intriguing alterations over the centuries involves the word *passion*. We still remember—
or we should—that passion indicates in its original Latin form suffering,
and has come to mean strong emotion or enthusiasm; it also signifies
anger and, important to the Christian story, is associated with the final
agony and ecstasy of Christ. But in our century the word has come to
mean, most immediately, sexual passion, and even an English professor like myself recalls first hearing the title of Mel Gibson's famous 2004
movie and muttering to myself, wide-eyed, "*The Passion of the WHAT?*"
Why, I wondered, would he make a movie about *that*?

A pastor once steadfast in ministering to the soul's needs who ends
in ministering to the body's desires: this fall has been told many times.
This might be the clerical tale that gains our attention most readily, or has

1. Peterson, *Working the Angles*, 2.

more staying power. In this chapter I would like to talk about the passion of the priest, but also bear in mind a balanced notion of what passion is. In a way, passion is a neutral concept, although it never feels neutral because it is by definition so exciting. But passion can be beneficial or distracting, an appetite that leads to fulfillment and joy or a draining ardor that drags restlessness and aching yearning in its wake. In chapter 8 I will deal more precisely with the fallout of destructive lust in clerical stories, but in this chapter I hope to stay in a less destructive but nevertheless equivocal site—the place where passion, defined broadly, grips a clerical character and either nourishes a ministry or damages it.

In 2004, while still Archbishop of Canterbury, Rowan Williams delivered a lecture called "The Christian Priest Today," full of invigorating injunctions about the difficulties faced by and virtues sought in Church of England priests of the twenty-first century. One of Williams's most stimulating ideas is that "[The priest must be] a place where lines of force intersect, where diverse interests and passions converge."[2] One can see why the Archbishop felt the need to press this point, since many Christians have come to regard clerics as a separate class, an elite detached from the concerns of ordinary church members. Williams uses, boldly I think, the word *passion* here, encouraging us to accept the fully human qualities of ordained ministers. But before we revel too much in the flesh-and-blood qualities of our pastors, he cautions us:

> Priests need detachment—not from human suffering or human delight, but from dependence on human achievement. . . . To be a point where lines of force converge and are knitted together, there must be a level of stillness in us that allows this to happen.

This seems to me an almost impossibly challenging commission for a mortal creature: to be a place where passions converge and yet a site of detachment and tranquility.

Extravagant Romance

The urtext for pastoral passion gone awry is *The Scarlet Letter*, a novel published by Nathaniel Hawthorne in 1850 and revealingly subtitled *A Romance*. Hawthorne was one of the architects of the nineteenth-century Romance, and the important detail to remember is that this type of

2. Williams, "Christian Priest."

Romance has nothing (or little) to do with amorousness or sexual long-ing. For Hawthorne and other literary innovators of his generation, the Romance was supremely about imagination, about stretching the human ability to conjure, embroider, dream, and desire. Hawthorne's Romance is more about quest, adventure, and trial than it is about interpersonal relations. And there is, peculiar to Hawthorne, always a kind of wild-ness, even a hint of supernatural confusion, which forces us to read his tales carefully. Hawthorne is a moral writer, but the lessons are (in my opinion) not in the least straightforward. Horton Davies cautions us, for example, to note the combination of "fascination and repulsion" in Hawthorne's attitude to Puritanism.[3] *The Scarlet Letter*, an extravagantly written and demanding book, is still widely read, especially in the United States, and frequently set as a school text even now. But it is also, I think, widely misread. This characterization of the adulterous couple, Arthur Dimmesdale and Hester Prynne, is all too typical.

> The clergyman epitomizes purity, goodness, perfected religious faith, and social/spiritual power. . . . Hester plays the perfect sab-oteur. Besides embodying universal aspects of the seductress—sultry beauty, sensuality, hauteur, and grace—she also reveals in her character all the temptations against which the "city upon the hill," and particularly its apostles, had to steel itself against.[4]

If *The Scarlet Letter* were only a tale of seduction, it would not oc-cupy such an elevated place in the literary canon. Nor should it simply be read as a metaphor of the Puritan settlers' relationship with the American environment (although this must be allowed as a consideration). Haw-thorne is a sophisticated writer, and when his narrator goes on about sin or the devil, for example, it is not always clear whether the narrator is mimicking the complacent attitude of the community or being candid. Subtle ironies abound in the novel: while we are never to take Hester Prynne's adulterous sin lightly, she is the most admirable character, marked by compassion, independence, intelligence, and courage. She is also the most fully-rounded character, replete as she is with sinful pride and explicitly aware of her physical attractions and irresistible aura of mystery. The Reverend Arthur Dimmesdale is described throughout as brilliant but flawed; pale, intellectual, overly sensitive, physically weak. We only encounter Hester and Arthur after their "fall," observing the

3. Davies, *Mirror of the Ministry*, 24.
4. Prioleau, "The Minister and the Seductress," 2.

aftermath of their sexual union, but it is reasonable to assume that Dimmesdale has always been an overly ambitious, cerebral, anemic man. It is not only his sexual shame but a pre-existing sense of inadequacy that leads to "the fasts and vigils of which he made a frequent practice, in order to keep the grossness of this earthly state from clogging and obscuring his spiritual lamp."[5] The narrator encourages our sympathy for several of the characters, but particularly for Dimmesdale, who is granted the adjective "poor" at least a dozen times: "Poor, miserable man!" (133).

Adultery is just one aspect of the passion which wraps up these strange characters—not only Hester and Arthur, but also their child Pearl and Hester's estranged husband Roger Chillingworth. The infamous "A" that Hester must wear on her gown signifies adultery at the start, but soon the letter transforms and shifts, both to reflect the complexity of Hester's character and the characters around her who are no less sinful (or even more so). Pearl, for example, dressed in gorgeous scarlet, is deliberately created by Hester as an incarnate "A" for all to see; she is both Hester's burning shame and the object of her obsessive love.

> She is my happiness—she is my torture, none the less! Pearl keeps me here in life! Pearl punishes me, too! See ye not, she is the scarlet letter, only capable of being loved. (100)

Those who do not know Hester's story believe the letter stands for "Able" because of her tireless service in the community; it is also said that after time passes "the scarlet letter had the effect of the cross on a nun's bosom" (145, 146). When Dimmesdale late one night believes he sees an ominous "A" burning as a message for him in the sky, others interpret the celestial message innocently, as "Angel" (142). When the town allows that Hester need no longer bear the sign of her punishment, she refuses to remove it. Among her reasons are that the letter is for Hester a "discipline to truth" (156) that she profoundly values and also her realization that the letter gives her fellow feeling with other sinners, "a sympathetic knowledge of the hidden sin in other hearts" (76–77). In proximity to sin, the letter burns; Hawthorne slyly makes it clear that the letter burns even in the vicinity of Christian ministers—and he does not mean Dimmesdale. Hester's "A" could also represent courageous Action; she tries to transfer her daring to Dimmesdale in a rousing line: "Act! Do anything, save to lie down and die!" (180).

5. Hawthorne, *The Scarlet Letter*, 107. References to subsequent passages are given parenthetically.

I make so much of the interpretive possibilities bound up in the scarlet letter in order to point out how many varied passions are embodied within Hester and Dimmesdale, for good or ill. And the narrow, cold, self-righteous colony needs their passions; most particularly, the puritanical church needs an injection of passion. "Meagre, indeed, and cold, was the sympathy that a transgressor might look for, from such bystanders, at the scaffold" is the description of the clergy at Hester's sentencing (43), and the narrator goes on:

> They were, doubtless, good men, just and sage. But, out of the whole human family, it would not have been easy to select the same number of wise and virtuous persons, who should be less capable of sitting in judgment on an erring woman's heart, and disentangling its mesh of good and evil, than the sages of rigid aspect towards whom Hester Prynne now turned her face. (57)

It could be said that Arthur Dimmesdale's one night of passion with Hester Prynne was the most likeable thing he ever did. It had been "a sin of passion, not of principle, nor even purpose" (200). All his other acts are compelled by the "framework of his order" that "inevitably hemmed him in." Hawthorne tell us that even an ordinary clergyman of the day would be "at the head of the social system" but Dimmesdale is no ordinary minister: he is the most highly regarded preacher of the colony. None of the others have anything like his homiletic fire, but his success arises not so much from his outstanding intellect as from his sorrows; "his power of experiencing and communicating emotion," we are told, was "kept in a state of preternatural activity by the prick and anguish of his daily life" (127). In other words, his powerful awareness of passion and sin enriches and enhances his preaching.

Arthur Dimmesdale manages a confession and a redemptive moment with Hester and Pearl just before he dies; his death results from the psychic and bodily damage he does to himself in attempting to hide his fully human self from the public eye. Hester, however, in her freely confessed sin, lives a long and worthy life. It is not the adultery which damns either of them; abused and mistreated passion on Dimmesdale's part ruins his life, while Hester achieves contentment because she owns her emotions, her principles, and her flaws.

Grief and Repentance

Arthur Miller's 1953 play *The Crucible* explores a similar era in American history as Hawthorne's *Scarlet Letter*. Although the clerical characters in *The Crucible*, Reverend Parris and Reverend Hale, are secondary, they are significant in that they represent the tyranny of the Salem witch hunts at the beginning of the action but switch their allegiance to the innocent victims of the trials at the conclusion. They know in the final act (Parris slower to come to realization than Hale, but then no less ashamed) that they have been instigators of injustice and are terrified at what they have unleashed. Hale in act 3 realizes that hysteria, lies, and greed are in play, not witchcraft, and in a highly dramatic moment at the end of the act shouts "I denounce these proceedings."[6] Unfortunately the campaign that the church instigated could not be stopped by the church once the legal system, such as it was in seventeenth-century New England, got under way.

It is refreshing to see clerical characters as rigid and unpromising as Parris and Hale learn so much about honesty and conciliation within the literary time frame of *The Crucible*. Parris looks like our villain from the start when the play's uneasy hero, the plain-speaking John Proctor, explains why he has ceased to attend church (and thus attracted the censure of the community):

> I have trouble enough without I come five mile to hear him preach only hellfire and bloody damnation. Take it to heart, Mr. Parris. There are many others who stay away from church these days because you hardly ever mention God any more. (26)

Parris is a harsh and inadequate minister who is nevertheless a good man trying to manage the town and his own spirit; throughout the play he is running scared because his daughter is one of the first girls to enter into a state of hysteric catatonia that is mistaken for bewitchment. Hale, on the other hand, while as rigidly dogmatic as Parris and apparently inflexible in his pursuit of devils, is accorded serious respect in Arthur Miller's stage directions:

> His goal is light, goodness and its preservation, and he knows the exaltation of the blessed whose intelligence, sharpened by

---

6. Miller, *The Crucible*, 115. References to subsequent passages are given parenthetically.

> minute examination of enormous tracts, is finally called upon
> to face what may be a bloody fight with the Fiend himself. (33)

In the stage directions Miller also notes that the following speech from
Hale has never received a laugh from the audience, which recognizes
that the cleric's pursuit of evil is based on the best intentions and a sharp
intelligence:

> Now let me instruct you. We cannot look to superstition in this.
> The Devil is precise; the marks of his presence are definite as
> stone, and I must tell you all that I shall not proceed unless you
> are prepared to believe me if I should find no bruise of hell upon
> her. (35)

The Devil *is* precise, but by the end of the play the viewers and readers
will identify the devil's marks in the governor's office and in the bitterly
mischievous hearts of bored or rejected girls, not in the supposed sins
of any of the condemned. Certainly Hale and Parris recognize this shift,
and they stand aghast as witnesses of murderous injustice. Their passionate goodness and concern for the moral well-being of the Puritan
community has been turned against them; they realize they are at fault
in persecuting innocence, but they have been swept up in political and
economic complaints that they had not realized would be so entangled in
a supposedly spiritual matter.

Passion in Plain Sight

A. N. Wilson, writing the introduction to the 1992 *Faber Book of Church
and Clergy* said one astonishing thing: in editing the anthology he felt he
was "compiling a portrait of a largely obsolete world."[7] Most of the works
that piqued his interest were Victorian. Similarly Douglas Alan Walrath
in a recent study of American clerical fiction can find little after 1930 that
interests him. God and his representatives, fictional and real, have been
"displaced," specifically by the cultural forces of modernism and postmodernism, Walrath claims; there has been a "cultural discrediting of
Christian faith."[8] While I do not dispute that the scores of clerical novels
in the nineteenth century have no current counterparts, that is not necessarily a bad thing. Even such a well-regarded author as Harriet Beecher

---

7. Wilson, "Introduction," *The Faber Book of Church and Clergy*, ix.

8. Walrath, *Displacing the Divine*, 272.

Stowe could write some fairly overcooked nonsense, like *The Minister's Wooing* (1859). Today illuminating novels and plays involving the church are still being written, and tales of clerical passion can be located if you are even mildly attentive. In England Wilson should have been aware of David Hare's 1990 play *Racing Demon*, for example, and that play's sympathetic portrayal of clerical commitment and anguish is all the more intriguing since Hare is known for his political dramas and not at all for his approval of religion.

Racing Demon exposes some of the same clerical dilemmas as in Hawthorne's and Miller's works, but given the location of an inner city London parish in the nineteen-eighties, the plot will not involve scaffolds or witchcraft. Hare's four Anglican priests, all trying to make a difference in a difficult ministry, show in their diverse approaches a passionate commitment to goodness. They also demonstrate the myriad ways in which that wholesome passion can be undermined, exploited, misrepresented, and pulled to pieces. The character who changes the most during the play is Tony, young, idealistic, and increasingly embittered that good Sunday morning attendance brings in "one percent of our whole catchment area."[9] Feeling that their team ministry is increasingly involved in social work, he longs to be representative of a supernatural religion and interferes aggressively with a parish family whose violence he believes he can combat with worship and prayer. Speaking to God, as many of the characters do in the play, Tony says in exasperation:

> I mean, can you tell me, is anything *right* with the Church? I mean, is the big joke that having lived and died on the Cross, Jesus would bequeath us—what?—total confusion, a host of good intentions, and an endlessly revolving Cyclostyle machine? (22)

The other three members of the pastoral team, Lionel, Streaky, and Harry, are faithful and effective pastors in their way, but Tony sees them as complacent. He cannot apprehend how impressive is the loyalty among the other team members, nor how valiant their attempts to be peacemakers. Tony believes he has a responsibility to parishioners "to give them some sense of joy" (10), but his methods become extreme; he instead causes great unhappiness, particularly for Lionel, victimized by the church hierarchy for not being charismatic enough, and for Frances, Tony's rejected girlfriend, pronounced a distraction in his new zealousness.

---

9. Hare, *Racing Demon*, 17. References to subsequent passages are given parenthetically.

This being an English play about an old denomination tied inextricably to the state, one of the issues in *Racing Demon* is that habitual reserve and institutional inertia can make it difficult to identify passion that is indeed present. Harry, for instance, utters a very plain statement about what the priest's job is: "There is people as they are. And there is people as they could be. The priest's job is to try to yank the two a little bit closer. It takes a good deal of time" (71). This is not uttered in exciting or inspirational language, but combined with other statements by Harry, we are able to identify how absolute is his love for the ministry: he is, he says, "only the channel through which God's love can pass. That makes me, as a person, totally irrelevant. As a person, nobody should even be conscious I'm there" (24). Donald "Streaky" Bacon is even less able to be expressive about his love of the ministry. He is unaffectedly happy and decent. "The whole thing's so clear. He's there. In people's happiness," he declares to himself. "The whole thing's so simple. Infinitely loving. Why do people find it so hard?" (63)

If there are villains in *Racing Demon*, they are the bishops, fearfully fighting against female ordination and taking out their frustrations on the priests. And the priests are pummeled additionally by church members.

> It can be pretty punishing. It gives you pause. You have to think all the time about what the job is. Mostly, in fact, it's just listening to the anger. One reason or another. . . . I've had three couples in the last week. They need somewhere to express their frustration. Everyone does. They don't realize it. But that's why they're drawn to a priest. They're furious. At their lives. At the system. At where they find themselves. And the vicar is the one man who can never hit back. (34–35)

Lionel believes the old Church has died and "the new Church is having its troubles being born" (32). His strategies for the new church are simple and viable but do not look inspirational enough to Tony and the bishops. For example, Lionel states artlessly that "The doors should be open. A priest should be like any other man. Only full of God's love" (67–68). The disgruntled ones want ministry that shouts success and smacks of intensity, and they cannot see the quiet but rather inarticulate passion that is already in place.

There's Sin and There's Sin

In 1994 British film director Antonia Bird created a gritty and realistic portrayal of contemporary Roman Catholic priests in Liverpool. *Priest* was well-received in the United Kingdom, but in the United States some Roman Catholics were offended by the film's frankness, especially in reference to the active sexuality of priests. For the film's star, Linus Roache, the story was not about sex but instead "compassion and forgiveness."[10] Father Greg, played by Roache, arrives in his rough new parish confident that he will encourage his people toward new heights of moral responsibility. Impatient with his fellow priest, Father Matthew (Tom Wilkinson), who leans left, dresses informally, and amiably encourages people to be open and discover their potential, Greg insists instead on the dignity of his office. "There's just sin," he says to Matthew; proceeding with precision to do his duties Father Greg quickly finds himself baffled and shut out by parishioners.[11]

Greg is hard on Matthew who, it turns out, has been for years sleeping with his housekeeper. Then in the confessional Greg is handed a miserable scenario he does not know how to act upon: a young girl is being repeatedly raped by her father, but the child refuses to report him and Father Greg cannot break the confessional's seal. Trying to drop hints to mother and teachers and thus solve the problem in the correct manner gets him nowhere, and he feels useless. The father threatens him. In a scene that is possibly one of those that certain viewers objected to, Father Greg weeps and yells at a Crucifix. Greg's obedience to the law of the church is, he realizes, ruining a girl's life. If he has decided at this juncture to break the rules of the confessional, it is too late; the mother has discovered the incest and hates the priest, damning him to hell in a very public scene.

Running parallel to this plot is the one involving Father Greg's hidden homosexuality. Taking off his collar one night when he is acutely lonely, he visits a gay bar, meets Graham (Robert Carlyle) and goes home with him. Greg thinks he can keep this aspect of his life behind locked doors, but his self-imposed rules (you can imagine him creating an inner set of justifications as he carefully removes his clerical collar and puts it in a drawer before setting out) are not nearly adequate. He and Graham

10. Lambert, "Father Figure."

11. *Priest*, directed by Antonia Bird, written by Jimmy McGovern (this and all subsequent quotation is my own transcription from the film).

fall in love; Graham demands openness and even comes to Eucharist but Greg refuses him. Humiliated by exposure as a gay priest in the tabloid papers, Greg attempts suicide. His bishop visits him, throws some grapes on his hospital bed, and says: "You say you want to carry on serving God. Well, that's good. The best way for you to serve God is to disappear. The best way you can serve God is to piss off out of my diocese. Is that clear?"

The people who want to stand with Greg are the other sexual sinners: Matthew and his lover, and Graham. Matthew (who has broken down Greg's door and prevented his suicide) insists that the only way to meet the scandal is to serve Eucharist together and weather this out. This is indeed what happens at the end of the film, although half the congregation abandons them and the only person who will take the host from Greg's hand (the communicants line up in front of Matthew) turns out, after a long hesitation, to be Lisa, the sexually abused girl he has felt such guilt about.

There is so much ostensible concentration on sex in this film that one could be excused for focusing on that issue—there are not one or two, but three instances of sexual wrongdoing in the scenario. But the very prevalence of sexual sin clears the way for the movie's real meaning. Antonia Bird demonstrates that sinful desires of all sorts are going to occur within human situations, but what signifies is patience, forgiveness, love, and humility. The sexual lives of both priests do involve love, not just sex, but there is no appropriate way that love and desire can be made known. In each case Greg and Matthew have been counseled to leave the church, but they do not want escape from this problem. Each recognizes their imperfection but each also wants to remain a priest. They love their work and love God, and they are both, in their contrasting ways, effective pastors—smart and resilient, even wise. Pledged to a nearly impossible vocation, the priests are expected to comply with standards of holiness that a person cannot attain every single day of his or her life.

Bird's use of the third plot strand—the one involving incest—helps to clarify the sexual issues in the film. Compared to the intimidating and hateful abusive father, Greg's and Matthew's sins are less destructive. No coercion is involved, no children are damaged. What is damaging is concealing normal human sexual desire; the furtiveness of the sexuality will eventually make these well-meaning and loving Catholics embittered and angry. Greg's own human fallibility, and the passions—wicked and virtuous—he discovers within himself make him, like Dimmesdale, a better pastor. He has been stiff and correct, but experience of pain brings him into true communication with God. The film's best speech bursts out of Greg as he tries to explain his frustrations to his lover Graham:

> He wasn't human enough, the son of God. He had certainty. Heaven, everlasting life, he knew it all with absolute certainty. Well, give me that, fine, no problem; you can crucify me as well. All the agonies of the world, no bloody problems whatsoever. Because I'd be certain that God exists. But I'm not certain. All I've got is faith. Something evil comes along. Grinning, sickening evil. And faith just runs away in terror.

It is possible that Greg's ministry could be saved by having a domestic partner to listen to such anguished speeches and a ministry partner like Matthew to offer loyal support. At the film's end, we do not know what will happen to these characters. The last scene of the film shows Greg gripped with violent weeping; the passion that he manifests here may be turned in several directions, positive or negative, or perhaps he will lock the passion away again.

As with *The Scarlet Letter*, *Priest* might first appeal to us because, to put it bluntly, we will always be interested in sex, and what could be more titillating than thinking about the sexual desires of high-minded clerics? The clash of longing and purity is irresistible as literary fodder. But as Arthur Miller is careful to demonstrate in *The Crucible*, if the combination of sex, religion, and morality makes a terrible mess, such conjunctions can hardly be avoided. The sexual passion of Arthur Dimmesdale in *The Scarlet Letter* is not separate from his other attributes but is inextricably bound up with them—he is a man of immense feelings and high thoughts. To thwart or crush such emotions and ideas is to ruin not only a human being, but also a ministry. In most of the works under scrutiny in this chapter, the ministry has been sound, even in Dimmesdale's case electrifying.

While some qualities of ministry in *Priest* or *Racing Demon* might make us uncomfortable, all the better. Candid contemplation of the pastor's ideas and character is necessary. The necessity of frankness, even bluntness about religion was reinforced for me recently when I was singing a hymn from the Iona Community. Their words for "Praise with Joy the World's Creator" insist that each member of the Trinity be seen in unexpected or even outrageous ways: Jesus Christ is an iconoclast, not only healing the sick but upsetting religion, and the Holy Spirit is associated with sacred foolishness. The hymn celebrates the variety of attributes that the Triune God enjoys. It is a passionate hymn to a passionate God. If pastors of honest passions are hounded from the church, then the church lies open to careerists and hypocrites—the subject of the next chapter.

The Book Against God

a Novel by James Wood

The Book Against God is the sole novel to date by one of our era's most astute literary critics, a writer described in *New York* magazine as "pretty much universally acknowledged—grudgingly, fawningly, eagerly, nervously, warningly, or mockingly, depending on which journals you subscribe to—as the best book critic currently classing up the back end of America's magazines."[1] James Wood has written regularly for *The Guardian*, *The New Republic*, and *The New Yorker*, holds a chair in literary criticism at Harvard, and is the author of several influential works of cultural criticism, among them *The Broken Estate: Essays on Literature and Belief* (2000) and *How Fiction Works* (2008). *The Book Against God* (2003) is usually labeled an autobiographical novel, and its plotline involving a young intellectual trying to come to terms with his own faltering sense of vocation, contrasted with his father's happy existence as an Anglican priest, does appear to have a corollary in Wood's own life as the son of intensely religious parents. And although the main character, Tom Bunting, tries to convince himself and the reader that the church is washed up and God must be rejected, he remains obsessed with faith. It may well be, strangely, the impact of Tom's father's constancy and integrity which the reader takes away from the novel.

Tom Bunting is wallowing in failure—failure to hold together a marriage; failure to make money; failure to finish a PhD in philosophy; even failure to wash. Tom is in revolt against the faith of his father, a beloved Anglican priest happily serving a small northern English town. It

1. Anderson, "How James Wood's *How Fiction Works* Works."

is important to know that Peter Bunting is not some happy simpleton but a keenly aware and intellectually capable man, once a theology professor, who gave up academe for the active life of faith and service. It becomes evident that Tom rebelliously rejects God because his father's faith is so pure and, equally important, because his parents' marriage is also a pure and lovely thing. Tom cannot manage any of it: marriage, faith, or real knowledge, and so he determines to reject God. He becomes a chronic liar, and this is the element that drives his wife away from him. He spends all his time writing a shadow dissertation called "The Book Against God," a kind of commonplace book with commentary, full of arguments about God based on Kierkegaard, Nietzsche, and the like.

James Wood's attitude toward Christianity and toward his characters Peter and Tom Bunting can seem puzzling, complicated by the book's status as an autobiographical novel and Wood's considerable status as a cultural critic who has written a book, after all, subtitled *Essays on Literature and Belief*. (The belief he describes in *The Broken Estate* might be better described, however, as a series of metaphysical skirmishes.) How much should we conflate Tom Bunting with James Wood, or does that get us anywhere at all? Occasionally Tom will speak of choral music or the scriptures with such real interest and remembered joy that you suspect Wood is encouraging the reader to see that Tom really is faithful and that his secularism is impossible. The words and actions of Tom's father are more inspiring than Tom's poor attempts at articulation. Here is Peter Bunting on his decision to become a priest:

> You know, not long before you were born, I had a crisis of faith. Curiously, it's why I became a priest. Or rather, I resolved the crisis by leaving the intellectualism of the university for the devotion of the priest's life. I didn't know the answers to any of my questions, and decided in the end that living a Christlike life was the only answer to them. . . . Theology was encouraging me to think of problems as intellectually soluble; and I saw that I needed instead to see life itself as a problem handed to me by God.[2]

Peter is eccentric and charming; he develops a highly ornate style of speech to cover his intrinsic shyness. He entertains with tales of his clerical tasks, including one colorful story about visiting a recently bereaved

2. Wood, *The Book Against God*, 225–26. Note that this is not the same James Wood as the co-creator of the show *Rev.*

wife and finding the corpse still propped up in a nearby chair. During Tom's stay with his parents he has occasion to notice how people are drawn to Peter for guidance, although he downplays his father's spiritual appeal:

> The visitors, the visitors! They came up the gravel path, past the graveyard with its look of tidy ruin, to ask for healing of one kind or another. Religion barely entered into it. In that traditional place, the priest was socially elevated. Going to Peter was a modern version of visiting the landowner to collect wages. Peter gave the parishioners the salary of his words, and rich words they often were. With gentle, undogmatic faith, he fit himself around the lives of his flock.[3]

In his parents' marriage Tom Bunting unconsciously identifies some of the richness and beauty that characterizes Peter Bunting's successful ministry:

> I was always struck by how closely they stood together. They had everything they needed. They had made a kind of joint-stock of each other's mannerisms so that the originator was no longer identifiable. For instance, I don't know which parent first began to purse his lips, but now they both did it. They communicated wordlessly. Sometimes, in the evenings, Sarah came into Peter's study, and with one hand vertical and another placed horizontally across it, made a letter T, while looking quizzically at her husband: it was the sign for a cup of tea. And though they drank tea every night, from the same art deco cups and saucers, the event seemed to give them the same pleasure every night; there was no death by repetition every night, quite the opposite, it was as if only by repetition they knew the exact weight of everything.[4]

Like the Bunting marriage, the good priest's relationship to the church is ordered by kindness, repetition, pleasure, intimacy. Neither do the Buntings take themselves too seriously. The goodness of the Buntings as a married couple and the goodness of Peter Bunting as a priest exist in this novel in a peculiar manner; after all, this is called *The Book Against God*. The novel begins with Tom in spiritual crisis and the reader expects a certain trajectory: the protagonist's death perhaps, or madness, or repentance. But none of these plot elements occur.

3. Ibid., 60.

4. Ibid., 45.

It is Peter Bunting who dies within the novel, and the death of this good father allows Tom some space for maneuvering. As a less successful spiritual being than his father, Tom is able to give himself permission in the father's absence to grow. Wood allows Tom a little grace note of illumination, bringing him (potentially) out of his immature navel-gazing state, but it is a small moment of hope. Tom's position is indeterminate as the novel closes. In a sense we have Peter presented to us as representative of the best sort of nineteenth-century cleric, with Tom functioning as the anxious modernist unbeliever of the twentieth century. The two centuries gently clash, although the nineteenth-century man is too kind and too well-mannered to acknowledge the animosity directed toward him.

The Canadian novelist David Adams Richards recently wrote a polemic about the antagonism toward Christianity evidenced in today's fiction.

> I have been bothered on occasion, especially reading younger people's novels, by the largeness of certain religious targets, the ease with which the mark is hit, and the smallness of the points sometimes made. It has become, in many movies and many books, the status quo of our Western society, and leaves out so many people I grew up loving.[5]

Richards says that this "anti-religious sniping has become more prevalent over my lifetime" and, I have no doubt, he does not mean to restrict his remarks to Canada. He finds this sniping intellectually thin, aesthetically limiting, and conformist. James Wood, who is such a splendid literary critic, succumbs in *The Book Against God* to the distrust of religion which has become nearly axiomatic in contemporary literature. Wood's novel could have been a fine one, but its stubborn contrariness about the clerical life pulls the novel's narrative voice off kilter. The reader's experience of Peter Bunting and his son Tom will likely remain in conflict with the portrayal the novelist apparently wants us to see.

---

5. Richards, "Canada's Literary Community Gets Religion All Wrong."

6

Failure, for Worse and for Better

Now by chance a priest was going down that road; and when he saw [the wounded man], he passed by on the other side. (Luke 10:31)

For it is true beyond a question that the testament or sacrament is given and received through the ministration of wicked priests no less completely than through the ministration of the most saintly. For who has any doubt that the gospel is preached by the ungodly? (Martin Luther, *The Babylonian Captivity of the Church*)[1]

Our desire to be preached to by the godly, to have the sacraments administered by mortals who approach perfection is deeply entrenched. Pastors will never be free from the stress of living up to standards that no mortal can truly attain. Conflict and especially hypocrisy all too often follow. Hypocrisy is an ancient and venerable subject ("ypocrisye" is a "zenne" on the sixth bough of Pride, and Pride is the First Head of the Beast, says the Middle English moral treatise the *Ayenbite of inwyt*)[2] and hypocrisy seems never so discernible as when it is stamped on the countenance of a cleric. In George Eliot's *Middlemarch*, it is from the sin of hypocrisy that Mary Garth wants to save her beloved Fred Vincy, inappropriately headed for a life in the church. As an ordinary man, Fred might be labeled merely a laggard or egoist, but in the church, Mary believes, Fred could be accused as a "great hypocrite" and she

1. Luther, *Babylonian Captivity*, 55–56.
2. Michel of Northgate, *Ayenbite of inwyt*.

would "defend any parish from having him for a clergyman."[3] Because of the tremendous emphasis on right living in most traditional depictions of church leadership, the erring cleric is an obvious choice for a writer wanting a quick illustration of hypocrisy.

Early versions of my chapter sported various titles: "Power, Hypocrisy, and the All Too Human" was one, and "The Pull of the World, or, Just a Career" was another. The changing titles indicated the struggle in which I was engaged, wishing as I did to discuss failed pastors who could not be described as wicked or calamitous, but who nevertheless were vain, weak, distracted, misguided, or just in it for the money and security. Such mixed creatures are more difficult to analyze than the plainly virtuous or the demonstrably wicked. Just how harmful are such literary pastors in the middle ground, those who are wrong but not deliberately malicious? One portrayal of clerical meanness is the notorious Reverend Brocklehurst in Charlotte Brontë's *Jane Eyre*. He is authoritarian, narrow-minded, unkind, and a dozen other unpleasant adjectives, but he is not intentionally brutal. He is following, in his own awful way, a sincere course of rigid and unloving religious doctrine. Children under his care do become ill and die, and he is appropriately punished for it. Jane Eyre, however, comes through the testing ground of Brocklehurst with courage and composure and finds an alternate minister in the unexpected person of another girl, Helen Burns. It is often the case with these inadequate but not evil ministers that their lack of spirituality and warmth prompts people quite easily to discard or ignore their teachings. St. John Rivers, Casaubon, Mr. Collins—these unloving and unlovable clerics are hardly inspirational, but neither do they manage to crush the faith of Christians in their vicinity. Ministry finds another way, and in some cases we may need to reassess and refine our definitions of success and failure.

Master of Mortification

When Jane Eyre is sent by her spiteful aunt to Lowood School, with its prison-like conditions, she comes under the jurisdiction of the Reverend Brocklehurst. In the most notable instance of hypocrisy in Charlotte Brontë's novel, Brocklehurst delivers a speech about mortification to Miss Temple, the gentle mistress of the school. Concerning the orphans in their care he states that "my mission is to mortify in these girls the lusts

3. Eliot, *Middlemarch*, 115.

of the flesh; to teach them to clothe themselves with shame-facedness and sobriety, not with braided hair and costly apparel," but the mission for the women of his family is transparently another matter altogether.[4] Brocklehurst's own wife and daughter enter, dressed in the height of style. Brontë, herself the restless and sometimes querulous daughter of a clergyman, delights in stoking the reader's outrage at Brocklehurst's flagrant misapplication of Christian mission. Brocklehurst's meanness about funding and harsh interpretation of Christian piety contribute to the spread of hunger and illness in the school and the eventual death of a number of the children.

Before Jane is sent to Lowood School, she has a confrontational interview with Brocklehurst that is one of the most carefully analyzed of all scenes in *Jane Eyre*. Among feminist scholars, one need only mention "chapter 4" and nod knowingly. Brocklehurst is described in "big bad wolf" terms—"What a face he had, now that it was almost on a level with mine! what a great nose! and what a mouth! and what large prominent teeth!" (39)—and he assumes from the start that Jane can be easily designated in terms of naughtiness, wickedness, and deceit. Interrogating Jane about death, hell, and appropriate biblical reading, he finds out that she values life and a sprightly story. He tells her she should read the Psalms instead of enjoying Revelation and Genesis, and she counters with the frank assertion that Psalms do not interest her. Instead of being impressed that such a young child has read and formed independent opinions of the books of the Bible, Brocklehurst instantly decides that Jane must undergo a special program of mortification at the school. Jane's forthright honesty is punished, and Brocklehurst's theology is shown throughout the chapter to be a sham. Speaking to Jane's pitiless aunt, Brocklehurst amazingly pronounces that "Consistency, madam, is the first of the Christian duties" (42).

Brocklehurst is an ogre in a fairy tale, and this is appropriate for his role in the novel, since Jane is only ten. Possibly the most quoted sentence in chapter 4 is this one:

> The handle turned, the door unclosed, and passing through and curtseying low, I looked up at—a black pillar!—such, at least, appeared to me, at first sight, the straight, narrow, sable-clad

---

4. Brontë, *Jane Eyre*, 76. References to subsequent passages are given parenthetically.

> shape standing erect on the rug: the grim face at the top was
> like a carved mask, placed above the shaft by way of capital. (38)

Sandra Gilbert and Susan Gubar, in their landmark study *The Madwoman in the Attic: The Woman Writer and the Nineteenth-Century
Literary Imagination* were among the first to focus forceful attention to
the description of Brocklehurst, "consistently described in phallic terms
[. . . and] almost as if here were a funereal and oddly Freudian piece of
furniture" and a "personification of the Victorian superego."[5] There is no
doubt that the passage can be read in terms of sexual threat and as a criticism of the heartlessness of the Victorian church—his reiterated black-
ness and his designation as a pillar of the church are obvious. What strikes
me in addition is that Brocklehurst is hardly even a human being. It takes
Jane a few moments to realize that "it was a man" but when he "turned
his head slowly towards where I stood" the sense that she is looking at a
monster remains strong. When he sits later she says that "bending from
the perpendicular, he installed his person in the arm-chair" (38–39), and
the impression is she is still testing the idea that he may not be human.
His conversation throughout is stiff and pretentious—"Humility is a
Christian grace, and one peculiarly appropriate to the pupils of Lowood;
I, therefore, direct that especial care shall be bestowed on its cultivation
amongst them" (41)—and the reader could be forgiven for judging him
an automaton who has digested this dialogue from a pious primer and
lacks the intellectual equipment to understand his own statements.

Brocklehurst was based on a historic minister, Reverend Wilson, in
charge of a Clergy Daughters' School that the Brontë girls attended, and
at which two of them died. During Brontë's life, Wilson was recognized
in the novel; one reader wrote with approval to the author, stating that
Wilson "deserved the chastisement he had got" (538n). This indicates
that as emblematic as Brocklehurst is, in Freudian and other terms, he
was also strangely real. That this grim-masked "it" was recognizable as
a living clergyman is a dispiriting realization about the Christian leadership of Brontë's time. If we consider Brocklehurst unique, we need only
turn to the last section of the novel, and see in Reverend St. John Rivers
(Jane's cousin and would-be suitor) a counterpart to Brocklehurst—less
hypocritical, but just as stiff and inhuman. Rivers says:

5. Gilbert and Gubar, *Madwoman in the Attic*, 343–44.

God and nature intended you for a missionary's wife. It is not
personal, but mental endowments they have given you: you are
formed for labour, not for love. A missionary's wife you must—
shall be. You shall be mine: I claim you—not for my pleasure,
but for my Sovereign's service. (464)

Casaubon

The clergyman as cold, unbending, unloving creature reappears in another of the Victorian era's great novels. Edward Casaubon in *Middlemarch* has become a byword for pedantry; the reader may have forgotten
he is a clergyman, since he never does anything in the least religious. If,
as Oliver Lovesey has said, *Middlemarch* presents "the crisis of profes-
sionalism in the nineteenth-century Church,"[6] Casaubon is the smooth
professional par excellence now indistinguishable from other learned
gentlemen. He has money from his family and status as the incumbent of
a large and important parish; what Casaubon does not have, it appears,
are any parish duties beyond the Sunday sermon. Once he has contracted
out ecclesiastical tasks to his curate, Mr. Tucker, Casaubon can dedicate
himself instead to a massive scholarly project, the "key to all mythologies," a treatise in what would now be the field of comparative religion.
Whether Casaubon's research topic is a good one—most readers decide it
is not, but George Eliot named Casaubon for a respected classicist of the
late Renaissance, and the irony that Isaac Casaubon's work is valued and
Edward's is not may be one of several types of irony—what we know with
certainty is that it is never completed. Indeed, we have no evidence that
he gets further than the accumulation of multitudinous notes.

   The scholar-priest was once a familiar personage, and to an extent
Casaubon in *Middlemarch* provides us with the supreme, if twisted, literary example. In our day, when we have few scholarly clerics, it may
be difficult to imagine the importance they once had. (Are there clerics today we could be tempted to set alongside John Donne or John
Henry Newman?) George Eliot would not condemn the notion of the
scholar-priest—after all, she had one of the most formidable intellectual
dispositions of her century—but a scholar-priest who produces nothing
is a symbol of ruin and waste. Add to this Casaubon's marriage to the
novel's heroine, Dorothea, a marriage described by another character in

---

6. Lovesey, *The Clerical Character in George Eliot's Fiction*, 84.

this manner: "if he chose to grow gray crunching bones in a cavern, he had no business to be luring a girl into his companionship."[7] And as a final blow, for most readers of *Middlemarch* Casaubon's ultimate offense is his attempt to exact a promise from Dorothea that as his widow she will devote herself to his research (research he has not allowed her to lay a hand to during his life).

There are enough strikes against poor Casaubon that one hardly needs to add to these other faults his complete inadequacy as a clergyman. But "poor Casaubon" he is, and that he is a clergyman is one of the most poignant and mitigating facts about him. Casaubon is miserable and casts about blindly for a wife, not knowing what else to do for his loneliness and alienation; his place in the church holds no comfort or sustenance for him at all. George Eliot encourages us to be compassionate about Casuabon; while the phrase "poor Dorothea" is used about fifteen times in the novel, we should know that "poor Mr. Casaubon" occurs no less than eight times. In one celebrated passage, often cited in relating George Eliot's doctrine of sympathy, the narrator deliberately breaks into the story and says, "but why always Dorothea?" and then goes on to insist Casaubon is "spiritually a-hungered like the rest of us" (278).

Although Casaubon is customarily described as cold and pedantic, and the evidence inclines us to judge him harshly, I would hazard that without Casaubon the most important ministry in *Middlemarch* would never happen. That ministry belongs to his wife and widow, Dorothea. She cannot be an ordained minister, and that ambition never crosses her mind (although, as I have pointed out in chapter 2, George Eliot's character Dinah in *Adam Bede* is a successful Methodist preacher). George Eliot's mature fiction develops idiosyncratic doctrines of love and compassion that function outside the Christian church; even were it possible for Dorothea to enter the pulpit, her author would not allow it. In any case, if Dorothea had not married the incompatible Casaubon, learned suffering and sympathy within that marriage, and then, feeling unfulfilled, turned to alleviate the needs of those around her whose suffering she now more fully understands, the key compassionate acts of *Middlemarch* would not occur. In helping Farebrother, Lydgate, and Rosamond Dorothea sets in motion a train of generous actions that Casaubon could never have dreamed of.

7. Eliot, *Middlemarch*, 360. References to subsequent passages are given parenthetically.

I mentioned above that George Eliot's naming of Casaubon and her description of his scholarly work may "be one of several types of irony." Her irony can be difficult to summarize quickly, but for a start, know that it is subtle and kind. If we dismiss Casaubon too quickly as dry and pathetic, George Eliot judges us severely for our lack of mercy. There is also the circumstance that Dorothea, who can be naïve and sentimental, has fuller sympathetic contact with the reader than Casaubon, and the narrator insists we notice that he has no advocate. And, since we never have direct access to the "key to all mythologies," we cannot be certain it is a failure. *Middlemarch* is a complex book, and its author would hope that our reading takes into account all these mitigating elements—and more. I do think that one of George Eliot's subtle ironies is this: the most promising minister in a book full of ministers (Farebrother, Casaubon, Cadwallader, Tyke) is a woman who would certainly never call herself a minister. In such a case, we could remember Martin Luther's assertion that "we are all priests, as many of us as are Christians."[8] The Christian community of *Middlemarch* is being served by ministers in surprising shapes.

Squandered Gifts

Margaret Oliphant was a contemporary of George Eliot and Anthony Trollope and presented clergy characters at least as often as they did. Her Chronicles of Carlingford series (1863–1876) can be compared to Trollope's Barchester Chronicles, written at a similar time and similarly consisting of six novels of clerical life. Her books *Salem Chapel, The Rector, The Doctor's Family, The Perpetual Curate, Miss Marjoribanks,* and *Phoebe Junior* were as successful as (if not more successful than) Trollope's, although his books are better known today. Oliphant for example received £1500 for *The Perpetual Curate* in 1864, while Trollope in 1861 received £1000 for *Framley Parsonage.*[9] In each case, the cash rewards for clerical entertainments were considerable.

I have discussed Trollope's clergymen in chapter 3, as figures of comedy. One difference between Oliphant and Trollope is the more distinct seriousness she exhibits on church matters. A comparison of the autobiographies of each author shows that Oliphant makes constant

8. Luther, *Babylonian Captivity*, 113.
9. Oliphant, *Autobiography*, 10; Trollope, *Autobiography*.

reference to God, worship, and prayer, while for Trollope the church was more functional. (No one, he writes in his *Autobiography*, "could have had less reason than myself to presume himself to be able to write about clergymen."[10] The prompt came from his publisher.) Despite—or as a result of—Oliphant's more intense investment in the church, her clerics in the Chronicles of Carlingford are no more admirable or heroic than most of Trollope's men. Oliphant's novels are caught up in tensions between Dissenting churches (called, more commonly, chapels) and the Church of England establishment, but many of these tensions relate to class, not theology. Clergy on both sides are flawed by their ambition, complacency, or excessive bookishness. As with Trollope, it is refreshing to see the wide range of personalities within the church, but Oliphant makes pointed reference to the need for church leaders to be fully engaged with the needs of their communities, rather than theoretical squabbles or schemes for personal advancement.

The last Carlingford novel, *Phoebe Junior*, can be taken as a good example of Oliphant's approach. Various clerical characters are presented for our inspection, and none of them are exactly inspiring. On the Dissenting side we have Beecham, a fashionable London chapel minister whose main interest is social-climbing. One of the first scenes in the novel is the arrival at his home of an unattractive bust for the mantelpiece. It venerates the head of the congregation's "leading member," the obnoxious industrialist Copperhead, and is a defective bust that Copperhead has had recast for himself, giving the cast-off to his minister, who feels obliged—and apparently pleased—to display it. A better chapel minister is Horace Northcote, who is smart but never appears to actually do anything. On the Church of England side is Reginald May, the somewhat weak and bland son of the overpopulous May family, who has followed his father into the church for no strong reason. Mr. May is at the center of the novel's drama; the widowed father of eight children, he is perpetually short of money, inclined to laziness, but apparently a charismatic presence and a good preacher, with the potential to be an intellectual force. He squanders his ministerial gifts and retreats into evasion and pomposity. Having borrowed heavily with no plans for repayment of the debt, he eventually becomes involved in forgery and goes mad with the guilt and inability to see his way out of the wrongdoing.

10. Trollope, *Autobiography*.

Oliphant's clerics are nearly always flawed, but far from wicked. One of their faults is usually an inability to realize the ramifications of their actions within family or community. Women are the ones who suffer for the prejudices, mistakes, and sins of both the Dissenting ministers and the Anglican clergymen. (The hero of the book ends up being the sprightly young Phoebe of the title, an unpromising coquette who turns out to have a talent for conciliation and saves Mr. May from scandal and ruin.) The clerics often exhibit arrogance and smugness. The "suave" Mr. May condescendingly tells Phoebe, a chapel-goer, that "in the Church, fortunately, what the people say has not to be studied, as your unfortunate pastors, I am informed, have to do"—in other words, May does not have to cater to the hoi polloi. About Mr. May we are told, rather slyly, that

> he was a very good preacher, and those articles of his were much admired as "thoughtful" papers, searching into many mental depths, and fathoming the religious soul with wonderful insight. Ladies especially admired them; the ladies who were intellectual, and found pleasure in the feeling of being more advanced than their neighbours.[11]

Oliphant's language here ("wonderful insight," "more advanced") is exaggerated and quietly mocking; not only is Mr. May's conceit indicted, but also that of his parishioners.

May's worst crime is, I think, his exploitation of a parishioner, Cotsdean, who reveres the minister and in turn is held in contempt by him. May borrows money through Cotsdean, and May's financial ruin will be shared by them both. May conveniently goes mad, I always feel, to avoid the consequences of this selfishness. Oliphant's writing here is detailed and subtle; every feature of the financial mismanagement is given in queasy detail. It is not so much May's idiocy about money that is the problem as the way he feels he has special dispensation to do as he wishes; Cotsdean's unquestioning respect props up that unwarranted sense of privilege. This is the telling sentence about May: "Providence, which he treated like some sort of neutral deity, and was so very sure of having on his side when he spoke to Cotsdean, did not feel so near to him, or so much under his command when Cotsdean was gone."[12] His parishioners exist to accentuate his special role in God's kingdom.

11. Oliphant, *Phoebe Junior*, 271, 245.
12. Ibid., 187.

Oliphant's people are better-rounded than Trollope's and her feminism is stimulating. Where Trollope's people tend to be easily divided into light and dark categories, Oliphant's are dubious and admirable simultaneously. As human beings I find her clerics engaging, but I would be loath to approach them for spiritual advice: they are not to be trusted. However, a woman like Phoebe may be on hand to provide ministry to the minister, or in the minister's stead; as in *Middlemarch*, a cleric's failure is an opportunity for women to shine.

Jane Austen's Church

One almost hesitates to discuss Jane Austen's clergymen, familiar as they are and hardly seeming to need analysis: several damn themselves so readily. The favorite Austen clergyman of many readers is the empty-headed, pretentious Mr. Collins, whom I have filed with the clerical clowns. Mr. Elton, in *Emma*, is a vain and selfish vicar looking for a wife with status and fortune, and who angrily responds to Emma, when she suggests he be partnered with her poor friend Harriet Smith, that everybody "has their level: but as for myself, I am not, I think, quite so much at a loss. I need not so totally despair of an equal alliance."[13] But there are other, and more admirable, clerics: Edward Ferrars and Henry Tilney in *Sense and Sensibility* and *Northanger Abbey* are good fellows, intelligent and decent, with Henry being an unusually sharp-witted and clever young man; a third cleric, Edmund Bertram in *Mansfield Park*, emerges ultimately as reliable and honorable, although he has his head turned for a time by an amoral charmer. These male leads are satisfactory prizes to be distributed to Austen's heroines, but I would wager that the detail of all three heroes being clergymen has escaped the average reader's memory. It should be significant that three of the six novels in the Austen canon conclude with marriage to a clergyman, but in truth, it is not.

Edward Ferrars, who has not yet taken orders in the greater part of *Sense and Sensibility*, is said to long for "domestic comfort and the quiet of private life" and at the conclusion he is described in terms of "the ready discharge of his duties," as well as his "increasing attachment to his wife and his home, and . . . the regular cheerfulness of his spirits."[14] Being a clergyman is nearly synonymous with country retirement (with some

13. Austen, *Emma*, 125.
14. Austen, *Sense and Sensibility*, 31, 313.

light charitable work thrown in). Henry Tilney is in orders throughout the plot of *Northanger Abbey*, but mentions the church rarely, and attends to his parish with only partial attention. The major discussion of Christian ordination takes place in *Mansfield Park*, in which Edmund Bertram's desire to enter the church is tested by the worldly and attractive Crawfords, who lose no opportunity to mock his vocation. "A clergyman is nothing" and "You really are fit for something better" are typical utterances of the beguiling but unprincipled Mary Crawford, and her brother Henry derides Edmund's earnestness with the comment that "he will have seven hundred a year, and nothing to do for it."[15] To be fair, the Crawfords' opinion has been encouraged by intimacy with their brother-in-law, Dr. Grant, an indolent clergyman known as a glutton and bully. Austen dispenses with Dr. Grant, cheerfully, when he brings on his own "apoplexy and death, by three great institutionary dinners in one week."[16]

Jane Austen knew the church well, as her father and two of her brothers were clergymen, but rather than reverence her famously understated irony is nearly always in play when she approaches this character type. As Laura Mooneyham White points out in her study of Austen's religious beliefs, the author did not seem to expect "supernatural virtue" or a special sense of vocation from clergymen.[17] On the first page of *Northanger Abbey* we are told that the heroine's father "was a clergyman, without being neglected, or poor, and a very respectable man, though his name was Richard."[18] In other words, he is a failure for this imaginative girl, who craves melodrama. Austen knows all the commonplace ideas about clerics and laughs at them; she has a female character in *Northanger Abbey* "confess herself very partial to the profession" and breathe an amorous sigh.[19] But, if we put aside the comic uses Austen makes of the clergy, and look at these men with a sterner eye, what we see, even in the good ones, is unsettling. Edward Ferrars confesses himself an "idle, helpless being"[20] in *Sense and Sensibility* and we have little evidence to contradict this, even though his good character is indisputable. Even the best of these clerical heroes, Henry Tilney, is more closely associated with

15. Austen, *Mansfield Park*, 120–21, 237.

16. Ibid., 453.

17. White, *Jane Austen's Anglicanism*, 20.

18. Austen, *Northanger Abbey*, 37.

19. Ibid., 57.

20. Austen, *Sense and Sensibility*, 98.

a handsome parsonage than a church; his future wife's visit to the parsonage is akin to Elizabeth Bennet's realization that Mr. Darcy is wonderful because his fine house, Pemberley, is wonderful. Exclaiming over the parlor and the sitting-room as, respectively, "the most comfortable room in the world" and "the prettiest room in the world,"[21] the girl finds that her esteem for the clerical beau is assured.

In Austen's world, then, clerics at their best seek comfort and honor and are rarely if ever seen preaching or administering the sacraments. Even parish duties such as visiting the sick or alleviating the needs of the poor are seldom mentioned; women are more likely to perform these tasks in an Austen novel. Although hesitant to align myself with an Austen rogue, I am more than half inclined to agree with Mary Crawford when she criticizes the profession.

> A clergyman has nothing to do but be slovenly and selfish—read the newspaper, watch the weather, and quarrel with his wife. His curate does all the work, and the business of his own life is to dine.[22]

Given the palette of misdemeanors and deficiencies Austen uses in her clerical portraits in the six novels, it is fair to suggest that Austen injects some of her own opinion into Mary Crawford's harsh judgment. The gentle and sensible heroine of *Mansfield Park*, Fanny Price, can do no more to amend Mary's judgment than to say that the gluttonous Dr. Grant surely cannot attend church so often and preach so regularly "without being the better for it himself."[23] In other words, even Fanny can see that the vicar is doing no good and all that can be hoped is that he stumbles upon a little spiritual self-edification.

Am I too unkind about these often delicious comic characters? Ang Lee's insightful film of *Sense and Sensibility* picks up on Edward Ferrars's rather inept, hapless charm and encourages actor Hugh Grant to exaggerate his mild ridiculousness, having Edward develop a strange kind of sideways shuffle when he is embarrassed and allowing him to be stabbed when sword-fighting with a precocious child. It is comparison with the viciousness of other members of his family that makes Edward's ineffectual geniality look attractive. None of the many clerics in Austen's work even briefly approach holiness and for the most part are simply not

21. Austen, *Northanger Abbey*, 213–14.
22. Austen, *Mansfield Park*, 136–37.
23. Ibid., 138.

religious. This should give us pause, particularly when considering the influential nature of her fiction, held in higher esteem today than perhaps at any other point in her literary existence. Her clergyman are a blow to the church—one we might be inclined to laugh off rather than wince at—but a blow nevertheless.

Failure?

In the past century there has been less interest in the well-rounded or even comic fictional cleric; we like our clergy very good or very bad. (Although there is still room for funny clerics on television.) One of the more intriguing instances of the failed cleric, someone who appears deficient but may be capable of good, is the young Lutheran minister in John Updike's story "Pigeon Feathers." A long and complicated story, it is one of Updike's most concerted examinations of faith, and concerns a young boy, David, haunted by the problem of death and the reality of the afterlife. At the conclusion, David is reassured after (horribly) he shoots a large number of pigeons on the family farm. He is required to do this, but he enters into the experience with increasing pleasure, which Updike describes in hallucinatory detail. In a strange but numinous moment, David examines a dead pigeon and its beauty restores his faith and calm. The narrator tells us about David's sudden awareness of the intricacy and brilliance of the bird's physical structure in a final sentence that is deftly constructed, and we must read it with care:

> [H]e was robed in this certainty: that the God who had lavished such craft upon these worthless birds would not destroy His whole Creation by refusing to let David live forever.[24]

In the tone of this sentence, we should hear David's callousness as well as his renewed religious faith. It is a barbed and troubling conclusion. Why should David live forever? Is he at all good or worthy? Why should anyone want so badly to live forever? And how could David deserve to be "robed" in certainty? Most particularly, why should we trust a character who, after a religious epiphany, can still call these birds worthless?

Keeping these questions in mind, we turn to the portrayal of Reverend Dobson, who teaches catechism to David and others at the local Lutheran church. When David grills the pastor about death and heaven,

24. Updike, "Pigeon Feathers," 33.

Dobson answers hesitantly and awkwardly and David is infuriated by the lack of assurance. The minister comes off as conscientious but shy. He gazes at David at one point "intently, but with an awkward, puzzled flicker of forgiveness." David sees him as a fraud; the reader likely sees it differently.

> In the minister's silence the shame that should have been his crept over David: the burden and fever of being a fraud were placed upon *him*, who was innocent, and it seemed, he knew, a confession of this guilt that on the way out he was unable to face Dobson's stirred gaze, though he felt it probing the side of his head.[25]

David, thinking the opposite is happening, displaces his own unacknowledged guilt and shame onto the minister, who silently accepts it. When David stares in outrage at his catechism book, where "short words like Duty, Love, Obey, Honor were stacked in the form of a cross," we are given a glimpse into the life of Dobson and, unfortunately, a glimpse of David's derision of these values.

Updike's story is one of failure, although the pastor fails in this case less because of his own unworthiness than the unworthiness of his parishioner. But no matter whose failure, the church has suffered a defeat.

A Relationship that Moves

At one point in Clint Eastwood's long career, it would have seemed strange indeed to discuss the Christian implications of his films, but in recent years, although Eastwood claims no particular religious adherence, there have been several noteworthy clerical roles. I discuss *Pale Rider,* which features his strangest and most important preacher, elsewhere, but in this chapter, among the mundane but sometimes efficacious failures, I would like to place two of his recent characters, the Catholic priests of *Million Dollar Baby* and *Gran Torino.* The function of the flawed but still relevant priests in *Million Dollar Baby* and *Gran Torino* is to act as conscience or goad for the main character in each movie. The protagonists have difficult and adversarial relationships with the priests, but ultimately that relationship prompts important changes in the protagonist and in the events that unfold.

25. Ibid., 23.

In *Million Dollar Baby* Eastwood's character, Frankie, refuses the moral guidance of Father Horvak (Brian F. O'Byrne) when the priest insists that Frankie must adhere to traditional Catholic doctrine about the sanctity of life. At the climax of the movie, Frankie wants to stop life support for his young friend and apprentice, Maggie, paralyzed after a boxing match. The debate between Eastwood's character and his priest is taken seriously, and indeed Frankie may even agree with the priest that his soul will be forfeit if he involves himself in Maggie's death. The conclusion of the film can be read as Frankie offering his soul for the repose of Maggie's own. In any case, while the conflict with Father Horvak is a no-win situation—like many of Eastwood's recent films, *Million Dollar Baby* is a tragedy—the moral and religious dilemma is treated with respect. The relationship between parishioner and priest is intriguing because they seem to heartily dislike and distrust each other. In earlier scenes Frankie taunts Father Horvak about doctrine and eventually exasperates the priest into angry obscenity. Yet Frankie appears at mass almost daily and he and the priest continue to argue—in other words, they are in relationship. Until Maggie arrives on the scene, one of the most sociable activities in Frankie's life has been tormenting Father Horvak, with Father Horvak displaying admirable forbearance.

I do not entirely agree with Roger Ebert's assessment that instead of the "negative spin" that most contemporary movies put on the clergy, in *Million Dollar Baby* Eastwood gives us a Catholic priest who is, for once, "a good man."[26] But while Father Horvak fails in narrowly defined ethical terms—he would deem both Maggie and Frankie lost—the church, overall, fares well in *Million Dollar Baby* in demonstrating a dynamic and significant, if troubled, relationship between a priest and parishioner. Eastwood's film *Gran Torino* more clearly presents a good priest in relationship with a difficult parishioner, although the rapport between parishioner and priest follows a winding and bumpy path and again the outcome is tragic. *Gran Torino*'s theme is—and Eastwood is well situated to work out this poignant irony—vengeance and how to break its cyclic nature. This time, the priest and the parishioner who are at odds at the beginning eventually move with great strides toward each other, and when at the conclusion Eastwood's character Walt Kowalski offers himself, without resistance, as a sacrificial death, the priest is standing with him in nonviolent contradiction of the thugs who terrorize their

---

26. Ebert, review of *Million Dollar Baby*.

neighborhood. (Police officers remove the priest from the final scene, but he has been willing to make the same moral statement as Walt.)

The beauty of *Gran Torino* is the distance Eastwood's character travels from his first to his last scenes with the priest, Father Janovich (Christopher Carley). Like an imperfect "Hound of Heaven," Father Janovich patiently but ineptly pursues Walt from the opening scenes of the movie. At the funeral of Walt's wife, Dorothy, Walt is shown snarling irreverently at the priest's simplistic pieties. Typical rude responses to the priest's resolute attempts to connect are these: "I think you're an over-educated twenty-seven-year-old virgin who likes to hold the hands of ladies who are superstitious and promise them eternity" and the dismissive "Why don't you go tend some of your other sheep?"[27] Urged by Father Janovich to come to confession, Walt growls:

> Well, I confess that I never really cared for church very much. The only reason I went was because of her. And I confess that I have no desire to confess to a boy just out of seminary.

Walt keeps up the assault on the priest in scene after scene.

> You get up and preach about life and death but all you know is what you learned in priest school. Right out of the rookie preacher's handbook. . . . What you know about life and death [is] pathetic.

It is, largely, the bare fact of Father Janovich's persistence that finally wins Walt over, and it is Walt's unexpected compassion for his beleaguered Hmong neighbors that convinces Father Janovich that Walt is a good man who does not need to be pestered about salvation. Instead, they work in silent agreement in the last scenes of the movie, trying to protect the family of Thao and Sue, the neighbors once called "swamp rats" and "zipperheads" by the intolerant Walt. The priest learns depth of commitment and the reality of suffering from Walt; Walt learns in response about submission and generosity. When Walt, in the movie's climactic scene, very publicly allows the gang members to shoot him (so they will be taken into custody and the cycle of vengeance will stop) he whispers "Hail Mary, full of grace" and falls back, arms outstretched. At the beginning of *Gran Torino* it would be implausible to imagine Walt

---

27. *Gran Torino*, directed by Clint Eastwood, written by Nick Schenk (this and all subsequent quotation is my own transcription from the film).

Kowalski in such a Christ-like position; the needs of his neighbors have prompted this altered character, but so has Father Janovich's persistence.

The priests in *Gran Torino* and *Million Dollar Baby* are problematic, as are all the pastors and ministers in this chapter. More human than holy, more flawed than inspirational, they make mistakes, lose their tempers, commit blunders. On occasion the ministry staggers on, and one is reminded that of the Thirty-nine Articles in the Church of England, the twenty-sixth admits that "evil be ever mingled with the good" and if we encounter wayward clergy we still "may use their Ministry."[28] Whether the boy in Updike's "Pigeon Feathers" has the maturity to recognize it, he has been offered loving if inadequate ministry. There are limits, however, to how deeply we should search for the good effects of defective pastors. I think of Eugene Peterson's clarion call for three new adjectives to modify the noun pastor. Amazingly, his provocative adjectives are "unbusy, subversive, apocalyptic."[29] The failed pastor is almost always busy doing mischief that has nothing to do with Christ's mission; the failed pastor would be baffled by the call to be subversive or revelatory. About Casaubon's ministry, or Brocklehurst's, I have no doubt: they may have meant well, but that intention is not nearly good enough, nor subversive or apocalyptic enough.

28. "Thirty-nine articles."
29. Peterson, *The Contemplative Pastor*, 16.

INTERLUDE

Doubt, a Parable

by John Patrick Shanley

That John Patrick Shanley considers his 2004 play *Doubt, a Parable* indicates an intellectual and religious concern unusual in the Broadway and Hollywood districts where his drama has enjoyed such success. Winner of the Pulitzer Prize and nominated for several Academy Awards when it was filmed by Shanley in 2008, *Doubt* explicitly aligns itself within a long tradition of teaching stories, most famously the parables of Christ in the Gospels. The parable as fictional narrative aiming to teach a spiritual or moral lesson is problematized by Shanley, because *Doubt* refuses to settle into easy conclusions (as, we must admit, many of Christ's parables similarly refuse to settle). The play has two main characters, a liberal priest and a more traditional nun, who are antagonists from the beginning. She discovers apparent wrongdoing on his part and sets out to expose him, no matter what the cost. When I teach this play, I always finish by asking students, so which is it? Which part is the "lesson"? Is the priest innocent and nun wicked, or vice versa? Do they both mean well? Is there a more complicated solution? Or can we possibly conclude that anyone in this tussle is the victor?

Sister Aloysius, the principal of a Catholic School in the Bronx, represents order and stern discipline. Father Flynn is youth, modernity, and reform (and may or may not be involved in an inappropriate sexual relationship with a male student). Flynn and Sister James, a naïve nun caught in the battle of wills between the other two, have a conversation about parables:

Sister James: Was your sermon directed at anyone in particular?

Flynn: What do you think?

Sister James: Did you make up that story about the pillow?

Flynn: Yes. You make up little stories to illustrate. In the tradition of the parable.

Sister James: Aren't the things that actually happen in life more worthy of interpretation than a made-up story?

Flynn: No. What actually happens in life is beyond interpretation. The truth makes for a bad sermon. It tends to be confusing and have no clear conclusion.[1]

One matter we might be tempted to construe, using Flynn's remarks, is his sexuality. A possible explanation for Flynn's relationship with a boy named Donald is that they are both gay and have become friends: Flynn could well be chaste. However, we can never know because everyone speaks obliquely about the issue of "interference" with Donald (as is necessary for the date of the action, 1964). Also, at the play's conclusion Flynn has been hounded out of the parish by Sister Aloysius's persecution (although he receives a promotion to a better parish) and we receive no parting words from him. The last words in the play are, significantly, from Sister Aloysius, who cries out in emotion, "I have doubts! I have such doubts!" (58). Following Father Flynn's suggestion, it does seem that the truth in this story "tends to be confusing and have no clear conclusion." The stories that Flynn and Aloysius have made up, hoping to serve a greater good, have repercussions, even to the point that Aloysius is willing to be damned. "In the pursuit of wrongdoing," she says in the play's final scene, "one steps away from God. Of course there's a price."

The tangled nature of truth and falseness throughout the play gives the story its strength. When Sister Aloysius cries out about her doubts at the end, we do not know for sure what it is she is doubting. Her own fitness to be a nun? Father Flynn's wrong? Whether God even exists? Is she aware that she has destroyed the happy and simple faith of Sister James? And when Father Flynn says in a sermon that "doubt can be a bond as powerful and sustaining as certainty" (6), is he serving the gospel honestly? Has twelve-year-old Donald Muller been protected or harmed

---

1. Shanley, *Doubt*, 38–39. References to subsequent passages are given parenthetically.

by these religious leaders? Shanley turns these questions over to the audience, making all of us responsible for the well-being of children like Donald and indeed the well-being of the church.

John Patrick Shanley's complication of the nature of parable follows the example of a challenging parable like the prodigal son in Luke 15. The manner in which each listener hears about prodigality may be different. The extravagance, or prodigality, can be seen both in the son's sin and the father's forgiveness. There is also prodigal bitterness and self-righteousness in the "good" son's response to his brother's return. Over the centuries we have lost the ability to see the deliberately shocking excess in the father's reaction to the lost son's return. This is no simple welcome home. This is a challenge to tradition and reason. The listener is forced to think about wild generosity and unrestricted love, just as in an earlier parable (also in Luke 15) Christ tells of the shepherd who will leave ninety-nine sheep in order to search for one that is lost.

We have heard these parables a thousand times, and if we accept them as straightforward we do Christ a disservice. These Gospel stories should still be thorny and rough, but years of repetition have worn off their sharp edges. Shanley in *Doubt* aims to reintroduce the prickliness of the parable. Questions interest him more than answers. In his preface to the play, written in 2005, he says:

> There is an uneasy time when belief has begun to slip, but hypocrisy has yet to take hold, when the consciousness is disturbed but not yet altered. It is the most dangerous, important, and ongoing experience of life. The beginning of change is the moment of Doubt. It is that crucial moment when I renew my humanity or become a lie. (ix)

In part, Shanley claims, he wrote the play because he could see that American culture was becoming too much a culture of certainty, "of judgment, and of verdict" (vii). If we can suspend this hazardous tendency toward judgment, we will see the clerical characters in *Doubt* in their wholeness.

Both Sister Aloysius and Father Flynn have a good deal to offer the church. Both are smart, sincere, and committed. She wants to retain the best of the past; he wants the church to become more welcoming and tolerant. Neither is wrong. Although he is easier to like, representing as he does openness and good humor, she has admirable qualities. She is candid, direct, sharply observant. Because they enter into increasingly hostile competition with each other (as a result not only of her determination to protect vulnerable children but also her resentment that Roman Catholic women must be limited in their clerical ambitions) the church loses the genuine contribution of each. Although Shanley's play might be interpreted carelessly as an attack on the church, this is not at all what it is. He dedicates the play to "the many orders of Roman Catholic nuns who have devoted their lives to serving others" and ends his dedication with the admonishment to the audience: "Though they have been much maligned and ridiculed, who among us has been so generous?" (v). Far from wishing these clerical characters, both female and male, to be "maligned and ridiculed," Shanley wants acceptance for the full humanness of nuns and priests. The church should be a place for Sister Aloysius and Father Flynn to serve with gladness; if the church insists on hierarchy and rigidity, Shanley hints, mere human beings will be frustrated in their desire to serve.

On the page, the character I am more likely to side with is Father Flynn, who seems flexible and sympathetic. When Shanley filmed the play and cast Meryl Streep as Sister Aloysius, he did a wonderful thing for the balance of uncertainty in the play—and a balance of uncertainty is what the drama must strive for. Streep's greatness as an actor gives Sister Aloysius stature and vulnerability that the play on its own does not necessarily grant her. By the end of the film version of *Doubt* I am more firmly invested in the beneficial doubt that Shanley wants to instill and that he once called, in an interview, a "hallmark of wisdom."[2] The full and rich fallibility of both priest and nun, most evident in the admirable film performances of Streep and Philip Seymour Hoffman, prompts in the audience—or it should—a corresponding full and rich compassion, which the real clerics of the Christian church urgently need and deserve.

2. Rabin, "Interview: John Patrick Shanley."

7

Disaster

Now the Lord is about to lay waste the earth and make it desolate, and he will twist its surface and scatter its inhabitants. And it shall be, as with the people, so with the priest. (Isa 24:1–2)

We have, if you will, a complete crew of bishops, deans, and priests; learned men, eminently learned, talented, gifted, humanly well-meaning; they all declaim—doing it well, very well, eminently well, or tolerably well, or badly—but not one of them is in the character of the Christianity of the New Testament. (Søren Kierkegaard, *Attack upon "Christendom"*)[1]

Everyone has a negative avatar of ministry that springs to mind when asked about disastrous pastors in literature or film. One example might be Reverend Thwackum in Henry Fielding's *Tom Jones,* who has "a great reputation for learning, religion, and sobriety of manners" but whose name belies his religiosity. As a child, Tom receives from Thwackum "so severe a whipping, that it possibly fell little short of the torture with which confessions are in some countries extorted from criminals." Thwackum's meditations, says Fielding wryly and stingingly, "were full of birch."[2] My memorable disasters are the priests in James Joyce's *A Portrait of the Artist as a Young Man* (1916). Although kindness and intelligence are not completely absent from Joyce's priesthood, more memorable are the horrific scenes of intellectual and spiritual bullying in the novel. As a

---

1. Kierkegaard, *Attack upon "Christendom,"* 29.
2. Fielding, *Tom Jones,* 136, 126, 133.

child, Stephen Dedalus is strapped by Father Dolan, who seems to take pleasure in punishing. As a teen, Stephen is subjected to the terrifying hellfire sermons of Father Arnall. In trying to convince the boys to steer clear of sin, Father Arnall offers a detailed sensuous trip through hell. This builds on Loyola's *Spiritual Exercises*, prompting the listener to a deeper understanding of a text using sensory stimuli and imagination. Father Arnall almost exclusively uses the negative aspects of this method. Nowhere does he suggest the boys try to imagine compassion or joy. The positive aspects of faith, the love which ought to be at the heart of Christianity, are given a half page, while the horrors of hell and judgment take up over twenty-five pages. While warning the schoolboys about the "poison of the eloquence" of Satan, Father Arnall provides an impressive specimen of his own poisonous eloquence:

> Every sense of the flesh is tortured and every faculty of the soul therewith: the eyes with impenetrable utter darkness, the nose with noisome odours, the ears with yells and howls and execrations, the taste with foul matter, leprous corruption, nameless suffocating filth, the touch with redhot goads and spikes, with cruel tongues of flame.[3]

The priests in Joyce's novel tempt Stephen toward the priesthood, not with notions of service or brotherly love but with power. As a young man Stephen is told by a priest that "no king or emperor on this earth has the power of the priest of God."[4] Even angels—even the Virgin Mary—are supposedly less powerful than any priest. Decades later, I easily recall my initial revulsion reading these scenes. In most of my assessments in this study, I can find mitigating or constructive elements in even the baddest literary pastors; with Joyce's priests I am stretched to the limits of my charity.

This chapter on spectacularly failed priests and ministers must serve a different function than the other chapters in this book, which often demonstrate how secular literature or film has missed the point or cheapened the personality and position of the cleric. This time the ruin must be taken on its own terms and faced: there *is* madness, mendacity, and devastation in Ibsen's *Brand*, Golding's *The Spire*, Maugham's "Rain," and Updike's *A Month of Sundays*. I have no wish to avoid the calamity in these works. But I do hope to make it clear that while it is sometimes the

3. Joyce, *A Portrait of the Artist*, 127, 131.

4. Ibid., 171.

cleric himself (and here the male pronoun is apt) who tumbles spectacularly from grace, these portrayals of highly dramatic failure can be meant to indict the church itself, through the symbolic person of the church leader.

Let us take on *Elmer Gantry* straightaway. While Sinclair Lewis's notorious and controversial 1927 novel supposedly targeted hypocrisy, materialism, and corruption in the Protestant church, the book is better seen as an exposé of what Douglas Alan Walrath and others call "commercial preaching"[5] in the early twentieth century. The novel was a timely satirical attack on the worst aspects of the evangelical movement of its time, but today feels oversimplified, sensational, and frenetic. (The first line is "Elmer Gantry was drunk" and the last is "We shall yet make these United States a moral nation!") The 1960 film, with a powerful performance by Burt Lancaster, is another matter; that luridly striking film still has advocates and is one of the reasons that "Elmer Gantry" can still be used as a term of recognition and somewhat titillated castigation. There has been enough analysis of Lewis's creation over the years, so I am going to pass over *Elmer Gantry* swiftly, in part because of the exaggerated nature of the character and also because I agree with Richard Brooks, the director of the 1960 film adaptation, who posted a warning at the beginning of his movie that the story was not about Christianity but about "revivalism." Whatever one calls it—commercial preaching or revivalism—Elmer Gantry is so far from being a representative pastor that he is an incompatible participant in my study.

Extremity and Madness

Passing on to a pastor who is no less difficult, but more subtle and intriguing, we have Henrik Ibsen's *Brand* (1865). Like some of the Norwegian playwright's other works, *Brand* was not meant to be performed. Instead the play is usually seen as a text for discussion and debate, although it did have an English stage debut in 1959 with Patrick McGoohan as Brand. The original is a verse drama, and English translations have been problematic, but Michael Meyer's translation (in unrhymed iambic pentameter) is palatable and retains some of the strange rhetorical power of the Norwegian. Ibsen intends the reader to be stirred up by his preacher; Brand is both appalling and admirable, and Ibsen wants us to feel conflict

5. Walrath, *Displacing the Divine*, 258.

and confusion when reading the play. The key words for me in reading *Brand* are *defiance* and *will*. Brand is unbelievably strong and stubborn, the kind of Old Testament prophet impossible to tolerate in any time, but particularly in the contemporary era. The paradoxical and twisted reactions the character provokes are superbly summed up by the equally provoking Shaw, who was an admirer. "Brand dies a saint, having caused more intense suffering by his saintliness than the most talented sinner could possibly have done with twice his opportunities."[6]

Brand's God is uncompromising, stern, and his love is hard. Brand, in imitation of the God he follows, refuses to provide comfort or acknowledge human frailty. This is a typical line from Brand, and one of the first he utters: "Go home. Your life is a way of death. / You do not know God, and God does not know you."[7] Brand's way of life is summed up in the phrase "All or Nothing," repeated at least eight times in the course of the drama, and this is the way in which he rebukes lesser mortals:

> You do not want
> To live your faith. For that you need a God
> Who'll keep one eye shut. That God is getting feeble
> Like the generation that worships him.
> Mine is a storm where yours is a gentle wind,
> Inflexible where yours is deaf, all-loving,
> Not all-doting. (27)

Brand is uncompromising even with his mother, whom he refuses to attend in her final illness unless she completely capitulates to his beliefs, and with his wife and child. All die in the play, and George Bernard Shaw has no compunction in stating that Brand in actuality murders them.[8] The climax of the play occurs at the end of Act Three, when Brand chooses between his genuine love for his child (who is dying and should move to a better climate) and his vocation. He chooses his vocation. Urged to make a humane decision by a physician, Brand snarls: "Humane! That word excuses all our weakness. / Was God humane towards Jesus Christ?" (60)

Brand's wife Agnes is a remarkable character, at first a courageous fellow Christian whose generous love helps to make Brand's ministry possible. Eventually she is driven into bitterness and misery, particularly when Brand insists that she give to the poor every last article of clothing

6. Shaw, *The Quintessence of Ibsenism*, 49.

7. Ibsen, *Brand*, 20. References to subsequent passages are given parenthetically.

8. Shaw, *The Quintessence of Ibsenism*, 53–54.

once belonging to their dead child. Agnes's dialogue is shattering, and she goes to her death broken and bereft: "The God you taught me to know is a warrior God. / How dare I go to him with my small sorrow?" (69)

The conclusion of this difficult play is ambiguous. In the final moments, Brand weeps, seeming to repent, in part, of his hardness. He also feels further from Christ than he has before, and struggles with doubt and indirection. Yet he is no less imperious and stubborn. He demands divine answers, even as a punishing avalanche is about to bury him: "Answer me, God, in the moment of death! / If not by Will, how can Man be redeemed?" (105). The play ends with a voice shouting in answer, "He is the God of Love" (105), which has always seemed to me an unfair conclusion. Yes, of course, we might say. But what are we supposed to do with the formidable character of Brand? Brand strikes me as an inhuman practitioner of a heartless Christianity, yet one who can draw followers to him by the sheer force of his will. Will fascinated both Ibsen and Shaw, and Brand's courageous will has such drawing power that some readers of *Brand* see his heroism as overtaking all else. Irving Sussman, for example, says:

> In blasting the image of God as an anthropomorphic grandfather type, Ibsen also blasted the accepted image of the clergyman as one willing to go along with the lowest common denominator. He cracked the old image and showed forth the New Minister, a man who accepts the option to pay the cost of discipleship, following the God who is not a puff of wind but a great storm, the same God who confronted man in the burning bush and on the hill of Calvary.[9]

Certainly the reader should be stirred by Brand's insistence that Christ's followers admit their unworthiness to take the painful route of servanthood. For Brand, Christian discipleship must be costly; the follower of Christ ought to be willing to give up everything and endure much that is humiliating and distressing. As a pastor, Brand is willing to set an example, even unto death. But the character is, ultimately, destructive. He creates death, not life.

---

9. Sussmann, *As Others See Us*, 111.

⌒⌒

Jocelin, the protagonist of William Golding's 1964 novel *The Spire*, is similarly able to sway people toward his strange vision, at least for a time. He is the Dean of a medieval cathedral based, most probably, on Salisbury Cathedral, which does feature England's tallest spire. By sheer power of his immense will Jocelin convinces the church hierarchy and hesitant workers that an enormous spire is "a diagram of prayer; and our spire will be a diagram of the highest prayer of all" and would "complete a stone bible, be the apocalypse in stone."[10] Preaching to the poor, he manages to deflect their own misery with his vain and improbable goal: "The people moaned and beat their breasts, not because they understood him, but because he spoke so urgently; and because it was a time of rain, floods, death and starvation" (66). Although the reader at first might be impressed by Jocelin's enormous ambition to honor God with a mighty spire, eventually we perceive his madness and his unfitness to lead. Not only is the project architecturally foolish (the church has no foundation that can bear the spire's weight), it should be seen that the spire is a phallic tribute to Jocelin's confused lust and also a Babel-like symbol of his arrogant overreaching. Golding's novel has captivated readers because of its surreal, even hallucinatory prose, taking us deep into Jocelin's obsession and forcing the reader to judge over and over just what is mad and what rational.

For example, seeing the world around him in terms of blood, lust, debauchery, and death, Jocelin promotes the church as a true sanctuary and for a time this image might be inspiring. He proclaims the cathedral as "the great house, the ark, the refuge, a ship to contain all these people and now fitted with a mast" (106). A wholly different novel, Dorothy L. Sayers's 1934 Lord Peter Wimsey mystery *The Nine Tailors*, offers the church building as just such a sanctuary; when a coastal marsh area is swamped by winter floods, detective work is suspended and the bells ring to summon people to safety inside a church. There the rector works graciously and hospitably to house and feed all who come. The huge difference between the Sayers vision of sanctuary and the corrosive vision offered by Golding is that in *The Nine Tailors* the goodness resides in the generosity of the cleric and his devoted service to his people. The cleric

10. Golding, *The Spire*, 120, 108. References to subsequent passages are given parenthetically.

in *The Spire* has nothing but egotism and foolishness to fill up a building that he mistakenly worships instead of a loving God.

Golding's allegorical novel becomes nightmarish, a man's rapturous offering to God tainted and finally destroyed by human vanity and ignorance. Irving Sussman has written that "the image of Father Jocelin is that of a clergyman who believed his ordination and vision was from God, that he was chosen to reach God at any cost."[11] What do we do when such a belief is so strong—yet so utterly wrong—that entire communities are dragged to ruin? People die in Jocelin's ambitious undertaking, and the reader finishes *The Spire* wondering whether there was a man of God inside Dean Jocelin at all.

Power and Lust

William Somerset Maugham's story "Rain" is one of his most celebrated works. Written in 1921 (first published as "Miss Thompson"), this story of a fanatical clergyman and the loose woman he desires to save became an immediate stage success. "Rain" was on Broadway by 1922 and ran for three years; later it would be adapted for film on three memorable occasions. I will discuss two of these films, both of which have become landmark treatments of the purportedly upright clergyman who does battle against the force of female sexuality—and loses. Gloria Swanson and Joan Crawford played the scandalous Sadie Thompson, who clashes with the sternly pious Mr. Davidson, in 1928 and 1932; Rita Hayworth's 1953 *Miss Sadie Thompson* strays from the original material. The original story, the stage adaptation, and the first two film adaptations are powerful depictions of a clash between spirit and flesh. Each character has become iconic. In early twentieth-century theatrical parlance, says critic Katie N. Johnson, characters named Sadie "threaten the very fabric of normative sexuality" and in more than a handful of plays and novels become symbolically linked to downpours, floods, or hurricanes.[12] In Maugham's story there is incessant rain, which could represent not only sexual temptation but also divine punishment or even, more innocuously, the natural world that cannot be tamed by a missionary's clerical strictures. Audience attitudes toward the fallen woman Sadie and the eventually ruined clergyman Mr. Davidson have always been complicated.

11. Sussmann, *As Others See Us*, 237.
12. Johnson, "Before Katrina: Archiving Performative Downpours," 352.

"Rain" is set on the South Pacific island of Pago Pago (which today boasts a Sadie Thompson Inn, so it appears this woman of dubious reputation has been forgiven). Mr. and Mrs. Davidson are (in most versions) missionaries bound for another island who are delayed by an outbreak of infectious disease; waiting alongside them are a physician and his wife, Dr. and Mrs. Mcphail, who represent normality. Dr. Mcphail observes the Davidsons with increasing aversion as they declare the superiority of their version of Christian mission over the supposed depravity of the native Samoans. The Davidsons have banned dancing on their island, covered the natives with modest "Mother Hubbard" dresses, and instituted economic sanctions against any who defy their moral leadership. Although Maugham's story avoids direct indication, the stage and movie adaptations strongly present the Davidson marriage as sexless. Both Davidsons are given to pronouncements that are dogmatic about sin and swift to judge.

> When we went there they had no sense of sin at all. They broke the commandments one after the other and never knew they were doing wrong. And I think that was the most difficult part of my work, to instil into the natives the sense of sin.[13]

Since they have been away from their island for some time, Davidson says self-righteously, "I expect to have my work cut out for me. I shall act and I shall act promptly. If the tree is rotten it shall be cut down and cast into the flames."

Sadie Thompson is a shabby woman traveling alone who may or may not be a prostitute; this identification is usually assumed but there is, in fact, no definite statement from Maugham about her way of life. She is loud, brash, and tawdry and her major entrance into the story is heralded by obnoxious music from a gramophone. For a time Sadie and Davidson deliberately face off at opposite ends of a moral arena. She is unafraid of hurling "a torrent of insult, foul and insolent" (99), while he offers her first his harsh judgment and then his own peculiar brand of salvation. In Maugham's story, Davidson is sinister and unflinching in his determination to be the agent of her rescue, whether she wants it or not.

> She's sinned, and she must suffer. I know what she'll endure. She'll be starved and tortured and humiliated. I want her to accept the punishment of man as a sacrifice to God. I want her to

13. Maugham, "Rain," 83. References to subsequent passages are given parenthetically.

accept it joyfully. She has an opportunity which is offered to very few of us. God is very good and very merciful. (110)

At the height of the drama, Sadie and Davidson have a showdown or duel which culminates, amazingly, in her hypnotic recitation of the Lord's Prayer. This is, at any rate, what takes place in the films; in Maugham's story much of the conflict between Sadie and Davidson happens behind the scenes, which heightens the suspicion that something deviant or salacious might also be occurring. Joan Crawford's Sadie (matched with Walter Huston's mad-looking Davidson) is a woman more forlorn and vulnerable than she at first appears. As he insists, in the crisis scene, that she accede to his prayer, Crawford stares at the imposing Huston with unblinking eyes, backs away, and then kneels at the bottom of a staircase, apparently to him. She thrives under the intensity of his attention. The 1928 Gloria Swanson film is silent, but both Swanson and Lionel Barrymore, as Davidson, are heroically powerful; the dueling scenes are eloquent in action and expression and the title cards tilt us in sympathy toward Sadie. (Christ-like aspects of her character are emphasized when she says, at a crisis point, "This is my finish," and also "Where is your mercy?" Another card reads "Three tortured days of loneliness, repentance, redemption.")[14]

If "Rain" ended there, the story would be intriguing enough. Davidson's methods are harsh but his dedication seems unquestionable. Perhaps Sadie has, against all odds, been reclaimed for God by this unlikely intervention from a smug, holier-than-thou creature who might be an instrument of deliverance in spite of himself. However, the story continues with a strange and obscure event. Out of our sight, Davidson does something to or with Sadie—he allows himself to be seduced or perhaps rapes her—we cannot know. In the next scene his body is found on the seashore: he has committed suicide. Mrs. Davidson and Sadie each take the news oddly, and our knowledge of what Davidson has done to Sadie must be inferred by our observation of the two women. In Maugham's story, the two women are hardened in their roles. Mrs. Davidson continues to be cold and stern; Sadie emerges from her room dressed in her original gaudy clothes and spits at Mrs. Davidson. Sadie then shrieks that all men are "filthy, dirty pigs" and the final paragraph of the story informs us that Dr. Mcphail gasps and, alone among the characters, "understood" (115):

14. *Sadie Thompson*, directed and written by Raoul Walsh (my transcription from the film).

in other words, he understands that Davidson fell into a deeper sexual sin than Sadie ever did. Maugham's presentation of the final scenario is harsh and unforgiving; Sadie's repentance is overturned as if it had never been and the Christian characters are proven as heartless hypocrites.

Unwilling to conclude on such a dark note, the stage and film versions of "Rain" allow the women a moment of mutual understanding and compassion. Both Swanson and Crawford show sadness instead of repulsion when given the news of Davidson's suicide, and in each case Sadie states her forgiveness, making it clear that the missionary has wronged her but now paid for his sin. Although it is out of character, Mrs. Davidson in the 1932 film offers recognition and kindness to Sadie with the lines, "I understand, Miss Thompson—I'm sorry for him, and I'm sorry for you."[15] Both Maugham's original story and the adaptations judge Davidson harshly and with finality; the films, however, present Sadie as less sinful and even bordering on redemption. Although I disagree with Katie N. Johnson, who sees Sadie as "one of the most exciting, willful and self-possessed harlot characters in the dramatic canon"[16]—largely because I see no firm evidence that she is a harlot—I do see Sadie as heroic in the strength she shows in the face of Davidson's multiple assaults. First he attacks her (as he has the South Pacific islanders under his care) with a pitiless and unbending religion; then he assumes that her vibrant sexuality is meant for him, and brutally takes it.

In a 1921 review of Maugham's short fiction, the *New York Times* declared "Rain" an unpleasant but forceful story: "this tale of a soul's tragedy."[17] It is not entirely clear whose soul is lost, according to the reviewer. Is Sadie lost, or Davidson, or both? Most people would assume that in the end it is Davidson, although Sadie would seem the most visible sinner at the start. But even at the beginning of *Sadie Thompson*, the 1928 version of "Rain," with Gloria Swanson, Davidson can be seen for the walking clerical disaster he will become. Director Raoul Walsh's silent version introduces the characters by having them write something in Sadie's autograph book. Davidson's message is telling: "The knife of reform is the only hope of a sin-sick world."[18] And who wields this dangerous

15. *Rain*, directed by Lewis Milestone, written by Maxwell Anderson (my transcription from the film).

16. Johnson, "After Katrina," 364.

17. Field, review of *The Trembling of a Leaf*, 150.

18. *Sadie Thompson*, directed and written by Raoul Walsh (my transcription from the film).

knife of reform? Davidson does, although we do not realize the full dev-astation in this statement until Davidson, after violating the woman he was meant to save, cuts his own throat.

A Perilous Second Chance

Nearly all the disastrous clerical examples in this chapter are marked with a strangely urgent sincerity. With the exception of the preposterously self-centered Elmer Gantry (and this is one reason I have separated his character from my other clerical disasters), these clerics are determined that they are sent by God to perform remarkable feats of justice and sal-vation. The minister in William Faulkner's rather terrifying but moving 1932 novel *Light in August* is a different kind of disaster. Gail Hightower is a defrocked Presbyterian minister who lives on among the same people who once locked him out of his own church (after his neglected, dis-turbed wife is implicated in scandal and dies, probably by her own hand). He has been a terrible pastor in his youth, wild in the pulpit and "using religion as though it were a dream."[19] Obsessed with his family history in the American Civil war, he lives in a fantasy of flashing hooves and guns, trying to work out his grandfather's death and ignoring the con-temporary human need around him. Faulkner says this about the chaos of Hightower's ministry: "It was as if he couldn't get religion and that galloping cavalry and his dead grandfather shot from the galloping horse untangled from each other, even in the pulpit" (62). The ministry is used by the young Hightower as a refuge, as his name might seem to imply:

> He believed with a calm joy that if ever there was shelter, it would be the Church; that if ever truth could walk naked and without shame or fear, it would be in the seminary. When he believed that he had heard the call it seemed to him that he could see his future, his life, intact and on all sides complete and inviolable, like a classic and serene vase, where the spirit could be born anew sheltered from the harsh gale of living and die so, peace-fully, with only the far sound of the circumvented wind, with scarce even a handful of rotting dust to be disposed of. (478)

Hightower's first name, Gail, is explicitly linked to the "harsh gale of living" that he attempts to avoid. His avoidance is marked also by

19. Faulkner, *Light in August*, 61. References to subsequent passages are given parenthetically.

the language of doubt in this passage: "could," "would," "seemed," and even "believed" are here hesitant and provisional, and the comparison of ministry to serene vase is laughably naïve. But as Faulkner well knows, the minister's other name can be either life-giving or warlike: Psalm 18:2 celebrates the Lord as rock, fortress, deliverer, strength, buckler, horn of salvation and high tower but Isaiah 2:12–15 uses the image of the high tower as admonishment. The "day of the Lord of hosts shall be upon every one that is proud and lofty" and "against every high tower" (I use the King James Version here, as Faulkner would have).

In *Light in August* Hightower has become a recluse with an uncertain grip on reality, eternally watching the street from the shelter of his study and declining to be a full participant in life. He has been forbearing, surviving beatings by the Ku Klux Klan, but refuses to do more than suffer in silence. Then, as an old man, he is given a second chance. He is called upon to be a mediator and save a life. There is a manhunt for the strangely named Joe Christmas, a lost soul caught between white and black worlds because he supposedly has "negro" blood in him, an unstable fact that he both accepts and despises. The story of Christmas's life is agonizing, full of abandonment, confusion, and alienation. He is finally ruined in an obscure act that contains elements of murder and suicide; he apparently kills his white lover (the crime is never definitely established) but makes no proper attempt to escape. Whatever his precise level of guilt, Joe Christmas's misery spreads and blights others, including Gail Hightower. Hightower is, however, drawn back into the land of the living.

In *Displacing the Divine* Douglas Alan Walrath ceases his analysis of Hightower in the middle of the novel, when Hightower is still a dim figure who is estranged both from his own sanity and the church. Indeed, Walrath sees him as "symbolizing a God who is as disconnected from the present world as he is."[20] But to end contemplation of Hightower prematurely is to miss Hightower's important second chance. Whether we see his second chance as yet another catastrophe or not is a matter of interpretation—Faulkner's novel is challenging and even the plot can be difficult to summarize with certainty. But Hightower has redemptive moments worth our consideration.

As one of the few people in Jefferson, Mississippi known to be sympathetic to African-Americans, Hightower is asked to provide an alibi for Joe Christmas. Joe may or may not be a murderer, but his supposed

20. Walrath, *Displacing the Divine*, 283.

mixed blood makes it impossible for him to expect a fair hearing. Hightower refuses to provide the alibi, but Joe Christmas nevertheless turns up at his house for a last stand, viewing the minister's dwelling as a natural refuge. Faced with the actual presence of Christmas, Hightower responds in heroic Christian manner, offering a belated alibi for Joe to the violent mob in pursuit. It is too late. Christmas himself smashes Hightower in the head, and then Hightower must watch the vicious killing of Christmas in his own house.

Is Hightower's offer of protection to the hunted man too late, or not? Does he finally act in accordance with his honorable profession? It is possible, but only just, to judge him charitably. The tone of Faulkner's novel must be taken into account, however, and that tone is dark irony and barely mitigated hopelessness. If anything mitigates Hightower's cowardice, it is his attendance at the birth of a poor girl's baby just before the death of Christmas; when he helps deliver the baby, he tries to offer thanksgiving after years of neglecting prayer. For the most part, however, *Light in August* offers Gail Hightower as an intelligent, privileged man of God who has squandered his gifts and out of cowardice hidden himself away from responsibility.

Breakdown

Nearly all the disastrous pastors in this chapter could be excused on grounds of lunacy, but where would that get us? Why are authors so interested in mad church leaders, maniacally convinced of their own significance, crazily intent on demonstrating mastery of some crackpot notion or other? A. N. Wilson's *The Vicar of Sorrows* (1993) is a case in point. Why is the mental breakdown of Reverend Francis Kreer, a vicar who long ago stopped believing in God and is now trying to reconcile the Bible with the content of *Who's Who*, worth our attention? *The Vicar of Sorrows* excavates territory cultivated by Kingsley Amis, George Orwell, and Evelyn Waugh; the novel is a caustic travelogue through a Britain that no longer functions well, if it ever did. Apparently no one takes God or the church seriously, particularly its churchmen. Francis Kreer sees his ministry as a fantasy, "the love of an idea of virtue rather than a realized virtue which he had been able to practice" and, more devastatingly, his Archdeacon is "inclined to believe that being 'good with people' was 'what the Gospel is all about.'"[21] At the core of *The Vicar of Sorrows* is an unbecoming sexual adventure, which ends up distracting the protagonist—and the reader—from the weightier issue of religious vocation.

Similar problems arise in John Updike's *A Month of Sundays*, one of several books in which Updike deploys ideas and characters from Hawthorne's *The Scarlet Letter*. Updike's clerical character, Tom Marshfield, caught in sexual scandal and temporarily relieved of his parish duties, has been shamed into going on retreat, yet he is not actually ashamed of his multiple fornications. The book takes the form of a sort of diary written on this month-long retreat and features four capricious private sermons, one for each week, that demonstrate Tom's impertinence and iconoclasm.

> But let us pray together that [the church's] recollected and adamantine walls explode, releasing us to the soft desert air of this Sunday morning. . . . Nay, not explode, but atomize, and vanish noiselessly; nay, not that either, but may its walls and beams and mortar turn to petals, petals of peony and magnolia, carnation and chrysanthemum.[22]

His fake sermons include a defense of adultery, a problematizing of (but longing for) miracles, and a disquisition on desert and wilderness places, where he begins to discover himself, alongside others who are lost. Tom claims, for all his problems with authority and fidelity, "I brim still, alas, with faith" (50) and sees his mixed-up religious life as "one long glad feast of inconvenience and reason" (28).

Tom's undisciplined but clever mind is interesting, but his lewd and immature sexual nature is not. One of his lovers, Alicia, has real insight, claiming (just before she blows the whistle on his exploits) that he is acting out a "personal psychodrama" on the congregation's time. "This isn't mean to be your show, it's theirs," she says, declaring also that he is "angriest *sane* man" she has ever met (40, emphasis in original). Whether Tom Marshfield is sane is (as in other books like *Light in August* and Ibsen's *Brand*) a matter for debate. I think it unlikely that he is completely sane, and the fact that he is figuratively aligned with a more tortured and noble clergyman, Arthur Dimmesdale from *The Scarlet Letter*, makes Tom's unrepentant shallow lustfulness all the more dismal. If the decadence of Tom Marshfield seems atypical, I direct you to the Starbridge

21. Wilson, *The Vicar of Sorrows*, 239, 193.

22. Updike, *A Month of Sundays*, 128. References to subsequent passages are given parenthetically.

series of novels by Susan Howatch, clever but disturbing novels that I would hesitatingly label clergy porn, if I could bring myself to read more than one of them and be certain of my judgment. Glamour and sexual charisma are key in the first of Howatch's series, *Glittering Images*. One character says, "I remember reading once about a Victorian clergyman who inspired all the women in his congregation to faint in their pews"[23] and throughout the novel Howatch hints strongly that what the church is all about is erotic compulsion. Events get out of control and before long the reader of *Glittering Images* is faced with adultery, bigamy, illegitimacy, binge drinking, spousal abuse, incest, and naturally, hypnosis.

It is neither the depravity of Tom Marshfield nor the obstinacy of Brand that is the fundamental problem, nor is it Reverend Davidson's insistence that he must be the sole path to salvation for Sadie Thompson. Lust, stubbornness, even ridiculously inflexible conviction can be managed, even forgiven. But nearly all the truly disastrous pastors one contemplates in literature are utterly lacking in humility, and this is harder to absolve. (Gail Hightower has the opposite problem; he has such exaggerated humility he has become a deserter from existence.) Interestingly, truly disastrous pastors arise more often in literature than in the cinema. One needs the spacious nature of the novel to explore the destructive fullness of arrogance that is, perhaps, the worst moral sickness a pastor can experience. It is instructive to encounter such cautionary portrayals of clerical self-absorption and egotism—they can function rather like medieval Doom paintings—but the drawback of books like *The Spire, Glittering Images, The Vicar of Sorrows*, or even the ingeniously written *A Month of Sundays* is that for many readers these are not portrayals of individual clerics but portraits of the church itself. The spectacularly failed priest often serves as shorthand for a debased church; I would venture to say that no one character type in fiction is assumed so automatically to be at one with his (or her) occupation. An arrogant minister is, to put it simply, seen as an arrogant church.

23. Howatch, *Glittering Images*, 353.

Pale Rider

directed by Clint Eastwood

The laconic hero called the Preacher in Clint Eastwood's 1985 film *Pale Rider* could be—and has been—analyzed as a Christ-figure, or we could alternatively see him as a darker figure in the way he emerges, on a pale horse, from the pages of Revelation. Appearing precisely when a girl, Megan, reads aloud "and behold a pale horse: and his name that sat on him was Death, and Hell followed with him" (Rev 6:8), the Preacher can be interpreted as a figure of retributive violence. Yet later in the film we see the scars of six bullets which have torn through the Preacher's body; he has seemingly returned from the dead. He is reluctant to use his gun, which is—for a time—locked away in a deposit box. Which is he: emissary of hell or peacekeeping savior? Sarah, a member of the community the Preacher comes to help, finally asks him, "Who are you? Who are you, really?" The answer: "It really doesn't matter, does it?"[1] And Sarah concedes that it does not. *Pale Rider* benefits from the blurred and mysterious multiple identities of Eastwood's main character. As Sara Anson Vaux puts it in her book about Eastwood, "*Pale Rider* does not yield to simplistic or convenient analysis."[2]

It is best to say at the outset that *Pale Rider*, like many of Eastwood's films, provokes theological questions better than it provides distinct answers. Eastwood is not a conventionally religious person, but in many of his films (*Unforgiven* being the best example) he has shown significant

1. *Pale Rider*, directed by Clint Eastwood, written by Michael Butler and Dennis Shryack (this and all subsequent quotation is my own transcription from the film).

2. Vaux, *The Ethical Vision of Clint Eastwood*, 55.

courage in exploring concepts of communion and mercy, although often the stories are unable to break free of a tragic engagement with violence. It is often assumed that Eastwood is exploring and challenging traditional American notions of justice, but Vaux in her study makes a case for righteousness as the value Eastwood upholds, and she also points out that Eucharist-like meals of healing and unity are at the center of several of his films.[3] His career as director and actor is hugely varied, but there is no doubt that Eastwood's films do reward theological investigation.

Pale Rider functions on at least two levels—a realistic level in which a heartless corporate mining company aims to crush small-time gold miners living in a peaceful colony, and a mystical or symbolic one. The wicked capitalists in town, and their hired gunslingers, come to see the Preacher as something unworldly. Cleverly, much of the dialogue consists of the standard Western crudeness, but this time it has an exact meaning. "I'll be damned," and "To hell with you" and "Jesus!" are lines with extra resonance when uttered in conjunction with the Preacher's character, whether you see him as coming from heaven or hell. On the other hand, the colony of peaceful miners sees him as their earthbound pastor and ask him about homely tasks like blessing their meals and performing marriages. When he thinks the Preacher is just a preacher, the capitalist villain, LaHood (Richard Dysart), curses his henchmen for allowing a spiritual leader into the area. Even an ordinary parson can be powerful: "Their spirit was nearly broken. And a man without spirit is whipped. But a preacher, he could give them faith." In his first confrontation with the town's evildoers, the Preacher fights defensively with a piece of wood, and also throws water on the aggressors. His hat is a cowboy variant of the Victorian shovel hat (broad-brimmed and associated with clergy), and his spurs make a distinctive ringing sound as he walks, rather like a sanctuary bell sounding during a worship service. The symbols are simple and suggestive.

The most distinctive mark of his vocation is the Preacher's collar, which he reveals wordlessly after his first fight with the bad guys. He only comments on or avers his pastoral identity if another character prompts him to do so, and then his answers are enigmatic: "There's a lot of sinners hereabouts. You wouldn't want me to leave before I finish my work, would you?" and "Thanks for stopping by, son" (the latter after he serves out a large helping of physical punishment to a belligerent thug). In one

3. Ibid., 46, 209.

of the rare sustained scenes of dialogue, the Preacher and the capitalist boss, LaHood, have a wry discussion about the benefits of a settled and conventional ministry.

> *LaHood*: It occurred to me it must be difficult for a man of faith to carry the message on an empty stomach, so to speak. I thought why not invite this devout and humble man to preach in town? Why not let the town be his parish? In fact why not build him a brand-new church?
>
> *Preacher*: I can see where a preacher'd be mighty tempted by an offer like that.

The Preacher's ambiguous pastoral persona keeps everyone guessing— both the other characters in the film and the viewing audience. He appears and disappears in an almost supernatural way, responding most noticeably to the calls of the young girl, Megan, whose very personal version of Psalm 23 ("Yea, though I walk through the valley of the shadow of death, I shall fear no evil. But I *am* afraid") summons him at the movie's beginning. If he is a preacher, one of his most important attributes is to strengthen the community's independent resolve and sustain their courage and faith; as one character says, after the Preacher has apparently disappeared again, "Before he left he said if anything happened, he hoped we'd do like he'd do if he was here."

Acting as an intermediary between the two mining interests, he tries to negotiate a peaceful settlement that will allow the small-time miners to renounce their claims for one thousand dollars apiece. Ultimately, this does not work, and the Preacher has to cast off his pastoral nature when he fetches his gun out of a Wells Fargo deposit box and stores his clerical collar inside. His showdown with the deputies summoned by LaHood is brutal and final, a total victory for the (now) unambiguously supernatural Preacher, who is never in danger for a moment. His final act is to shoot Stockburn, the evil marshal, with the precise same pattern of six bullets we have seen in the scars on the Preacher's body. The number of bullets seems to demand symbolic explanation, but I agree with Adele Reinhartz when she states that such details ultimately do not "illuminate the film but may in fact lead us astray." She continues: "In the final analysis, we are left with a sense both of salvation and of mystery."[4]

---

4. Reinhartz, *Scripture on the Silver Screen*, 166, 173.

Pale Rider offers no obvious or direct lessons for today's church—it is a fantasia on Western themes with provocative but probably misleading biblical overtones. Yet Clint Eastwood's Preacher persona is a favorite with me. This is because his Preacher is allowed to be enigmatic and unpredictable in a way movie preachers are rarely allowed. Normally if a filmmaker flashes a clerical collar to the movie viewer, a stock response is expected: sanctimony, inhibition, conformity. Eastwood's Preacher is a strangely romantic figure that, to be fathomed at all, must be carefully scrutinized, and then generously and only provisionally interpreted. The famed steeliness of Eastwood's characterization is also in play; it is invigorating to see a clerical character who is fearless, unfaltering, and resolutely on the side of the oppressed.

8

Frustration

The Collar on Screen

Put on sackcloth and lament, you priests; wail, you ministers of the altar.
(Joel 1:13)

Anybody who preaches a sermon without realizing that he's heading straight
for Scylla and Charybdis ought to try a safer more productive line of work, like
laying eggs for instance. (Frederick Buechner, *Wishful Thinking:
A Theological ABC*)[1]

The "frustration" of my title might belong to television or movie pastors, struggling to reconcile a high calling with the distressing experiences of parish life and the insufficiencies of their own sinful selves.
But more likely the frustration is experienced by the intelligent viewer,
hoping to see a complex and nuanced portrayal of the ministry and
instead encountering yet another collection of clerical clichés. While I
have analyzed television and film representations of clergy throughout
this book, this chapter aims at a more particular inquiry into the ways
in which filmmakers and television producers make use of the clerical
type. I say "make use of" deliberately. While plays, novels, and even poetry have often created profound and intense clerical characters, movies
and (especially) television have tended to employ the pastor for quick,
even cheap purposes, lacking in detail and devoid of real humanity. As

1. Buechner, *Wishful Thinking*, 87.

Ann Paietta has said in her encyclopedia of screen portrayals of clergy, "religious figures in both movies and television tend toward being either miraculously pure or despicably evil and hypocritical."[2]

The criticisms above come from my cinephile self, not even my Christian self. I value intricacy, depth, and surprise in characters, plots, cinematography. When we add theological vacuity to the thin characterization and trite plot scenarios of most clerical screen portrayals, the conclusions are depressing indeed. In Garry Marshall's 2004 film *Raising Helen*, a Lutheran pastor (John Corbett) amiably concurs with a statement about the existence of heaven, hell, and purgatory, apparently unaware that purgatory is outside the realm of acceptable Lutheran doctrine. In this movie Pastor Dan functions as a two-dimensional exemplar of goodness (and good looks) to be given as a romantic reward to the heroine, Helen (Kate Hudson) if she grows up and learns to take responsibility. The short-lived nineties television drama *Nothing Sacred* allegedly was canceled because conservative Catholics thought it too heterodox. The more likely reason is that it was boring and humorless, the clerical characters ineffectual and unreal. In trying to humanize priests and nuns and make them approachable, the show's creators instead made them vague and neutral, talking incessantly about their vocations but rarely seen at work or worship. A classy soap opera, *Nothing Sacred* featured irrelevant shots of Father Ray (Kevin Anderson) taking his shirt off or worrying about the reappearance of a girlfriend from his secular life. The entire "reality" mini-series *God or the Girl* (2006) revolved around the perception that entering the church primarily involves sacrifice and renunciation. *God or the Girl* follows four young men contemplating the priesthood of the Roman Catholic Church. There is great emphasis placed on duty, discipline, personal holiness, and giving up women (as you can see from the title)—to the point where the female viewer can see that women must only exist as hindrances and objects of temptation, never as fellow Christians or, heaven forbid, potential fellow ministers. In the series there is little emphasis on service, justice, peace, or the restoration of wholeness to God's wounded creation.

One could fill many pages with theologically weak, creatively barren examples from television and film. Most of these examples are, however, unworthy of close scrutiny. Very few American television programs with central clergy characters, for instance, have lasted longer than one

2. Paietta, *Saints, Clergy, and Other Religious Figures*, 1.

season. The public has, seemingly, managed to recognize the inconsequence of the characters and the unreality of the plots. Father Mulcahy was an interesting minor character in the eleven years of *M*A*S*H*, but the brief run of the program *AfterMASH*, which attempted to give him a more prominent role, indicates that the character was not strong enough to sustain attention. *The Flying Nun* was broadcast for three seasons, and did help to build bridges between an increasingly liberated sixties audience and a Roman Catholic Church perceived as patriarchal and oppressive. Nevertheless *The Flying Nun* was, for the most part, a "cheery and not particularly controversial"[3] situation comedy involving a young and idealist character in weekly conflict with a peevish older character. Such "fish out of water" scenarios, in which fresh but quirky ideas are gradually seen to have their place in the order of things, are commonplace in television comedy. *Hell Town, Have Faith, Good News, The Book of Daniel,* and *Amazing Grace* all survived one season or less on American television, although as of this writing another comedy called *Soul Man*, starring Cedric the Entertainer (and not to be confused with the earlier *Soul Man*, starring Dan Aykroyd) is entering its second season. Usually such programs are reluctant to abandon the standard features of commercial television—conspicuous consumption, violence, romantic encounter, family conflict—many of which are an odd fit with a church setting. *The Book of Daniel* in its first four episodes (after which it was canceled) embraced plot elements like drugs, the mafia, and embezzlement. A tone of hysteria and melodrama was immediately established; the characters would never have been able to settle into anything resembling an authentic minister's family. One tagline for the series was this: "Sex. Drugs. Stolen Money and Martinis. Family can really test your faith."

My intention is to locate and examine some of the more original and valuable moments in film and television's interaction with the clergy. For example, *The Book of Daniel* (in many respects a failure) had a lovely recurring role for Jesus (played by Garret Dillahunt), emphasizing his intimate yet unassuming friendship with the Episcopalian minister Daniel (played by Aidan Quinn). This friendship, which did not provide Daniel with easy answers or getaway plans, was the most interesting thing about *The Book of Daniel*. Jesus is with Daniel nearly always (in the episode where Daniel cannot see Jesus he is lost and bereft). At one point, when one of Daniel's sons gives him bad news, Daniel reels and Jesus puts out a

---

3. Wolff, *The Church on TV*, 26.

hand and sets him upright again. This is a typical move. Jesus is constant and abiding, mostly listening, occasionally offering a sharp question, but never a rebuke. Nothing Jesus says is very controversial, but his slightly ironic tone is a surprise. What is also surprising is Daniel's tone with Jesus: often spiky and cranky. However, the frankness and the closeness of the relationship are refreshing. Also refreshing is the candid presentation of sexual attraction in the otherwise conventional movie *Raising Helen* (Pastor Dan's "I'm a sexy man of God" scene is worth a look) and in the beloved British television comedy *The Vicar of Dibley*, which in Series Three allowed Reverend Geraldine Granger a touching but ultimately doomed love affair.

Uptight Protestant, Tortured Catholic

In case I seem to have claimed out of hand that the public rejects screen clergymen or that the screen is inimical to portrayals of full-blooded pastors with integrity, let us test two memorable screen clerics: John Lithgow's Reverend Shaw Moore in *Footloose* (1984) and Richard Chamberlain's Father Ralph de Bricassart in *The Thorn Birds* (1983). Something about these two powerful characters has caught the public imagination; when I was researching this book, many people mentioned these clerics to me as noteworthy examples. What registers with me now about Lithgow's and Chamberlain's characters is the strangeness of the typology that has become associated with them. The pastor in *Footloose* is generally remembered as authoritarian, humorless, and inflexible. Having banned dancing in his parish (because his son was killed in an accident after a dance), Reverend Moore is seen as representative of unthinking adherence to law and judgment. Father Ralph in *The Thorn Birds*, vacillating between his love for a woman and his priestly vows, is usually regarded as tortured and romantic, even heroic; the *New York Times* reviewer congratulated Chamberlain for conveying the priest's "ordeal with conviction and, more impressive, believability."[4] The lure of watching Father Ralph struggle (unsuccessfully) with his desire for a beautiful woman was strong enough that *The Thorn Birds* became one of the most popular mini-series in television history: 42 percent of American households were tuned in.[5]

4. O'Connor, "Strong Performances."
5. Robertson, "Winning Miniseries."

Having recently renewed my acquaintance with both of these now-venerable screen projects, I found myself puzzled by the accepted assessments. In *The Thorn Birds* I could not see that the Roman Catholic Church was more than a convenient plot device to deny Father Ralph happiness with Meggie, and thus keep viewer interest artificially stimulated. Ralph has no particular interest in serving Christ, although he has no objection to him either. Primarily interested in self, Father Ralph does, against all probability, become a cardinal, possibly because he looks good in red. One can watch many hours of *The Thorn Birds* without catching Father Ralph doing the things priests are generally required to do: counsel those in distress, study the scriptures, preside at Holy Communion, help the needy. Instead, there are many conversations about ambition. Ascending the Catholic hierarchy does not appear overly different from climbing the corporate ladder. *The Thorn Birds* is an enjoyable melodramatic study of desire and power, but the clerical identity of Father Ralph is merely plot machinery, and one learns nothing real of the ministry. In *Footloose* I found Reverend Shaw Moore surprisingly accommodating in his moral stance; at the conclusion he listens thoughtfully to the arguments from the dance-loving teenagers (and even from his wife and daughter) and succumbs quickly and with grace. Unexpectedly, Moore is for me the most complex and sympathetic character in the 1984 version of *Footloose*; in an early scene when he finds his daughter and others at the drive-in dancing to a radio, he turns the radio off gently and says nothing. Lithgow's face is full of shame and hurt. This pastor honestly believes that his moral strictures will turn his community into a close and loving family, and he also believes (wrongly, but touchingly) that he is solely responsible for the spiritual welfare of his people. Moore is a cultured man, who has, after all, named his troublemaking daughter Ariel (and not Esther or Mary). He loves books and classical music and becomes dismayed when the members of his parish take his injunctions to a minatory extreme.

Crude Distinctions

There can be, then, gratifying moments of illumination in these well-known and apparently settled presentations of clerical character. Would that there were more. All too often directors bring a clergyman on screen to signal sexual timidity. Take, for instance, Hugh Grant as the nervous clergyman in *Sirens* (1994). The plot involves an Anglican cleric, Anthony

Campion, sent to an Australian community to deal with a famous artist who is painting scandalous and provocative pictures. Campion, and in particular his wife, become fascinated by the beauty and sensuality of the artist's trio of nude models, and the film turns out to be a paean to the unashamed freedom of sensual expression that Campion and his wife have, of course, been missing. The notion that a cleric must by definition be sexually repressed also makes possible the comedy of *The Missionary* (1982). The stereotype requires that a missionary be terrified or clueless about sex, and thus when Reverend Charles Fortescue (Michael Palin) responds with enthusiasm in his mission to London prostitutes, all of the audience's expectations are inverted in a titillating manner. One of the promotional lines for the movie on its release was "He gave his body to save their souls."

Another common use of the clerical stereotype is to set up a crude distinction between the secular world and the world of the spirit. Sometimes this is sheer comic device, but occasionally filmmakers attempt a serious or semi-serious investigation of the apparent dissimilarity between the religious life and "real" life. The premise that the church is an excellent place to hide from reality is the foundational principle of the Whoopi Goldberg *Sister Act* comedies of the nineties. When Goldberg's smart-mouthed, worldly Deloris needs to escape from the Mafia, she becomes Sister Mary Clarence, and her singular unsuitability for the role is the genesis of much of the mayhem. In one of Gregory Peck's first movies, *The Keys of the Kingdom* (1944), we see a classic instance of the church used as escape. Francis Chisholm, as a young man, is uncertain about whether he should enter the church or not, but when his childhood sweetheart, Nora, goes to the bad, Chisholm immediately takes his vows as a Roman Catholic priest. Chisholm has the reputation of being ineffectual as a priest (which Gregory Peck's robust and confident persona belies) and nobody holds out hope that he will be of use to the church. Thus he is shipped off to an impoverished and nearly-forgotten mission site in China, where, apparently, he will do no harm.

Eventually Father Chisholm's goodness wins the support of crusty nuns, warm-hearted soldiers, and wealthy mandarins, and he does beneficial work, educating children and protecting villagers during a civil war. So it is not always a bad thing when characters find sanctuary in the church. But in one of the movie's secondary characters, Mother Maria-Veronica (Rosa Stradner), we see the pattern once again, and this repetition should give us pause. She is a wealthy German aristocrat who has entered the church as self-imposed penance for her family's long heritage of arrogance and class segregation, forcing herself to believe that all God's children are equal, while palpably hating the idea.

A Clean Cosmos

From 1996 to 2007, a TV series which seemed suitable for wholesome Christian family viewing was *7th Heaven*, created by Brenda Hampton, produced by Aaron Spelling, and starring Stephen Collins as Reverend Eric Camden. The series on the WB and later the CW networks followed the growth of the Camden family, with Eric and his wife Annie eventually parenting seven children plus Happy the dog. Camden is the pastor of a community church in a white-picket-fence area of a California town. The show is a throwback, resembling *Little House on the Prairie* or *The Waltons* more than programs of its own era. Family values in *7th Heaven* are uncomplicated and obvious: mothers stay home, marriage and babies bring happiness, and there are few serious moral crises beyond the terror of heavy petting and bullies at school.

As a minister Eric Camden is well meaning but rather clued out. He often needs to be taught gentle lessons in appropriate Christian forbearance and trust by his wife and children. This is a bothersome portrayal: the cleric as docile fool and mild bumbler, whose theological education does not really amount to anything useful. At night on his bedside table you can see books like *Religion and Law*. On his wife's bedside table there are no books, and she is exhausted but happy after a day caring for the children. She has no time to read, nor need for it; she is a natural domestic minister, a success in her suitably limited household realm. Watching *7th Heaven*, one might come to the conclusion that being a clergyman means that you ladle out advice in a preposterously spacious study and that it is acceptable to spy on your kids to see if they are involved in malefactions down at the ice cream parlor. You rarely see Eric Camden involved in intellectual work, like sermon preparation, or the sacramental work of administering the Eucharist. Snippets of sermons are brief.

The clean cosmos of *7th Heaven* seems to me almost unrelated to the world in which actual pastoral families exist. Watching the Camden parents obsessively fuss about their children and dating, especially in the early seasons, is like watching the 1951 atomic bomb preparedness film *Duck and Cover*, or, at best, a slightly updated *Brady Bunch*. In later seasons the show's creators attempted to tackle tougher issues like drunk driving and single parent families, but would not approach the hot topics of abortion or sexual orientation, partly because, as Richard Wolff says, the target audience for *7th Heaven* was teenaged girls.[6]

One wonders if the show would have persisted for eleven years on one of the three major networks of the time. The retreat of Reverend Camden and his brood into simplistic values reminiscent of the fifties is a particularly egregious version of using the church as escape. Is the twenty-first century, with all its complexity, greed, violence, and danger, getting you down? Turn back to the church. This bland model of Christianity is akin to the "friendly" congregation that Douglas John Hall assesses critically in *The End of Christendom and the Future of Christianity*:

> In time, the friendly church wears thin. Those who are looking for meaning (and that is the most gripping search of humanity in our context) are not likely to find it in such churches. For one thing, part of the secret of their being reputedly friendly is their consistent avoidance of deeper human concerns, which are usually divisive. A superficial friendliness is no substitute for depth of meaning, or even of genuine community.[7]

Congregations where weighty and difficult matters are being openly discussed inevitably experience division and conflict. If Christians refuse to face toward the darkness, they cannot hope fully to understand or serve the provoking Christ who said in Luke 14:26 (and half a dozen similar places in the Gospels), "Whoever comes to me and does not hate father and mother, wife and children, brothers and sisters, yes, and even life itself, cannot be my disciple."

The squeaky-clean cleric—overly conscious of the role of moral exemplar, sanctimoniously guarding the gates of a prim Christendom—can be that most dangerous kind of church leader: someone who has labeled faults as gifts. In Barbara Brown Taylor's frank memoir *Leaving Church* (2006), which recounts her life as a popular Episcopal priest and her decision to resign from the ministry, she recalls that "one of the things that almost killed me was becoming a professional holy person."[8] To think of

---

6. Wolff, *The Church on TV*, 181.

7. Hall, *The End of Christendom and the Future of Christianity*, 26–27.

8. Taylor, *Leaving Church*, 226.

oneself, at any point, as a "professional holy person" is a grave thing for a minister to do.

God Squad

One of the rare instances of recent American movie-making which runs counter to this stereotype of the church as bland and escapist is Edward Norton's comedy *Keeping the Faith* (2000), in which he and Ben Stiller play childhood friends who grow up to become, respectively, Father Brian and Rabbi Jake. The last half of the film devolves into a more typical relationship movie, with a focus on sex, misunderstandings, and betrayed loyalties, but the first hour offers a refreshing view of these funny, complicated young men at work in the church and synagogue, talking about their work and enjoying it. These are faithful and hip clerics devoted to God and their communities. Their vocations are at the forefront of the movie, even though the standard romantic triangle plot interferes for a time. (The sexual temptation to which Father Brian almost succumbs is handled convincingly and humorously.)

Beginning with a delightful sequence about the boys' youthful fascination with religion (collecting Heroes of the Torah cards, cheerfully offering coffee to streetwalkers), Norton's film moves into their seminary training and early ministries. Guided by two patient elders who occasionally roll their eyes but offer steady support, Brian and Jake are cheeky, charming, and hard-working. They play basketball, calling themselves the God Squad, and Brian in an amusing scene flashes his clerical collar to a store clerk in order to get a reasonable price on equipment for their new Jewish-Catholic drop-in center. (Don, the clerk: "Oh man, what is that? What is it with that? Is that thing real?"[9]) Jake halts the liturgy to encourage his congregation to sing with more feeling ("It's a joyous song, a prayer about praising the Lord, telling the Lord how much we love him, or her") and Brian, taking confessions, is calm and accepting. They try to make their preaching approachable; one of Brian's sermons has this conclusion:

> And it's very important to understand the difference between religion and faith. Because faith is not about having the right answers. Faith is a feeling. Faith is a hunch, really. It's a hunch

9. *Keeping the Faith*, directed by Edward Norton, written by Stuart Blumberg (this and all subsequent quotation is my own transcription from the film).

that there is something bigger connecting it all, connecting us all together. And that feeling, that hunch, is God.

Jake is trying to be amiable about his synagogue's obsessive interest in finding him a nice Jewish girl to marry, and neutralizes potentially difficult situations with well-timed jokes. Helping a boy learning to chant prayers for his Bar Mitzvah, Rabbi Jake responds to the boy's worry that he "sucks" with "Okay. Yes, you do. You suck, but that's okay." He urges him to "embrace the suckiness." Instead of being defensive about stereotypical Jewish attributes like acquisitiveness, Jake cheerfully defuses tension with jokes about "doing a hostile takeover of Congregation Bertov Sholem." My favorite lines in this oddly thoughtful Hollywood comedy are these:

> *Jake*: Jews want their rabbis to be the Jews they don't have the time to be.

> *Brian*: Catholics want their priests to be the Catholics they don't have the discipline to be.

Without sacrificing comedy, Edward Norton in *Keeping the Faith* presents the ministry as an evolving, dynamic career for intelligent, even clever young men. (Yes, men. But we will let it go this time.) This confidence and joy in ministry seemed so unusual when I first saw this movie that I felt I had to watch it again immediately to see if I had imagined that joy.

The notion that God's work can be done by the unworthy, and that we may still benefit from the ministry of the fallen (as stated in the Thirty-nine Articles and in Luther's *Babylonian Captivity of the Church*) is more fittingly explored in a novel, one assumes, which has the space to stretch out and explore the particulars and fine distinctions of a personality like, for example, Dimmesdale in *The Scarlet Letter*. Edward Norton's movie *Keeping the Faith* is unusual enough in its insistence that intelligent, socially-engaged young people can find a robust, satisfying career in religious leadership. Even more unusual is a film that attempts, in approximately two hours, to explore a more compromised church leader, one whose sins and strengths are bound together in a complex tangle. One can enumerate such ambitious films on the fingers of one hand.

A Violent Faith

In Robert Duvall's celebrated 1998 film *The Apostle*, which he wrote, directed, and financed in addition to taking the lead role, he plays a hot-headed and charismatic Pentecostal preacher from the South. Fleeing a violent crime—he has hit with a baseball bat the youth minister with whom his wife is having an affair—he abandons his old identity but does not abandon ministry. This is because he cannot. Preaching is embedded in the personality of Sonny Dewey, who reinvents himself as the Apostle E. F. As Adele Reinhartz says, Sonny is "profoundly convinced that the Holy Spirit has empowered his endeavors throughout his entire life" and "derives his way of thinking and the vocabulary for articulating his view of the world directly from the Bible."[10] Sonny is steeped in religion and unshakeable in his certainty about his vocation to bring people to the Lord.

He is also, unmistakably, a violent and volatile man. Roger Ebert in his review stated that the character was "flawed, with a quick temper, but he's a good man."[11] Adele Reinhartz sees the film dividing into two, with Sonny experiencing a transformation from sin to redemption: when he goes on the run after the murderous assault on Horace, the youth minister, he crosses a bridge on foot, which Reinhartz sees as "metaphorically crossing over from his old life to a new."[12] Janet Maslin in the *New York Times* had the most positive assessment of the character, noting his "kindly manner and beatific smile." Maslin also states that the preacher's assault on Horace is "fate" dealing him a "career-ending crisis."[13]

I find *The Apostle* more troubling. Duvall's character is, ultimately, sincere in his faith and resolutely driven to secure souls for the Lord, but his charm does not work on me. Even when he becomes the Apostle, the man is manipulative, cunning, and lacking in warmth. At the center of the film is a scene where Sonny Dewey fasts and prays in a tent and then baptizes himself, in a river, into his new identity as the Apostle E. F. While other critics may find this a profound transformation I could not decide if Sonny was praying or scheming in the tent, and was unimpressed with the audacity of the self-baptism. (There is a friend at Sonny's re-baptism,

---

10. Reinhartz, *Scripture on the Silver Screen*, 116, 119.

11. Ebert, review of *The Apostle*.

12. Reinhartz, *Scripture on the Silver Screen*, 116.

13. Maslin, "Man of Strong Passion."

who could conceivably have performed the sacrament if Sonny truly thinks of the church as a community of Christians, rather than as a "one way road to heaven" which he controls.) Although his wife's adultery is apparently the act which sets the plot in motion, Sonny has admitted that he has a history of womanizing, and in his "redeemed" life we see him pursue a new flame (Miranda Richardson) with almost indecent ardor.

"One Way Road to Heaven" is the name of his new church (or, as he prefers, his temple). One positive element of the church is that is un-selfconsciously integrated; Sonny has been brought up on the rhythms of southern black preaching, and he naturally attracts a black congregation. He does not seem to see color, and it is also true that his work in the new church is fueled by intense apostolic energy and an increasingly apparent humility. One scene of delivering free groceries anonymously to the poor is meant to impress; the benefits of that scene might be outweighed by the one in which we witness him peddling specially-blessed scarves on the radio. At the film's conclusion, Sonny goes peacefully with the police when they catch up with him, but I was only persuaded to see him as a humbled man when, behind the final credits, Sonny genially labors with a prison work crew, leading the other prisoners in a call-and-response chant glorifying the name of Jesus.

Despite this conclusion, the viewer is well advised to keep asking what sort of church leader insists on calling his ministry the "One Way Road to Heaven." Sonny's ministry is manic and shallow. He teaches children to recite the books of the Bible in order, and uses the physical object of the Bible like a magic talisman to stop an antagonist from bulldozing his new church. The final preaching scene before Sonny is taken into custody has attracted comment; Duvall presents a long, emotional worship service in which, as Janet Maslin writes, "Sonny preaches his heart out." My northern heart must be to blame, but I did not respond; the preaching was thin, repetitive, frantic and lacking in thoughtfulness.

The viewers' responses to *The Apostle* depend very much on denominational background, ease with preaching that is melodramatic and extemporaneous, and attitude toward concepts like "personal Savior" and "Holy Ghost power"—this last phrase is used by Sonny continually.[14] At one point, trying to acquire a radio spot in his new Louisiana community, Sonny explains to the station owner that he has a "background in holi-

14. *The Apostle*, directed and written by Robert Duvall (this and all subsequent quotation is my own transcription from the film).

ness." Even once I recognized that Sonny's use of "Holiness" designates the movement still occasionally called Holy Rollers and associated with the Pentecostal movement, Sonny's phrase festered in my consciousness. Trying (and failing) to imagine myself saying to anyone, "I have a background in holiness," I did not know whether to be impressed or distressed by the Apostle's confident effrontery. Duvall himself addressed this matter in an interview:

> Some religious people might ask why I would make such a movie and emphasize that this evangelical preacher has weaknesses. And my answer is that we either accept weaknesses in good people or we have to tear pages out of the bible.[15]

Duvall is a Christian Scientist but created this southern Pentecostal preacher in all sincerity. In an interview he spoke of his desire to catch the spontaneity of that kind of church: "I love the directness of these people. They relate directly with God, not going through anything."[16] Even accepting that premise, Sonny's violent personality should give us pause. Sonny does not merely give into one isolated act of violence; in the second half of the movie, when he is supposedly on the way to redemption, he delivers a vicious beating to an antagonist. Adele Reinhartz calls this a fist fight but this designation is as false as Janet Maslin's notion that fate hands Sonny the baseball bat that leads to the death of Horace. Neither Sonny nor the Apostle has a mere temper; the excessive violence in the man's character continues, suppressed or not, throughout the film. Late in the film we see Sonny pray for Horace's recovery, but this is too little, too late. He never fully recognizes the brutality within himself, seeing it instead as momentary weakness.

Duvall had a tough time getting *The Apostle* made. As Roger Ebert puts it, "The major studios turned him down (of course, it's about something, which scares them)."[17] This movie *is* about something, and it is an unusually well-developed portrait of a full-blooded preacher. The lessons of the film are less palatable to me than to other commentators, but *The Apostle* is still that rare film that insists that the church is worth our full attention, and that fallen human beings can nevertheless do God's work of ministry, although success, and holiness, are not assured.

15. Quoted in Blizek and Burke, "The Apostle: An Interview."

16. Ibid.

17. Ebert, review of *The Apostle*.

The Best of Britain

One of the most pleasurable clerical excursions in recent years has been to visit Dibley. There an Anglican vicar, Geraldine Granger (Dawn French) provides both humor and poignancy, the first (for example) in the infamous Christmas lunch incident, where Geraldine accepts too many invitations and has to be taken home in a front-end loader, and the latter in the Make Poverty History episode, with its serious insistence that viewers give their full attention to the impoverished of Africa. Like many British comedies, *The Vicar of Dibley* is irreverent and farcical, but the show (which ran in irregular fashion on BBC TV from 1994 to 2000, with occasional specials in the following years) had a genuine contribution to make. It was created soon after the first women were ordained in the Church of England (1992), and Richard Curtis, the creator of the series, has stated that he deliberately wanted to enter the fray and use comedy to disarm opponents to the ordination of women.[18]

Geraldine comes out swinging in the first episode with the terrific lines: "You were expecting a bloke: beard, Bible, bad breath. And instead you've got a babe with a bob cut and a magnificent bosom."[19] The assessment of the female vicar by the ultra-conservative chair of the Dibley parish council, David Horton (Gary Waldhorn), is this: "You're a good woman with a good heart but you should be running a cake stand, not a church."[20] However, Geraldine is confident, funny, vulnerable, and in love with Jesus. She calls herself the "vixter" and is eventually called, with affection, "Mrs. God." Her typical fashion statement is a black shirt, cross, long white wool vest, and black and white polka dot pants. Eventually even David Horton will be won over by her joyful style of preaching, her commitment to the poor, and her ability to bring people into the church. After Geraldine interferes with local council elections to help the poor and elderly get a bus service, she and David have this exchange:

> *David*: I will not be undermined by a left-wing priest spreading hard-core Marxism in my constituency. What was the socialist tract you were spouting from the pulpit last week?
>
> *Geraldine*: I've got a feeling it was the Sermon on the Mount.

18. "The Real Vicars of Dibley," featurette, DVD.

19. *The Vicar of Dibley*, "Arrival," season 1, written by Richard Curtis (this and all subsequent quotation is my own transcription from the series).

20. *The Vicar of Dibley*, "Animals," season 1, written by Richard Curtis.

David: I'm sorry—Jesus did not tell rich people to give all their money away.

Geraldine: I think you'll find that he did, actually.[21]

Since the main body of *The Vicar of Dibley* consisted of twenty episodes lasting less than thirty minutes each, one can only expect so much. As with many screen portrayals of clergy, sermons appear to be only a few moments long. Even given its brevity, Geraldine's first sermon in Dibley provides a bold statement of her personal creed as a vicar:

> I was convinced that naturally I would become a supermodel. . . . And then one day I read the Sermon on the Mount and it was so fantastic. That was it. . . . So here I am. At your service. Totally yours. Any time, any day. Although if you come to see me first thing in the morning, wear dark glasses. Because if you see me first thing in the morning before my face falls into place, I look frighteningly like [hefty British comedian] Bernard Manning.[22]

"So here I am. At your service. Totally yours. Any time, any day" is probably a foolish thing for a new vicar to say. But the commitment and generosity of Geraldine Granger are valuable to have on view, especially in England, where there are often grave suspicions about the supposed idlers in the pay of the state church. Geraldine's antics can be ridiculous but are nearly always performed in aid of the needy of her parish. For example, in the episode "Community Spirit" Geraldine promises pop star Kylie Minogue a front row seat in heaven if she will open the church fête. In the final series, off-color sex jokes escalate and Geraldine must endure an all-male parish council; that she manages to smile and spar through all this aggravation underscores her considerable tolerance and good will. This is not to say that Geraldine's personality is anodyne; when the parish council in the first episode is about to bow to David's will and send a letter to the Bishop requesting a male vicar, Geraldine's response is sad, but dignified: "Well, you certainly know how to wind a girl."[23]

Especially given the challenges women in the Church of England were facing in the first years of ordination, Geraldine's buoyant patience and ability with clever comebacks were exhilarating to watch. Challenged

---

21. *The Vicar of Dibley*, "Election," season 1, written by Richard Curtis and Paul Mayhew-Archer.

22. *The Vicar of Dibley*, "Arrival," season 1, written by Richard Curtis.

23. Ibid.

by David Horton with the disparaging comment, "I didn't know flirting was on the syllabus of theological colleges," Geraldine's acerbic but good-natured rejoinder is "Oh yes, it's the whole second year."[24] She knows she is worthy of a position of responsibility and influence, but she also must wrestle with her own shortcomings and unruly desires. This blend of the vulnerable and the mature was, ultimately, a service to the Church of England and, one assumes, has affected other denominations. In 2007, when the number of female ordinands overtook male for the first time in Britain, the *Guardian* called this the "*Vicar of Dibley* effect":

> A Church of England spokesman said a possible reason for the rise was the continued popularity of the BBC programme *The Vicar of Dibley*, starring Dawn French, which could have encouraged women who already had a sense of calling.[25]

For detractors who saw *The Vicar of Dibley* as inhabiting the sheltered never-never-land of a sleepy rural parish, and thus hardly connecting to the high stress urban environments of the majority of today's viewers, the current BBC TV show *Rev.* is a valuable corrective. It is also sometimes startlingly frank, with rude language, lots of drinking, and bouts of real despair. This is not your grandmother's Church of England. The theme song for *Rev.* is a strangely upbeat, possibly ironic version of the old African-American tune "Couldn't Hear Nobody Pray," more usually heard in a cathartically mournful arrangement. (The song involves a repeated call-and-response of "I couldn't hear nobody pray / On the mountain / I couldn't hear nobody pray / In the valley.") Here "Couldn't Hear Nobody Pray" is almost painful in its intimation that nobody in Reverend Adam Smallbone's parish is praying (except him), and his wan smile at the end of the credits indicates he wearily accepts this. However, Adam Smallbone's prayer life is tangible and crucial to his survival in the tough St. Saviour's parish; the viewer who dismisses the show for its apparent crudeness will miss something quite marvelous.

24. *The Vicar of Dibley*, "Community Spirit," season 1, written by Richard Curtis and Paul Mayhew-Archer.
25. Butt, "*Vicar of Dibley* Effect."

Created by Tom Hollander and James Wood, *Rev.* in its two seasons so far has been more successful with the critics than *The Vicar of Dibley* (*Rev.* has won a BAFTA award for best situation comedy, which *Dibley* never did), and its ratings respectable. Hollander plays Smallbone, in charge of a nearly-deserted East London parish, trying with desperate cheerfulness to live on a small stipend and enjoy marriage with his often-disgruntled but generally supportive wife, Alex. Wood has stated that he and Hollander intended realistically to "depict the joys and irritations of day-to-day church business" in a way that previous British clerical comedies had not managed to do.[26] The first major scene of the first series, which I provide below at some length, gives a lovely indication of the program's tone, irreverent and remarkably poignant. Adam in the first scene has invited his tiny congregation for a "vicarage warming" from the pulpit. It is now the morning after the party. Adam enters the kitchen, where Alex is seated. She looks rumpled and holds a cup of something hot.

> *Adam*: Oh, my God. [He has his clerical shirt on, open at the neck, with clerical collar dangling. He looks terrible and is practically whispering.]
>
> *Alex*: Taking the Lord's name? [She is propping up her head on her hand.]
>
> *Adam*: It's a dialogue, actually, darling. [Opening a drawer at random.] Where do we keep the aspirin in this house?
>
> *Alex*: End. [She points.]
>
> *Adam*: Whose bird table is that? [The camera pulls back to reveal the entire kitchen, towels and balloons on the floor, and in the middle, a large bird feeder.]
>
> *Alex*: Ours now. [Pause.] A surprise housewarming gift from Colin. [When Alex says "Colin" her voice goes up in pitch and accentuates the name.]
>
> *Adam*: Isn't it from next door? [Alex lifts her head in surprise, looks left out the window.] I didn't get too drunk, did I?
>
> *Alex*: You were fine. [She amiably stresses the word *fine*.] Everyone was very impressed you can still do the splits. [Pause.] Nigel is really quite unbelievably strange, isn't he?

26. Wood, "The Writer."

Adam: [Adam begins to smile.] Yes! Imagine sharing an office with him.

Alex: And Adoha.

Adam: She won't stop flirting with me. She keeps pulling me into those big bazoomas like the Death Star. [Look of hilarious incredulity on Alex's face. Adam gives an embarrassed, snorting little laugh.] It's terrifying. [Doorbell rings.]

Alex: If that's Colin this early, tell him we're not open yet.

Adam: It won't be Colin. [Opens door.] Hello, Colin.

Colin: Vicar, you'd better come quick! There's been a disaster at the church!

Adam: OK, shh. [Makes quieting motion with hands.]

Alex: Hello, Colin.

Adam: Yes, it's Colin.

Colin: Hello, Mrs. Vicarage. Off for another day saving lives?

Alex: I'm a solicitor, Colin. [Kisses Adam.] Bye, darling.

Adam: Bye, darling.

Colin: Bye, darling. [Looks as if he expects Alex to kiss him too. Is disappointed. Alex leaves.] Come on, Vicar!

Adam: Yes, OK, coming. [They walk.]

Colin: Cracking piss-up last night. Previous vicar never let me in his house.

Adam: Thanks for the bird table.

Colin: Eh? Oh, yeah. Nice one.

Adam: So, what's the problem?

Colin: You'll see at the church. It's a scandal, vicar.

Adam: Ok, is it a scandal, or is it just a pigeon like last time?[27]

The homeless, often drunk Colin will reappear at the vicarage door frequently and always inconveniently in the coming episodes and, against

27. *Rev.*, season 1, episode 1, directed by Peter Cattaneo, written by James Wood (my transcription).

all probability, he and Adam become friends, sitting on a bench behind the church building, drinking ale and smoking cigarettes. Another person who knocks at the door is the addict Mick, always with an unlikely swindle to cadge a handout. Adam's lay reader, Nigel, is pompous and terrible with people; Adoha is the middle-aged, lascivious groupie looking for any chance to call Adam "darling." These people are the core of Adam's tiny congregation, St. Saviour's, and sometimes they are not the core so much as the entirety. Watching over them and constantly criticizing Adam for his dismal collection plates is Archdeacon Robert (Simon McBurney), a cleverly witty but cruel cataloguer of Adam's faults.

It may seem trivial, but the television and movie depiction of a pastor's dwelling is worth consideration. Typically in an American movie or television show, the minister and his family will live in sit-com affluence. The ministers' houses in *7th Heaven* and *The Book of Daniel* are, to my eye, almost laughably posh, featuring colonial styling, doric columns, and large manicured lawns. If we think this is just upper middle class white America, the domestic setting for the African-American minister's family in *Soul Man* resembles the comfortable living room from *The Cosby Show* (and recall that Cosby's character was an obstetrician); even the supposedly downscale black neighborhood of *The Preacher's Wife* offers the minister a massive old house with large bedrooms and oak trim. Admittedly I have not visited the homes of American or British clerics, but I know the homes of dozens of Canadian pastors. None has such impressive square footage nor such massive stainless steel refrigerators. Compared to their American television counterparts, Adam and Alex Smallbone in *Rev.* live in something close to squalor—their house is lower middle class, cluttered, and decidedly small and plain (just as the vicarage in *The Vicar of Dibley* is a small Tudor cottage).

Unusual for a traditional situation comedy, but becoming more common, *Rev.* allows its characters some fierce alterations of character, for better or worse. Adam is intelligent and faithful, but hesitant and meek. His good ideas are stolen by another vicar, his sermon receives a vicious online review, and he becomes tongue-tied and maladroit on national television. Having come from a more tranquil parish in Suffolk, Adam is criticized by his father-in-law: "Why anyone would choose to move from Suffolk to Heroin Alley is quite beyond me."[28] At the end of

---

28. *Rev.*, season 2, episode 7, directed by Peter Cattaneo, written by James Wood and Sam Bain (my transcription).

the first season, Adam hits bottom with several days of heavy drinking and total gloom, making a fool of himself in public and flirting with the principal of the local parish school, his long-suffering friend Ellie. At the conclusion of the second season, exhausted by the Christmas rush and smarting not only from the death of an elderly parishioner but additionally a fight with Colin, Adam loses control at midnight mass and lets loose with an angry, absurd parody of "The Twelve Days of Christmas." Again, the scene is worth giving at length. Adam's "Christmas episode," as he later calls it, is prompted by raucous interruptions from pub-goers who have arrived at the church expecting it to be a revel like the Last Night of the Proms. The line from the Eucharistic Prayer that Adam is trying to deliver before being drowned out is "Great is the mystery of faith." He murmurs it, turns around, and the worship service stops. He then sings, with perceptible frustration, his song:

> On the first day of Christmas my true love gave to me
> Ten office parties, 5000 mince pies,
> Forty-five hospital visits, one multi-faith ecumenical event.
> Too much to do.
>
> Every day I get up at 5:30. Then my friend died, but I missed it.
> But I said I'd be there. But I missed it.
> And then a man who I thought was my mate
> Came round and hit me in the face.
> One black eye.
>
> Mince pies, mince pies, mince pies, mince pies. More mince pies.
> Mince pies, mince pies, mince pies, mince pies. More mince pies.
> And they cost £2.90 for six. Can you believe it?
> Mince pies, mince pies, mince pies. More mince pies.
> Can you believe it?[29]

The next morning—Christmas morning—there is hardly anyone in attendance at worship. But following the service there is a "ways-and-strays" lunch that brings back many of the people with whom Adam has been at odds, and he is reconciled with them. A particularly bright moment occurs after Adam forgives Colin for giving him a black eye; Colin shouts out, "I'm forgiven. We're all forgiven!" This episode ends with an intentional tableau which parallels the Last Supper, centering Adam at the table with his few parishioners and some strangers who have nowhere

29. Ibid.

to go on Christmas Day. The end of the previous episode also featured a careful tableau when five of the characters wander separately into the church sanctuary and sit in different places, nursing their wounds. All of these characters have undergone individual strains in the episode, and their presence in the sanctuary signals not only their need for healing but the genuine reality that this shabby church community can facilitate that healing.

Every episode of *Rev.* features scenes of Adam Smallbone at prayer: as he washes dishes, walks the streets of London, sits in a pew on a weekday morning. He offers everything in his life in conversation with God—his need for more sexual energy to keep his marriage going, the church's money problems, his own sense of futility. Adam is not always a good man—in the episode where he desperately wants to win an ecumenical football match he is spectacularly awful. But his complete honesty with God and the natural tenor of his prayer life are exemplary. One of the best prayers is heard in the very first episode of *Rev.* It follows a riotous and vulgar outburst to his wife about how exasperating Adam's job is.

> This is not easy, OK, Alex, this job. [Adam frustrated and unusually agitated.] All that happens all day, every day, all the time, is that people want something from me. Which is fine [when he says "fine," a trace of his customary sweet nature comes through], it's a vocation. But I do have to depend on a whole lot of volunteers, some of whom can't even wipe their own arses.

Following this, Adam is chagrined; walking to the church building, he prays, apologizing to God.

> I'm sorry, Lord, that was wrong. I shouldn't have talked about people's arses like that. It was a grotesque succession of images. I'm just finding everything a bit difficult. . . . How did I get into this situation? I'm supposed to walk with the broken, aren't I? Not horse-trade with an admittedly rather pretty headmistress, that toxic MP, and Gemma the barmaid. [Shot from overhead as Adam turns his face skyward.] And why do you want me to be a fundraiser the whole time? Why have you given me this huge, crumbling building, and now this window to deal with? It's such a burden. Let's face it, it's not a terribly good window, really, is it? Speak to me, Lord, your servant listens.[30]

---

30. *Rev.*, season 1, episode 1, directed by Peter Cattaneo, written by James Wood (my transcription).

The grittiness of Adam Smallbone's ministry and the pain experienced by him and his community bring us closer to Christ's own ministry than most cinematic portrayals of the clergy. Adam is deeply flawed but committed to the church; as one watches the two available seasons of *Rev.* the essence of his ministry shines more brightly. That message is profound humility, of a sort we rarely encounter in any century, but even more rarely in our own. Geraldine Granger in *The Vicar of Dibley* told her congregation, "So here I am. At your service. Totally yours. Any time, any day," and similarly Adam Smallbone is formed to serve. This totalizing concept of service creates trouble in his marriage, which is (after all) another of his callings. That this profound steadfastness and sacrifice often go terribly wrong is a reality; but that imperfect humility is a necessity in church leadership is a lesson we badly need to hear and see.

Richard Wolff in his book *The Church on TV* claims that representations of church leaders on television have had little impact, positive or negative, over the years, partly because few church-centered programs have been successful. One reason that religion and television are not a good fit, he says, is that television narrative demands a "steady state" that remains from episode to episode.[31] The steady state of most television shows, given their relative brevity of twenty or fifty minutes, demands repetitive, minor-league conflict (comic or otherwise), and the types of conflict television utilizes and the types of conflict the church actually experiences are usually remote from each other. Speaking about American television, Wolff notes that shows featuring clergy have nearly always conformed to Hollywood trends and thus have offered nothing distinctive. Liturgy and worship, prayer and spiritual contemplation, for example, are hardly ever shown, and thus the potentially distinct character of the church-centered show is lost.

The pressures to simplify and conform, Wolff hints, are less strenuous for cinema, which can present a more spacious narrative, but Ann Paietta disagrees, stating that on both the small and large screen clerics are "either saints or sinners" with little nuance.[32] In addition the Mo-

31. Wolff, *The Church on TV*, 211.
32. Paietta, *Saints, Clergy, and Other Religious Figures*, 1.

tion Picture Production Code, in effect from the thirties to the sixties, discouraged complex, critical, or naturalistic presentations of the church, since the Code required optimism and respect in movies involving religion. Even today, Wolff concludes that most screen portrayals of church leaders are cheery and inoffensive; he does not seem worried about that. But we should be worried. The bland and unrealistic nature of (particularly) American screen depictions of the church must surely have an impact on the viewing public (British film and television, as I hope has been obvious in my discussion, is usually more original and more daring). In 1961, Martin Marty hoped that cultural depictions of the church might evangelize (actually "pre-evangelize") in an unthreatening way, and the curious might be drawn to Christianity.[33] Fifty years later, I see little justification for Marty's hope (admittedly he said this function would never extend beyond "preparing the soil") apart from uncommon achievements like *Rev.*, *The Vicar of Dibley*, and *Keeping the Faith*. Larry Witham tells of two clerics who felt "the call" after seeing the film *Becket* in 1964. Since that era he claims that "religious figures have virtually disappeared from movie plots."[34] That which survives is not exactly inspirational.

33. Marty, *The Improper Opinion*, 139.
34. Witham, *Who Shall Lead Them?*, 12, 185.

The Bing Crosby and Richard Burton Movie Priests

In 1944, *Going My Way*, a genial little movie about two Roman Catholic priests in a big city parish, won the Oscar for best picture, plus six other Oscars. The movie was so popular, and earned such warm acclaim, that in 1945 a similar movie, *The Bells of St. Mary's*, was made by the same director, Leo McCarey. The vital element in the success of these movies was the rather odd choice of singer Bing Crosby to star as Father O'Malley, the easy-going priest who must clear away the proverbial cobwebs with his new style of ministry: informal, intuitive, natural. These movies actually managed to alter the image of North American Christianity in considerable ways. McCarey's movies were friendly and accessible, and his concept of the church harmonized with his style: unthreatening and mainstream. At the time this must have seemed like a good idea.

It is not easy now to grasp the high regard these films once commanded. Today the Father O'Malley pictures look pallid. The conflicts are hardly earthshaking: young Father O'Malley must prove his mettle against old-fashioned Father Fitzgibbon in *Going My Way* and against cranky capitalist Horace P. Bogardus in *The Bells of St. Mary's*. Hearts must be turned, and there is never any doubt that hearts will indeed turn. In each case O'Malley gently manages the allegedly difficult parish children, taking them to the movies and turning them into choirs or sports teams with ease. He helps young women navigate the dangers of the big city, reconciles separated couples, and (in *Going My Way*) writes a song that saves the church from financial ruin. In both movies, there is a lot of singing, some of it religious but most of it the optimistic light-hearted popular song associated with Bing Crosby, whose dialogue was always so natural and musical that it seemed he would meander again into song at any moment. The songs are sentimental, about swinging on stars and taking the road to Rainbowville. This has some charm. But no sermons, no sacraments are on view in either movie: instead we are given a little light counseling, singing, and sports. The most sacred elements in each movie are the sheltered and peaceful churchyards and parish offices. A haven of quiet and decorum in a noisy cityscape, the church represents repose and protection, but also, unfortunately, escape.

I would personally be inclined to dismiss these movies, but for the fact that they have a distinct place in the history of American films about the ministry, and there is the awkward fact of those Academy Awards. Anthony Burke Smith has written extensively about Catholicism on the screen, and he says that "Crosby's performance as a cleric hip to the ways of the world set a new standard for the representation of Catholicism in the popular imagination."[1] The reviews at the time were almost universally positive, with a writer in *The Christian Herald* stating that the film "transcends all bounds of sect or creed in its human, wholesome handling of the politics and problems common to any Church of God."[2] Even in 2013, Richard A. Blake in the *Journal of Religion and Film* defended Leo McCarey for films that offer "the possibility of redemption for anyone" and emphasized the consistent theme of conversion in all of McCarey's films, including the Bing Crosby O'Malley films.[3]

Some Roman Catholic commentators assert that the O'Malley movies had a huge impact on the manner in which Catholics were treated in American society. *Going My Way* "directly challenges [the] image of Catholicism as dangerous or mysterious," says Smith, with Father O'Malley "recognizable enough with his love of sports and popular music to be American but different enough as a Catholic priest to suggest the nourishing of distinctive subcultures."[4] Colleen McDannell points out the strong Roman Catholic influence in the creation and administration of the Hollywood Production Code, which expected, among other things that "the top-billed star speak for morality and to respect all lawful authorities. There was to be no cynical contempt for middle-class social

---

1. Smith, "America's Favorite Priest," 108.
2. Quoted in Smith, "America's Favorite Priest," 117.
3. Blake, "The Sins of Leo McCarey."
4. Smith, "America's Favorite Priest," 111, 121.

standards, no morbid or depressing themes." Whereas Roman Catholics before this time could be identified in the popular imagination as outsiders, secondary citizens, or even symbols of decadence, from the nineteen-thirties to the sixties as the Production Code was enforced, Catholicism became more and more "the American religion" at least as far as movies were concerned.[5]

In *The Bells of St. Mary's* Father O'Malley goes to visit the nuns next door for the first time and accidentally sits on a kitten, which later climbs into his straw boater and cavorts on the mantelpiece behind the priest. This delights the nuns and baffles the priest, who cannot tell at first why they are laughing; the priest is made likeable and the nuns humanized. The fact that Father O'Malley wears a boater at all is a significant step forward in popular acceptance; instead of the dour little caps worn by movie priests like Barry Fitzgerald, the dapper straw hat worn by Bing Crosby at a jaunty angle signals approachability and friendliness. Crosby's open-faced enjoyment of living in the moment is evident at all times, and there is even a thoughtful if brief condemnation of acquisitiveness in *Going My Way* when the son of the local capitalist says to the priests in exasperation: "You haven't got anything and you don't want anything."[6] This is both refreshingly right and glaringly wrong. In consumerist terms, the church should be (thankfully) out of step, but then what do we do with the fact that both of the Father O'Malley movies obsessively worry about new or improved church buildings? And if the capitalist cannot see that the church does have something—community, grace, mercy, guidance—then the church is failing to fulfill its mission. The church should also want something, eternally: to promote the worship of God, to help the largest possible number of bodies and souls.

There is only so far one can go with contemplative or theological matters in simplistic movies like these, and McCarey must have recognized that even in the second film he was reaching the limits of believability. Perhaps this is why he introduces in *The Bells of St. Mary's* Sister Benedict as a sort of innocently romantic sparring partner for Father O'Malley, so that we get a toned-down Beatrice and Benedick situation, albeit with none of the fireworks of Shakespeare's *Much Ado About Nothing*. Ostensibly Sister Benedict represents a different educational

5. McDannell, "Introduction," *Catholics in the Movies*, 17, 14.

6. *Going My Way*, directed and written by Leo McCarey (my transcription from the film).

philosophy than Father O'Malley, but since Ingrid Bergman at her most lustrous was cast in the role of the nun, it is impossible that rivulets of erotic interest should not make themselves known, to the audience at least if not to Bing Crosby. That Ingrid Bergman and Bing Crosby would appeal to audiences as their secular selves is evident in the poster for *The Bells of St. Mary's*, which features both of them in civilian clothes although each wears clerical garb throughout the entire movie.

The church in the nineteen-forties needed to be made approachable, affable, normal and these Bing Crosby movies did help to make that change possible. Anthony Burke Smith has said that the change could even be called "a movie infatuation with Roman Catholicism" and "a veritable Catholicization of the American imagination in the middle years of the twentieth century," although I would emphasize the Catholic nature of the Father O'Malley films less than Smith.[7] Seventy years later, that approachable, affable, normal church has long since become stale, predictable, and collusive with the dominant culture. Bing Crosby tried to resurrect the priest role one more time, in 1959, in the film *Say One For Me*, and this time, the audience stayed away. By the sixties a completely different clerical character was called for.

In quick succession, in 1964 and 1965, actor Richard Burton made three powerful films that featured him as a priest of some sort: *Becket* and *The Night of the Iguana* in 1964 and *The Sandpiper* in 1965. Burton's choices of acting project, especially later in his career, were notoriously rash, partly because during his two marriages to Elizabeth Taylor they had a large family and entourage to support. (Burton's well-documented drinking problem also had a role in his bad decisions.) These three projects occurred during his most successful years; after the late sixties Burton was rarely cast in an acclaimed film. Although Burton's depiction of clerical character cannot be narrowed to such a precise type as Bing Crosby's celebrated priest, it is worth considering Burton's clerical movies as indicative of the sixties, just as Crosby's were indicative of the forties.

The Night of the Iguana and *The Sandpiper* are linked in their presentation of struggling Protestant pastors tempted by extramarital pleasures

7. Smith, *The Look of Catholics*, 1.

of the flesh, while *Becket* is different in its focus on a historical character, a legendary Catholic priest who moves from hedonism to sainthood. All three Burton movies, however, are similar in their emphasis on strong passion—passion so strong that in two of the films (*Becket* and *Iguana*) the viewer assuredly seeks for a more searing word: *fury* comes to mind. Even in the more modest *The Sandpiper* (which has never enjoyed the critical standing of the other films, although it is a good movie) the Reverend Edward Hewitt displays throughout a quiet agony and distinct spiritual unease that are riveting. In all these films Burton, one of the cleverest actors of his day, presents men of formidable intellectual ability who chafe at standard clerical roles, strain at conformist expectations, and demonstrate no small amount of pride and ambition. To focus on the place of sexual desire in these roles is too crude, as significant as desire is to the characters and to the plots. Equally important in these Burton portrayals is the presentation of ministry as exertion, even anguish. The church in the sixties would be severely tested by secular culture, and these Richard Burton movies demonstrate early on the critical challenges the church would have to face. Intriguingly, most mainstream cultural depictions of sixties-type counterculture upheaval would not actually appear until the seventies (*Easy Rider* is usually considered the vanguard counterculture film, and it was not released until 1969), but Burton encapsulates some of the turmoil early on.

The opening scene of John Huston's film of *The Night of the Iguana* differs significantly from the 1961 play by Tennessee Williams. Whereas all of Williams's play is set in nineteen-forties Mexico, which stands for a place both primitive and beautiful in its remoteness, Huston's version offers a dramatic overture explicitly showing us the crack-up in the United States of the Reverend T. Lawrence Shannon, as he loves to call himself. In a conventional sixties Episcopal church filled with establishment parishioners (shot in extreme close-up, making them look bug-eyed and malevolent), Shannon begins a sermon based on Proverbs 25:28: "He that hath no rule over his own spirit is like a city that is broken down, and without walls." He begins conventionally and calmly, asking "How many of us here can say: I rule my own spirit?" But soon he falters, and almost immediately is overcome with tremendous anger. The rest of his "sermon" is offered as a howl of outrage.

> All right! You know! That's why you're here. To see this city with
> its broken walls. Wherever two or three are gathered together

in my name is what the scripture says. But that's not why you're here. Let's change the words. Let's rewrite the order of the Morning Prayer. Wherever two or three or twenty or thirty or two hundred or three hundred are gathered together to make whispered comment, to sit in judgement upon . . . the condition of, of . . . what . . . of a man of God. I said man of God! And I mean it![8]

Although everyone knows that Shannon is involved in a sex scandal, Shannon goes on to rave, incoherently, on the nobility of his ancestry, both ecclesiastical and adventurous. When he gets to his adventurous ancestors, he becomes agitated.

Men with men's hearts! Wild and free hearts! Men! They knew hunger and they fed their appetites! They fed their appetites! Appetites that I have inherited! I defy you! Shannon defies you! Get out your tomahawks! Get out your scalping knives! Sharpen your scalping knives! Scalp me! I will not and cannot continue to conduct services in praise and worship of this angry, petulant old man in whom you believe. You turn your backs on the God of love and compassion and invent for yourself this cruel, senile, delinquent who blames the world and all that he created for his own faults. Close your windows. Close your doors. Close your hearts against the truth about God!

Descending from the pulpit, Shannon chases the already fleeing congregation out of the church building. Burton shouts most of this melodramatic speech in a richly sonorous monotone, looking crazed but also powerful and active.

This speech was fashioned by John Huston and the other screenwriter, Anthony Veiller, from frenzied reminiscences of his fall from grace that Shannon offers later in the stage version of *The Night of the Iguana*. Huston makes Shannon a more sympathetic mad clergyman than in Williams's original play. Tennessee Williams, for example, never provides Shannon with a reference to the "God of love." His Shannon instead offers a personal definition of God as "a terrific electric storm," also exemplified as "oblivious majesty."[9] The screenplay, on the other hand, allows Shannon to pronounce judgment on "man's inhumanity to God," declaring that "we've poisoned his world." Huston also provides a

8. *The Night of the Iguana*, directed by John Huston, adaptation by John Huston and Anthony Veiller (this and all subsequent quotation is my own transcription from the film).

9. Williams, *The Night of the Iguana*, 304–5.

supplementary scene of suffering and atonement for Shannon when he walks on broken glass, unmindful of the pain.

In the original play, the iguana is a symbol of wildness confined and distressed (it has been captured and tied up by two Mexican boys). Reading Tennessee Williams's play, one is struck by the aptness of the symbol for nearly all of the characters: the lusty and vulgar hotel owner Maxine, the virginal redemptive figure Hannah and her ancient grandfather Nonno, as well as Shannon himself. These characters are a mixture of deviance and geniality, but Williams strongly stresses their flaws. Huston emphasizes the characters' humane qualities, and generally makes everyone more sane and attractive. The film director encourages Burton to use his amazing presence, physical and vocal, to make Shannon's line of self-justifying, panicky claptrap seem feasible, almost majestic. At the end of the film, the iguana's escape from bondage is most discernibly Shannon's escape from restriction and guilt.

Burton's clergyman in *The Sandpiper* is a milder version of T. Lawrence Shannon. Similarly tempted by sex outside marriage and disgruntled by the conventionality of his role, Edward Hewitt differs in keeping a firm grip on his sanity, worrying about his obligations and responsibilities. This makes sense, given that *The Sandpiper* was directed by the relatively placid Vincente Minnelli as opposed to the intense John Huston.

Edward Hewitt, a cleric in charge of a parochial school, encounters the free-spirited, unmarried, artistic mother of a student (she happens to be the enthralling and very attractive Elizabeth Taylor) and has an affair with her. The affair is handled with delicacy, and poses a number of unexpected moral problems. Elizabeth Taylor's character, Laura Reynolds, represents vitality and joy: she brings the dry and dutiful minister back to an appreciation of the vibrancy of living, she opens his eyes to art and nature, and she is the most courageous person in the movie. She is a healthy, vigorous, admirable pagan and the church people look extremely dull alongside her. The symbolic creature at the heart of this movie is a sandpiper with a broken wing that Laura treats and brings back to health; as with the iguana, it does not take an extensive search to come up with the notion that Reverend Hewitt is the broken and pitiful creature who must be healed by Laura's exuberant, unrestrained love.

Hewitt is torn between his passion for Laura Reynolds and sense of duty to his wife Claire, played by an icy Eva Marie Saint. It must be admitted that *The Sandpiper* deals to an extent in clichés, but one scene in particular, during which the estranged husband and wife have a painful conversation about their marriage and shared ministry, moves beyond the predictable. The dilemma of the minister's wife—someone who has become an invisible and unglamorous partner in the daily drudgery of church work—is well delineated here. At the same time Edward Hewitt finally reveals his conviction that his life and ministry have become corrupt. This involves the obvious sin of adultery. But just as important, I think, is his shame that he has become a church manager, or as Eugene Peterson puts it, a "religious shopkeeper."[10] One of the traps this ministry couple in *The Sandpiper* has fallen into is that they have become fundraisers. As Hewitt says to his wife, "I'm a sloganeer, a keeper of the treasury." Claire Hewitt sees her own trawling for donations as stooping to "petty tasks and busy little trivialities" and she recalls their youthful sense of shared mission: "We were God's sweet fools. We were going to minister to the poor, live in perfect trust, one with another, to trace in our lives the gentle footsteps of Francis of Assisi."[11] *The Sandpiper* does not solve these disappointments and dilemmas at the end of the film but the three main characters are left, more or less, in their place of sorrow and uncertainty, which is refreshing.

In Hewitt's farewell sermon he thanks younger people for teaching him "reverence for life, no matter what form it takes. Reverence also for the needs of each individual and his right to move as swiftly along the path of enlightenment as his ability permits." This elegantly phrased countercultural injunction is supplemented by Hewitt's final statement, learned from Laura, that

> total adjustment to society is quite as bad as total maladjustment. That principled disobedience of unjust law is more Christian, more truly law-abiding, than unprincipled respect. That only freedom can tame the wild, rebellious, palpitating heart of man. Encagement, never. That life, unfettered, moves towards life. And love, to love. That in the full blaze of God's cleansing sunlight, men and women are purely innocent, and therefore most purely beautiful.

10. Peterson, *Working the Angles*, 1.

11. *The Sandpiper*, directed by Vincente Minnelli, written by Dalton Trumbo and Michael Wilson (this and all subsequent quotation is my own transcription from the film).

All of the Richard Burton clerical movies, with remarkable effectiveness, prompt the viewer to ask what a pastor is for. In *The Night of the Iguana* and *The Sandpiper* the ministers have succumbed to unsuitable sexual desire as well as personal ambition and arrogance; they become estranged from their congregations and neglect the worship of God. The outsized nature of the minister's personality in *Iguana* and *Sandpiper* is more of a problem than the adultery, and the pressure to conform to a stale institutional church has wreaked havoc with whatever good impulses these clergymen once had. It may be easy to blame Edward Hewitt in *The Sandpiper* for shallowness, in allowing himself to become a fund-raiser for a building project, but the fact that such building projects recur in film after film—in American cinema in any case—indicates that the building project is not such a simple issue after all. The need to have a bigger, better church building (or sometimes parochial school) is a feature of a large number of movies about clerical characters; *Boys' Town*, *The Bishop's Wife*, *The Preacher's Wife*, *Going My Way*, and *The Bells of St. Mary's* all revolve around this plot point. The sin that believing the church is a building is one of the easiest to fall into, and one of the most debilitating problems congregations can face. *The Sandpiper* realizes this. *(Going My Way* does not.) Ultimately *The Sandpiper* can be appreciated for its presentation of an intelligent pastor who struggles with many of the same issues as everyone else, and who honestly is trying to serve God in addition to finding personal fulfillment and happiness. That insistence that personal fulfillment and service to God might be combined is refreshing.

Richard Burton's role in *Becket* precisely delineates the widely-held opposing view about the clergy: that worldly happiness and spiritual duty are miles apart. Thomas Becket's friend and eventual enemy, King Henry II, puts Becket's youthful character well: "He's read books, you know, it's amazing. He's drunk and wenched his way through London but he's thinking all the time."[12] Eventually Becket will resist the worldly charms of being chancellor and archbishop and tell the king "you have introduced me to deeper obligations." As I said in my discussion of *Becket* in chapter 1, this story to a certain extent presents the skirmish between church and state as a power struggle rather than a religious one: a test of wills between two strong individuals. But if we focus on Richard Burton's performance more than on Jean Anouilh's play (or Edward Anhalt's English version),

---

12. Anouilh, *Becket*, directed by Peter Glenville, English adaptation by Edward Anhalt (this and all subsequent quotation is my own transcription from the film).

we can see that being made archbishop gives Becket, unexpectedly and suddenly, true happiness. Burton allows Becket's personality to expand and exude confidence and fulfillment in the church years. It should be ridiculous that a man who is not even a priest should be made arch-bishop—and it is—but almost immediately Burton's Becket completely inhabits the role, relishing it. When he gives away all his possessions to the poor, he turns to God in a casual, joyous prayer:

> Dear Lord, I wish there were something I really regretted part-ing with so that I might offer it to you. But forgive me Lord, it's like going on a holiday. I've never enjoyed myself so much in my whole life. Lord, are you sure you're not laughing at me? It all seems far too easy.

The scene in *Becket* that everyone remembers—and is, in my opin-ion, the best reason for watching the film—is Burton's marvelous per-formance of the excommunication scene. The king's man, Gilbert, has killed a priest, and Becket wants justice; the king is protecting Gilbert. Becket responds with excommunication for Lord Gilbert, which the king expects is inconsequential. Instead, the excommunication erupts with awful intensity and force. The language of the scene is largely accurate for a true excommunication, but Richard Burton makes the act utterly his own. His face is set in hardness, his eyes unmoving and pitiless.

> We do here and now separate him from the precious body and blood of Christ and from the society of all Christians. We ex-clude him from our Holy Mother Church and all her sacraments in heaven or on earth. We declare him excommunicate and anathema. We cast him into the outer darkness. We judge him damned with the devil and his fallen angels and all the reprobate to eternal fire and everlasting pain.

It is clear after this powerful scene that Becket will do anything for the church. No sacrifice will be too great.

In *The Night of the Iguana*, Reverend Shannon's key word is *fantastic*. When Shannon mutters this to himself repetitively he is trying to differ-entiate and judge the gap between the real and fantasy. It might have been preferable for Tennessee Williams to use another word, since fantastic has too many connotations that get in the way of understanding what Shannon needs to express. Shannon sees the world of people as they are and then glimpses the realm of people as they should be and the differ-ence is painful. Richard Burton's movie priests excel at demonstrating the gaps, strains, wounds, and frustrations of the clerical personality. It is not so much the life or the duties that frustrate, but the pressures on human character. It is telling that in each of Burton's films the priest leaves the ministry and that this leavetaking does not happen in the confines of a church office with the writing of a careful letter but instead happens, dramatically, in the worship space itself. Becket leaves the ministry unwillingly, stabbed to death near the altar by agents of a king who could not bear to be opposed. In *The Sandpiper* and *The Night of the Iguana* the two priests use the pulpit as the place to announce their separation from the church, and the fact that they use the worship space for this dramatic announcement communicates that they do not, in fact, want to leave, but feel compelled to do so by forces outside of themselves. In all three movies the expression on Richard Burton's face during these scenes is similar—his character is unwilling to relinquish a vocation that he truly loves.

9

Clergy Wives and Daughters

The Concealed Collar

He must manage his own household well, keeping his children submissive and respectful in every way—for if someone does not know how to manage his own household, how can he take care of God's church? (1 Tim 3:4–5)

> *Agnes: Brand!*
> *Brand:* I love you.
> *Agnes:* Your love is hard.
> *Brand:* Too hard?
> *Agnes:* Do not ask. I follow where you lead.
> *Brand:* You are my wife, and I have the right to demand
> That you devote yourself wholly to our calling. (Henrik Ibsen, *Brand*)[1]

For centuries, if women desired a place in the leadership of the church, the limitations were obvious. Roman Catholic women could have a distinct, if subordinate, place in their hierarchy, but for Protestants, the opportunities were few. Certainly women could find a place in music or children's ministries, often on a volunteer basis. For most of the twentieth century it was possible to enter the diaconal ministry in many Methodist, Presbyterian, and Lutheran churches. In 1936, the United Church of Canada, the largest Protestant denomination in Canada, ordained its first

---

1. Ibsen, *Brand*, 76.

woman, Lydia Gruchy, for a ministry of word and sacrament, and in subsequent decades other mainstream churches around the world gradually accepted female leadership. The situation for conservative evangelicals has varied widely, particularly since many of these churches are independent and not governed through national or international bodies. But as recently as 1994 the Southern Baptist Convention, the largest Protestant denomination in the United States, decided that the only step it was willing to take was to allow local jurisdictions to make their own decrees about the ordination of women.[2]

There is a strong literary and cinematic tradition exploring the lives of nuns; the cultural analysis of fictional nuns is an exceptional situation that needs more attention than I can offer here. For Protestant women, until quite recently the closest approach to church leadership has been as the wife or a daughter of a clergyman, and the literary and cinematic record follows suit. There are many significant cultural representations of these very specific clergy situations—one thinks of the ambitious wives in Anthony Trollope's clerical novels—and while the clergy wife in these works is sometimes in accord with her husband, performing significant ministry tasks herself or at least acquiescing gracefully, many other depictions convey frustration and resentment. In more than a few cases, there is a strange "secret" ministry of the wife that is more authentic than the husband's efforts, and in several spectacular instances there is defiance, insurrection, or ruination. This chapter will consider a range of literary depictions of women who are connected with the pulpit at one remove. These wives and daughters are associated with a man of the cloth and share in the joys and frustrations of that work, while experiencing in addition a distinctive set of joys and frustrations known only to clergy-women of this very peculiar sort.

Happy and Fulfilled

In Eugene Peterson's 2011 memoir, *The Pastor,* we learn intriguing things about this well-known pastor, writer, and teacher—but we learn *amazing* things about what ministry has meant for his wife. Before he met her, in the fifties, Jan Peterson had "prayed for a vocation as a pastor's wife."[3] Eugene Peterson at the time was not especially interested in a call to min-

2. Christensen, "Chronology of Women's Ordination."
3. Peterson, *The Pastor,* 18.

istry, but he then entered the field partly for love of her. Presbyterian women could be ordained starting in 1956, and the Petersons married in 1958. But it was still unusual for women to enter the ministry and there was a strong preference for female clergy to be unmarried. The employment situation for women in the church today is vastly improved. But would ordination ever have been desirable for Jan Peterson? Eugene Peterson writes that Jan's particular ministry as a clergy wife

> meant participation in an intricate web of hospitality, living at the intersection of human need and God's grace, inhabiting a community where men and women who didn't fit were welcomed, where neglected children were noticed, where the stories of Jesus were told, and people who had no stories found that they did have stories, stories that were part of the Jesus story. Being a pastor's wife would place her strategically yet unobtrusively at a heavily trafficked intersection between heaven and earth.[4]

According to her husband, Jan Peterson has been a joyful and willing participant in this volunteer ministry, or (if you will) a co-minister with him. At the heart of Eugene Peterson's description of his wife's gifts is *hospitality*. Freed from most administrative tasks and unburdened by a formal job description or supervisory council, Jan could invent her own ministry. Eugene Peterson is insistent that we understand her commitment to hospitality in a profound, even radical sense. He is disposed to say that Jan's work has been more fruitful than his, her faith more grounded. For Jan Peterson, the informal and neighborly character of her work has been essential. If *hospitality* is the most important defining word here, then *unobtrusive* may be the next most important.

> If Jan had to give a name to what she was doing, it would probably be something on the order of "hanging around this intersection between heaven and earth and seeing what there is to be done." But she would never have described it as "church work."[5]

It is unusual for a clergy wife to appear so satisfied with this unofficial conception of her activities. As a pastor's wife myself, with an individual career of my own, I came to this section of *The Pastor* and flinched. I had to leave off reading and contemplate my reaction; later I could more patiently return to the book and consider Jan Peterson's vocation. Part

4. Ibid., 95.
5. Ibid., 194.

of my frustration involves the *unobtrusive* nature of such a ministry. As George Eliot says about the "unhistoric acts" of women—many of them like pastoral acts—at the conclusion of *Middlemarch,* "that things are not so ill with you and me as they might have been, is half owing to the number who lived faithfully a hidden life, and rest in unvisited tombs."[6] Eliot's sentence is known for its ambiguous conjunction of praise and regret, and its recognition of the mixed blessing that is the semi-invisibility of a woman's work. (Attend to the complex nuances involved in the phrases "not so ill," "half owing," and "hidden life" in Eliot's sentence.) Yet Jan Peterson's would seem to be the experience of a clergy spouse at its best: fulfilling, valuable, and valued. And the fact that she does not crave recognition and praise is refreshing and salutary, at least to some degree.

One is tempted to say that such happy experiences over the generations must have been rare. But that statement is too glib. The contented and fulfilled type occurs, to an extent, in Anthony Trollope's *The Warden*; Archdeacon Grantly and his wife Susan discuss parish affairs most efficiently and happily in bed, where he listens carefully to her counsels "though he considered himself entitled to give counsel to every other being whom he met" and where she, amusingly, continues to address him as "archdeacon."[7] In Charles Dickens's *Our Mutual Friend*, when the minister Mr. Milvey is consulted by the Boffins about adopting an orphan, the minister immediately calls in his wife and they embark upon a careful consultation of worthy candidates. And in Oliver Goldsmith's *The Vicar of Wakefield*—a book whose volatile ironic tones must be handled with care—the beginning of the book is dominated by a portrayal of the vicar's idyllic marriage.

> To do her justice, she was a good-natured notable woman; and as for breeding, there were few country ladies who could shew more. She could read any English book without much spelling, but for pickling, preserving, and cookery, none could excel her.[8]

When Dr. Primrose, the vicar, informs us disingenuously that their "year was spent in moral or rural amusements; in visiting our rich neighbours, and relieving such as were poor," the reader must decide whether this is an innocent novel of sentiment or a more mixed mode of literature,

6. Eliot, *Middlemarch*, 838.
7. Trollope, *The Warden*, 11.
8. Goldsmith, *The Vicar of Wakefield*, 1.

involving satire and scorn. (I have analyzed the Primrose situation more fully in chapter 3.)

The happy, fulfilled clergy spouse is most often found in the pages of mass market or escapist literature. The Steeple Hill imprint of the Harlequin romance empire and several other publishers offer inspirational romances, an unapologetically wholesome category of fiction that caters to conservative Christian readers. A startlingly popular sub-genre of the inspirational romance is the pastor romance, with a number involving the additional sub-genre of the murder mystery. In the past five years there have been titles like *Too Little, Too Late* by Victoria Christopher Murray and *A Matter of Wife and Death* by Ginger Kolbaba, all of them catalogued in my local library as "Spouses of clergy—Fiction." For example, Steeple Hill's title *The Maverick Preacher* by Victoria Bylin (2009) features the handsome Joshua Blue, a preacher who needs to learn humility and discovers it at the hands of beautiful, stubborn Adie. "She loved this man. She wanted to feed him and kiss him and bind up his wounds, except she couldn't give him what he needed most—a woman who shared his faith."[9] *The Preacher's Wife* by Cheryl St. John (2009) offers a companionable marriage between two widowed (and attractive) adults. Samuel Hart is a minister who asks Josie to marry him so that his children can have a mother; she is seeking a life's work with value and significance. Reverend Hart kneels to pray before having marital relations with Josie; the plot turns on the axis of duty and responsibility until Josie discovers that "strong and tender" feelings have arisen.[10] A more literary version of this type is *This Fine Life* by Eva Marie Everson (2010), a title from the Baker Publishing Group, a Christian press in Grand Rapids, Michigan. Mariette is a spoiled child of the middle class who as a teenager falls in love with and marries Thayne Scott, to be dismayed when Thayne declares his intention to enter the ministry after a year of marriage.

In all these inspirational romances there are slight tensions between clergy husband and wife (more fully developed in the Everson novel) that are, in the end, easily and conclusively resolved by the husband's more expressive dealings with his wife added to the wife's acceptance of the sovereignty of God in her own life. This satisfied female acceptance of a peaceful coexistence with God and pastor husband generally revolves around the pleasures of motherhood and a modest amount of enthusiastic

9. Bylin, *The Maverick Preacher*, 205.
10. St. John, *The Preacher's Wife*, 157.

community service. I will say little more about this sub-genre of clergy fiction, beyond the observations that, first, the rapidly growing popularity of these series would be scope for intriguing sociological research (there being too little literary merit to warrant further attention in my present study), and, second, that most of these stories can only succeed because they are historical fiction—the St. John and Bylin stories are set in the nineteenth century and the Everson book in the nineteen-sixties.

These titles are akin to the influential movie *A Man Called Peter* (1955), with Richard Todd as the Presbyterian preaching marvel Peter Marshall, based on the 1951 memoir by Marshall's wife Catherine. Catherine Marshall worshiped Peter Marshall, and the success of biography and movie—the book sold millions and was one of the key American titles of the mid-century—should not be underestimated when considering the consequences for an entire generation of clergy wives (and for women who were inculcated by Catherine Marshall to conceive of marriage to a clergyman as an exalted ideal). Both sentimental biography and hagiographic movie put considerable distance between the man in the pulpit and the woman in the pew. I use those gendered nouns deliberately, as this is precisely the active/passive binary enacted. In scene after scene Peter Marshall stands in authority, looking down on the attentive wife who is delighted to be saturated with his wisdom. Catherine Marshall's book is full of sententious descriptions like this one: "Into our marriage came an ever-deepening fusion of heart and mind . . . the most melodious harmony there is."[11] *A Man Called Peter* is wholesome, unquestioning, unrealistic, dull, and probably still comforting for many contemplating the facts of clergy marriage even today. The misplaced veneration for the male minister that is the central tenet of that movie rips at the fabric of Christian purpose.

Clergy Daughters: Frivolity or Exploitation

Before carrying on to literary categories of clergy wife other than the happily fulfilled or acquiescent, we should take in a sub-category of women twice removed from clerical power: the daughters. This is a small assembly, and that is just as well, as it is a depressing one. For example, it is not as credible that a team ministry could be envisioned for a clergy daughter, as it just might be with a wife; a daughter until recently would

11. Marshall, *A Man Called Peter*, 248.

automatically be expected to serve several steps behind a pastor, not at his side. (Sisters are in a similar position. One such clerical adjunct can be found in *The African Queen,* the novel by C. S. Forester and the film by John Huston. The missionary's sister, Rose Sayer, played memorably by Katharine Hepburn in the film, enters the story as a dutiful, inhibsited helpmeet. However, she undergoes a transformation, becoming independent, passionate, and fearless. In Huston's film, at any rate, Rose Sayer must abandon her half-clerical identity in order to become truly alive.) The clerical daughter with an inclination toward ministry has an uphill struggle to be taken seriously; it is no wonder that the standard trope invoked is a girl who instead is egocentric, troublemaking, even promiscuous. If we ponder the daughters of Mr. Brocklehurst in Charlotte Brontë's *Jane Eyre* we find that their entire accomplishment is to devote themselves to the acquisition of finery and social position. We see this often in the clergy daughters of Margaret Oliphant's and Anthony Trollope's novels.

But there are clergy daughters in literature who devote their lives to their father's ministries; the paradigmatic case is Dorothy Hare in George Orwell's *A Clergyman's Daughter.* Published in 1936, Orwell's novel, surprising as it may seem, examines an individual learning to survive after a devastating loss of faith. And although Orwell was known to be a committed socialist, not a Christian, Dorothy's passage from faith to atheism is shown to be exceedingly painful: "And yet after all—and here lay the trouble—she *was* the same girl. Beliefs change, thoughts change, but there is some inner part of the soul that does not change. Faith vanishes, but the need for faith remains the same as before."[12] In addition to investigating the dilemma of unbelief, *A Clergyman's Daughter* allows Orwell to plunge a female character into the world of indigence he himself experienced and reported in *The Road to Wigan Pier* and *Down and Out in Paris and London.* These two elements—the portrayal of painful unbelief and the female experience of Depression-era poverty and vagrancy—are the most important facets of Orwell's book. But an additional feature of interest is Orwell's description of the exploitation of a clergy daughter in the Church of England.

Dorothy Hare is the only child of a widowed Church of England rector, Charles Hare. "Unable to afford a curate, he left the dirty work of the parish entirely to his wife, and after her death (she died in 1921) to

12. Orwell, *A Clergyman's Daughter,* 315.

Dorothy."[13] Hare, due to unsuitable investments, has acquired large debts but Dorothy is the one who suffers because of these debts. She is expected to run her father's household without adequate means, and her father ignores her distress. She does a cheerless and endless round of parish tasks for which she receives little or no thanks. Orwell's outlandish plot solution for Dorothy's dilemma is to provide her with amnesia. The trauma of her miserable life causes her to lose her identity, and she spends a year wandering England in harsh circumstances. She becomes an itinerant hop-picker, a beggar, and finally (in an "elevation" of status once her family in some measure recovers her) a teacher in a ghastly school suggestive of Dickens.

The absurdity of Orwell's scenario aside, Dorothy's story is poignant and frightening. Even when she is "safe" at home in the rectory, at the novel's beginning and end, the atmosphere of petty tragedy is, in its way, as upsetting as the apparently more devastating situation of starvation and homelessness in the novel's mid-section. Here is a typical day in Dorothy's existence as a clergyman's daughter:

> "Visiting," because of the distances she had to bicycle from house to house, took up nearly half of Dorothy's day. Every day of her life, except on Sundays, she made from half a dozen to a dozen visits at parishioners' cottages. She penetrated into cramped interiors and sat on lumpy, dust-diffusing chairs gossiping with overworked, blowsy housewives; she spent hurried half-hours giving a hand with the mending and the ironing, and read chapters from the Gospels, and readjusted bandages on "bad legs" and condoled with sufferers from morning-sickness; she played ride a cock-horse with sour-smelling children who grimed the bosom of her dress with their sticky little fingers; she gave advice about ailing aspidistras, and suggested names for babies, and drank "nice cups of tea" innumerable—for the working women always wanted her to have a "nice cup of tea," out of a teapot endlessly stewing.
>
> Much of it was profoundly discouraging work.[14]

After reading Orwell's staggering catalogue of tedious duties the reader should experience a distinct sensation of being winded. Dorothy's life is exhausting. But how beneficial is her work? The euphemistic

13. Ibid., 23.
14. Ibid., 56–57.

phrases in quotation marks (*visiting, bad legs, nice cup of tea*) highlight the lack of honesty or profundity in this daily round. This is not to say that Dorothy's tasks are pointless; they are tasks necessary to Christian ministry. The problem here is twofold: she has no partner in her work (her father cannot be bothered with such duties) and she is unpaid. Dorothy, whose spirit has been surviving on a blurring of the boundaries between nature-worship and Christianity, suffers a crisis of religious apprehension when she realizes she is only able to believe in God in the presence of sunlight or the pleasant scent of favorite plants.

Orwell's novel has never been popular. One reason must be that Dorothy is left in a more cruel position at the novel's end than she was at the beginning. She is performing the same parish tasks, apparently willingly, but she no longer believes in God. She convinces herself that "faith and no faith are very much the same provided that one is doing what is customary, useful and acceptable." Dorothy is not unintelligent, and she has at least one friend who protests her acquiescence to "years of calculated hypocrisy."[15] But she cannot conceive a way out of her situation; more devastating is that she does not care to.

Rebellion: Comic and Tragic

The exploitation and loss that Dorothy experiences in *A Clergyman's Daughter* bring to mind the striking words of Catherine Mumford Booth (founder, with her husband William Booth, of the Salvation Army). In her 1859 work *Female Ministry: A Woman's Right to Preach the Gospel*, Booth writes bitterly of the misapplication of scripture in regard to a woman's place in the church (most famously, the injunction in 1 Corinthians 14:34 for women to "keep silence in the churches"). This misapplication, says Booth, "has resulted in more loss to the Church, evil to the world, and dishonour to God, than any of the errors we have already referred to." Over 150 years ago, Booth could see that this suppression of female capability guaranteed that the hard work and devout service that Christian women naturally wanted to offer would be unacknowledged and unappreciated, their generosity taken advantage of.

> We cannot be blind to the supreme selfishness of making her
> so welcome to the hidden toil and self-sacrifice, the hewing
> of wood and the drawing of water, the watching and waiting,

15. Ibid., 319, 307.

the reproach and persecution attaching to her Master's service, without allowing her a tittle of the honour which He has attached to the ministration of His gospel. Here, again, man's theory and God's order are at variance.[16]

There are several types of clerical wife in fiction who rebel against the limitations and frustrations of their lives and marriages. One common type rebels for our entertainment and is a staple of literary comedy. In one of P. G. Wodehouse's clergy stories, a curate's fiancée, feeling obliged to "take a few pints of soup to the deserving poor," nevertheless mutters saucily that it is "amazing the way these bimbos absorb soup. Like sponges."[17] Another comic rebel is Griselda in Agatha Christie's first Miss Marple novel, *The Murder at the Vicarage*. She is the young and "most distractingly pretty" wife of the narrator, Reverend Leonard Clement:

> She is incompetent in every way and extremely trying to live with. She treats the parish as a kind of huge joke arranged for her amusement. I have endeavored to form her mind and failed. I am more than ever convinced that celibacy is desirable for the clergy. I have frequently hinted as much to Griselda, but she has only laughed.

Clement almost immediately gives up trying to form Griselda for her proper role. Asked early in the novel what she will be doing with her afternoon, Griselda's capricious response is "My duty as the Vicaress. Tea and scandal at four-thirty."[18] Griselda persists throughout the novel as a force of natural vitality and unadorned truthfulness. Although the Clement marriage is, I think, an eventual success, Leonard Clement's perturbed comment that "celibacy is desirable for the clergy" is indicative of a theme that runs through much fiction involving Church of England clerics. One sees this frequently in the novels of Barbara Pym. Her clerics are often attractive and desired by the women of the parish, but they are better off unmarried. Even when they are married, enough havoc is created that celibacy is invoked as the ideal. I wonder if many disordered clergy marriages in fiction can be attributed to wistful advocacy for the Apostle Paul's ostensibly undistracted state: "it is well for them to remain unmarried as I am" (1 Cor 7:8).

16. Booth, *Female Ministry*, 23, 14–15.
17. Wodehouse, *Clergy Omnibus*, 87.
18. Christie, *The Murder at the Vicarage*, 2, 5.

Alan Bennett, in his 1988 play *Bed Among the Lentils*, in the *Talking Heads* series of dramas (monologues written for venerable members of the British theater establishment, in this case Maggie Smith), offers an amusingly unhappy clergy wife named Susan.

> One of the unsolved mysteries of life, or the unsolved mysteries of my life, is why the vicar's wife is expected to go to church at all. A barrister's wife doesn't have to go to court, an actor's wife isn't at every performance, so why have I always got to be on parade? Not to mention the larger question of whether one believes in God in the first place. It's assumed that being the vicar's wife one does but the question had never actually come up, not with Geoffrey anyway. I can understand why, of course. To look at me, the hair, the flat chest, the wan smile, you'd think I was just cut out for God. And maybe I am. I'd just like to have been asked that's all. Not that it matters of course. So long as you can run a tight jumble sale you can believe in what you like.[19]

Susan has become, accidentally, a rebel, and an unrepentant one. To compensate for her husband's insensitivity, her disappointment in the church, and the exasperations inherent in the parish flower rota, Susan has turned to alcohol. When she feels the need to drive furtively to another town to buy sherry, she patronizes the shop of a handsome young Hindu man, and they embark on an affair. At the end of the play, Susan is attending Alcoholics Anonymous, but not because her husband has discovered her secrets. Susan's lover, Ramesh Ramesh, has commented sadly on her inebriation and this has propelled her to seek help. Geoffrey remains oblivious about Susan's life and instead capitalizes on Susan's newfound sobriety in his sermons and parish prayers. "The mileage in it is endless," she says.

> I've caught the other young, upwardly mobile parsons sneaking looks at me now and again and you can see them thinking why weren't they smart enough to marry an alcoholic or better still a drug addict, problem wives whom they could do a nice redemption job on, right there on their own doorstep.[20]

Bennett's play is a humorous glance at a distinctive predicament for clergy wives (and, in recent years, clergy spouses). The clergy wife is expected to replicate her husband's attributes and beliefs; she was also, until recently,

---

19. Bennett, *Bed Among the Lentils*, 3.
20. Ibid., 13.

expected to contribute a handsome share of her time to congregational duties. The notion that a clergy spouse might want to exercise independence in opinion and occupation has been unusual enough that the resultant tension provides an automatic situation for comedy or highly charged drama.

We can see this in the television show *The Book of Daniel*, the short-lived NBC drama in which the Episcopal minister's wife, Judith, is rarely seen without her comforting martini glass in hand. But one of the most powerful depictions of an unhappy clergy marriage has been Joanna Trollope's *The Rector's Wife*, a novel immediately popular on its release in 1991 and even more so after a successful 1994 television movie starring Lindsay Duncan. According to *The Independent*, Trollope's novel sold 750,000 copies in the nineties alone,[21] making *The Rector's Wife* perhaps the most influential portrayal of a clergy marriage since *A Man Called Peter*.

The portrayal is a grim one as it relates to Peter Bouverie, the rector in question. Peter is in charge of a five point rural parish in England; he and his wife Anna have three children and are impoverished, wearing clothes donated to church jumble sales. Anna does translation work of a tedious nature at home to supplement their income. They are told by the powerful members of the parish that a working clergy wife is unacceptable, so Peter wants her to take on work that can be "invisible." When Peter fails to win a recommendation for an archdeacon's seat he becomes increasingly dull and embittered.

> There is no gaiety in Peter, she thought, bending her face to the wafer, no real pleasure in living, just an anxious shrinking from everything except duty; obligation has become his Rule, he clings to it, it stops him drowning. The communion wafer glued itself to the roof of her mouth.[22]

In part because they need the money and in part to assert her independence, Anna takes a job as a grocery clerk, even though the foremost member in their parish tells her such a job is "out of the question." Anna is fed up with "clergy wife" functioning as "a separate category of human being"; she notes in exasperation that women of her village speak and act

---

21. Thackray, "Best Selling Books."
22. Trollope, *The Rector's Wife*, 12, 37.

differently when she approaches, "as if she were a headmistress. But she was worse than a headmistress; she was the Rector's wife."[23]

The narrative is emotionally skewed toward Anna's predicament. She is vivacious and honest; Peter is evasive and defeatist. At the book's climax Anna has decided to leave Peter as a result of a serious of domestic betrayals. He has sided against Anna with the parish "groupies"—the women who crave opportunities to serve the rector—and he has forced Anna's resignation from the grocery store. Before she can leave Peter, he dies in a car crash, almost certainly a suicidal act, and Anna is liberated into a new existence that may or may not involve the church. It is unlikely, however, that the church will play a large role in her new life.

Although her own husband has not been able to recognize her predicament, one of Peter's fellow clerics easily notices Anna's exasperation throughout the book. He says, "It's an assumption—and not a generous assumption—that not only is a clergy wife expected to live by almost exaggerated standards of rectitude, but that she is somehow immune to the devices and desires of all other human hearts."[24] Trollope takes the well-known phrase from *The Book of Common Prayer*—"We have followed too much the devices and desires of our own hearts"—and overturns its confessional intention. For Anna to be a fulfilled and useful human being, following the devices and desires of her own heart is precisely what is called for. Her uncertainty, muddled humility, and risk-taking are admirable. The devices and desires of her very human heart, Trollope indicates, would actually have made Anna the better rector, because she has courage and an instinct for personal relationships that her despondent husband never demonstrated.

Early in the book, the narrator compares Anna's faith with Peter's. Peter has asserted that he is the religious professional and his decisions are not to be questioned. Her religious impulses are squashed and derided; she is directed toward quiet and dutiful service. But Anna's wondering and questioning offers a marked contrast to Peter's dullness.

> Anxiously, Anna had sometimes wondered if Peter had lost his faith. As for herself, she was uncertain she had ever had any, and yet, for all that, she sometimes joyfully felt that she knew what it was about.[25]

23. Ibid., 69, 32, 7.
24. Ibid., 139–40.
25. Ibid., 25.

The Woman Wears the Collar

Although the comparative aspect of *The Rector's Wife* is not a major premise in the novel—Anna's need for freedom and passion is more prominent—the clerical wife who in fact has the real talent for ministry can be seen in a number of works. The husband has status and the wife is unpaid, but as far as authentic and vital ministry goes, the reader or viewer has weighed the husband in the balance and found him wanting. An example of this type is the harsh minister in George Roy Hill's 1966 film *Hawaii*, played by Max von Sydow. He is a dry defender of tradition for its own sake, a man profoundly repressive of creativity, freedom, and sensuality. He is arrogant and sanctimonious, in love with the law. Although Von Sydow's Reverend Abner Hale considers himself unquestionably "God's instrument on earth," throughout the movie it is his wife Jeruscha (Julie Andrews) who is the authentic exemplar of Christian conduct.[26] Over and over Jeruscha has to teach Abner compassion, and sometimes he unbends. But it does not take hold, and later his wife has to teach him again. Abner is not completely despicable: he shows himself to be vulnerable and capable of some remorse. But ultimately he is a pastor of the law, and not of love. His sort closes doors, pronounces judgments, denies hope.

A more hopeful and humorous depiction of this kind of clergy marriage appears in the 1947 movie *The Bishop's Wife* and its 1996 remake *The Preacher's Wife*. In each movie the cleric has become distracted away from the most important aspects of being a man of God; both Bishop Henry Brougham (1947) and Pastor Henry Biggs (1996) have become busy, somber administrators with fundraising for new buildings as their primary endeavor. While the husband wanders, lost in the moral disarray that building projects can become, the wife carries on in her loving way. She manages the household, cares for people, preserves friendships, observes needs, and is willing to enjoy and learn and bend. With the help of a good-looking angel, the marriage is mended and church work is set back on the right path of providing meaningful worship and tending to the needs of the community. The wife in each of these movies does not, interestingly, need the reminders that the angel is sent to bring. She has never strayed.

26. *Hawaii*, directed by George Roy Hill, written by Dalton Trumbo and Daniel Taradash.

In this category, one of the fullest and strangest theatrical portrayals of a clergy marriage comes unexpectedly from George Bernard Shaw, an iconoclast with little patience for organized religion or conventional ethical thought. It is probably the distinct weirdness of Shaw's thinking that makes him so percipient about the future of marriage in his 1898 play *Candida*. Decades ahead of its time in its proposals about female individuality and marital honesty, Shaw's play is, however, awkward for today's feminists to embrace because of the way Candida, his strong female character, insists on submitting to male mastery and tending male weakness, at least to a degree. Candida is rather like Barbara in Shaw's *Major Barbara*, who swings strangely from assertive leader to feminine bystander concerned with homemaking and children. When reading or watching Shaw we have to grapple with his idiosyncratic conception of human will, or the life force, usually embodied in women, rather as we have to grapple with his idiosyncratic punctuation. Shaw's women are certainly strong and intelligent, but his idea of what they are ultimately good for is strangely constrained: usually he sees them as an animating force to get the world peopled and improved. His women and his men are bound in tight and odd relation to each other—often not erotic so much as procreative and motivational—and it is a commonplace of Shaw criticism to note that his people do not behave and talk like real people at all. They are provocateurs, symbols. He called himself a battering ram; one critic has called him "much less an artist or a philosopher than an intense rhetorician."[27]

In this play the marriage of the Morells, James and Candida, has been happy and successful. He is a popular Christian socialist preacher and she appears contented in her role as adored wife, mother, muse, and manager. In Act One, James Morell holds out their marriage to his curate, Lexy, as an ideal: "Ah, my boy, get married: get married to a good woman; and then youll understand. Thats a foretaste of what will be best in the Kingdom of Heaven we are trying to establish on earth."[28] We know even before Candida arrives on the stage that she is the central force in this parson's house. Her beauty is renowned, the minor characters are obsessed with her, and her husband responds with "everybody loves her: they cant help it" (149) after a young admirer, Eugene Marchbanks,

---

27. Carpenter, "The Quintessence of Shaw's Ethical Position," 492.

28. Shaw, *Candida*, 137 (with Shaw's idiosyncratic punctuation). References to subsequent passages are given parenthetically.

declares his passion for her. Shaw's description of Candida in the stage directions of Act One is fascinating: the cornerstone of her character, he writes, is "maternal indulgence," but he also insists on her serenity, courage, largeness of mind, dignity of character, and—importantly—capability of manipulating people for selfish ends (144).

This play turns from a general examination of marriage to a specific examination of clergy marriage when Candida is called upon to choose between a parson and a poet, or, if you like, a man of principles and a man (really, a boy) of passion. Eugene Marchbanks claims her for the forces of passion, asserting that as a vicar's wife she has been "fed on metaphors, sermons, stale perorations, mere rhetoric" (151). Ultimately, since Shaw is less interested in the church than in his own ethical system involving the strength of the human will, Candida's ties to the church are revealed to be less significant than her perceived need to take care of the man who needs her most. The one that needs her most is, surprisingly, the prosperous Morell rather than the immature Marchbanks. However, en route to the typically thorny Shavian conclusion (where the Morells embrace but the audience wonders what model of marriage they have just been convinced to fall for) there are some dazzling speeches on the nature of clergy marriage.

> Why must you go out every night lecturing and talking? I hardly have one evening a week with you. Of course what you say is all very true; but it does no good: they dont mind what you say to them one little bit. They think they agree with you; but whats the use of their agreeing with you if they go and do just the opposite of what you tell them the moment your back is turned? Look at your congregation at St. Dominic's! Why do they come to hear you talking about Christianity every Sunday? Why, just because theyve been so full of business and money-making for six days that they want to forget all about it and have a rest on the seventh; so that they can go back fresh and make money harder than ever! You positively help them at it instead of hindering them. (163)

Candida, it turns out, has been (and will continue to be) fully supportive of a pastoral enterprise that she ultimately thinks is foolhardy or, even worse, duplicitous. Candida is committed enough to this ministry to state that Morell's words are "true" but she is sharp enough to notice that few social or moral improvements ensue. To a certain extent Shaw is here criticizing the mixture of socialism and religion in Morell's character;

as a keen Fabian and atheist Shaw preferred his politics unsullied with
Christian complication. Morell is in over his head, attempting to create
an egalitarian Christian society to which Shaw cannot assent. However, I
agree with William Irvine that it is a mistake to see Morell as too much of
a fool. Candida's love for Morell only makes sense, Irvine says, if "he has
been, in some respects at least, stronger and wiser than she."[29]

Candida's speeches about the challenges of her life and the problematic, even counterproductive, nature of Morell's Christian socialist
ministry do not indicate any interest in renouncing it. These are just the
sort of challenges that Shaw's characters relish, so that they may defiantly
continue their sometimes irrational exertions. And ultimately Candida
proves right Morell's naïve assertion in Act One: their marriage is a foretaste of heavenly harmony. But that is not because they are perfectly
happy or perfectly suited. Their partnership involves his fall and her rise;
his weakness, admitted so movingly in his anguished cry of "Candida!" in
the last act, is matched by her magnanimous generosity.

In this sense, although it is unlikely that Shaw would countenance
such a reading, the play can be seen as symbolic of the successful union
of Christ and his church. Morell, as the church, needs more than he can
give; blessedly he has the divine Candida to sustain him. In any other
playwright's hands, this portrayal of clergy marriage where a wife's role
is to give and give and give would be unbearably cloying or painful. In
Shaw's hands, this marriage works, because one should never confuse
Shaw's situations with realistic ones and also because Candida's nobility
and insight are so manifest. Shaw's women choose their roles. They often
move away from a relatively autonomous existence and elect to be apparently subservient. But to think of Candida as a servant, one must be
careful to qualify the description. There is nothing about Candida that
is meek or submissive; she exudes power and strength. If Candida is a
servant it is the kind of vibrant servant that the Old Testament prophets
are, or the apostle Paul—confident and purposeful.

Candida has a fiery final speech about how this eminent clergyman's
household functions. It is not a speech of complaint or rebellion, but a
truth-telling that allows the relations between the Morells to be grasped.

> Ask the tradesmen who want to worry James and spoil his beau-
> tiful sermons who it is that puts them off. When there is money
> to give, he gives it: when there is money to refuse, I refuse it. I

29. Irvine, "On *Candida*," 499.

> build a castle of comfort and indulgence and love for him, and
> stand sentinel always to keep little vulgar cares out. I make him
> master here, though he does not know it, and could not tell you
> a moment ago how it came to be so. (181)

Ostensibly, it is love that fuels Candida's ministry to her husband so that
he in turn can minister to society—at one point in Act Two she says,
"Put your trust in my love for you, James; for if that went, I should care
very little for your sermons: mere phrases that you cheat yourself and
others with every day" (165). But love as a vitalizing force never sits quite
right in Shaw's work—he is one of those unusual writers who does not
know what to do with romantic or erotic love. Nevertheless, Candida's
love as the foundation for her ministry to the minister is credible and
rather wonderful.

A Strange Separation

In the odd and mysterious little story "The Minister's Black Veil" by Nathaniel Hawthorne, first published in 1836, the minister in question, Mr.
Hooper, eccentrically and chillingly adopts a veil for his face, refusing to
relate his reasons or show his face for his entire life. The reason that is giv-
en at Hooper's death is that all human beings have veiled their true hearts
and his action was a symbolic reminder of this duplicity. The person who
approaches most nearly to the heart of the mystery is Hooper's beautiful
"plighted wife," Elizabeth, who courageously cajoles and questions the
minister. Hooper attempts to bind Elizabeth to him, saying that the veil is
only for his mortal life, not for all eternity. But she refuses to marry him
if he will not let her see beneath the veil. They part. Hawthorne, in his
enigmatic style, closes the scene by writing this:

> But even amid his grief, Mr. Hooper smiled to think that only
> a material emblem had separated him from happiness, though
> the horrors, which it shadowed forth, must be drawn darkly
> between the fondest of lovers.[30]

The minister's fiancée is not allowed into the inner sanctum of
doctrines and theories that govern Hooper's life. The sacrifice of a happy
marriage is apparently justified, in the exercise of this moral experiment, or so Hooper's smile tells the reader. Hawthorne's dark allegory is

30. Hawthorne, "The Minister's Black Veil," 6.

profoundly rooted in his dark Romanticism, but a secondary allegory—involving the inevitable separation of a minister from all human beings, even his wife—is applicable. This stark separation between minister and wife is also at the heart of Ibsen's devastating play *Brand*, discussed in chapter 8, in which the blazing fanaticism of the husband immolates his affectionate wife Agnes. As Brand's mother, son, and wife die, he explicitly insists that he must choose his vocation over love for them.

A work which emphasizes the female responsibility for discord in a clergy marriage is Ingmar Bergman's 1996 novel *Private Confessions*, suggested by the marriage of Bergman's parents. Henrik and Anna are a Lutheran pastor and his wife in the early twentieth century; their marriage is a misery. (His parents' unhappy marriage is reiterated in several Bergman screenplays.) Henrik is an overwrought man who loses his sanity when Anna confesses her infidelity; both are tortured souls and highly self-destructive. The pastor husband represents sterility, lovelessness, and demand. Bergman's sympathies are largely with the wife and mother, who represents for him passion and freedom, but neither partner in the marriage is admirable. Although Bergman's own father eventually became chaplain to the King of Sweden, in this novel Anna presents her pastor husband as an utter failure as a human being: "I know he's a good priest. He's a conscientious spiritual adviser and has helped a great many people. But inside all that, he is a lamentable terrified wretch."[31]

In *Jane Eyre* St. John Rivers, determined to become a missionary in India and take Jane with him, proposes marriage solely so she can accompany him in the role of "helpmeet and fellow-labourer." The icy argument that Rivers offers to Jane ("you are formed for labour, not for love"[32]) is designed to humble her and appeal only to her sense of duty; he has no amorous feelings for her. This situation echoes Susan's lines, cited above, from Bennett's *Bed Among the Lentils*: "To look at me, the hair, the flat chest, the wan smile, you'd think I was just cut out for God." This sad joke has fueled stories about pastors for centuries: the pastor's wife is a failure as a woman, unsuitable for passion. One sees the stamina of the stereo-

31. Bergman, *Private Confessions*, 29.
32. Brontë, *Jane Eyre*, 464.

type, for example, in the many filmed versions of Somerset Maugham's story "Rain," which has at its center the pulsating and lustful conversion battle between the disreputable Sadie Thompson and the upright minister Mr. Davidson. Mrs. Davidson in all the films is the epitome of the priggish, unforgiving killjoy. At least Mr. Davidson, with his lust, is rendered human. The spousal divide in these works of literature is absolute and even horrible.

As might be expected, the fiction involving clergy marriage offers numerous depictions of disgruntled women. (There seems to be no interest so far in the literary portrayal of the male clergy spouse, even though many denominations have ordained women for decades.) There are women whose spirits are crushed and those whose lack of fitness for the role creates comedy. Some women become the de facto ministers of the parish due to the inadequacies of their husbands or fathers. But there are also clergy wives like Jan Peterson and her fictional counterparts who find gratification in this very particular line of volunteer work. All of these models will continue to circulate in literature, because the combined complexities of ministry and marriage create a highly charged situation that we cannot help but find interesting. What one hopes to see less frequently is the portrayal of the clerical marriage that is marked by significant rupture: the moral and theological rupture of the Hawthorne and Ibsen works, or the romantic and erotic rupture in Brontë, Bergman, and Maugham. The rebellious or frustrated wives in literature at least know their messy situations for what they are, but the destructive clergy marriages I have mentioned at the conclusion are not functional in the least. These are hellish unions, made all the more macabre by the smiling ghostly remembrance of Peter and Catherine Marshall's "ever-deepening fusion of heart and mind . . . the most melodious harmony there is."[33]

33. Marshall, *A Man Called Peter*, 248.

INTERLUDE

The Bell

by Iris Murdoch

Iris Murdoch can be seen as the twentieth century's George Eliot, a seriously moral writer unwilling to subscribe to religious belief who nevertheless borrows respectfully from the Christian tradition. The origins of Murdoch's philosophical writings on the Good can be traced not only to Plato, but also to Christ. Like George Eliot, Murdoch knew a great deal about the Christian church and was capable of presenting it with sympathy and understanding. Also like Eliot, Murdoch's novels can be profoundly cerebral, intellectual exercises that sometimes place within the mouths of unlikely characters pronouncements that are much too weighty. Some of Murdoch's characters are awkwardly weighted down with symbolism or with ethical problems their author wants them to work through. Her 1958 novel *The Bell* is one of her fleshier outings, although still satisfyingly intelligent. The characters are human and often humorous and when she allows them to breathe, the novel is convincing.

The Bell concerns two religious communities, neighboring and interrelated, as well as several of the peripheral personalities who become attached to religious houses. (One of the intriguing things about *The Bell* is that who is marginal or central to the communities is less certain as the action closes, and in some cases they have exchanged places.) The conventional community, into which the reader is not really encouraged to enter, is an Abbey of nuns; existing alongside the Abbey is a collection of idealistic laypeople trying to live harmoniously and equitably on the land (rather new, in 1958) and who, it quickly becomes clear, can neither live in the world nor successfully leave it. The thorny personalities, doubts, and desires of the various characters thwart the intentions of harmony and service that underlie both communities, and the bell itself comes to represent a complicated range of concepts for the characters, although suppressed or misguided sexual desire is perhaps the most obvious. For Dora, a sort of Everywoman and natural pagan who wanders into the orbit of this group of believers, the bell is both religious and sexual: "the truth-telling voice that must not be silenced." At one point she is alone with the bell in the dark.

> She pressed her palm gently against it as if supplicating. . . . Fascinated, Dora knelt down on the ground and thrust her arm inside it. It was black inside and alarmingly like an inhabited cave. Very lightly she touched the great clapper, hanging profoundly still in the interior.[1]

At the head of the lay community is the magnetic Michael Meade, a fallen candidate for the priesthood struggling with his homosexuality. Contrasted with Michael, and vying with him for leadership, is a muscular Christian named James Tayper Pace, whose plain emphasis on work and responsibility contrasts with Michael's sensitive and contemplative approach. Of all the people in the novel, Michael's faith is the most profound, but he is also one of the most troubled characters, and his attractiveness to others, male and female, and his own agonized struggles with sexual desire distract him from his religious purpose. *The Bell* has much else going on, but for my purposes at present, the reader is directed to Murdoch's careful delineation of the two leadership styles represented by Michael and James.

Murdoch exhibits her cleverness by having Michael and James, in successive sermons, duplicate what the reader is attempting to do: they interpret the bell. James's sermon involving the bell is, predictably, straightforward. He requires the bell to be a witness, a voice acknowledging innocence and preaching renunciation (135). He moves out from his interpretation of the symbolism of the bell to state that the chief requirement of a good life "is to live without an image of oneself" (131). James Tayper Pace is one of those church leaders who provides helpful rules for living, discourages questions, and expects followers to conform. Michael's sermon involves the importance of self-knowledge and is the opposite of James's sermon in almost every regard. The bell is useful for him in that he sees it as announcing its subjection to the force of gravity;

---

1. Murdoch, *The Bell*, 266–67. References to subsequent passages are given parenthetically.

individuals likewise must be in touch with the forces within their person-alities. Both James and Michael are preaching on the chief requirement of a good life, and for Michael it is that "one should have some conception of one's capacities" (200).

James Tayper Pace, then, preaches abjection and renunciation, while Michael preaches wholeness and knowledge, but the expectations of the liberal reader about the various successes of these approaches are frustrated. At the end of the novel, surely, honesty and knowledge should win. But it is James who has the equipment to be the better leader. The community would likely function well under his simple, unreflective guidance. Michael is too subtle. (Due to various events in the plot, the community falls apart, so there is no leadership to observe and judge at the conclusion. Michael and Dora, once representatives of Christianity and paganism, are all that is left: on their own in the abandoned com-munity building, they are quietly and independently trying to sort out what to do next.)

Michael neither has full self-knowledge nor is he able to act on such knowledge as he has. He wants to accept his homosexuality but is never able to. Too cerebral, he is entangled within and fascinated by the idea of his own unhappiness. At the novel's end, Michael comes to this conclu-sion: "there is a God, but I do not believe in Him" (308). This is the kind of roundabout agnostic answer—an answer that is really a dilemma—that Murdoch relishes. One problem with this busy religious community is that while they are trying to live in harmony with nature, there is too much human commotion for harmony to be possible. When nearly ev-eryone leaves at the end, suddenly (and temporarily) Michael and Dora can experience the earth's healing properties. "A curious dream-like peace" descends and "owls hooted closer to the house" (300).

While Dora still believes that conventional religion is destructive—she speaks of religion as a "machine of sin and repentance which was alien to her nature" (303)—and although Michael's existence outside the faith is going to be difficult, Murdoch suggests that some dialectic of inside and outside might have real applicability. Her two religious communities can be seen as intensely experienced miniature versions of the Christian church. She is respectful of the church and the difficulty in being its leaders; she acknowledges the power of the Christian mes-sage to those who can hear it. But the person who represents health and happiness is Dora, living outside religion, the only one to experience in a thorough way the joy and physical well-being that other characters experience intermittently (if at all). But Dora is unusual, if not unique. The other agnostics and atheists in the novel are less appealing as characters. Dora's friend Noel represents them when he says, pompously: "No good comes in the end of untrue beliefs. There is no God and there is no judgement, except the judgement that each one of us makes for himself" (186). Self-centered and smug, Noel is neither interesting nor convincing.

The theme of Christian leadership is only one element that Murdoch explores in *The Bell*, and not the most important. Her explorations of guilt and the corruption of innocence are foremost in importance, and the range of opinions expressed throughout the novel about the roles of women is refreshing and startling for the time. But her examination of what it means to be inside and outside the community of the church, and what it means to lead a church community, is often shrewd and refreshing. It is evident, for instance, that many of the people supposedly "enclosed" are healthier and more aware than the "free" people outside. The open sexuality of the outside world is threatening and destructive at the same time as it is the best reason to stay in the outside world. Within religious community, several of the characters hope to evade the seductive and damaging nature of power, and find that power games follow them inside. Murdoch says, "Those who hope, by retiring from the world, to earn a holiday from human frailty, in themselves and others, are usually disappointed" (85).

10

The Canadian Collar

The high priest ... is able to deal gently with the ignorant and wayward, since he himself is subject to weakness; and because of this he must offer sacrifice for his own sins as well as for those of the people. (Heb 5:2–3)

There is a palpable sense of dissatisfaction and boredom with ecclesiastic business as usual. (Douglas John Hall, *The End of Christendom and the Future of Christianity*)[1]

If we look to literature as one way of understanding Canadian Christianity, it should quickly become obvious that Canadians have a remarkably different relationship to the church than do Americans or Britons. Although Canadians as individuals have a respectable record of religious observance—more on that in a moment—the literary profile of religion in the nation is distinctly less colorful, although also less acrimonious, than in those other jurisdictions. (My assertion is based on Canadian literature in English and does not take French-Canadian writing into account.) There must be a number of intriguing reasons for this more restrained literary presence, but one of the most important is the Canadian tendency to be quietly suspicious but generally courteous about institutions, and that includes the Christian church. Taking this mildly iconoclastic tendency to an uncharacteristic extreme, Canadian theologian Douglas John Hall has called for followers of Christ to carry out willing and joyful disestablishment from organized Christendom because

---

1. Hall, *The End of Christendom and the Future of Christianity*, 29.

"commitment to the established institutional model of the church—to Christendom in its various institutional forms—is the single most important cause of inertia."[2] Although such radical disestablishment thinking is relatively unusual in Canada, it is nevertheless fitting that a Canadian theologian should make this observation about the banality of institutional life. Canadians generally have the ability to look beyond the figure of the minister, beyond church buildings, beyond synods, when they turn their attention to religious matters. This openness to varieties of religious experience does, however, make the interaction between literature and the Christian church in Canada challenging to locate and analyze with precision.

The analysis of membership or weekly church attendance figures in various nations can only take us so far, but the statistics do provide a glimpse of the differences between Canada, the United States, and the United Kingdom. Worship habits of people in the United Kingdom are thoroughly surveyed, in part because of the Church of England's status as a national church. However, even with (or because of) the eminence of the national church, weekly attendance according to the official Church Census on May 8, 2005 was only 6.3 percent of the population. The survey by the British organization Tearfund uses a different methodology and estimates attendance in the United Kingdom as 10.1 percent in the same year. [3] In the United States, George Barna stated that as recently as 1993 an astonishing 66 percent of Americans claimed weekly attendance at Christian worship, but this self-reported high percentage by subjects of Barna's study is questionable, to say the least.[4] The Gallup Poll is more conservative, stating that figures representing Americans who claimed to attend "church or synagogue within the last seven days . . . have generally been in the 40 percent to 45 percent range" for the latter part of the twentieth century.[5] The Canadian situation, as one might expect, moderates between the British and American extremes. Statistics Canada in 1998 reported that weekly church attendance was 22 percent but another Statistics Canada study in 2006 created a "religiosity index" (combining the four dimensions of affiliation, attendance, personal practices, and importance of religion). "Based on these criteria, 40 percent of Canadi-

2. Ibid., 7.

3. Ashworth and Farthing, *Churchgoing in the UK*, 41.

4. Barna, *Virtual America*, table 89.

5. Newport, "Estimating Americans' Worship Behavior."

ans have a low degree of religiosity, 31 percent are moderately religious and 29 percent are highly religious."[6]

Even though the 2005 Tearfund study found that 39 percent of Britons now "claim to have no religion,"[7] British cultural conventions of the Christian cleric are vigorous and recognizable. There are distinct personality types one expects to encounter if reading a book or watching a television program featuring British clergy; there are, for example, the farcical examples played by Rowan Atkinson or encountered on a series like *Father Ted*. In 1950, a British writer stated his opinion that "the parson today . . . is the recognised butt only needing to trip at his entrance upon the stage to set up a roar of appreciative laughter."[8] However, British culture also provides the clever clerics found in mysteries by G. K. Chesterton and Ellis Peters. When approaching the American scene we are not likely to experience difficulty in identifying representative figures. There are the evangelical tricksters like Elmer Gantry and homely good sorts like Father Tim in Jan Karon's novels. Recent studies by Douglas Alan Walrath (*Displacing the Divine: The Minister in the Mirror of American Fiction*) and G. Lee Ramsey Jr. (*Preachers and Misfits, Prophets and Thieves*) indicate a healthy scholarly interest in American clerical fiction.

Asked about similar clerical types in Canadian literature, most commentators would likely be confounded. There are no automatic expectations, and this is, to some extent, a good thing. Yet it is startling to read this comment in a recent British anthology—

> No account of the English-speaking peoples, whether historical, sociological or cultural, would be complete without mention of the clergy. Many people may have been ignorant of theology, indifferent to ecclesiastical affairs, absent from public worship, but the clerical presence has been inescapable.

—and then apply this dictum to Canada.[9] Such automatic associations are not possible. My aim is not to unduly emphasize statistical analysis of the intersection of Canadian religious and literary life, nor is it to dwell upon comparisons to British and American experiences. These opening remarks serve, I hope, to stimulate inquiry about the way Canadian

---

6. Clark, "Patterns of Religious Attendance," 23; Schellenberg and Clark, "Who's Religious?," 4.

7. Ashworth and Farthing, *Churchgoing in the UK*, 4.

8. Christmas, *The Parson in English Literature*, 316.

9. Chapman, *Godly and Righteous, Peevish and Perverse*, vii.

Christian experience has been related in the nation's fiction. Both the British and American experiences have been energetically, if not thoroughly, researched. And although a study of literary clergy can only be one step toward a thorough understanding of Canadian religion, it is a step that has not been taken. There is scarcely any scholarly material about the presence of the minister in Canadian literature. But Canadian novelists have indeed used pastors as shorthand for religious experience, and it is worthwhile to attempt to decipher that shorthand.

"He Thinks He's Failed"

Canadian literary clerics, one is not surprised to find out, are rarely charismatic or fiery, nor are they often involved in scandal or miraculous feats. The bleakly comic villain of Miriam Toews's celebrated 2004 novel *A Complicated Kindness*, the Mennonite pastor nicknamed The Mouth of Darkness, is a startling exception, but the cruelty (and pathos) of that character is so atypical in the gallery of Canadian clerical portrayals that I have chosen to disregard it. Alice Munro's story "Wild Swans" might be held up as a dramatization of clerical wrongdoing, but there is no indication in the story that the man who molests the protagonist actually is a minister, although he claims he is.

More usually, the Canadian literary minister is the conduit of small surprises and delicate insights. I offer, as a preliminary illustration, Mr. Troy in Margaret Laurence's novel *The Stone Angel* (1964). Mr. Troy is the well-meaning but ineffectual clergyman forced upon the ferocious protagonist, Hagar Shipley, by Hagar's conventional daughter-in-law Doris. Laurence's well-known novel is plentifully furnished with biblical allusions, starting with the Old Testament names of the protagonist and her husband (Hagar and Bram) and ending on the last page with the "glass, full of water to be had for the taking,"[10] an image of baptism or communion. But Hagar herself, whose powerful personality dominates the narrative, makes it distinctly clear that she has no patience for the institution that is the church. When Mr. Troy makes the last of his visits to the ailing Hagar, he offers to pray with her, and Hagar says, typically, "I've held out this long. I may as well hold out a while longer" (290). Although Hagar does have conversations with God, they are argumentative, and

10. Laurence, *The Stone Angel*, 308. References to subsequent passages are given parenthetically.

her final acquiescence to God (which might more accurately be called a partial concession) is framed by the words *"Bless me or not, Lord, just as You please, for I'll not beg"* (307, emphasis in original). *The Stone Angel* is one of Canada's flagship fictional works and Hagar has been called "one of the most compelling figures in our literature."[11] Like many Canadian works the novel is attentive to, even immersed in, religious issues—but not ecclesiastical issues.

However, to conclude that Hagar Shipley's faith is ruggedly individual to the last would be to miss something beautifully suggestive about the function of Mr. Troy, at first glance an anemic, overly nice clergyman offered up by the novel to indicate the church's contemporary irrelevance. Mr. Troy's final visit to Hagar is initially as unpromising as the preceding visits—he reaches out with platitudes and she slaps him down. He leaves her hospital room feeling defeated; Hagar notices this and says, "He thinks he's failed, and I can't muster words to reassure him, so he must go uncomforted" (293). But he has not failed. Enclosed within his visit is Hagar's epiphany about the causes of unhappiness in her life: that she has never spoken "the heart's truth" and that "pride was my wilderness, and the demon that led me there was fear" (292).

What Mr. Troy has done to occasion this illumination—arguably the climax of the book, if a moderately modernist novel can be said to have a climax—is to sing a hymn for Hagar, at her rude command. She asks him to sing "All People that on Earth Do Dwell."

> "All right, then." He clasps and unclasps his hands. He flushes warmly, and peeks around to see if anyone might be listening, as though he'd pass out if they were. But I perceive now that there's some fibre in him. He'll do it, even if it kills him. Good for him. I can admire that.
>
> Then he opens his mouth and sings, and I'm the one who's taken aback now. He should sing always, and never speak. He should chant his sermons. The fumbling of his speech is gone. His voice is firm and sure. (291)

Hagar will later admit to Doris: "He sang for me, and it did me good" (293). Mr. Troy is the facilitator of Hagar's moment of insight. He does not know he has done good; he is unassuming to the point of invisibility; he has no earthly status or power. He is a particularly Canadian means of grace.

11. Callaghan, "The Writings of Margaret Laurence," 131.

While I will not claim that ministers like Mr. Troy recur with great frequency, I do think he is characteristic. Canadian fictional clergy are both less inspiring and less destructive than their counterparts in British or American literature. There are no Canadian clerics, to my knowledge, who freely face a firing squad, like Greene's priest in *The Power and the Glory*. But there are also few who register as high on the scale of destructiveness as Fathers Dolan and Arnell in Joyce's *A Portrait of the Artist as a Young Man*. While this might prompt some readers to consider the Canadian minister as a middling sort, effective at compromise but deficient at inspiration, instead I offer the possibility that Canadian literary ministers are of particular benefit because that they point away from clerical personality toward issues more deeply involving ministry, worship, and belief.

The Early Twentieth Century: Melodrama and Satire

Despite the vigorous life of the churches in nineteenth-century Canada— one has only to glance at *A Concise History of Christianity in Canada* and see the references to revivalism, Tractarianism, temperance, and schism—there are few significant portraits of clerics in the fiction that has survived from that era. Although clerical types exist in Thomas Chandler Halliburton's Sam Slick stories of the eighteen-thirties and forties, it is the fiction of Ralph Connor that provides Canada with its first significant literary ministers. Connor was the pen name of prominent Presbyterian minister Charles William Gordon. As Ralph Connor he was a literary star. Sales during his lifetime have been estimated at thirty million copies. As a church leader, Charles William Gordon was also a star of sorts. A respected arbitrator in public disputes, he was asked to chair the influential Joint Council of Industry after the 1919 Winnipeg Strike. When the United Church of Canada integrated most Methodists, Presbyterians, and Congregationalists in 1925, forming Canada's largest Protestant body, he was a key proponent of union. He preached at the League of Nations in Geneva in 1932.

His fiction made him a millionaire. Connor's novels were successful because, says Keith Wilson, to the readers of his era they seemed full of "humour and dramatic realism" and were considered "portraits of the raw, turbulent" life of the West.[12] Connor would have concurred.

12. Wilson, *Charles William Gordon*, 28–31, 40–48, 28.

But an additional function of his fiction, Connor stated, was to display Christianity "in its true light as a synonym for all that is virile, straight, honourable, withal tender and gentle in true men and women."[13] He saw his novels as an extension of his ministry and was unashamed of their romantic appeal.

To readers of our era the Connor novels are less likely to seem romantic than sentimental, less realistic than formulaic. It is true, as David B. Marshall says, that many Connor novels "in essence were secular sermons." But it is not their preachy quality that makes them less palatable today. The problem is that the novels are thinly characterized and clumsily structured. One of Connor's best-remembered books is *The Man from Glengarry* (1901), which tries to include everything at once, and with no noticeable attempt at harmony: religious faith, wilderness, the Canadian character, adventure and action, family relations. It may not even be clear which character *is* the man from Glengarry. The novel is at its midpoint when it settles down to be "about" Ranald Macdonald, only son of Black Hugh Macdonald, a rough lumberman from the Ontario backwoods. But it is the first half of the novel, which serves as the joint portrait of a community and, more specifically, a faith community, where Connor's power makes itself evident.

The first part of *The Man from Glengarry* is dominated by the presence of the Presbyterian church in the vicinity of the "Indian Lands," north of the Ottawa Valley, and by the ministry of Reverend Alexander Murray and his wife. Reverend Murray is a supreme figure of authority and fear; the narrator calls him "superb." Murray sees all, and he has set himself up as the Law.

> There was not a man of them but he could fling out of the door and over the fence if he so wished; and they knew, too, that he would be prompt to do it if occasion rose. Hence they waited for the word of God with all due reverence and fear.[14]

Under his command the community has built a new church and on his watch a spontaneous religious revival happens in the community. The Great Revival carries on for months, and when Murray's health breaks down from the stress of daily preaching, others carry on. Despite the heroic language surrounding Murray, it becomes evident early in the novel

---

13. Quoted in Marshall, *Secularizing the Faith*, 140.

14. Connor, *The Man from Glengarry*, 128, 123. References to subsequent passages are given parenthetically.

that the true sources of strength in Murray's church are the many ministries carried on by his wife. It is Mrs. Murray who takes the evening Bible study classes and does preparatory lessons for the young men who go on to study the ministry. She reports for duty at the hard places: praying at death beds, helping those who wrestle with doubt, urging them toward forgiveness and reconciliation. In one exciting chapter she outraces wolves on a night-time gallop to minister to her neighbors. Mrs. Murray is worn to a shadow at the conclusion of the book, but we never see her rest. Reverend Murray may be commanding and apparently "superb," but Mrs. Murray is of a higher order. Her words "fall from lips touched with the fire of God" (244).

It might seem peculiar that Connor should portray Reverend Murray so severely, given that the author was a minister himself. (Inquiries about the Murrays can be answered by the possibility that they are based on C. W. Gordon's own parents.) But what emerges from *The Man from Glengarry* is the sense that the dynamic presence of the church does not depend upon one minister, no matter how "superb." For example, a visiting preacher who brings the Great Revival a message of love, not law, is a necessary complement to Murray's message of reverence and fear. Together, these two messages in juxtaposition bring about the important conversion scene of the book (257), when Ranald's father Black Hugh Macdonald "comes to the Lord." And the people of Murray's congregation themselves are the source of much of the intensity of the Great Revival. But the decisive force in this backwoods Presbyterian congregation is a minister who is not ordained: Mrs. Murray.

The Man from Glengarry, clichéd as it is, has a strange and tense vivacity, at least in sections. To an extent this is because it is not the man but the woman from Glengarry, Mrs. Murray, who is the hero. Partly it is that the Presbyterian congregation is simultaneously of two minds: splendidly stalwart in its adherence to tradition and startlingly open to illumination from unexpected, even unsanctioned sources. And for the purposes of this study, what the reader encounters is the insight that ministry happens not because of one traditional man, but rather that ministries thrive when they are plural, communal, spontaneous, even feminine.

Like Ralph Connor's, Stephen Leacock's once-mighty status in Canadian literature is now difficult to fathom and evaluate. He is one of those nineteenth and early twentieth century writers who have not fared well in our times. This is unfortunate, because many Leacock tales are remarkably enduring, his wit still perceptive and entertaining. There are numerous Leacock stories, but two stories centered on clergymen from the collection *Arcadian Adventures with the Idle Rich* (1914) will suffice to demonstrate Leacock's individual brand of charm, satire, and insight.

"The Rival Churches of St. Asaph and St. Osoph" and "The Ministrations of the Rev. Uttermust Dumfarthing" were published in the era of Connor's popularity, but Leacock's purpose and manner could not be more different. Where Connor is unsophisticated and traditional, Leacock's sharp, urbane stories sit comfortably alongside Anthony Trollope's very British annals of clerical Barchester. The austere Reverend Murray in *The Man from Glengarry* bears no resemblance to the first Leacock minister encountered in *Arcadian Adventures*. This is the spiritual leader of St. Asaph's church (tellingly located on Plutoria Avenue, in a city likely modeled on Chicago or Toronto), the Reverend Edward Fareforth Furlong.

> St. Asaph's is episcopal. As a consequence it has in it and about it all those things which go to make up the episcopal church—brass tablets let into its walls, blackbirds singing in its elm trees, parishioners who dine at eight o'clock, and a rector who wears a little crucifix and dances the tango.[15]

Here we have the Christian church held up for satirical scrutiny, even at Canada's relatively young age. St. Asaph's Anglican Church is the town's leading congregation because it embraces materialism and excuses its members from thinking about ethical or spiritual issues. Of Reverend Furlong Leacock's narrator wryly states (205–6): "No man was known to preach shorter sermons or to explain away the book of Genesis more agreeably."

The rival church, St. Osoph's, is led by the Reverend Dr. McTeague, dry and intellectual. Completely unworldly, he does not perceive his parishioners' impatience; trying to get rid of him, they reduce his salary

---

15. Leacock, *Arcadian Adventures*, 201. References to subsequent passages are given parenthetically.

by half but he does not notice. His Presbyterian congregation once took doctrine very seriously indeed:

> St. Osoph's is only presbyterian in a special sense. It is, in fact, too presbyterian to be any longer connected with any other body whatsoever. It seceded some forty years ago from the original body to which it belonged, and later on, with three other churches, it seceded from the group of seceding congregations. Still later it fell into a difference with the three other churches on the question of eternal punishment, the word "eternal" not appearing to the elders of St. Osoph's to designate a sufficiently long period. The dispute ended in a secession which left the church of St. Osoph practically isolated in a world of sin whose approaching fate it neither denied nor deplored. (202–3)

But commercial interests and worldly aspirations are now as observable at St. Osoph's as at St. Asaph's. When McTeague suffers a stroke, the town's obituary writers rush him into the tomb when he is not dead, and the St. Osoph's trustees hurry to appoint the Reverend Uttermust Dumfarthing to the pulpit. Although Dumfarthing is a very different preacher than Furlong at St. Asaph's, he quickly steals Furlong's followers. Dumfarthing preaches sin and punishment. One Sunday he tells his listeners that at least seventy percent of them are destined for hell. "The congregation was so swelled next Sunday that the minister raised the percentage to eighty-five, and everybody went away delighted" (238). Damnation is a sideshow, an extravaganza. Although the satire in Leacock's stories may now seem mild, on the book's release a 1914 review in *The Spectator* warned that it might "shock fastidious readers."[16]

Both churches are swept by trends and vicissitudes, by market values and popularity ratings, and financial instability worries the two sets of trustees. The solution, they decide, is a merger, based on the model of two rum distilleries in the community (257). The trustees become stockholders in a new united church, and they argue vociferously over lines of accountability and organizational structure. When that is settled, they turn to the "minor" issue of religious belief, and vote happily in favor of this doctrine: "no form of eternal punishment shall be declared valid if displeasing to a three-fifths majority of the holders of bonds" (267).

At the end of these two stories, the Reverend Dr. McTeague is unpredictably brought back into the pulpit, but by this time the pastoral

16. Quoted in "Selected Reviews," 208.

leadership of United Churches Limited is inconsequential. The incorporated, commercial entity that is the modern church is secure; the ministers are valuable only as purveyors of entertainment. In one telling scene Reverend Furlong's father suggests that the world needs an "entirely new Bible" because "for the market of today this Bible . . . is too heavy" (227). This literary view of the Christian community as inimical to Christian doctrine and established Christian practice is one that will become more prevalent as the twentieth century advances. Leacock would never have heard of "Christianity Lite" in his time, but he would have recognized its symptoms. What is surprising about Leacock's 1914 stories about St. Asaph's and St. Osoph's is their percipience. How contemporary this situation looks to us.

The Social Gospel and Realism

Two eminent Canadian novels of the thirties and forties provide intriguing indications for the road ahead. On the one hand Morley Callaghan's *Such is My Beloved* (1934) continues the tradition of simple, well-meaning ministers going back to Oliver Goldsmith's *The Vicar of Wakefield* (1766) and Anthony Trollope's *The Warden* (1855), a tradition that continues today in Jan Karon's novels. This category of minister will never go out of style; naïveté and pure, unthinking conviction are always useful in a certain type of literature. On the other hand we encounter Sinclair Ross's *As For Me and My House* (1941), a landmark of Canadian realism, with its bitter and compromised small-town minister, Philip Bentley. Callaghan's Father Dowling is a type of Christ figure, offering himself as a sacrifice to save the souls of two prostitutes he clumsily befriends. Ross's Philip Bentley is usually seen as a spiritual failure, an artist who enters the church merely to make a living and who embarks on an unhappy existence of religious and even sexual hypocrisy. These two novels are among the handful of Canadian books that have been fitted out for accepted critical positions, but the standard interpretations accorded them, I believe, have been received too easily. Callaghan's portrait of a good pastor and Ross's portrait of a bad one might have been accorded wrong places in the canon of Canadian fiction.

What follows is a typical passage from *Such is My Beloved*, in which Father Dowling partakes of some lightweight soul-searching. He has been questioned by his parishioners and chastised by his church superiors about the excessive (and highly visible) amount of his time that is being spent with two streetwalkers.

> As he reached the corner and stood looking across at a drug store, he knew that in his thoughts he could not obey the Bishop and this disturbed him. He decided to go into the drug store and have a soft drink and he sat there staring at the marble counter, blinking his eyes and pondering his wilful lack of obedience. The Bishop had said that his love had degenerated. "How could God have loved those girls if not for themselves? How otherwise then could I have loved them?" he asked himself. And if God was able to love all souls without distinction in His divine way in spite of their failures, their lusts and avariciousness and their miserable condition, wasn't he, a simple priest, through his love of these two girls, loving the whole world, too? He began to smile, and he felt very confident with a swift rush of marvellous joyfulness.[17]

As with the portrayal of the cleric in Georges Bernanos's *Diary of a Country Priest*, published just after Callaghan's novel, there is a breach between the discernment of the reader and the almost outlandish innocence of the priest. In Callaghan, the reader does not know whether to laugh or cry over Father Dowling's ill-advised charitable work on behalf of streetwalkers who do not welcome his help; the level of irony is hard to ascertain. If we are to view Father Dowling's stubborn but stupid good works as "heroic," as does critic F. Hale, who also terms the priest "gifted,"[18] then we might expect the representation of the church hierarchy to be in marked contrast. The Bishop should be venal, for example. But the Bishop who tries to steer Father Dowling back to reality is inhabited by an active conscience, although he certainly is too comfortable and too powerful. The reader who accepts that Father Dowling represents true Christian action in a profane world needs also to face the fact that Callaghan allows Father Dowling to slip into insanity at the novel's end. Why is Dowling insane? It is not that he has been treated cruelly; other characters in the book—even his Bishop—have been tolerant of his quixotic ways.

The flat modernist style of *Such is My Beloved* may now seem ineffective, but one must come to grips with the conception that Dowling's action is sincerely offered by Callaghan as ideal Christian behavior. But taking a step back from Callaghan's strange little parable, one might well

17. Callaghan, *Such is My Beloved*, 133.
18. Hale, "The Postfigurative Christ," 46, 28.

ask: What could Father Dowling in reality have accomplished? Critics like Hale see Dowling as representative of Callaghan's own social gospel views, but surely Callaghan inadvertently undercuts his own best intentions. Note in the passage quoted above that, while pondering his ethical life, Father Dowling has a soft drink in a drug store. The description of him trying to think through his situation is diluted by the dullness of him "blinking his eyes" and by his lurching toward confidence with a "swift rush of marvellous joyfulness" based on nothing in particular. If Father Dowling is the best the Christian faith has to offer, then what is the point of the church staggering on at all?

Philip Bentley, in *As For Me and My House*, would never claim to approximate the best the Christian faith has to offer. Nor does his wife, the legendary Mrs. Bentley (whose mysterious narrative persona has occasioned much ink in Canadian academe), make many claims for Philip's goodness. According to Mrs. Bentley, Philip does not believe. She unequivocally names him *hypocrite* and *failure* several times in the first pages of the book and vocabulary like *feeble, tedious,* and *depressed* also makes an early arrival. In one of the novel's well-known scenes, Mrs. Bentley analyzes Philip's drawings of his congregation in Horizon (probably in Saskatchewan) saying that "everything is distorted, intensified, alive with thin, cold, bitter life." The people he sketches have "ugly, wretched faces, big-mouthed, mean-eyed."[19]

Since Mrs. Bentley goes confidently on to demonstrate what Philip's drawings say about his personality, how petty and cramped he has become, we might neglect the opportunity to take Philip's drawings on their own terms. Because of Philip's status as a clergyman, the inclination is to focus our critical energy on his hypocrisy. The involuntary reaction is indictment; a hypocritical clergyman stands out in sharp relief in any narrative. But Philip's drawings (like Mrs. Bentley's recurring use of a metaphor of false-fronted stores) also point to the considerable hypocrisy and callousness of the prairie people he has been called to serve. These people are robustly resistant to redemption. Philip is to offer spiritual guidance to parishioners who do not want it.

Nearly all the critics on this novel judge Philip harshly for his aridity and hypocrisy; W. H. New dismisses Philip as a minister who "does not believe in his church and cannot comfort the people."[20] A few critics will

19. Ross, *As For Me and My House*, 7, 21–23, 10, 14, 17.
20. New, *Articulating West*, 62.

remind us that Mrs. Bentley controls the narrative and that we cannot say with certainty "whether her assessments of Philip are correct."[21] Mrs. Bentley is, however, our only source of information in *As For Me and My House*, and we must invest in her tale. At the novel's conclusion, when the Bentleys leave the town of Horizon to take up a new city life as owners of a used bookstore, Mrs. Bentley, surprised, reports the good send-off they receive: "It turns out now that all along they've liked us. Philip, they tell me, was always such an earnest, straightforward man."[22] This farewell may or may not be heartfelt, but one can find evidence in the novel that the Bentleys have in fact done their duty. Mrs. Bentley makes calls in the community; they do their best to comfort the farmer Joe Lawson and his wife when their son dies. One night Mrs. Bentley is certain that Philip is having a tryst with his parishioner Judith; it transpires he is indeed sitting, for the second night, with the dying man he has claimed to be visiting. Even Mrs. Bentley occasionally admits that Philip is conscientious in his ministry. Could it be that Philip is holding to some notion of vocation and duty that is not completely derisory?

There are two scenes early in the novel that help us investigate the possibility that Philip is not such a failure as a minister. In the novel's first chapter we receive word about the meaning of the title.

> His sermon for tomorrow is spread out on the little table by the bed, the text that he always uses for his first Sunday. *As For Me and My House We Will Serve the Lord*. It's a stalwart, four-square, Christian sermon. It nails his colours to the mast. It declares to the town his creed, lets them know what they may expect. The Word of God as revealed in Holy Writ—Christ Crucified—salvation through His Grace—those are the things that Philip stands for.[23]

Philip's sermon is based on Joshua 24.

> Now therefore revere the Lord, and serve him in sincerity and in faithfulness; put away the gods that your ancestors served beyond the River and in Egypt, and serve the Lord. Now if you are unwilling to serve the Lord, choose this day whom you will serve, whether the gods your ancestors served in the region beyond the River or the gods of the Amorites in whose land you

21. Calder, "Sinclair Ross."
22. Ross, *As For Me and My House*, 215.
23. Ibid., 7.

are living; but as for me and my household, we will serve the
Lord. (Josh 24:14–15)

This is the passage on which Philip always preaches in a new town; out of
thousands of more celebrated scriptural readings he has chosen this one
as his creed. The text is about choice. Joshua has chosen to serve God, and
others may emulate him if they wish. This is not an ecstatic text about
redemption, but obedience. The word *serve* is used repeatedly. If Philip
were a fraud, surely he would choose a flashier text to impress his listeners. None of Mrs. Bentley's harsh or suggestive vocabulary is brought
into play when describing Philip's keystone sermon. Where she might
insinuate or limit, instead she uses straightforward verbs (*nails, declares,
stands*) and positive adjectives (*stalwart, four-square*). The sermon is on
the bed-side table, presumably so Philip can continue to reflect on this
text. Yes, it is possible to question the sincerity of Philip's sermon, but
there is no certain evidence that Philip does not mean what he says.

Not all pastors have the same gifts nor serve the same purpose.
Philip is not capable of being inspirational or comforting. But Philip
does represent serious obedience, and allows his parishioners to choose
whether they will follow suit with their own obedience. Aside from his
alleged unbelief (which we learn of, almost exclusively, through his wife)
and from his apparent but ultimately unproven affair with Judith, there
is little to condemn Philip's ministry. He is dry and cool, certainly. But he
would not appear to be uncaring.

A second enlightening scene follows a few pages later, when Mrs.
Bentley has a dream about Philip.

> Only last night I was lying half-awake, thinking about him, a
> little uneasy; and then drowsing off I seemed to see him in the
> pulpit, turning through the pages of the Bible. The church was
> filled. I was sitting tense, dreading something, all my muscles
> tight and aching. It seemed hours that he kept on, searching
> vainly for his text; and then with a laugh he seized the Bible
> suddenly, and hurled it crashing down among the pews.[24]

Mrs. Bentley interprets this dream in terms of Philip's "rage and bitterness." Yet the strain in the dream belongs to her; she is tense, full of dread,
her muscles aching. Philip, on the other hand, is resolutely searching the
Bible for answers, and when he hurls the Bible with a crash it might be
a judgment on others. If it were a moment of self-reproach or loathing,

24. Ibid., 21–22.

would he hurl it down among the pews, or do something more indicative of himself?

Any analysis of *As For Me and My House* has to deal with its definitive ambiguity, an unusual phrase I use deliberately. A large portion of the story's reason for existence is ambiguity: Who is Mrs. Bentley? Is she as insightful as she believes she is? Is the Bentley marriage a failure, or is this her perception? None of the questions can be answered, and the continued vitality of these questions ensures the continued vitality of this amazingly sophisticated prairie novel.

The critical interpretations that promote Philip Bentley as a prominent example of failure and hypocrisy—"the preacher who has lost his vision of a new world can see the fallen world only as it is in all its pettiness"[25]—should be opened up. If we question much about Mrs. Bentley's narrative, we should allow for the possibility that Philip is not a failure, or not a complete failure. While not the best kind of pastor, a specimen that represents obedience, seriousness, and presence is not to be dismissed absolutely.

Robertson Davies

Northrop Frye has said that

> Religion has been a major—perhaps the major—cultural force in Canada, at least down to the last generation or two. The churches not only influenced the cultural climate but took an active part in the production of poetry and fiction, as the popularity of Ralph Connor reminds us. But the effective religious factors in Canada were doctrinal and evangelical, those that stressed the arguments of religion at the expense of its imagery.[26]

This claim is now very much a historical one. Even in 1965 Frye identified religion as a major cultural force that had lasted only until the turn of the twentieth century or (at best) the end of the Depression. His final sentence above marks the limit of the religious influence he claims: religion in Canadian literature could once be traced by its intellectual, argumentative life, but it made no imaginative or creative contribution. In that same era, Pierre Berton's *The Comfortable Pew* (1965) lambasted Canadian religion for its alliance with the establishment and its lack of

25. Latham, "Sinclair Ross: An Annotated Bibliography," 366.

26. Frye, "Conclusion to *A Literary History of Canada*," 227.

vitality. "Religion today," he wrote, "has become as conservative a force as the force the original Christians were in conflict with."[27]

In the seventies, one Canadian writer in particular strove to bring Christian religion into a more central and affirmative position in fiction. The religion that interested Robertson Davies was, however, unconventional. Not obviously devoted to Christian ideals (although a keen analyst of the denominational landscape), Davies wanted to bring larger notions of faith and belief into play in his writings. Born a Presbyterian, he eventually moved to the margins of orthodox Christianity, incorporating within his own worldview mythology, magic, and psychology. His character Dunstable (later Dunstan) Ramsay speaks in *Fifth Business* (1970) of his "childhood notion that religion was much nearer in spirit to the *Arabian Nights* than it was to anything encouraged by St. James Presbyterian Church."[28] Dave Little argues that in the work of Davies the search for self is primary and that Davies eventually became convinced that such a quest was a religious one.[29]

Given this awareness of Davies's unusual interests, one might not expect many portrayals of clergy or of church matters. Yet Davies wrote some of the most interesting clergy fiction in Canadian history. One of the key figures in his Cornish Trilogy (1981–88) is Simon Darcourt, an Anglican scholar-priest who stands as the moral arbiter of at least two books of the trilogy. And Davies's most celebrated work, *Fifth Business*, offers a number of distinct ministers. The ministers Amasa Dempster, Padre Blazon, and Joel Surgeoner are minor characters who have real consequence, and there are also ersatz or manqué ministers to be found in two major characters, the supposed madwoman Mary Dempster and the narrator Dunstan Ramsay. Amasa Dempster is a small-town Baptist preacher, Padre Blazon a rascally European Jesuit, Joel Surgeoner a missionary to Toronto's destitute. Mary Dempster is, according to Ramsay, a healer or saint, and Ramsay himself becomes a kind of lay theologian. Because Ramsay supposes that Mary Dempster performs three miracles in his life, he dedicates himself to a lifelong study of miracles. Indeed, *Fifth Business* can be seen as a search for the answer to this question: Can a miracle happen in Canada? Yes, the mature Dunstan eventually believes, it can.

27. Berton, *The Comfortable Pew*, 94.
28. Davies, *Fifth Business*, 119.
29. Little, *Catching the Wind in a Net*, 149.

Amasa and Mary Dempster are at the heart of the instigating action of *Fifth Business,* and therefore of the two books that follow in the Deptford Trilogy, *The Manticore* (1972) and *World of Wonders* (1975).The Dempsters go for a walk in 1908 and get in the way of a snowball thrown at Ramsay by his friend Boy Staunton. The snowball has a rock concealed within it; Mary, who is pregnant, is struck and goes into premature labor. The various plots of the Deptford Trilogy all extend outward from the snowball hurtling toward Reverend Dempster and his young, unsuitable wife.

"Poor, silly Mrs. Dempster." "Poor Amasa Dempster."[30] These are the refrains heard in the opening pages of *Fifth Business.* Amasa is unworldly. Although his wife is ill and he has a three-pound newborn son, he is liable to "drop to his knees at any time" (38). Ramsay's sensible Presbyterian mother is impatient with the Baptist parson: "Amasa Dempster just won't believe that there's a time to talk about God and a time to trust God and keep your mouth shut" (22). Although the ten-year-old Ramsay concurs in the general consensus that Dempster is ineffectual, the boy also sees in the Dempsters the first marital affection, even passion, he has ever witnessed. Several years later, in one of the plot's pivotal episodes, Mary Dempster, having gone "simple," is found copulating in the town's gravel pit with a tramp. The shocks of the gravel pit incident are many, but in terms of the present study, readers should note Reverend Amasa Dempster's response to his wife's public shame: he takes her courteously by the arm and gently walks home with her.

Dempster dies five years later in the 1918 flu epidemic, but in Dunstan Ramsay's eyes, the family ministry does not die with him, because Mary Dempster is an agent of salvation. The tramp to whom she offers herself, we find out later, considers he has been saved by her complete and utter sacrifice. He becomes Joel Surgeoner, missionary to Toronto's toughest and neediest. Ramsay will come to see Mary's supposedly profane action as her first miracle; there is a sizeable narrative gap (about eighty pages) between the gravel pit incident and our awareness of Surgeoner's salvation, and we need this time, as does Ramsay, to process the notion of Deptford's gravel pit as an allegory of hell. Mary's descent can be seen as akin to the apocryphal descent in some Orthodox traditions of the mother of God into Hell, where harrowing and salvation take place.

30. Davies, *Fifth Business,* 10, 19. References to subsequent passages are given parenthetically.

Mary Dempster's first miracle is the salvation of Surgeoner; her second is the resurrection of Ramsay's brother; her third is the saving vision of the Madonna that Ramsay receives at Passchendaele. Whether Mary is accepted by the reader as a saint, a healer, or a minister of sorts is to some extent beside the point. (In 1913, what could such status really mean to a Canadian Protestant woman?) The intriguing realization is that Mrs. Dempster, long before the gravel pit episode, is rejected as unfit even to be a parson's wife. Yet for Dunstan Ramsay, Mary Dempster enacts a powerful ministry. This is what Ramsay says of her, looking back at his teen years:

> I do not know how to express it, but she was a wise woman, and though she was only ten years older than myself, and thus about twenty-six at this time, she seemed to me to have a breadth of outlook and a clarity of vision that were strange and wonderful; I cannot remember examples that satisfactorily explain what I mean, and at the time I did not know in what her special quality lay, but I recognize now that it was her lack of fear, of apprehension, of assumption that whatever happened was inevitably going to lead to some worse state of affairs, that astonished and enriched me. (49–50)

Mary Dempster, unlike everyone else that Ramsay meets, represents absolute faith. Her youth, femininity, and madness make her an impossible instrument for the Christian church to recognize. But it would seem that God makes use of Mrs. Dempster's holiness; Ramsay believes she is ministering to him and those around him, and Ramsay is among Davies's most scrupulous narrators.

It could be argued that Mary Dempster is a kind of subversive bishop who will pass on her strange underground ministry to Dunstan Ramsay, and in the other books of the Deptford Trilogy we do observe the way Ramsay ministers, often roughly, to others. As Stephen Bonnycastle writes, "The religion of these novels proposes a new ideal, something primitive and sublime, in which society and its institutions are insignificant."[31] The Deptford Trilogy sketches a surprising new church, with eccentric and unexpected leaders. But I would like now to turn to another clerical character in the work of Robertson Davies: the scholar-priest Simon Darcourt.

---

31. Bonnycastle, "Robertson Davies and the Ethics of Monologue," 170.

If we merely give Simon Darcourt a glance—and this is a distinct possibility because Davies fills his narratives with exotic and bizarre individuals who overshadow a quiet man like Darcourt—we might be tempted to accord him a place in the literary pantheon of mild-mannered clergymen, usually of the Anglican variety. Darcourt himself concedes that his character is unprepossessing: "I was the man many people thought of immediately whenever a parson, often in a distant suburb, fell ill with the flu and somebody had to be jobbed in at short notice to turn the crank of the dogma-mill."[32] However, what he actually represents is an almost lost conception of the scholar-priest, a vocation that he considers the highest calling.

Darcourt defends "the notion of religion as a mode of thought and feeling that could consume the best intellectual efforts of an able man" (55). He is like Dunstan Ramsay in his conviction that the boundaries of religion should be widened, but where Ramsay moves toward magic, Darcourt is an advocate of intellectual curiosity of a more exacting academic sort. They are both advocates of self-knowledge in the religious quest.

> I had become convinced, in some words Einstein was fond of, that the serious research scholar is the only deeply religious human being. Having discovered how hard it is to save the souls of others (did I ever, in my nine years of parish work among both poor and not-so-poor, really save anybody's soul?) I wanted to give all the time I could spare to saving my own soul. (55)

Darcourt is unsuited to parish work because he cannot bear sentiment. His intellectual curiosity leads him into unconventional studies. Unusual for an Anglican of his generation, he is keen to reclaim the female presence in Deity. He can be impatient and abrupt.

Darcourt's characteristics might mark him as an unsuitable cleric, but he emerges as the moral center of the Cornish Trilogy. He functions, for example, as a model creative force: in two of the novels he produces books and in the other a libretto. He also functions as a facilitator, a confessor or truth-teller for the other characters in the various complicated plots. Darcourt is the one who can be trusted; he is honest, insightful, and relatively untarnished in terms of the lusts and deceptions that drive the action.

---

32. Davies, *The Rebel Angels*, 237–38. References to subsequent passages are given parenthetically.

But most importantly Darcourt represents a principle of equilibrium. If the main question of *Fifth Business* is "can a miracle happen in Canada?" then the main question of *The Rebel Angels* is "how do we connect 'our root to our crown'?" (197–198). Many of the characters in *The Rebel Angels* believe that our heads and our bottoms make up the totality of who we are. So Ozias Froats the biologist is studying excrement to understand human personality; Clement Hollier as a paleo-psychologist is studying filth therapy. Many of these characters are extremists. Darcourt understands and is sympathetic to their researches and passions, and devotes his time to patiently making sense of their mess. He is balanced, even wise.

Although I have chosen *The Rebel Angels* as the book in the Cornish Trilogy which presents Simon Darcourt's ministry most evidently, in *The Lyre of Orpheus* there is a section which makes his stance nicely lucid:

> [Simon Darcourt] had reservations about many of the things which he, as a clergyman, was expected to believe and endorse publicly, but about the virtues of baptism he had no doubt. Its solely Christian implications apart, it was the acceptance of a new life into a society that thereby declared that it had a place for that new life; it was an assertion of an attitude toward life that was expressed in the Creed which was a part of the service in a form archaic and compressed and full of noble implication. The parents and godparents might think they did not believe that Creed, as they recited it, but it was plain to Darcourt that they were living in a society which had its roots in that Creed; if there had been no Creed, and no cause for the formulation of that Creed, vast portions of civilization would never have come into being, and those who smiled at the Creed or disregarded it altogether nevertheless stood firmly on its foundation. The Creed was one of the great signposts in the journey of mankind from a primitive society toward whatever was to come, and though the signpost might be falling behind in the march of civilization, it had marked a great advance from which there could be no permanent retreat.[33]

Robertson Davies in old age stated in an interview that he had expanded his idea of a conventional God "and I now feel a sort of recognition of the whole of life as involved and intermingled."[34] Simon Darcourt stands

---

33. Davies, *The Lyre of Orpheus*, 355–6.
34. Quoted in Grant, "Discovering Robertson Davies," 947.

for a widening and liberalization of what the church and ministry can encompass. Toward the secular world he sends the message that the church still has intellectual consequence; to the church he argues for the importance of apparently secular, even profane inquiry. Davies worked hard in his lifetime to promote serious (and merry) discourse about Canadian religious thought and feeling. His challenging contribution was unusual in North American letters of his time; there were few novels in Canada in the seventies and eighties that featured the church in any light at all.

Fresh Voices

Alice Munro's 1990 story "Pictures of the Ice" focuses on the final days of elderly minister Austin Cobbett, a man with a "careful, quiet kind of religion" who comes up against an antagonist representing "a stricter, more ferocious kind of Christianity." Pretending to retire to Hawaii, Austin instead takes a call to remote Shaft Lake, where he intends to "wear himself out, quick, quick, on people as thankless as possible."[35] The goodness of Austin Cobbett cannot, apparently, survive. He dies, either suicidally or accidentally, after a few weeks in the northern parish where he has retreated to immolate himself. Alice Munro occasionally includes ministers in her renowned stories of Canadian life, but putting one near the center of the story, as she does in "Pictures of the Ice," is unusual. Munro's interest in the church, as Nora Foster Stovel has identified, is usually limited to the anthropological. In *Lives of Girls and Women*, for example, Munro's main character "characterizes denominations in terms of their social status, rather than their religious faith" and the ministers encountered by the girl offer a limited choice between decorum and theatricality (see Munro's story "Age of Faith").[36] Stovel has noted a similar anthropological tendency in some of Margaret Laurence's works. While Laurence, as we have seen in *The Stone Angel*, was more explicitly engaged with Christian matters than most other Canadian novelists, her novels *The Fire-Dwellers*, *A Jest of God*, and *The Diviners* nevertheless feature protagonists distanced from the church, working out religious questions on their own, casting a skeptical eye on ecclesiastical matters.

The concluding sentence of William Closson James's study of Canadian literature and religion, *Locations of the Sacred*, is this:

35. Munro, "Pictures of the Ice," 155, 165.
36. Stovel, "Temples and Tabernacles."

> Religion in Canada late in the twentieth-century is highly
> personal and individual, characterized more by an eclectic
> spirituality cobbled together from various sources rather than a
> monolithic and unitary superordinating system of belief.

While James does identify a search for transcendence in Canadian fiction, he claims the quest is "focussed on this-worldly reality or presence." His study follows interesting trails of religious feeling, imagery, and rebellion in Canadian culture, but he refuses to look in conventional places for these trails. Organized Christianity, and its ministers, has no appeal for him; the sacred in Canada, he says, is "difficult to locate." [37] The assumption is that the sacred is not much in evidence in the churches themselves. Alice Munro does bear out James's contention. When religion appears in Canadian fiction of the late twentieth century, it is often unhoused and individual. This is not, however, its only means of appearance.

In *Restless Churches* (2004) Reginald Bibby urges Canadian Christians to take the notion of a religious Renaissance seriously. He suggests that the churches should be sending out search parties for former adherents who were not as lost as they might appear. The churches "have assumed that those family members and friends have dropped out when they haven't. They have assumed that they were not receptive when they are." [38] By the end of the century Christianity in Canada was, feasibly, just unrecognized enough in Canadian culture that it could be intriguing again. The church began to edge back into literary endeavor.

In 1999, Warren Cariou published two novellas as *The Exalted Company of Roadside Martyrs*. The second novella, "Lazarus," features as its protagonist Father Silvan, a man who feels he has second-hand faith and is propelled toward something near madness when he unintentionally brings back to life Lucius, a man he hates, and is then revered for this miracle. After trying to destroy himself by drowning, Father Silvan interprets his failure to drown as a kind of baptism into resolution. His resolution is a reversal of his initial saving act: he wants to obstruct Lucius—former degenerate, now evangelist—in his new holy life. When

---

37. James, *Locations of the Sacred*, 243, xii, xiv.
38. Bibby, *Restless Churches*, 181.

that fails, Father Silvan reverses again and joins forces with Lazarus, as he renames Lucius, in an evangelical crusade. People are, apparently, healed at their worship services, but to Father Silvan the people are healed by his own doubt.

> "That's the kind of man I am," I said. "No hero, no spiritual leader, no healer. I don't even have any faith. And the moment when it happened, when I lost it—or when I realized it had never been there at all—was when I touched your face. Here in this bloody room. It wasn't a conversion, a resurrection. It was the moment when doubt gained a foothold in my soul."[39]

Cariou's "Lazarus" is a strangely Protestant story in one sense, although it is immersed in miracles, saints, and a character named Guadeloupe. Father Silvan arrives out of a tradition that reveres its priests, providing them with special status and reverence. However, the narrative strips Silvan of any godliness he or his position might once have had, and he descends into a hellish landscape of unbelief and murderous impulses. With the priest removed from his central position in his little Christian community, what follows for that community is not spiritual chaos but a beneficial dispersal of the leadership. The faith carries on, in the unlikely missionary fervor of the former bootlegger, Lucius, who upon his return from death becomes an earnest proselytizer for God. Father Silvan describes the spontaneous power of belief to be found among the sometimes astonishing individuals in his community:

> I would have thought that in our secular age an oversupply of belief would be the last of our problems. But now I see that belief is everywhere. It has been suppressed for too long, and it springs out from people's souls before they even know it, latching onto whatever sensational legends are near at hand. (160)

Cariou's story is carnivalesque, darkly comic, and peppered with irony and satire. It is not for this reader to assert with certainty that miracles do or do not happen in the lives of Father Silvan and Lucius/ Lazarus. But Cariou does supply a powerful portrait of a church that will find vital leadership any which way. It does seem as if the lost soul, Lucius, in becoming a fervent missionary, has been touched by the Holy Spirit. The notion is outrageous, impossible—but somehow Lucius has become righteous. He becomes the minister that the church needs when

39. Cariou, *The Exalted Company of Roadside Martyrs*, 253. References to subsequent passages are given parenthetically.

the designated officials of the church have failed. And in the portrait of Father Silvan himself, Cariou gives us a wonderful example of a clerical type who ministers in spite of himself. Father Silvan, deeply flawed and profoundly damaged, is forced into an intense spiritual realignment. While feeling only hatred and negativity—he believes he has healed Lucius with some "dark shape of negative power" (245)—his actions have been overturned into goodness. Cariou's story gives us an extreme instance of a priest whose life and actions should not be successful. But Father Silvan's value does not arise from himself; despite his own unbelief, a powerful ministry arrives and happens anyway.

At the conclusion of the novella "Lazarus," Father Silvan is, at least in part, still sneering at the believers in miracles, still in despair at his own lack of conviction. "So much credulity, so little time," he says on the last page (267). In a reversal of what would be expected of a Roman Catholic priest, he has tumbled into an abyss of doubt while the people of the church are the providers of comfort and grace to him. Despite his profound desire to escape the reality of faith, he cannot.

> I have learned that everyone wants to believe. It is an innate need, inexplicable and eternal, like our requirement for food or for sexual gratification. This is why, despite my frailties, I am indispensable. My curse can become a blessing—not for me, but for the legions of believers. They will keep coming to me, and their needs will keep pouring into the chasm of my disbelief. And they will never fill it up. (267)

In Marina Endicott's novel *Good to a Fault* (2008), the Anglican priest Paul Tippett appears at first to be within the critically accepted lineage of almost feeble clerics like Amasa Dempster in *Fifth Business* or even the hypocritical, troubled ones like Philip Bentley in *As For Me and My House*. Paul is clumsy and stilted in his conversations, self-conscious, painfully aware of himself as a fool. He sees "his own ridiculous self" all too well, and has no idea how to make known his romantic feelings for Clara, the novel's heroine. Visiting Paul in his church office, Clara wonders how he manages to advise parishioners when "his own life seemed to be a shambles."[40] Emotionally battered by a bad marriage, Paul feels lost and inept when he is summoned before the Bishop because his ex-wife is reported to have published journalistic pieces that are inappropriately sexual.

But Endicott's narrative presence is patient with, even loyal to Tippett, allowing the relationship with Clara to develop, revealing the Bishop as intelligent and compassionate, and most of all urging us to be forbearing with this unpromising cleric. And we discover that even in his most depressed state, Tippett is principled. He firmly refuses to be obsessed with "dignity or authority or respect" (93). Several sermons and worship services are provided by Endicott in careful detail—decidedly rare in such novels—and in one chapter, "Service," the author describes Tippett's pastoral joy as shining from his "pure face." The direction and quality of his preaching is clear and stirring, and his customary clumsiness disappears. Looking at his parishioners, his expression is genuine and loving, as if "they'd come over to his house by surprise" (135).

Tippett is a throwback to another age and time. He possesses the classical learning that was once expected of a priest, but in late twentieth-century Saskatoon this learning is an impediment. He muses that what success he has achieved derives from what he calls his "opposite action" effect (48): parish matters seem to resolve through an inversion of his own best intentions. If successful North American religion is increasingly dominated by commercial values or prosperity theology, Tippett is badly out of step: "Paul had an unassuming smile, acknowledging his own inadequacy but relying on your great mercy and goodness" (137).

Tippett's humility and genuineness gradually win over Clara, his parishioners, and the book's readers. In one of the novel's great set-pieces, Tippett hosts a Christmas party for the members of his congregation. He has little idea how to host such an event, and the chapter, rife with bad smells, misbehavior, and old antagonisms, appears headed for disaster. (Indeed, an elaborate cake does come spectacularly to grief.) Yet, due to Tippett's instinctive and reckless desire to be a generous host, and to his artless goodwill, the Christmas party becomes an ecstatic celebration of the highest sort, binding the people together in honest and surprisingly holy communion.

---

40. Endicott, *Good to a Fault*, 92, 18. References to subsequent passages are given parenthetically.

A similar averted disaster happens during a Sunday morning service when a drunken man wanders into church and up the aisle, in the midst of the celebration of communion. Embarrassment and paralysis would appear to be the best of several possible horrible outcomes; the reader expects confrontation, perhaps violence or sacrilege. Instead, Tippett steps aside from the expected order of the liturgy and ministers to the man, even though it means that the service halts and the congregation must wait.

> "Are you in trouble?" Paul asked.
>
> The man's head lifted. His eyes stared into Paul's, their focus coming slowly home, resolving into human sense and pain.
>
> Down in the pews the congregation shifted. Clara could feel the cowardly anxiety of well-off people in the presence of disaster. And felt it herself. Paul was talking so quietly that no one could hear the words. The man answered, louder but unintelligible. He was swaying now. He bent down to hold the rail. Paul lifted the movable section, took the man's arm and helped him out the side door to the vestry. . . .
>
> Paul was gone a long time. (75)

Paul Tippett has no idea how good a minister he actually is. In one section of the novel we learn of his private conviction that "he lived on God, that the earth itself was God itself." However, he is rarely confident enough to share with others the vitality of this bond. Only the reader is party to the scene where "Paul lifted his face to feel the sun and thanked God, thanked God, as he did almost all the time" (140). Nevertheless, Tippett is so genuine and compassionate that his gifts tumble out anyway, in spite of himself.

While the well-developed and distinctive clerics of Cariou and Endicott indicate a deepening of the Canadian literary understanding of ministry, this is still an embryonic and limited stage. Both of these recent books were well reviewed, but there has been no real critical attention paid to Cariou's and Endicott's presentation of the church. Recently Ontario's Exile Editions published an anthology of the sort that has been circulating in Great Britain for years. *The Exile Book of Priests, Pastors, Nuns and Pentecostals: Stories of Preachers and Preaching* (2010) apparently belongs in the affectionate British tradition of, for example, the various editions of *The Faber Book of Church and Clergy*. However, the reader who expects this will be misled. The book is not friendly to clergy, nor is it overly enlightening or provocative. The editor provides a dismissive introduction that assumes the worst: "You know from the newspapers, and you will be reminded in the pages that follow, that the seven lovely deadlies—avarice, sloth, lust, gluttony, envy, pride and wrath—do not respect the cloth."[41] The collection is vague, flippant, anchorless.

In 2007 the CBC comedy show *Little Mosque on the Prairie* first aired. (Its last episode was broadcast in early 2012.) For the first three seasons a key character is Reverend Duncan Magee, an Anglican minister who provides a worship space for the slightly fraught Muslim community in the small town of Mercy, Saskatchewan. Magee, resisting the town's suspicion and prejudice, shares his church building with the Muslims and becomes a friend of their Imam, Amaar Rashid, commiserating with him about the skirmishes inherent in all congregational life. Although the series, created by Zarqa Nawaz, is light-hearted and farcical, there are moments in the first seasons that provide much-needed examples of inter-faith education and understanding. Many of these feature Reverend Magee. In the episode "Eid's A Wonderful Life" in season two, when an Anglican Christmas event is a failure and the bustling Muslim community has a catering problem for their Eid al-hada feast, the two congregations come together, feeding and comforting each other.

In the fourth season the producers, perhaps sensing that this good Christian pastor did not generate enough tension to allow the plot's premises to function, send Magee away to northern Canada, and a new Anglican minister appears. Reverend William Thorne is arrogant, intolerant, and hilariously rude. The basis for comedy is assured. But the foundation for more fully understanding Canadian clerics and the Canadian variety of the Christian church is fractured.

Because little has been written about the presence of the clergy in Canadian fiction, any analysis of clerical typology in our literature must be provisional. The fictional examples chosen for this study are somewhat unsystematic and personal, but I believe they are a good indication of Canadian attitudes toward church and clergy. My suggestion so far is that ministry in our fiction often arrives from unexpected sources and has surprisingly beneficial achievements. Canadian fiction recognizes and

41. Fiorito, "Introduction," *The Exile Book of Priests*, xiv.

encourages ministry that is valuable because it is unconventional, even though (or because) the ministers in question often cannot believe in their own value. They are, however, principled. Unlike clerical characters in other traditions, Canadian ministers are not memorable for their own personalities but direct attention toward more important matters such as compassion, humility, and patience. These characters prompt us to think about worship at its most genuine and least ecclesiastical.

Lights and Shadows of Clerical Life

by William Cheetham

O f all the books read for *The Collar*, this virtually unknown novel was one of the most resonant for me, and it was also the one that turned up nothing when I typed the author's name into an Internet search engine. That the author was a Canadian minister in the nineteenth century is clear. His preface is dated "Brockville, Ontario, 1879" and this is its first sentence:

> The following pages have been written during an inevitable temporary cessation of stated ministerial labor, and in the sincere hope that they may do some good, and in some humble measure further the interests of truth, and promote the glory of God.[1]

The word "inevitable" alongside "temporary" is intriguing. While writing the novel, William Cheetham was not carrying out the duties of an ordained minister, but he expected to resume them. However, "inevitable" has a sting in it. Does ministry go hand-in-hand with illness, or with the sort of exhaustion that ends in lengthy rest cures? Or (given the parish scheming and treachery that is central to *Lights and Shadows*) has Cheetham been the victim of a plot? Is he out of a job, nursing his wounds after being unseated from a parish? I have not been able to find any more information about William Cheetham except that he was a Baptist minister in Brockville, and that he authored one other book, *Christianity Reviewed* in 1896, dedicated to his only son, whose death,

---

1. Cheetham, *Lights and Shadows of Clerical Life*, iii.

"deeply lamented, gave forth the germ and quickening from which these pages have sprung."[2]

To write and publish a novel in Canada in 1879 was impressive, and to write one of this level of sophistication was even more so. (In 1879, the place in which I live had been a province, rather than a territory, for a mere nine years, and the copyright of Cheetham's book was filed, remarkably, with Canada's Ministry of Agriculture.) Like Anthony Trollope and Margaret Oliphant, writing their clerical novels in England, William Cheetham has a sharp eye for the hypocrisies and incongruities that arise when the ideals of Christian life collide with the fallen nature of the human beings who fill the pews and pulpits. Like Trollope and Oliphant, Cheetham writes prose that is elegant and assured, but his fervent belief that the church ought to be providing more illumination and guidance adds a piquant and sorrowful quality to the book. Trollope's and Oliphant's clerical novels are more firmly identifiable as social comedies.

Early in the novel, while readying himself to leave the shelter of the seminary, Paul Vincent, the novel's hero, bursts out with this to a fellow student:

> I am beginning to experience the first dawn of the very practical idea that, possibly, there is a good deal of trickery and unreality in the world; that things are not always what they seem; that men are perpetually engaged in carrying out their little schemes for personal and selfish ends; that the question is not, how to secure the greatest good for the greatest number, but how can I secure my own individual advancement and profit? That the glory of God the chief end of man is perpetually lost sight of; that there is more truth than poetry in the statement that the 'heart is deceitful above all things and desperately wicked'; that the Church itself is not free from the blighting, blasting contagion of trickery and devilishness, which reigns supreme in the world.[3]

The novel records the first four or five years of Paul Vincent's career as an ordained minister. After being summoned on two long and tiring journeys to "supply the church" in distant communities seeking a "likely candidate for the office of pastor" (19), Mr. Vincent indulges in the outburst above. The dishonesty he encounters on these trial visits leaves him

2. Cheetham, *Christianity Reviewed*, 4.

3. Cheetham, *Lights and Shadows*, 65. References to subsequent passages are given parenthetically.

feeling sullied and suspicious. The author offers such sharply detailed (and probably autobiographical) scenes of seminarian embarrassment as Mr. Vincent's suspicion that the seams will split on his one good suit. This occurs while he tries to submit cheerfully to the "demonstrations of delight" offered by the children of a congregation's ruling deacon. After pulling Mr. Vincent's hair, they "trod upon his new boots and corns; whirled round him, catching hold of the tails of his fine new frock coat" (22).

Finally called to a decent church at the town of Crossberry, Mr. Vincent spends two happy years there. Then he is forcefully pursued by representatives of a church at Battlemount, a large, important, but more troubled community. Although Mr. Vincent has no desire to leave Crossberry, whose name suggests a burden willingly carried because of the beauty and sweetness within it, he eventually gives in to the insistent pressure placed on him by Battlemount, a place we know can only be the site of hardship and hostility. Why Mr. Vincent accedes to the aggressive courtship maneuvers of Battlemount, why he leaves a beloved parish, is one of this novel's absorbing enigmas. Ostensibly Mr. Vincent accepts the call to Battlemount because he feels this is where God wants him to serve, even though he would prefer to stay where he is. But there is in the vigorous pursuit of Mr. Vincent a strong element of seduction, even abduction and violation. William Cheetham presents the minister as an exquisite and delicate idealist whose charms somehow arouse and challenge the belligerent leaders of Battlemount's congregation.

The small reservations Mr. Vincent has about Crossberry—the congregation is, for example, gripped in unthinking class segregation with the rich occupying choice seats and the poor banished to drafty galleries above—are made more urgent and evident in his next charge. Cheetham's novel will not allow Mr. Vincent (or the reader) to remain comfortable. Anodyne notions of Christian life can arise only to be banished. Crossberry is pleasant, yes, but is this pleasant living the one that Mr. Vincent—or any pastor of merit—was called to fulfill? In any case, even Crossberry prompts Mr. Vincent to wonder "what God thinks of people who profess to have so much reverence for His word, and yet so perpetually, and with such horrible uniformity, violate it" (122). Unfavorable observations become even more common in Battlemount:

> It was with no small concern, however, that he saw that the expectations of the people were wholly fixed upon himself; that

the great work that was to be done was expected to be done mainly, if not exclusively, by him, unaided and alone. (227)

As I was reading *Lights and Shadows of Clerical Life*, in a first edition that had belonged to the man who in 1947 became the first president of one of my university's predecessor colleges and retrieved from our library's deep storage, I constantly ran across intriguing sentences I would copy out and send electronically across town to my husband in his church office. They offer shrewd warnings and dark reminders.

> A minister can scarcely refer to money in any shape, or in any connection, however innocent, without incurring the liability of being charged with mercenary feelings. (85)

> It is singular, too, how curiously and complacently good men can look on, and never utter a word of kindly expostulation or warning, while his pastor is visibly working himself to death. (95)

> The man who is good for nothing, whether in the world or in the church, is always grumbling, and finding fault; while he who is usefully employed has no time for, and no temptation to, such undignified occupation. (147)

As old and obscure as this novel is, and as overwrought as the language sometimes is, Cheetham's characters were to me utterly recognizable and the situations all too up-to-date. Specifically, Cheetham is very accurate on contention between the pastor and the congregation's "leading members."

In this novel the domineering head deacon, the wonderfully named Hezekiah Shankey, suddenly and arbitrarily demands the resignation of Mr. Vincent after two successful years in the pulpit at Battlemount. This is a pure exercise in power. By the force of his personality and his pocketbook, Deacon Shankey leads for a time a flourishing campaign against the pastor. This is despite the fact that another hostile deacon, Mr. Cheesman, freely admits that he has "nothing particular to urge against the Pastor, except that he has refused to take the advice of the officers of the church" (294). Shankey, Cheesman, and the other deacons are transparent in their bid to maintain absolute control of the organization, stating publicly that they are the largest contributors to the funds of the church. One of the first tactics in Deacon Shankey's plot is to tell the treasurer that he will immediately "reduce his subscription fifty percent" (250).

Throughout this miserable time Paul Vincent takes the moral high ground, refusing to debate or argue with the mutinous deacons, serving the community as faithfully as ever. But he does not neglect the opportunity to chastise, subtly, the insubordinate and wayward from the pulpit. In one key sermon he reminds his parishioners that the Christian life is holy and should bring out the highest qualities of human beings. "This life is a reality; not a sentiment, not a social convenience or adjunct, not simply a creed, but a life in Him who is the highest embodiment of life" (209). It is possible that the congregation is ill at ease with Mr. Vincent's learning (not always worn lightly); as Deacon Cheesman says, "we do not like to feel that there is a great distance between him and us, mentally and spiritually" (294). However there is no firm evidence that any lapse of Mr. Vincent's has been the cause of dissent. On the contrary, the narrator states plainly that "we may venture to affirm that Mr. Shankey had no tangible or sufficient reason for the course he was pursuing" (261).

This power struggle between affluent lay leaders and ordained clergy is painfully familiar to anyone involved with the church in any era. Along with the circumstance that people offer even in 1879 the phrase "it has always been so" (96) as sufficient reason to continue well-worn practices, the fight for congregational control makes Cheetham's novel seem in some respects as if it were written in our day.

I have undertaken such a detailed sketch of *Lights and Shadows of Clerical Life* because it is unusual to have the actual dilemmas of church life offered as the central drama of a novel. And for once the scandal is not sexual. Neither is the dilemma that faces Mr. Vincent as farfetched as the one on which Margaret Oliphant's *Phoebe Junior*, for example, rests. In that 1876 novel there is a highly colored instance of forgery and embezzlement on the part of the clergyman, Mr. May, followed by "mental shock" and narrowly averted disgrace. Additionally, in Oliphant's and Anthony Trollope's clerical novels there is considerable distance between author and subject. Both Oliphant and Trollope present the church as a fascinating organization, full of entangled loyalties, flagrant ambitions, outmoded practices, and stubbornly held prejudices. In some regards the church for Oliphant and Trollope could be the law, or a medical establishment or school. Complicated human schemes and inevitable human weaknesses are what interest these other authors (both of whom, it must be said, are better than Cheetham at bringing appropriate female complications into the action). But for William Cheetham, the crisis of leadership in Battlemount is not just another specimen of wry or leisurely social comedy. Cheetham is passionate about the situation of Paul Vincent, angry about his betrayal, and shocked at the weakness of his supporters.

The novel's conclusion is unconvincing. Vincent is saved from his persecutors by an eloquent speech from a retired pastor, Reverend Jeremiah Gamble. If this member of his own brotherhood had not conveniently intervened to save him, what would have happened? I think that Cheetham knows that the destruction of a clerical career was the more likely outcome. Cheetham often uses the word "realism" in both this novel and his later study *Christianity Reviewed*. It is a term of the highest approbation to him. That he is unable to offer a realistic solution to the cruel situation in which Mr. Vincent, through no fault of his own, is placed indicates just how alarming and capricious the conditions of clerical life were—and continue to be.

Once the Victorian era closed, for some reason never completely understood, there were few novels that dared, or bothered, to offer the drama of church life as their central theme. (Marilynne Robinson's *Gilead* and *Home* are noted exceptions.) Yet the drama of the clerical life is undeniable. The reader may say that, as a clergy spouse, I am too close to such lives to be an objective arbiter. Still, I recall that in the ten days or so following the birth of our youngest son, in 2002, my husband was called upon to conduct four funerals, and I briefly wondered if we would lose our minds. Just this past week, I have been in two cafés where at nearby tables pastors unknown to me were obviously recounting various skulduggeries in their parishes to sympathetic friends. (The words "presbytery" and "worship committee" indicated their careers.) The job is a frustrating one, and William Cheetham took the bold step in 1879 of making his grievances public in a stylish and intelligent novel. Cheetham presents ministers used as puppets and punching bags; he takes upon himself the leadership of a vigorous campaign for their better care and handling. This is no less needed today, not merely because clergy are worth protecting, but because the church as a whole suffers in these painful situations. This is how William Cheetham puts it:

> The church's wellbeing and the pastor's are indefeasibly identical. They stand or fall together. If one be injured, the other will be equally affected. If one be blessed, the other will share the blessing. Lower the character and standing of the pastor, and you lower the character and standing of the church. (73–74)

Corpus permixtum

The Latin term *corpus permixtum* means "mixed body"—both bad and good—and Augustine was fond of describing the Christian church in this way. Weighing in on controversies about purity in the church leadership of his own time, the fourth century, Augustine admitted that priests may fail and show themselves unworthy. However, the sanctity of the sacraments and their efficacy as priests need not be in question. The concept of *corpus permixtum* is still very useful, not least because of its emphasis on the body: the church is Christ's body, and the church is full of fallible and exceedingly individual human bodies, including the bodies of its priests and ministers. The Christian ministry is absolutely and thoroughly embodied; no two embodiments can possibly be the same. For this reason I have avoided using words like *image* in *The Collar*. These are not clerical images I have been collecting and pursuing, but embodied pastors.

The reader may respond that I have been invoking fictional examples: how is it possible in such a case to speak of embodiment? If I thought literature was only about images and patterns, words and style, I certainly would not bother with this study. But literature—if it is doing what it ought—is warm-blooded and breathing, and at some level I insist that these characters *are* real people. Some are more affecting than others, but literary characters could not enter our hearts and lives the way they sometimes do if they were bits of rhetoric or scenery. I think of the one time that Sherlock Holmes failed in a disguise and was caught out by the one adversary he truly respected, Irene Adler. Trying to uncover her secrets, Holmes has dressed as an elderly clergyman and entered her house. The clever woman is reluctant at first "to think evil of such a dear, kind old clergyman," but nevertheless realizes she is being tricked and quickly turns Holmes's trickery back upon himself. Holmes is ashamed of impersonating an honorable cleric and bestows all the honor of the case on Irene Adler.[1]

I like my literary pastors credible, ambiguous, and perfectly imperfect. In *The Improper Opinion*, Martin Marty's old book about the church and the mass media (written when, or so it now seems, such media were relatively innocuous), he points out that the commercial media will always try to shape "proper opinion"—conformity, compliance—in its audience, while the church must do the opposite. Christianity, says Marty, needs to be on the side of "improper opinion," working with paradox, foolishness, and contrariness. Similarly, when secular culture tries to describe or expose the Christian church the results will be mere presentation, he says, not communication. Communication is dialogue, but the entertainment and news industry is not interested in dialogue. It wants to sway us with monologue.[2] Thus the most valuable depictions of clergy—the ones found in art, not the mass media—will be messy, complicated, and prickly. The more prickly, the more real. A pastor who is not incarnate is of no use to anyone. A novel, play, or film which offers pastors who are not fully human is similarly of little use.

For these reasons I have struggled against categories of clergy in this study. I have arranged and organized them as needed for the reader's comprehension, but tried not to be excessive in categorization. Some of the clerical characters I have studied refused to stay in one chapter, and that is for the best. Many of them refused to stay in any chapter at all, and so I wrote the Interludes, granting them their independence. No real pastor is made up of one element, or even ten elements. Why not accept that they may be comprised of a bit of Parson Yorick, a little of Mr. Beebe, a lot of Monsignor Quixote, and hopefully a whole lot of something entirely individual and unique?

One of my regrets is that I have not been able to venture toward clerics from other religions. At least one Jewish rabbi appears, but it would have been lovely to do more of this. Buddhist and Christian monks, Muslim and Christian clerics—these people surely share many of the same duties, frustrations, and joys. I have wished, however, not to overstep

1. Doyle, "A Scandal in Bohemia," 130.
2. Marty, *The Improper Opinion*, 32, 13, 86.

my bounds, and I may have been uneven in my attitude toward various Christian denominations. If so, my apologies. But although my own Lutheran beliefs and practices direct my exploration, I do hope that my ranging through other denominations has been reliable and stimulating. I want *The Collar* to be as accessible and supple as possible.

As I wrote this book, another phrase percolated within my thinking from time to time: *with* (or *without*) *benefit of clergy*. The origin of this expression lies, interestingly, in the struggle between Henry II and Thomas Becket, discussed several times in this book. In the twelfth century these two stubborn and titanic personalities fought over church and state power. After Archbishop Becket was murdered and King Henry felt the need to atone, it was settled that the church could, in some instances, control its own legal jurisdiction. To invoke benefit of clergy meant originally a request to have a case tried in an ecclesiastical court, not a civil court, and was intended to protect clerics and recognize their distinct situations. Soon, however, it became common to use a test of literacy to determine if someone pleading benefit of clergy was indeed a cleric, and eventually the literacy test became a huge loophole in the English legal system. For hundreds of years it had nothing to do with being of the clergy; the benefit of clergy rule was not finally abolished until the nineteenth century.

In 1890 Rudyard Kipling wrote about the relationship of an Englishman living with, and having a child with, a Muslim woman in India. Kipling's story "Without Benefit of Clergy" is one of the first major instances of the way the term is often used today; it now implies a conjugal relationship that exists outside the blessing of the church. The phrase in some dictionaries is still defined solely in the ancient way (the Oxford English Dictionary has no entry for this contemporary use of *benefit of clergy*) but generally it is now understand that the concept involves not a literacy test but (once again) the sanction and mandate of the church, and in particular, *without benefit of clergy* suggests a couple who is living together.

Think about the circumstance that for hundreds of years the notion of enjoying benefit of clergy has indicated, in the main, either literacy or marriage. Yet neither of these notions has anything to do with the essential qualities and tasks of Christian ministry. Much of what distracts or exercises us about the ordained ministry is likewise beside the point: wearing a clerical collar, being male, or demonstrating upright, even superhuman behavior. I must admit that this phrase also tickles me because it gets to the heart of two items which often become tangled up in our perceptions of the ministry: words and sex. Naturally we expect our pastors to be literate, but we want much more than that: we need them to be eloquent and inspiring, using enthralling language every Sunday morning to convince us to stagger on toward goodness for another week. We want not just articulate pastors, but women and men who will transform and convert us. And when a minister presides over romantic and sexual unions, we are reminded that ministers surely have romantic and sexual interests of their own, and this will never fail to fascinate us. Otherwise, why has Susan Howatch sold so many copies of the sensational and oversexed Starbridge series of clerical novels, and why are Robert Browning's vivacious poems about libidinous clergy (a monk leering at a luscious woman, a dying bishop forgetting to call his sons "nephews"[3]) so entertaining? Pondering our obsession with clerical sex, I have decided that now is as good a time as any to just get over it.

I have also worried occasionally about the efficacy of clerical characters at the opposite end of the literary spectrum, those who shine so brightly we must avert our eyes. There are several ministers in *The Collar* who could be analyzed as Christ figures (Dinah Morris in *Adam Bede*, the Preacher in *Pale Rider*, the martyrs of *Romero* and *Becket*) and perhaps do not belong in this book at all. Take the least serious one as an example, Clint Eastwood's Preacher in *Pale Rider*: what good does it do the viewer to recognize his pastoral characteristics when the Preacher turns out to be invincible and perhaps even immortal? What is the sense of a saintly, flawless pastor? Perhaps it is wiser to turn away our gaze from perfection, especially if there is danger that such interpretation ruins us for the realism of our actual pastors. Dinah Morris and Archbishop Romero are so inspirational and courageous that your week-kneed, absent-minded real-life ministers may begin to look like walking catastrophes, when really they are well-meaning human animals minding the store for God as best they can.

---

3. Browning, "Soliloquy of the Spanish Cloister" and "The Bishop Orders His Tomb at Saint Praxed's Church."

In the early stages of Herman Melville's *Moby Dick*, we come upon a chapter called "The Pulpit." The focus of this brief section of the novel is Father Mapple, chaplain to the sailing community, once a sailor and now a respected old man of the cloth. On entering his chapel, Father Mapple casts his eyes up to the pulpit which is (like many pulpits once were) very lofty. This pulpit is so lofty that it resembles the bow of a ship and Father Mapple climbs into it by way of a rope ladder, which he pulls up after himself. Melville's narrator wonders if this signifies the minister's "spiritual withdrawal" but then decides on a more momentous explanation:

> What could be more full of meaning?—for the pulpit is ever this earth's foremost part; all the rest comes in its rear; the pulpit leads the world. From thence it is the storm of God's quick wrath is first descried, and the bow must bear the earliest brunt. From thence it is the God of breezes fair or foul is first invoked for favourable winds. Yes, the world's a ship on its passage out, and not a voyage complete; and the pulpit is its prow.[4]

Then Father Mapple begins to preach (unsurprisingly, about Jonah), and his sermon, saturated with the idiosyncratic language of the sailors, justifies the extraordinary confidence of the narrator. Every sentence is in a seagoing vernacular, with references to keels and top-gallants, pilots and bulwarks. His sermon concerns obedience, but concludes hopefully and joyfully with emphasis on God's mercy: "Delight is to him, whom all the waves of the billows of the seas of the boisterous mob can never shake from this sure Keel of the Ages."[5]

There are still pulpits that must be, unfortunately, climbed into. I have watched, with misgiving, vicars in English churches ascend steep stairs and wondered if their homiletics would be similarly imposing and lordly. Pastors have told me stories of their internship days in old rural Canadian churches and the horror of leaving the pulpit, forgetting the stairs, and plummeting to ignominy. The pastor in *Moby Dick* lives up to his elevated position, but he does so by being absorbed into the congregation. Father Mapple's language is neither haughty nor grand; ironically it is the workaday idiom which makes his message exceptional and exalted.

4. Melville, *Moby Dick*, 35.
5. Ibid., 43.

Although my field is literature, I have attempted to keep my ideas in *The Collar* grounded in scripture. In particular, I knew I had to pay attention to the pastoral epistles, but working with the epistles to Timothy and Titus has been a mixed blessing. I flinch, as a pastor's spouse, from the disparaging tone of "for if someone does not know how to manage his own household, how can he take care of God's church?" (1 Tim 3:5). The emphasis on prudence, godliness, uprightness, and righteousness can begin to sound like a provocative taunt: *so you think you can live up to this?* The words *purity* or *pure* are used many times and there is an extremity in the language that can be unnerving—"Show yourself in *all* respects a model of good works" (Titus 2:7, my emphasis). Eugene Peterson's warning sounds in my head: "Many a Christian has lost his or her soul in the act of being ordained."[6]

So I turn instead to one of the less alarming verses: "Be persistent whether the time is favorable or unfavorable" (2 Tim 4:2). The average pastor should be able to handle this. Persistence is feasible, as are love and patience. Most pastors should also be able to carry out gentleness and hospitality. And then I remind myself once again that we are all ministers, and that Christians in general—not just the ordained sort—can take instruction from the pastoral epistles. If the challenges are large, so is the assembly of the priesthood of all believers.

Eugene Peterson has written that many congregations do not want pastors at all, but instead "managers of their religious company. They want a pastor they can follow so they won't have to bother with following Jesus anymore."[7] Peterson is frighteningly perceptive, and both pastors and laity should be concerned about members who drift away from Christ's centrality. Christ's message can be unnerving: all of that *righteousness* and *godliness* is hard to live up to, but in the company of our fellow ministers, ordained and not, we should be able to accomplish at least some of this, with God's grace.

The time may be favorable or unfavorable, I would not care to say, but persistent is the call and God is the caller. Let the congregation say Amen.

6. Peterson, *The Unnecessary Pastor*, 14.
7. Ibid., 4.

Bibliography

7th Heaven. Created by Brenda Hampton. Produced by Aaron Spelling. With Stephen Collins and Catherine Hicks. WB and CW Television Networks, 1996–2007.

The African Queen. Directed by John Huston. Written by James Agee and John Huston. Based on the novel by C. S. Forester. With Humphrey Bogart and Katharine Hepburn. United Artists, 1951.

Anderson, Sam. "How James Wood's *How Fiction Works* Works (and Why it Sometimes Doesn't)." *New York Magazine*, August 3, 2008.

The Apostle. Directed by Robert Duvall. Written by Robert Duvall. With Robert Duvall, Farrah Fawcett, and Miranda Richardson. October Films, 1998.

Ashworth, Jacinta, and Ian Farthing. *Churchgoing in the UK*. Middlesex: Tearfund, 2007.

Auden, W. H. "The Guilty Vicarage: Notes on the Detective Story, by an Addict." 1948. In *Detective Fiction: A Collection of Critical Essays*, edited by Robin W. Winks, 15–24. Englewood Cliffs, NJ: Prentice-Hall, 1980.

Austen, Jane. *Emma*. 1815. London: Penguin, 1996.

———. *Mansfield Park*. 1814. Harmondsworth: Penguin, 1985.

———. *Northanger Abbey*. 1818. Harmondsworth: Penguin, 1985.

———. *Pride and Prejudice*. 1813. Oxford: Oxford University Press, 1998.

———. *Sense and Sensibility*. 1811. New York: Signet, 1997.

"The Autochef." *Wallace and Gromit's Cracking Contraptions*. Directed by Loyd Price and Christopher Sadler. Aardman Animations, 2002.

Barna, George. *Virtual America: What Every Church Leader Needs to Know About Ministering in an Age of Spiritual and Technological Revolution*. Ventura, CA: Regal, 1994.

Beerbohm, Max. "A Clergyman." In *And Even Now*, 238–41. New York: E. P. Dutton, 1921.

Becket. Directed by Peter Glenville. Written by Edward Anhalt. Based on the play by Jean Anouilh. With Peter O'Toole and Richard Burton. Paramount, 1964.

Begley, Ann M. "Georges Bernanos' Love Affair with God." *Religion and Literature* 33. 3 (Autumn 2001) 37–52.

The Bells of St. Mary's. Directed by Leo McCarey. Written by Dudley Nichols. With Bing Crosby, Ingrid Bergman, and Henry Travers. RKO Pictures, 1945.

Bennett, Alan. *Bed Among the Lentils*. London: Samuel French, 1988.

Bergman, Ingmar. *Private Confessions*. 1996. Translated by Joan Tate. New York: Arcade, 1997.

Bernanos, Georges. *The Diary of a Country Priest*. 1936. Translated by Pamela Morris. London: Collins/Fontana, 1956.

Berton, Pierre. *The Comfortable Pew: A Critical Look at Christianity and the Religious Establishment in the New Age.* Toronto: McClelland & Stewart, 1965.

Bibby, Reginald. *Restless Churches.* Toronto: Novalis, 2004.

The Bishop's Wife. Directed by Henry Koster. Written by Leonardo Bercovici and Robert E. Sherwood. With Loretta Young, David Niven, and Cary Grant. RKO Pictures, 1947.

Blake, Richard A. "The Sins of Leo McCarey." *Journal of Religion and Film* 17.1 (April 2013). Online: unomaha.edu/jrf.

Blizek, Bill, and Ronald Burke. "The Apostle: An Interview with Robert Duvall." *Journal of Religion and Film* 2.1 (April 1998).

Bonhoeffer, Dietrich. *Life Together.* 1938. Translated by John W. Doberstein. San Francisco: Harper and Row, 1954.

————. *Sanctorum Communio: A Theological Study of the Sociology of the Church.* 1930. Translated by Reinhard Krauss and Nancy Lukens. Minneapolis: Augsburg Fortress, 1998.

Bonnycastle, Stephen. "Robertson Davies and the Ethics of Monologue." In *Robertson Davies: An Appreciation*, edited by Elspeth Cameron, 140–75. Peterborough, ON: Broadview, 1991.

The Book of Daniel. Created by Jack Kenny. With Aidan Quinn and Susanna Thompson. NBC Television, 2005–2006.

Booth, Catherine Mumford. *Female Ministry: A Woman's Right to Preach the Gospel.* London: Morgan & Chase, 1859.

Bosco, Mark. *Graham Greene's Catholic Imagination.* Oxford: Oxford University Press/American Academy of Religion, 2005.

Bottum, Joseph. "God and the Detectives: Religious Mysteries, a Perplexing Case." *Books and Culture: A Christian Review* (September/October 2011) 1–11.

Brockman, James. R. *The Word Remains: A Life of Oscar Romero.* Maryknoll, NY: Orbis, 1982.

Brontë, Charlotte. *Jane Eyre.* 1847. London: Penguin, 2006.

Browning, Robert. "Soliloquy of the Spanish Cloister" and "The Bishop Orders His Tomb at Saint Praxed's Church." In *Selected Poems*, edited by Daniel Karlin, 27–29, 45–48. London: Penguin, 1989.

Buechner, Frederick. *Wishful Thinking: A Theological ABC.* New York: Harper and Row, 1973.

Butt, Riazat. "*Vicar of Dibley* Effect: More Women than Men Ordained." *The Guardian* November 14, 2007.

Byatt, A. S. *Babel Tower.* London: Chatto & Windus, 1996.

————. *Still Life.* London: Penguin, 1985.

————. *The Virgin in the Garden.* 1978. London: Penguin, 1981.

————. *A Whistling Woman.* London: Chatto & Windus, 2002.

Bylin, Victoria. *The Maverick Preacher.* New York: Steeple Hill, 2009.

Calder, Alison. "Sinclair Ross." *The Literary Encyclopedia.* 2002.

Callaghan, Barry. "The Writings of Margaret Laurence." In *Margaret Laurence: The Writer and Her Critics*, edited by William New, 126–31. Toronto: McGraw-Hill Ryerson, 1977.

Callaghan, Morley. *Such is My Beloved.* 1934. Toronto: McClelland & Stewart, 1957.

Cariou, Warren. *The Exalted Company of Roadside Martyrs.* Regina, SK: Coteau, 1999.

Carpenter, Charles A. "The Quintessence of Shaw's Ethical Position." In *Eight Modern Plays,* edited by Anthony Caputi, 491–97. New York: Norton, 1991.

Chapman, Raymond. Introduction to *Godly and Righteous, Peevish and Perverse: Clergy and Religious in Literature and Letters.* Grand Rapids: Eerdmans, 2002.

Cheetham, William. *Christianity Reviewed.* Brockville, ON: Recorder Printing Company, 1896.

———. *Lights and Shadows of Clerical Life.* Montreal: Lovell, 1879.

Chesterton, G. K. *The Annotated Innocence of Father Brown.* Edited by Martin Gardner. Mineola, NY: Dover, 1998.

———. "Bacon and Shakespeare, Again." In *Collected Works of G. K. Chesterton,* vol. 29, 418–21. San Francisco: Ignatius, 1988.

———. "A Defence of Detective Stories." In *The Defendant,* 155–62. London: Dent, 1901.

———. "The Divine Detective." In *A Miscellany of Men,* 235–40. London: Methuen, 1912.

———."The World of Sherlock Holmes." In *Collected Works of G. K. Chesterton,* vol. 24, 237–40. San Francisco: Ignatius, 1991.

Christensen, Martin. "Chronology of Women's Ordination." *Worldwide Guide to Women in Leadership,* 2005.

Christie, Agatha. *The Murder at the Vicarage.* New York: Dodd, Mead, 1930.

Christmas, F. E. *The Parson in English Literature.* London: Hodder and Stoughton, 1950.

Clark, Warren. "Patterns of Religious Attendance." *Canadian Social Trends* (Winter 2000) 23–27.

Connor, Ralph [Charles William Gordon]. *The Man from Glengarry: A Tale of the Ottawa.* Chicago: Fleming Revell, 1901.

Coote, Stephen. Introduction to *The Vicar of Wakefield,* 7–24. Harmondsworth: Penguin, 1982.

Dahl, Roald. *The Vicar of Nibbleswicke.* London: Penguin, 1991.

Davies, Horton. *A Mirror of the Ministry in Modern Novels.* New York: Oxford University Press, 1959.

Davies, Robertson. *Fifth Business.* 1970. In *The Deptford Trilogy.* London: Penguin, 1983.

———. *The Lyre of Orpheus.* Toronto: Macmillan, 1988.

———. *The Rebel Angels.* Toronto: Macmillan, 1981.

Dawn, Marva. *The Sense of the Call: A Sabbath Way of Life for Those Who Serve God, the Church, and the World.* Grand Rapids: Eerdmans, 2006.

Dead Man Walking. Directed by Tim Robbins. Written by Tim Robbins. With Susan Sarandon and Sean Penn. Polygram Films, 1995.

Dickens, Charles. *Bleak House.* 1853. London: Penguin, 1996.

———. *Our Mutual Friend.* 1865. London: Penguin, 1997.

Dostoyevsky, Fyodor. *The Brothers Karamazov.* 1880. London: Penguin, 2003.

Doubt. Directed by John Patrick Shanley. Written by John Patrick Shanley. With Meryl Streep, Philip Seymour Hoffman, and Amy Adams. Miramax Films, 2008.

Doyle, Arthur Conan. "A Scandal in Bohemia." In *Sherlock Holmes: The Complete Facsimile Edition,* 117–31. London: Wordsworth, 1989.

Doyle, James. Preface to *The Lives of the Fathers, Martyrs, and Principal Saints,* by Alban Butler. New York: Archbishop's House, 1895, 7–15.

Ebert, Roger. Review of *The Apostle.* January 30, 1998.

————. Review of *Million Dollar Baby*. December 14, 2004. Online: rogerebert.com

Eco, Umberto. *The Name of the Rose*. 1980. Translated by William Weaver. New York: Harcourt Brace Jovanovich, 1983.

Eliot, George. *Adam Bede*. 1859. London: Penguin, 1980.

————. *Middlemarch*. 1871–1872. London: Penguin, 1994.

————. *Scenes of Clerical Life*. 1857. London: Penguin, 1998.

Eliot, T. S. "Choruses from *The Rock*." *Collected Poems: 1909–1962*. London: Faber, 1963, 159–85.

————. *George Herbert*. London: British Council/Longmans Green, 1962.

————. *Murder in the Cathedral*. New York: Harcourt Brace, 1935.

Ellmann, Richard. *Edwardians and Late Victorians*. New York: Columbia University Press, 1960.

Elmer Gantry. Directed by Richard Brooks. Written by Richard Brooks. With Burt Lancaster and Jean Simmons. United Artists, 1960.

Endicott, Marina. *Good to a Fault*. 2008. Toronto: Harper Perennial, 2010.

Everson, Eva Marie. *This Fine Life*. Grand Rapids: Baker, 2010.

Father Ted. Created by Graham Linehan and Arthur Mathews. With Dermot Morgan. Channel Four Television, 1995–1998.

Faulkner, William. *Light in August*. 1932. New York: Vintage: 1985.

Field, Louise Maunsell. Review of *The Trembling of a Leaf* by W. Somerset Maugham. In *W. Somerset Maugham: The Critical Heritage*, edited by Anthony Curtis and John Whitehead, 148–51. London: Routledge, 1987.

Fielding, Henry. *The History of Tom Jones, a Foundling*. 1749. London: Penguin, 1985.

Fiorito, Joe. Introduction to *The Exile Book of Priests, Pastors, Nuns and Pentecostals: Stories of Preachers and Preaching*. Holstein, ON: Exile Editions, 2010, xi–xv.

Fish, Stanley. *The Living Temple*. Berkeley: University of California Press, 1978.

Flaubert, Gustave. *Madame Bovary*. Translated and edited by Paul de Man. New York: Norton, 1965.

The Flying Nun. Created by Harry Ackerman, Max Wylie, and Bernard Slade. With Sally Field. ABC Television, 1967–1970.

Footloose. Directed by Herbert Ross. Written by Dean Pitchford. With John Lithgow and Kevin Bacon. Paramount Pictures, 1984.

Forster, E. M. *A Room with a View*. 1908. New York: Penguin, 2000.

Four Weddings and a Funeral. Directed by Mike Newell. Written by Richard Curtis. With Hugh Grant and Rowan Atkinson. Channel Four Films, 1994.

Frye, Northrop. "Conclusion to *A Literary History of Canada*." 1965. In *The Bush Garden: Essays on the Canadian Imagination*, 213–51. Toronto: Anansi, 1971.

Gilbert, Sandra, and Susan Gubar. *The Madwoman in the Attic: The Woman Writer and the Nineteenth-Century Literary Imagination*, 2nd ed. New Haven: Yale University Press, 2000.

God or the Girl. Created by Stephen David, David Eilenberg, and Darryl M. Silver. With Joe Adair and Steve Horvath. A & E Television, 2006.

Going My Way. Directed by Leo McCarey. Written by Leo McCarey. With Bing Crosby and Barry Fitzgerald. Paramount Films, 1944.

Golding, William. *The Spire*. 1964. London: Faber, 2005.

Goldsmith, Oliver. *The Vicar of Wakefield*. 1766. Harmondsworth: Penguin, 1982.

Gran Torino. Directed by Clint Eastwood. Written by Nick Schenk. With Clint Eastwood and Christopher Carley. Warner Bros., 2008.

Grant, Judith Skelton. "Discovering Robertson Davies." *University of Toronto Quarterly* 78.4 (2009) 931–48.

Greene, Graham. *Monsignor Quixote*. London: Penguin, 1982.

———. *The Power and the Glory*. 1940. London: Penguin, 1992.

Haight, Gordon S. *George Eliot: A Biography*. Oxford: Oxford University Press, 1968.

Hale, F. "The Postfigurative Christ in Morley Callaghan's *Such is My Beloved*." *Acta Theologica* 25.1 (2005) 28–49.

Hall, Douglas John. *Bound and Free: A Theologian's Journey*. Minneapolis: Fortress, 2005.

———. *The End of Christendom and the Future of Christianity*. 1997. Eugene, OR: Wipf and Stock, 2002.

Hare, David. *Racing Demon*. London: Faber, 1990.

Hawaii. Directed by George Roy Hill. Written by Dalton Trumbo and Daniel Taradash. Based on the novel by James A. Michener. With Max von Sydow and Julie Andrews. United Artists, 1966.

Hawthorne, Nathaniel. "The Minister's Black Veil: A Parable." 1837. In *Twice-Told Tales*, 47–66. Boston: Osgood, 1876.

———. *The Scarlet Letter*. 1850. New York: Signet, 1999.

Heavens Above! Directed by John Boulting and Roy Boulting. Written by John Boulting and Frank Harvey. With Peter Sellers and Isabel Jeans. British Lion Films, 1963.

Herbert, George. *The Country Parson, The Temple*. Edited by John N. Wall. Mahwah, NJ: Paulist, 1981.

Hinde, Thomas. *A Field Guide to the English Country Parson*. London: Heinemann, 1983.

Hodgson, Peter C. *Theology in the Fiction of George Eliot*. London: SCM, 2001.

Hoen, Matthew. "Georges Bernanos." *Library of Catholic Authors*, 2009.

Howatch, Susan. *Glittering Images*. New York: Knopf, 1987.

I Confess. Directed by Alfred Hitchcock. Written by George Tabori and William Archibald. With Montgomery Clift and Anne Baxter. Warner Bros., 1953.

Ibsen, Henrik. *Brand*. 1865. Translated by Michael Meyer. London: Hart-Davis, 1960.

Irvine, William. "On *Candida*." 1949. In *Eight Modern Plays*, edited by Anthony Caputi, 497–501. New York: Norton, 1991.

James, William Closson. *Locations of the Sacred: Essays on Religion, Literature, and Canadian Culture*. Waterloo, ON: Wilfrid Laurier University Press, 1998.

The Mission. Directed by Roland Joffe. Written by Robert Bolt. With Jeremy Irons and Robert DeNiro. Warner Bros., 1986.

Johnson, Katie N. "Before Katrina: Archiving Performative Downpours and Fallen Women Named Sadie in *Rain* and *The Deluge*." *Modern Drama* 52.3 (Fall 2009) 351–68.

Joyce, James. *A Portrait of the Artist as a Young Man*. 1916. New York: Penguin, 1993.

Karon, Jan. *A Light in the Window*. 1995. New York: Penguin, 1996.

———. *At Home in Mitford*. 1994. New York: Penguin, 1996.

———. *Out to Canaan*. 1997. New York: Penguin, 1998.

Keeping the Faith. Directed by Edward Norton. Written by Stuart Blumberg. With Ben Stiller, Edward Norton, Jenna Elfman. Touchstone Pictures, 2000.

Keeping Mum. Directed by Niall Johnson. Written by Richard Russo. With Rowan Atkinson, Maggie Smith, Kristin Scott Thomas. ThinkFilm, 2005.

Keillor, Garrison. *Pontoon*. New York: Viking Penguin, 2007.

The Keys of the Kingdom. Directed by John M. Stahl. Written by Joseph L. Mankiewicz and Nunnally Johnson. Based on the novel by A. J. Cronin. With Gregory Peck and Rosa Stradner. Twentieth Century Fox Films, 1944.

Kierkegaard, Søren. *Attack upon "Christendom."* 1854–1855. Translated by Walter Lowrie. Princeton: Princeton University Press, 1946.

Kipling, Rudyard. "Without Benefit of Clergy." In *Selected Stories,* edited by Andrew Rutherford, 213–31. London: Penguin, 1987.

Lambert, Pam. "Father Figure: Unruffled Linus Roache Finds Himself in the Eye of the Storm over *Priest.*" *People* 43.17 (May 1, 1995).

Lane, Anthony. Review of *Priest.* In *Nobody's Perfect: Writings from the New Yorker,* 109–113. New York: Knopf, 2002.

Latham, David. "Sinclair Ross: An Annotated Bibliography." In *The Annotated Bibliography of Canada's Major Authors,* vol. 3. Edited by Robert Lecker and Jack David. Downsview, ON: ECW, 1981.

Laurence, Margaret. *The Stone Angel.* 1964. Toronto: McClelland & Stewart, 1968.

Leacock, Stephen. *Arcadian Adventures with the Idle Rich.* New York: J. Lane, 1914.

Lewis, Sinclair. *Elmer Gantry.* 1927. New York: Signet, 1970.

Lewis-Anthony, Justin. *If You Meet George Herbert on the Road, Kill Him.* London: Mowbray, 2009.

Little, Dave. *Catching the Wind in a Net: The Religious Vision of Robertson Davies.* Toronto: ECW, 1996.

Little Mosque on the Prairie. Created by Zarqa Nawaz. Canadian Broadcasting Corporation, 2007–2012.

Lovesey, Oliver. *The Clerical Character in George Eliot's Fiction.* Victoria, BC: English Literary Studies, 1991.

Luther, Martin. "Fourteen Consolations." 1520. In *Luther's Works,* vol. 42, 119–166. Philadelphia: Fortress, 1959.

———. "The Babylonian Captivity of the Church." 1520. In *Luther's Works,* vol. 36, 11–126. Philadelphia: Fortress, 1959.

MacFarlane, Robert. "A Very Bad Case of Birds on the Brain." Review of *A Whistling Woman* by A. S. Byatt. *The Guardian,* September 15, 2002.

A Man Called Peter. Directed by Henry Koster. Written by Eleanore Griffin. Based on the book by Catherine Marshall. With Richard Todd and Jean Peters. Twentieth Century Fox, 1955.

Marshall, Catherine. *A Man Called Peter: The Story of Peter Marshall.* 1951. Grand Rapids: Baker, 2002.

Marshall, David B. *Secularizing the Faith: Canadian Protestant Clergy and the Crisis of Belief, 1850–1940.* Toronto: University of Toronto Press, 1992.

Marty, Martin. *The Improper Opinion: Mass Media and the Christian Faith.* Philadelphia: Westminster, 1961.

M*A*S*H. "Dear Dad." Season 1, Episode 12. Directed by Gene Reynolds. Written by Larry Gelbart. With Alan Alda and William Christopher. CBS Television, 1972.

M*A*S*H. "Rainbow Bridge." Season 3, Episode 2. Directed by Hy Averback. Written by Larry Gelbart and Laurence Marks. With Alan Alda and William Christopher. CBS Television, 1974.

Maslin, Janet. "Man of Strong Passion, Earthly and Otherwise." Review of *The Apostle.* *New York Times,* October 9, 1997.

Maugham, W. Somerset. "Rain." In *Short Stories,* 73–115. London: Minerva, 1994.

McDannell, Colleen. Introduction to *Catholics in the Movies*. Oxford: Oxford University Press, 2008, 3–31.

McSweeney, Kerry. *Middlemarch*. Unwin Critical Library. London: Allen & Unwin, 1984.

Melville, Herman. *Moby Dick*. 1851. Oxford: Oxford University Press, 1988.

Michel of Northgate. "Ayenbite of inwyt." *Corpus of Middle English Prose and Verse*. University of Michigan.

Miller, Arthur. *The Crucible*. 1952. New York: Penguin, 2003.

Miller, Karl. "Ladies in Distress." Review of *Excellent Women* and *Quartet in Autumn* by Barbara Pym. *New York Review of Books* 25.17, November 9, 1978.

Million Dollar Baby. Directed by Clint Eastwood. Written by Paul Haggis. With Clint Eastwood, Morgan Freeman, and Hillary Swank. Warner Bros., 2004.

The Missionary. Directed by Richard Loncraine. Written by Michael Palin. With Michael Palin. Handmaid Films, 1982.

Moseley, Merritt. "A Few Words about Barbara Pym." *The Sewanee Review* 98.1 (Winter 1990) 75–87.

Munro, Alice. "Age of Faith." In *Lives of Girls and Women*. Toronto: McGraw-Hill Ryerson, 1971, 77–97.

———. "Pictures of the Ice." In *Friend of My Youth*. Toronto: McClelland & Stewart, 1990, 137–55.

———. "Wild Swans." In *Who Do You Think You Are?* Toronto: Macmillan, 1978, 56–66.

Murdoch, Iris. *The Bell*. 1958. London: Penguin, 1962.

Murphy, Rachel. Review of *The Diary of a Country Priest* by Georges Bernanos. *Catholic Fiction*, February 9, 2006.

Murphy, Terrence, and Roberto Perin. *A Concise History of Christianity in Canada*. Toronto: Oxford University Press, 1996.

The Name of the Rose. Directed by Jean-Jacques Annaud. Written by Andrew Birkin et al. With Sean Connery. France 3 Cinema/Twentieth Century Fox Films, 1986.

New, W. H. *Articulating West: Essays on Purpose and Form in Modern Canadian Literature*. Toronto: New Press, 1972.

Newport, Frank. "Estimating Americans' Worship Behavior." *The Gallup Poll*, January 3, 2006.

The Night of the Iguana. Directed by John Huston. Written by John Huston and Anthony Veiller. With Richard Burton, Ava Gardner, and Deborah Kerr. MGM, 1964.

Nothing Sacred. Created by Bill Cain and David Manson. With Kevin Anderson. ABC Television, 1997–1998.

O'Connor, John. "Strong Performances Help *Thorn Birds* Soar." *New York Times*, March 27, 1983.

Oliphant, Margaret. *The Autobiography of Margaret Oliphant*. Peterborough, ON: Broadview, 2002.

———. *Phoebe Junior. A Last Chronicle of Carlingford*. 1876. Peterborough, ON: Broadview, 2002.

Orwell, George. *A Clergyman's Daughter*. 1936. New York: Harcourt, n.d.

Paietta, Ann C. *Saints, Clergy, and Other Religious Figures on Film and Television, 1895–2003*. Jefferson, NC: McFarland, 2005.

Pale Rider. Directed by Clint Eastwood. Written by Michael Butler and Dennis Shryack. With Clint Eastwood and Sydney Penny. Warner Bros., 1985.

Paton, Alan. *Cry, the Beloved Country.* 1948. New York: Scribner, 2003.

Peters, Ellis [Edith Pargeter]. *Brother Cadfael's Penance.* 1994. London: Headline, 1994.

Peterson, Eugene. *The Contemplative Pastor: Returning to the Art of Spiritual Direction.* 1989. Grand Rapids: Eerdmans, 1993.

———. *Five Smooth Stones for Pastoral Work.* 1980. Grand Rapids: Eerdmans, 1992.

———. *The Pastor: A Memoir.* New York: HarperCollins, 2011.

———. *Working the Angles: The Shape of Pastoral Integrity.* Grand Rapids: Eerdmans, 1987.

Peterson, Eugene, and Marva Dawn. *The Unnecessary Pastor: Rediscovering the Call.* Grand Rapids: Eerdmans, 2000.

The Preacher's Wife. Directed by Penny Marshall. Written by Nat Mauldin and Allan Scott. With Whitney Houston, Courtney B. Vance, and Denzel Washington. Touchstone Pictures, 1996.

Priest. Directed by Antonia Bird. Written by Jimmy McGovern. With Linus Roache, Tom Wilkinson, and Robert Carlyle. BBC Films, 1994.

Prioleau, Elizabeth. "The Minister and the Seductress in American Fiction: The Adamic Myth Redux." *Journal of American Culture* 16.4 (Winter 1993) 1–6.

Pym, Barbara. *Crampton Hodnet.* New York: E. P. Dutton, 1985.

———. *The Barbara Pym Omnibus: Some Tame Gazelle, Excellent Women, Jane and Prudence.* London: Pan, 1994.

Rabin, Nathan. "Interview: John Patrick Shanley." *A. V. Club*, January 13, 2009.

Rain. Directed by Lewis Milestone. Written by Maxwell Anderson. With Joan Crawford and Walter Huston. United Artists, 1932.

Raising Helen. Directed by Garry Marshall. Written by Jack Amiel and Michael Begler. With Kate Hudson and John Corbett. Buena Vista Pictures, 2004.

Ramsey, G. Lee, Jr. *Preachers and Misfits, Prophets and Thieves: The Minister in Southern Fiction.* Louisville: Westminster John Knox, 2008.

"The Real Vicars of Dibley." DVD featurette. *The Vicar of Dibley.* Third series. BBC Video, 2003.

Reinhartz, Adele. *Scripture on the Silver Screen.* Louisville: Westminster John Knox, 2003.

"Reputations Revisited." *Times Literary Supplement,* January 21, 1977, 66–68.

Rev. Created by Tom Hollander and James Wood. With Tom Hollander, Olivia Colman, and Simon McBurney. Series one and two. BBC TV, 2010–2011.

Rhys, Grace. Introduction to *Scenes of Clerical Life.* London: Everyman's Library, 1910.

Richards, David Adams. "Canada's Literary Community Gets Religion All Wrong." *The Globe and Mail,* August 14, 2009. Online: theglobeandmail.com.

Ricks, Christopher. "Introductory Essay." 1967. In *The Life and Opinions of Tristram Shandy, Gentleman,* xi–xxxii. London: Penguin, 1997.

Robertson, Ed. "How to Create a Winning Miniseries." *Media Life,* June 29, 2005.

Robinson, Marilynne. *Gilead.* New York: Harper Perennial, 2004.

Romero. Directed by John Duigan. Written by John Sacret Young. With Raul Julia. Paulist Pictures, 1989.

Romero, Oscar. *The Violence of Love.* Translated by James R. Brockman. Rifton, NY: Plough, 2011.

Ross, Sinclair. *As for Me and My House.* 1941. Toronto: McClelland & Stewart, 1989.

Sadie Thompson. Directed by Raoul Walsh. Written by Raoul Walsh. Based on Maugham's "Rain." With Gloria Swanson and Lionel Barrymore. United Artists, 1928.

The Sandpiper. Directed by Vincente Minnelli. Written by Dalton Trumbo and Michael Wilson. With Richard Burton, Elizabeth Taylor, and Eva Marie Saint. MGM, 1965.

Sayers, Dorothy L. Introduction to *The Omnibus of Crime,* 9–38. New York: Harcourt, Brace, 1929.

Schellenberg, Grant, and Warren Clark. "Who's Religious?" *Canadian Social Trends* (Summer 2006) 2–9.

"Selected Reviews." Stephen Leacock, *Arcadian Adventures with the Idle Rich.* Critical edition, edited by D. M. R. Bentley. Ottawa: Tecumseh, 2002, 207–15.

Sense and Sensibility. Directed by Ang Lee. Written by Emma Thompson. With Emma Thompson, Kate Winslet, Hugh Grant. Columbia Pictures, 1995.

Shanley, John Patrick. *Doubt: A Parable.* New York: Theatre Communications Group, 2005.

Shaw, George Bernard. *Candida.* 1898. In *Eight Modern Plays,* edited by Anthony Caputi. New York: Norton, 1991, 133–82.

———. *The Quintessence of Ibsenism.* London: Walter Scott, 1891.

Sirens. Directed by John Duigan. Written by John Duigan. With Hugh Grant and Tara Fitzgerald. Miramax Films, 1994.

Smith, Anthony Burke. "America's Favorite Priest: *Going My Way.*" In Colleen McDannell, *Catholics in the Movies,* 107–26. Oxford: Oxford University Press, 2008.

———. *The Look of Catholics: Portrayals in Popular Culture from the Great Depression to the Cold War.* Lawrence: University Press of Kansas, 2010.

St. John, Cheryl. *The Preacher's Wife.* New York: Steeple Hill, 2009.

Sterne, Laurence. *The Life and Opinions of Tristram Shandy, Gentleman.* 1759–1767. London: Penguin, 1997.

Stott, John. *The Preacher's Portrait.* Grand Rapids: Eerdmans, 1961.

Stovel, Nora Foster. "Temples and Tabernacles: Alternative Religions in the Fictional Microcosms of Robertson Davies, Margaret Laurence, and Alice Munro." *International Fiction Revew* 31.1 (2004).

Sussman, Irving. *As Others See Us: A Look at the Rabbi, Priest and Minister Through the Eyes of Literature.* New York: Sheed and Ward, 1971.

Taylor, Barbara Brown. *Leaving Church: A Memoir of Faith.* New York: HarperCollins, 2006.

Taylor, Will. "Rowan Atkinson: Church of England Clerics are 'Smug and Arrogant.'" *The Telegraph,* September 25, 2011.

Thackray, Rachelle. "The Fifty Best Selling Books of the 1990s." *The Independent,* September 26, 1998.

"Thirty-nine Articles of Religion." *Book of Common Prayer.* Anglican Church of Canada.

The Thorn Birds. Directed by Daryl Duke. Written by Carmen Culver and Lee Stanley. Based on the novel by Colleen McCullough. With Rachel Ward and Richard Chamberlain. ABC Television, 1983.

Trollope, Anthony. *An Autobiography.* 1883.

———. *The Warden.* 1855. New York: Dover, 1998.

Trollope, Joanna. *The Rector's Wife.* 1991. London: Black Swan, 1992.

Twain, Mark. *The Adventures of Huckleberry Finn*. 1885. Peterborough, ON: Broadview, 2011.

Updike, John. *A Month of Sundays*. New York: Fawcett Crest, 1974.

———. "Pigeon Feathers." 1960. In *The Early Stories: 1953–1975*, 13–33. New York: Ballantine, 2003.

Vaux, Sara Anson. *The Ethical Vision of Clint Eastwood*. Grand Rapids: Eerdmans, 2012.

The Vicar of Dibley. Created by Richard Curtis and Paul Mayhew-Archer. With Dawn French. Series one to three. BBC Television, 1997–2000.

Wall, John N. Introduction to *The Country Parson, The Temple*, by George Herbert, 1–51. Mahwah, NJ: Paulist, 1981.

Walrath, Douglas Alan. *Displacing the Divine: The Minister in the Mirror of American Fiction*. New York: Columbia University Press, 2010.

White, Hal. *The Mysteries of Reverend Dean*. Savage, MN: Lighthouse, 2008.

White, Laura Mooneyham. *Jane Austen's Anglicanism*. Farnham, Surrey: Ashgate, 2011.

Williams, Rowan. "The Christian Priest Today." May 28, 2004. *Archbishop of Canterbury*.

Williams, Tennessee. *The Night of the Iguana*. 1961. In *The Theatre of Tennessee Williams*. Vol. 4. New York: New Directions, 1993.

Wilson, A. N. Introduction to *The Faber Book of Church and Clergy*, vii–x. London: Faber, 1992.

———. *The Vicar of Sorrows*. New York: Norton, 1994.

Wilson, Keith. *Charles William Gordon*. Winnipeg: Peguis, 1981.

Winner, Lauren. "Sherry with Father Tim: A Conversation about Jan Karon's Fiction." *Books and Culture*, December 2007.

Witham, Larry A. *Who Shall Lead Them? The Future of Ministry in America*. New York: Oxford University Press, 2005.

Wodehouse, P. G. *The Clergy Omnibus*. London: Hutchinson, 1992.

Wolberg, Kristine A. *"All Possible Art": George Herbert's* The Country Parson. Madison, NJ: Fairleigh Dickinson University Press, 2008.

Wolff, Richard. *The Church on TV: Portrayals of Priests, Pastors and Nuns on American Television Series*. New York: Continuum, 2010.

Wood, James. "The Writer of TV Comedy *Rev.*, James Wood, Talks about the Show." *The Daily Mail*, November 5, 2011. Online: dailymail.co.uk.

Wood, James. "Acts of Devotion." Review of *Gilead* by Marilynne Robinson. *New York Times*, November 28, 2004. Online: nytimes.com.

———. *The Book Against God: A Novel*. New York: Farrar, Straus and Giroux, 2003.

———. *The Broken Estate: Essays on Literature and Belief*. New York: Modern Library, 2000.

———. *How Fiction Works*. New York: Farrar, Straus and Giroux, 2008.

Index

7th Heaven, 8, 187–88, 199

"Aaron" (Herbert), 15
Adam Bede (Eliot), 53–56, 61, 63,
    144, 280
"Affliction" (Herbert), 17
African Queen, The, 223
AfterMASH, 183
"Age of Faith" (Munro), 262
"All People that on Earth do Dwell"
    (hymn), 245
All Possible Art (Wolberg), 20
Amazing Grace (television show),
    183
"America's Favorite Priest" (Smith),
    206
Amis, Kingsley, 173
Anderson, Kevin, 182
Anderson, Maxwell, 170
Anderson, Sam, 135
Andrews, Julie, 230
Anhalt, Edward. *See* Anouilh, Jean
Annaud, Jean-Jacques, 113
Anouilh, Jean, 23–31, 208–9,
    213–15, 276, 280
Apostle, The, 191–93; interview
    with Blizek and Burke, 193;
    review by Ebert, 191, 193;
    review by Maslin, 191–93
Arabian Nights, 257
*Arcadian Adventures with the Idle
    Rich* (Leacock), 249–51;
    review in *The Spectator*, 250

Aristotle, 112
Articulating West (New), 253
As for Me and My House (Ross), 9,
    251, 253–56, 265
As Others See Us (Sussman), 165,
    167
Ashworth, Jacinta, 242–43
At Home in Mitford (Karon), 94–95
Atkinson, Rowan, 3, 86–88, 243
Attack upon Christendom
    (Kierkegaard), 7
Auden, W. H., 97–100, 106
Austen, Jane, 2, 4, 62, 66, 70, 78, 92,
    140, 148–51
*Autobiography of Margaret
    Oliphant, The* (Oliphant),
    145
Autobiography, An (Trollope),
    145–46
"Autochef, The," 3–4
"Ayenbite of inwyt" (Michel of
    Northgate), 139

Babel Tower (Byatt), 44, 46–47
"Babylonian Captivity of the
    Church, The" (Luther), 7,
    139, 145, 190
"Bacon and Shakespeare, Again"
    (Chesterton), 106
Baring-Gould, Sabine, 24
Barna, George, 242
Barrymore, Lionel, 169

Becket (Anouilh), 23, 28–31, 203, 208–9, 213–15, 279, 280

Bed Among the Lentils (Bennett), 227–28, 235

Beerbohm, Max, 1

"Before Katrina" (Johnson), 167, 170

Begley, Ann M., 39, 41

Bell, The (Murdoch), 237–40

Bells of St Mary's, The, 3, 8, 205–8, 213

Bennett, Alan, 227–28, 235

Bergman, Ingmar, 235–36

Bergman, Ingrid, 208

Bernanos, Georges, 36, 39–42, 252

Berton, Pierre, 256–57

Bibby, Reginald, 263

Bird, Antonia, 130–32

"Bishop Orders His Tomb at Saint Praxed's Church, The" (Browning), 280

Bishop's Wife, The, 213, 230

Blake, Richard A., 206

Bleak House (Dickens), 77–79, 115

Blizek, Bill, 193

"Blue Cross, The" (Chesterton), 102–4, 106

Blumberg, Stuart, 189–90

Bolt, Robert, 27

Bonhoeffer, Dietrich, 6, 24, 43, 60

Bonnycastle, Stephen, 259

Book Against God, The (Wood), 135–38

Book of Common Prayer, The, 10, 155, 190, 229

Book of Daniel, The, 183–84, 199, 228

Book of Martyrs, The (Foxe), 23

Booth, Catherine Mumford, 225–26

Bosco, Mark, 41

Bottum, Joseph, 99

Boulting, John, and Roy Boulting, 85–86, 89

Bound and Free (Hall), 59

Boys' Town, 213

Brand (Ibsen), 162–65, 174–75, 217, 235

Bresson, Robert, 39

Brideshead Revisited (Waugh), 104

Brockman, James R., 25

Broken Estate, The (Wood), 135–36

Brontë, Charlotte, 2, 140–43, 155, 223, 235–46

Brooks, Richard, 163

Brother Cadfael's Penance (Peters), 108–11

Brothers Karamazov, The (Dostoyevsky), 2

Browning, Robert, 280

Buechner, Frederick, 181

Burke, Ronald, 193

Burnt Norton (Eliot), 28

Burton, Richard, 3, 28–31, 208–15

Butler, Alban, 24

Butler, Michael, 177–80

Butt, Riazat, 196

Byatt, A. S., 44–48, 56, 59

Bylin, Victoria, 221–22

Calder, Alison, 254

Callaghan, Barry, 245

Callaghan, Morley, 251–53

Camus, Albert, 41

"Canada's Literary Community Gets Religion All Wrong" (Richards), 138

Candida (Shaw), 7–8, 231–34

Canterbury Tales, The (Chaucer), 28

Cariou, Warren, 263–65, 267

Carley, Christopher, 154

Carlyle, Robert, 130

Carpenter, Charles A., 231

Casaubon, Isaac, 48

Catching the Wind in a Net (Little), 257

Catholics in the Movies, introduction (McDannell), 206–7

Cattaneo, Peter, 198–201

Cecil, David, 92

Cervantes Saavedra, Miguel de, 76, 81, 83

Chamberlain, Richard, 184–85

Chaplin, Charlie, 81

Chapman, Raymond, 243

Charles Willliam Gordon (Wilson), 246

Chaucer, Geoffrey, 2, 28

Cheetham, William, 11, 271–76

Chesterton, G. K., 97–107, 111, 113, 243

"Choruses from *The Rock*" (Eliot), 37

Christensen, Martin, 218

"Christian Priest Today, The" (Williams), 60, 122

Christianity Reviewed (Cheetham), 271–72, 276

Christie, Agatha, 100, 226

Christmas Carol, A (Dickens), 62

Christmas, F. E., 243

"Chronology of Women's Ordination" (Christensen), 218

Church on TV, The (Wolff), 183, 188, 202

Churchgoing in the UK (Ashworth and Farthing), 242–43

Clark, Warren, 242–43

Clergy Omnibus, The (Wodehouse), 226

"Clergyman, A" (Beerbohm), 1

Clergyman's Daughter, A (Orwell), 223–25

Clerical Character in George Eliot's Fiction, The (Lovesey), 63, 143

Clift, Montgomery, 100

"Collar, The" (Herbert), 10, 13–21

Collins, Stephen, 187–88

Comfortable Pew, The (Berton), 256–57

Common Life, A (Karon), 94

Complicated Kindness, A (Toews), 244

"Conclusion to *A Literary History of Canada*" (Frye), 256

Connery, Sean, 113

Connor, Ralph (Charles William Gordon), 246–49

Contagion, 115

Contemplative Pastor, The (Peterson), 2, 155

Coote, Stephen, 72–74

Corbett, John, 182

Cosby Show, The, 199

Country Parson, The (Herbert), 6, 18–21; introduction by John N. Wall, 19

Crampton Hodnet (Pym), 93–94

Crash, 115

Crawford, Joan, 167, 169–70

Crosby, Bing, 3, 205–8

Crucible, The (Miller), 4, 126–28, 132

Cry, the Beloved Country (Paton), 115–19

Curtis, Richard, 86–87, 194–97, 199, 202

Dahl, Roald, 88–89

Davies, Horton, 10, 32, 40, 123

Davies, Robertson, 23–24, 256–62, 265

Dawn, Marva, 7

Dead Man Walking, 60

"Defence of Detective Stories, A" (Chesterton), 97

Defoe, Daniel, 71

Diary of a Country Priest, The (Bernanos), 36, 39–42, 252; review by Murphy, 39

Dickens, Charles, 62, 77–79, 115, 220, 224

Dillahunt, Garret, 183–84

"Discovering Robertson Davies" (Grant), 261

Displacing the Divine (Walrath), 127, 163, 172, 243

"Divine Detective, The" (Chesterton), 98

Diviners, The (Laurence), 262

Doctor's Family, The (Oliphant), 145

Don Quixote (Cervantes), 76, 81, 83

Donne, John, 14–15, 143

Dostoyevsky, Fyodor, 2

Doubt (Shanley), 4, 157–60; film adaptation, 4, 157, 160

Down and Out in Paris and London (Orwell), 223

Doyle, Arthur Conan, 100–2, 106, 112–13, 277

Doyle, James, 24

Duigan, John, 25–31, 185–86

Duncan, Lindsay, 228

Duvall, Robert, 191–93

Dyck, Paul, 16

Dysart, Richard, 178

Eastwood, Clint, 152–55, 177–80, 280

Ebert, Roger, 153, 191, 193

Eco, Umberto, 100, 111–13

Edwardians and Late Victorians (Ellmann), 58

Eliot, George, 2, 34, 48–56, 59, 61–68, 115, 139–40, 143–45, 148, 220, 237

Eliot, T. S., 14, 28–31, 37, 279

Ellmann, Richard, 58

Elmer Gantry (Lewis), 10, 163, 171, 243; film adaptation, 163

Emma (Austen), 4, 66, 148

End of Christendom and the Future of Christianity, The (Hall), 188, 241–42

End of the Affair, The (Greene), 32, 81

Endicott, Marina, 265–67

"Estimating Americans' Worship Behavior" (Newport), 242

Ethical Vision of Clint Eastwood, The (Vaux), 177–78

Everson, Eva Marie, 221–22

Exalted Company of Roadside Martyrs, The (Cariou), 263–65

Exile Book of Priests, Pastors, Nuns and Pentecostals, introduction (Fiorito), 267–68

Faber Book of Church and Clergy, introduction (Wilson), 127, 268

Farthing, Ian, 242–43

"Father Figure" (Lambert), 130

Father Ted, 8, 70, 243

Faulkner, William, 32, 171–75

Female Ministry (Booth), 225–26

Feuerbach, Ludwig, 62

"Few Words about Barbara Pym, A" (Moseley), 92

Field Guide to the English Country Parson, A (Hinde), 97

Field, Louise Maunsell, 170

Fielding, Henry, 71, 161

Fifth Business (Davies), 23–24, 256–61, 265

"Fifty Best Selling Books of the 1990s" (Thackray), 228

Fiorito, Joe, 267–68

Fire-Dwellers, The (Laurence), 262

Fish, Stanley, 14

Fitzgerald, Barry, 207

Fitzgerald, F. Scott, 41

Five Smooth Stones for Pastoral Work (Peterson), 6

Flaubert, Gustave, 2–3
Flying Nun, The, 183
Footloose, 184–85
Ford, Ford Madox, 41
Forester, C. S., 223
Forster, E. M., 4, 56–59, 278
Four Weddings and a Funeral, 3,
  86–87
"Fourteen Consolations" (Luther),
  23
Framley Parsonage (Trollope), 145
French, Dawn, 8, 184, 194–97, 202
Frye, Northrop, 256

George Eliot (Haight), 61–62
George Herbert (Eliot), 14
"Georges Bernanos" (Hoen), 41
"Georges Bernanos' Love Affair
  with God" (Begley), 39, 41
Gibson, Mel, 121
Gilbert, Sandra, 142
Gilead (Robinson), 8–9, 24, 34–37,
  276; review by Wood, 36
Glenville, Peter, 28–31, 208–9,
  213–15
Glittering Images (Howatch), 175
"God and the Detectives"
  (Bottum), 99
God or the Girl, 182
*Godly and Righteous, Peevish and
  Perverse* (Chapman), 243
Going My Way, 8, 205–8, 213
Goldberg, Whoopi, 186
Golding, William, 162, 166–67, 175
Goldsmith, Oliver, 71–74, 80,
  220–21
Good News, 183
Good Soldier, The (Ford), 41
Good to a Fault (Endicott), 265–67
Gordon, Charles William. *See*
  Connor, Ralph
*Graham Greene's Catholic
  Imagination* (Bosco), 41
Gran Torino, 152–55

Grant, Hugh, 150, 185–86
Grant, Judith Skelton, 261
Great Gatsby, The (Fitzgerald), 41
"Great Sermon Handicap, The"
  (Wodehouse), 10
Greeley, Andrew, 99
Greene, Graham, 1–2, 9, 31–34, 36,
  41, 81–84, 89, 246, 276
Gubar, Susan, 142
"Guilty Vicarage, The" (Auden),
  97–100, 106

Haight, Gordon S., 61–62
Hale, F., 252–53
Hall, Douglas John, 59, 188,
  241–42
Halliburton, Thomas Chandler, 246
Hamlet (Shakespeare), 76
"Hammer of God, The"
  (Chesterton), 106
Hampton, Brenda, 187–88
Hare, David, 128–29, 132
Harvey, Frank, 85–86, 89
Have Faith, 183
Hawaii, 230
Hawthorne, Nathaniel, 4, 8,
  122–26, 131–32, 174, 190,
  234–36
Heart of the Matter, The (Greene),
  31, 81
Heavens Above!, 85–86, 89
Hell Town, 183
Hemingway, Ernest, 40
Hepburn, Katharine, 223
Herbert, George, 6, 10, 13–21
Hill, George Roy, 230
Hinde, Thomas, 97
Hitchcock, Alfred, 100
Hodgson, Peter C., 55
Hoen, Matthew, 41
Hoffman, Philip Seymour, 160
Hollander, Tom, 196–203
Home (Robinson), 36, 276
Hopkins, Gerard Manley, 24

"Hound of Heaven, The"
    (Thompson), 154
How Fiction Works (Wood), 8, 135
"How James Wood's *How Fiction
    Works* Works" (Anderson),
    135
"How to Create a Winning
    Miniseries" (Robertson), 184
Howatch, Susan, 175, 280
Huckleberry Finn (Twain), 7
Hudson, Kate, 182
Huston, John, 208–11, 213–15, 223
Huston, Walter, 169

I Confess, 100
Ibsen, Henrik, 162–65, 174–75,
    217, 235–36
*If You Meet George Herbert on the
    Road* (Lewis–Anthony), 5,
    9, 18
Improper Opinion, The (Marty),
    203, 278
Innocence of Father Brown, The
    (Chesterton), 102–6
Iona Community, 133
Irons, Jeremy, 27
Irvine, William, 233

Jacobi, Derek, 100
James, William Closson, 262–63
Jane and Prudence (Pym), 91–92
Jane Austen's Anglicanism (White),
    149
Jane Eyre (Brontë), 140–43, 155,
    223, 235–36
Jest of God, A (Laurence), 262
Joffe, Roland, 27–30
Johnson, Katie N., 167, 170
Johnson, Niall, 87–88
Joyce, James, 32, 40, 161–62, 246
Julia, Raul, 25–26

Karon, Jan, 9, 91–92, 94–96, 243,
    251

Keeping Mum, 87–88
Keeping the Faith, 189–90, 203
Keillor, Garrison, 70
Keys of the Kingdom, The, 3,
    186–87
Kierkegaard, Søren, 7, 136, 161
King Lear (Shakespeare), 45
Kipling, Rudyard, 279
Kolbaba, Ginger, 221

"Ladies in Distress" (Miller),
    96
Lambert, Pam, 130
Lancaster, Burt, 163
Larkin, Philip, 92
Latham, David, 256
Laurence, Margaret, 244–46, 262
"Lazarus" (Cariou), 263–65
Leacock, Stephen, 249–51
Leaving Church (Taylor), 6–7,
    188–89
Lee, Ang, 150
Lewis, Sinclair, 10, 163, 171
Lewis-Anthony, Justin, 5, 9, 18
Life of Our Lord, The (Dickens), 62
Life Together (Bonhoeffer), 6, 60
Light in August (Faulkner), 171–75
Light in the Window, A (Karon),
    91–92
Lights and Shadows of Clerical Life
    (Cheetham), 11, 271–76
Lithgow, John, 184–85
Little House on the Prairie, 187
Little Mosque on the Prairie, 268
Little, Dave, 257
*Lives of the Fathers, Martyrs
    and other Principal Saints*
    (Butler), 24; preface by
    Doyle, 24
Lives of the Saints (Baring-Gould),
    24
Living Temple, The (Fish), 14
Locations of the Sacred (James),
    262–63

Loncraine, Richard, 186
Look of Catholics, The (Smith), 208
Lovesey, Oliver, 63, 143
Loyola, Ignatius, 162
Luther, Martin, 7, 23, 139, 145, 190
Lyre of Orpheus, The (Davies), 261

M*A*S*H, 71, 183
MacFarlane, Robert, 44
Madame Bovary (Flaubert), 2–3
Madwoman in the Attic, The
    (Gilbert and Gubar), 142
Major Barbara (Shaw), 9, 231
Man Called Peter, A (Marshall),
    222, 228, 236; film adapta-
    tion, 3, 22
Man from Glengarry, The (Connor),
    247–48
Mansfield Park (Austen), 148–50
Manticore, The (Davies), 258
Marshall, Catherine, 222, 228, 236
Marshall, David B., 247
Marshall, Garry, 182
Marshall, Penny, 230
Marty, Martin, 203, 278
Martyrs Mirror, The, 23
Maslin, Janet, 191–93
Matilda (Dahl), 88
Matter of Wife and Death, A
    (Kolbaba), 221
Maugham, W. Somerset, 162,
    167–71, 175, 236
Mauriac, François, 41
Maverick Preacher, The (Bylin), 221
Mayhew-Archer, Paul, 195–96
McBurney, Simon, 199
McCarey, Leo, 205–8
McDannell, Colleen, 206–7
McGoohan, Patrick, 163
McGovern, Jimmy, 130–32
McInerny, Ralph, 99
McSweeney, Kerry, 51
Melville, Herman, 281
Meyer, Michael, 163

Michel of Northgate, 139
Middlemarch (Eliot), 34, 48–54,
    63–64, 115, 139, 143–45, 220
Middlemarch (McSweeney), 51
Milestone, Lewis, 169–70
Mill on the Floss, The (Eliot), 61
Miller, Arthur, 4, 126–28, 132
Miller, Karl, 96
Million Dollar Baby, 152–55; re-
    view by Ebert, 153
Milton, John, 43
"Minister and the Seductress in
    American Fiction, The"
    (Prioleau), 123
"Minister's Black Veil, The"
    (Hawthorne), 234–35
Minister's Wooing, The (Stowe), 128
"Ministrations of the Rev.
    Uttermust Dumfarthing,
    The" (Leacock), 249
Minnelli, Vincente, 208–9, 211–13,
    215
*Mirror of the Ministry in Modern
    Novels, A* (Davies), 10, 32,
    40, 123
Miss Marjoribanks (Oliphant), 145
Mission, The, 27–30
Missionary, The, 186
Moby Dick (Melville), 281
Moll Flanders (Defoe), 71
Monsignor Quixote (Greene),
    81–84, 89, 278
Month of Sundays, A (Updike), 8,
    162, 174–75
Morbid Taste for Bones, A (Peters),
    108
Moseley, Merritt, 92
Much Ado about Nothing
    (Shakespeare), 207
Munro, Alice, 244, 262–63
Murder at the Vicarage, The
    (Christie), 226
Murder in the Cathedral (Eliot),
    28–31, 37, 279

Murdoch, Iris, 237–40
Murphy, Rachel, 39
Murphy, Terrence, 246
Murray, Victoria Christopher, 221
Mysteries of Reverend Dean, The
(White), 101, 106

Name of the Rose, The (Eco), 100,
111–13; film adaptation, 113
Nawaz, Zarqa, 268
New, W. H., 253
Newell, Mike, 3, 86–87
Newman, John Henry, 143
Newport, Frank, 242
Nietzsche, Friedrich, 136
Night of the Iguana, The (Williams),
9, 208–11, 213–15; film
adaptation, 208–11, 213–15
Nine Tailors, The (Sayers), 166
Northanger Abbey (Austen),
148–50
Norton, Edward, 189–90
Not the Nine O'Clock News, 87
Nothing Sacred, 182

O'Byrne, Brian F., 153
O'Connor, John, 184
O'Toole, Peter, 28
Oliphant, Margaret, 11, 145–48,
272, 275
Omnibus of Crime, The, introduc-
tion (Sayers), 97
"On *Candida*" (Irvine), 233
"On His Blindness" (Milton), 43
Orwell, George, 173, 223–25
Our Man in Havana (Greene), 81
Our Mutual Friend (Dickens), 220
Out to Canaan (Karon), 95

Paietta, Ann C., 202–3
Pale Rider, 152, 177–80, 280
Palin, Michael, 186
Pargeter, Edith. *See* Peters, Ellis

Parson in English Literature, The
(Christmas), 243
Passion of the Christ, The, 121
Pastor, The (Peterson), 7, 218–20
Paton, Alan, 115–19
"Patterns of Religious Attendance"
(Clark), 242
Peck, Gregory, 3, 186–87
Perin, Roberto, 246
Perpetual Curate, The (Oliphant),
145
Peters, Ellis (Edith Pargeter), 100,
107–11, 113, 243
Peterson, Eugene, 2, 6, 7, 69–70,
121, 155, 212, 218–20, 236,
282
Phoebe Junior (Oliphant), 11,
145–48, 275
"Pictures of the Ice" (Munro), 262
"Pied Beauty" (Hopkins), 24
"Pigeon Feathers" (Updike),
151–52, 155
Plato, 237
Poetics (Aristotle), 112
Pontoon (Keillor), 70
*Portrait of the Artist as a Young
Man, A* (Joyce), 161, 246
"Postfigurative Christ, The" (Hale),
252–53
Powell, Anthony, 44
Power and the Glory, The (Greene),
1–2, 9, 31–34, 81–82, 246
"Praise with Joy the World's
Creator" (hymn), 133
Preacher's Portrait, The (Stott), 6
Preacher's Wife, The (1996 film), 3,
199, 213, 230
Preacher's Wife, The (St. John), 221
*Preachers and Misfits, Prophets and
Thieves* (Ramsey), 7, 243
Pride and Prejudice (Austen),
70–71, 78, 140, 150
Priest (1994 film), 3, 130–32
Priest (2011 film), 3

Priest to the Temple, The. See *The Country Parson*
"Priesthood, The" (Herbert), 15, 17
Prioleau, Elizabeth, 123
Private Confessions (Bergman), 235
Pym, Barbara, 9, 91–96, 226

"Queer Feet, The" (Chesterton), 104–6
Quinn, Aidan, 183–84
Quintessence of Ibsenism, The (Shaw), 164
"Quintessence of Shaw's Ethical Position, The" (Carpenter), 231

Rabin, Nathan, 160
Racing Demon (Hare), 128–29, 132
Rain (1932 film), 167, 169–70, 236
"Rain" (Maugham), 162, 167–71, 175, 236; review by Field, 170
Raising Helen, 172, 184
Ramsey, G. Lee, Jr., 7, 243
"Real Vicars of Dibley, The," 194
Rebel Angels, The (Davies), 260–62
Rector, The (Oliphant), 145
Rector's Wife, The (Trollope), 228–30
Reinhartz, Adele, 179–191
"Reputations Revisited," 92
Restless Churches (Bibby), 263
Rev., 3, 34, 196–203
Rhys, Grace, 61
Richards, David Adams, 138
Richardson, Miranda, 192
Ricks, Christopher, 77
"Rival Churches of St. Asaph and St. Osoph, The" (Leacock), 249
Roache, Linus, 130
Road to Wigan Pier, The (Orwell), 223
Robbins, Tim, 60

"Robertson Davies and the Ethics of Monologue" (Bonnycastle), 259
Robertson, Ed, 184
Robinson, Marilynne, 2, 8–9, 24, 34–37, 276
Romeo and Juliet (Shakespeare), 56
Romero, 25–31, 280
Romero, Oscar, 25–31, 280
Room with a View, A (Forster), 4, 56–59, 278
Ross, Herbert, 184–85
Ross, Sinclair, 9, 251, 253–56, 265
"Rowan Atkinson" (Taylor), 87

Sadie Thompson (1928 film), 167, 169–79, 236
Saint, Eva Marie, 211–12
Saints, Clergy, and Other Religious Figures on Film and Television (Paietta), 202–3
Salem Chapel (Oliphant), 145
Sanctorum Communio (Bonhoeffer), 43
Sandpiper, The, 208–9, 211–13, 215
Sartre, Jean-Paul, 41
Say One for Me, 208
Sayers, Dorothy L., 97–98, 166
"Scandal in Bohemia, A" (Doyle), 277
Scarlet Letter, The (Hawthorne), 4, 8, 122–26, 128, 131–32, 174, 190
Scenes of Clerical Life (Eliot), 61–68; introduction by Rhys, 61
Schellenberg, Grant, 243
Schenk, Nick, 154
Scripture on the Silver Screen (Reinhartz),179, 191
Secularizing the Faith (Marshall), 247
Sellers, Peter, 84–86

Sense and Sensibility (Austen), 148–50; film adaptation, 150
Sense of the Call, The (Dawn), 7
Shakespeare, William, 2, 45, 56, 76, 207
Shanley, John Patrick, 4, 157–60; interview with Rabin, 160
Shaw, George Bernard, 7–9, 164–66, 231–34
"Sherry with Father Tim" (Winner), 95
Shryack, Dennis, 177–80
"Sinclair Ross" (Calder), 254
"Sinclair Ross" (Latham), 256
"Sins of Leo McCarey" (Blake), 206
Sirens, 185–86
Sister Act, 186
Smith, Anthony Burke, 206, 208
Smith, Maggie, 227
"Soliloquy of the Spanish Cloister" (Browning), 280
Some Tame Gazelle (Pym), 93–94
Soul Man, 199
Spire, The (Golding), 162, 166–67, 175
Spiritual Exercises (Loyola), 162
St. John, Cheryl, 221–22
Stahl, John M., 186–87
Sterne, Laurence, 71, 74–77, 89, 278
Still Life (Byatt), 44–46
Stiller, Ben, 189–90
Stone Angel, The (Laurence), 244–46
"Story of a Panic, The" (Forster), 57–58
Stott, John, 6
Stovel, Nora Foster, 262
Stowe, Harriet Beecher, 128
Stradner, Rosa, 186–87
Strauss, David Friedrich, 62
Streep, Meryl, 160
"Strong Performances Help *Thorn Birds* Soar" (O'Connor), 184

Such is My Beloved (Callaghan), 251–53
Sussman, Irving, 165, 167
Swanson, Gloria, 167, 169–70
Syriana, 115

Taradash, Daniel, 230
Taylor, Barbara Brown, 6–7, 188–89
Taylor, Elizabeth, 208, 211–12
Taylor, Will, 87
Temple, The (Herbert), 13–21; introduction by John N. Wall, 19
"Temples and Tabernacles" (Stovel), 262
Thackray, Rachelle, 228
Theology in the Fiction of George Eliot (Hodgson), 55
Third Man, The (Greene), 81
"Thirty-nine Articles of Religion, The," 10, 155, 190
This Fine Life (Everson), 221
Thompson, Francis, 154
Thorn Birds, The, 184–85
Todd, Richard, 222
Toews, Miriam, 244
Tom Jones (Fielding), 71, 161
Too Little, Too Late (Murray), 221
Traffic, 115
Tristram Shandy (Sterne), 71, 74–77, 89, 278; introductory essay by Ricks, 77
Trollope, Anthony, 65, 79–81, 108, 145–46, 148, 218, 220, 249, 272, 275
Trollope, Joanna, 228–30
Trumbo, Dalton, 211–13, 215, 230
Twain, Mark, 7

Unforgiven, 177
Unnecessary Pastor, The (Peterson and Dawn), 282

Updike, John, 8, 151–52, 155, 162, 174–75

Vaux, Sara Anson, 177–78
Veiller, Anthony, 208–11, 213–15
Vicar of Dibley, The, 3, 8, 86, 184, 194–97, 199, 202–3; "Vicar of Dibley effect," 196
Vicar of Nibbleswicke, The (Dahl), 88–89
Vicar of Sorrows, The (Wilson), 173–74
Vicar of Wakefield, The (Goldsmith), 71–74, 80, 220–21, 251; introduction by Coote, 72–74
Violence of Love, The (Romero), 25–27
Virgin in the Garden, The (Byatt), 44–48
Virtual America (Barna), 242
von Sydow, Max, 3, 230

Waldhorn, Gary, 194
Wall, John N., Jr., 19
Wallace and Gromit's Cracking Contraptions, 3–4
Walrath, Douglas Alan, 127, 163, 172, 243
Walsh, Raoul, 169–70
Waltons, The, 187
Warden, The (Trollope), 79–81, 220, 251
Waste Land, The (Eliot), 37
Waugh, Evelyn, 82, 104, 173
Whistling Woman, A (Byatt), 44; review by MacFarlane, 44
White, Hal, 101, 106

White, Laura Mooneyham, 149
Who Shall Lead Them? (Witham), 5, 203
"Who's Religious?" (Schellenberg and Clark), 242–43
"Wild Swans" (Munro), 244
Wilkinson, Tom, 130
Williams, Robin, 3
Williams, Rowan, 60, 122
Williams, Tennessee, 9, 208–11, 213–15
Wilson, A. N., 127–28, 173–74
Wilson, Keith, 246
Wilson, Michael, 211–13, 215
"Windows, The" (Herbert), 15, 17
Winner, Lauren, 95
Wishful Thinking (Buechner), 181
Witches, The (Dahl), 88
Witham, Larry A., 5, 203
"Without Benefit of Clergy" (Kipling), 279
Wodehouse, P. G., 10, 226
Wolberg, Kristine A., 20
Wolff, Richard, 183, 188, 202
Wood, James (novelist and critic), 8, 36, 135–38
Wood, James (television writer), 196–203
Word Remains, The (Brockman), 25
Working the Angles (Peterson), 121, 212
"World of Sherlock Holmes, The" (Chesterton), 107
World of Wonders (Davies), 258
"Writer of TV Comedy *Rev.*, James Wood" (Wood), 197
"Writings of Margaret Laurence, The" (Callaghan), 245

Scripture Index

OLD TESTAMENT

Genesis	141
Joshua	
24:14–15	254–55
Proverbs	
25:28	209
Psalms	141
18:2	172
23	179
Isaiah	
2:12–15	172
24:1–2	161
Ezekiel	112
Joel	
1:13	181
Jonah	281

NEW TESTAMENT

Mark	
4:18–19	121
Luke	
1:79	24
10:31	139
14:26	188
15	159
John	
15:18–19	29–30
17:13–19	109–10
17:26	109–10
Acts	
17:6	70
1 Corinthians	
1:27–29	69
4:10	70
4:13	70
7:8	226
14:34	225
Galatians	
3:28	12

Ephesians

3:8–9   97, 101, 105, 113

1 Timothy   6

2:5–6   59–60
3:4–5   217, 282

2 Timothy

1:8   23
2:5   6
2:23–25   43
4:1–5   1
4:2   282

Titus   6

2:7   282

Hebrews

5:2–3   241

Revelation   141

6:8   177